Software Engineering
Analysis and Verification

T. G. Lewis
Oregon State University

Reston Publishing Company, Inc. A Prentice-Hall Company, Reston, Virginia

To Madeline Rubin, whose name makes a difference.

Library of Congress Cataloging in Publication Data

Lewis, Theodore Gyle,
  Software engineering.

  Includes bibliographical references and index.
  1. Electronic digital computers—Programming.
2. Computer programs—Verification. I. Title.
QA76.6.L477   001.64'2   81-22637
ISBN 0-8359-7023-X   AACR2

Contents

Preface

I wrote this book for two purposes: (1) to use in a two-quarter or one-semester course on software engineering at the upper division level of a computer science curriculum, and (2) to give an alternative method of formal verification of single and multiple process computer software.

The first goal has been achieved by teaching these ideas to upper division students at Oregon State University for the past five years. The material has evolved from the ideas of my contemporaries (testing and proof of correctness) into a completely new and original method that combines pragmatic testing with mathematical proof of correctness. I have found that using common algorithms such as searching, sorting, hashing, etc. as examples of the new method is an effective way of teaching the method as well as reviewing these useful algorithms in greater detail than normally provided in other textbooks. In addition, I have included a number of new algorithms that have not previously been published; for example, the perfect hashing program is an original contribution.

My second goal grew out of dissatisfaction with the field of software verification. First, the idea that humans can formally prove a program correct by rewriting it as a system of assertions seems totally inadequate to me. What makes predicate logic any more viable as an artifact of programming than the actual source code itself? Second, I wanted to capture the essence of what a programmer does when debugging a program by traditional testing methods because this seems to me to be the most effective means of verification. However, pragmatic testing lacked the rigor and formalism of proof-of-correctness. In this book, therefore, I introduce the notion of a "program calculus" which is applied directly to the most obvious artifact: the source program itself. The early chapters of the book show how to do this and the remaining chapters merely apply the new verification technique, relentlessly.

Some readers may question the wisdom of combining performance, algorithms, verification, and concurrent programming into a single book on software engineering. My defense is quite simple: why not? Software is software regardless of artificial boundaries put in place by tradition. If a verification technique is any good at all, it ought to be useful across the breadth of computer science. The new method presented here does indeed apply equally well to, say, single process and concurrent process systems. Indeed, one of the nice features of the new method is the way it ties together both single and multiple process software under a unified theory of verification. This book is not for those who must limit their understanding to narrowly defined ''areas'' of computer science.

I owe a lot to the people who have contributed their time and understanding to this project. Larry Benincasa, Carol King, and Ellen Cherry at Reston all had the courage and desire to publish this book in spite of the fact that it does not fall into a narrowly defined category. Donna Norvell did a great job of typing, and several reviewers (unknown to me) made valuable suggestions. I also want to thank my students M. Harris, D. Buck, and others for finding and correcting errors in the manuscript.

T. G. Lewis

0

Survey of Software Life-Cycle Models

INTRODUCTION

Software development modeling is in rapid flux. A variety of models exist, but few proven formulas are known. For this reason, we survey and compare several models rather than give an in-depth analysis of only one model. For a critical evaluation of the state of software life-cycle modeling, see the Moranda reference at the end of this chapter.

In this chapter we identify the major cause of the rising cost of software development by comparing various software development process models. We hope to show that cost and effort can be reduced through careful control of program specification, implementation, testing, and enhancement throughout the software life cycle. Once the source of cost and effort is identified, we can develop a theory and technique for coping with it. This is what the remainder of the book attempts to do: to reduce the cost and effort of software development through systematic application of a few well-chosen software engineering analysis techniques.

SOFTWARE DEVELOPMENT PROCESS

A *life cycle* is a profile of a project beginning at time t. A *software life cycle* is a profile of a software project. We usually view a software life cycle as a collection of *phases*. The phases of a large-scale software life cycle may total more than 100% of the effort due to their overlap (see Figure 0-1). The phases are:

Functional specifications	20%
Design and coding	15%
Test and certification	20%
Development extension	10%
Program modifications	25%
Program maintenance	20%
Project management	10%
	120%

These phases account for total effort, but as shown in Figure 0-1, they may begin slightly before the official life cycle begins. Our concern will be with the part of the life cycle that begins at some arbitrary point in time, say $t = 0$, and continues in time, indefinitely.

The total effort, K, of a software life cycle is the sum total of effort used to complete a life cycle. Effort is measured in units of people-years, MY, and the rate of expenditure of effort is measured in people-years/year, MY/YR.

The cost of software development can be estimated when the development time, t_d, the power, dy/dt, and the unit cost per person-year, $\$U$, are known.

$$\$DEV = \$U \left(\frac{dy}{dt}\right) t_d$$

For example, suppose we are given:

$$\$U = \$25,000/MY$$

$$\frac{dy}{dt} = 3MY/YR$$

$$t_d = 1.2YR$$

Thus,

$$\$DEV = 25,000(3)(1.2) = \$90,000$$

This represents the cost of development only. In Figure 0-1, the development time is used to normalize the time scale. Hence, when the value of t/t_d equals 1.0, a new system is ready for release as a completed product.

It is not clear from Figure 0-1 exactly where t/t_d equals 1.0. Indeed, it is not altogether obvious that the power curves are shaped as we have shown them in the figure. These shapes, regardless of their mathematical nature, have a combined effect as shown by the envelope curves in Figure 0-2.

The most interesting feature of the envelope curve is the location of development time. This curve suggests that t/t_d equals 1.0 at the maximum point of the software life-cycle curve. Recall that this point is reached by the combined efforts of all phases.

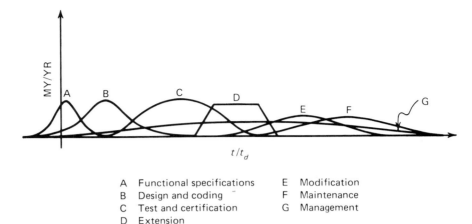

A Functional specifications   E Modification
B Design and coding   F Maintenance
C Test and certification   G Management
D Extension

Figure 0-1. Phases of a software life cycle.

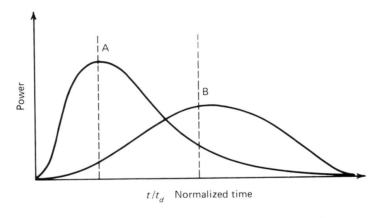

t/t_d Normalized time

A Development time for an accelerated or "short" project
B Development time for a "long" project

Figure 0-2. Software life-cycle envelope curve.

Many models have been proposed to explain the software life-cycle envelope curve (see references at end of chapter). Several parameters that appear to be most influential in determining the shape of the curves at each phase, and ultimately the shape of the envelope curve, are listed below.

T = the state of technology. A few of the items that affect technology are: (1) unstructured versus structured programming, (2) batch versus interactive development systems, and (3) automated versus hand-test method.

K = the applied effort (total) expended throughout the life cycle, measured in person-units, MY.

t_d = the time spent on developing the code, certifying it, and releasing it. This does not include modification, maintenance, or management. If additional extension time is needed (as indicated in Figure 0-1), it is not reflected in the time estimate, t_d.

In the following sections we develop and investigate several proposals for computing estimates of software life-cycle parameters. These parameters can then be used to predict the behavior of software throughout its entire lifetime. For example, we can ask, "How much will it cost?" and "How long will it take?" before a software project begins.

The Norden-Rayleigh Model

The Norden-Rayleigh model has been studied extensively by Putnam. Indeed, the model was used to study the life cycles of several large-scale data-processing projects for the U.S. military. The following analysis and values were obtained from these life cycles and may *not* apply to new situations. For a critical evaluation of this and other models, see the article by Moranda.

Putnam developed a life-cycle envelope curve from the Rayleigh formula:

$$\frac{dy}{dt} = (2Kat) \exp(-at^2)$$

In this formula, we must know the development time, t_d, and the total effort, K (the area under the envelope curve), before the other variables are computed.

$\frac{dy}{dt}$ = rate of change (expenditure of effort), i.e., the power of the life-cycle envelope.

K = total effort, i.e., the area under the curve,

$$K = \int_0^\infty \left(\frac{dy}{dt}\right) dt$$

a = intensity of the life cycle. This parameter determines the shape of the envelope curve by moving the maximum to the left or right. In Putnam's model,

$$a = \frac{1}{2t_d}$$

t_d = development time corresponding with (roughly) the peak of the power envelope.

t = time

Putnam verified several interesting facts concerning the software envelope curve. First, the development effort almost always equaled 40% of the total effort:

$$K_d = \int_0^{t_d} \left(\frac{dy}{dt}\right) dt = 0.40K$$

Thus, we can immediately compute the costs of both development and total effort:

$$\$TOTAL = \$U(K)$$
$$\$DEV \quad = (0.40)(\$TOTAL)$$

These useful formulas are derived from the helpful relationships given below:

$$y = K[1 - \exp(-at^2)]$$

which is the instantaneous power expenditure at time t in the life cycle. The empirically derived maximum suggests that peak power is reached at $t = t_d$. The reader can also show that

$$\lim_{t \to \infty} y = K \qquad (* \text{ total effort } *)$$

Putnam was able to further classify the military software he studied by noting the similarity of life-cycle curves. Two quantities showed high correlation with systems thought to be "difficult" and "complex." Thus, if the difficulty, D, was small, then the software project was classified as "easy." If D was large, the corresponding software was termed "hard" to do. Thus,

$$D = \frac{K}{t_d^2}$$

The gradient of the envelope curve is dominated by the complexity quantity, C.

$$C = \frac{K}{t_d^3}$$

Putnam found that whenever "new" systems were plotted on the same graph with "modified" and "highly revised" systems, they coincided with complexity values 8, 15, and 27, respectively.

C	Type of System Studied
8	new systems
15	modified systems
27	major revisions

This suggests a "difficulty gradient" related to the problem of understanding a program. The more complex a program is, the more difficult it is to modify. Hence, the complexity quantity may provide a way to begin an analysis of software life-cycle costs. This is indeed what was done in order to derive the following equation of state.

The software size equation

$$S_s = TK^{1/3}t_d^{4/3}$$

where S_s is the number of lines of source code in a piece of software developed in time t_d by total effort K, using a level of technology given by the constant T.

Putnam's size equation was used to evaluate several large-scale software systems *after the fact*. When curve-fitting techniques were used to estimate T, the values 4980 and 10040 were obtained:

$T = 4980$. The environment consisted of a batch development computer system, unstructured coding methods, "fuzzy" design requirements, and restricted access to the test machine.

$T = 10040$. The environment consisted of an on-line interactive development system, structured coding methods, well-defined requirements, and unrestricted access to the test machine.

These ideas are illustrated in the following example. Suppose a microcomputer system is to be developed in two years. The project manager determines that this project is of moderate complexity; hence she estimates $C = 15$. We want to know in advance what the expended effort will be, and how much it will cost to develop the software from $t = 0$ to $t = t_d = 2$ years.

(a) What is the expected effort, K?

$$\frac{K}{t_d^3} = C = 15; \text{ hence } K = 120MY$$

(b) Assume $\$U = 25,000/MY$. What are the relative costs, $\$TOTAL$ and $\$DEV$?

$$\$TOTAL = (25,000)(120) = \$3\ M$$
$$\$DEV\ \ \ = (0.40)(3\ M)\ \ \ = \$1.2\ M$$

(c) What is the expected size, S_s? Assume old technology, $T = 4980$.

$$S_s = (4980)(120)^{1/3}(2)^{4/3} = 61,851 \text{ lines of code}$$

(d) Assume two bytes per line of code: What is the size of memory required?

$$(2)(61,851) \doteq 128 \text{ kilobytes}$$

We can see from the example that the sizing equation relates the total effort to the finished product size. It means that given a technology and a fixed length of time, a fixed number of lines of source code can be produced. The amount of code does not vary with language or personality of programmers. Such an assumption may not be true in individual cases, but Putnam's results appear to be *accurate in the large*.

The size equation is nonlinear in total effort, K, and development time, t_d. As it turns out, these two parameters can be traded off, one for the other. The trade-off is nonlinear, however, due to the nonlinear nature of the sizing equation.

Conservation of agony law

$$Kt_d{}^4 = \text{constant}$$

We can use the conservation law above to study the effects of a compressed development time schedule. Suppose the microcomputer project illustrated above is compressed by 25%. Now,

$$t_d = 1.5\,YR$$

Since the conservation law holds, we find the constant:

$$(120)(2)^4 = 1920 \quad \text{(before compression)}$$

Using 1920,

$$K = (1920)(1.5^4) = 376.4MY \quad \text{(after time compression)}$$

Thus the result of a 25% acceleration in the development schedule is devastating to the cost of the software.

$$\$TOTAL = \$9.4\ M$$
$$\$DEV\ \ \ = \$3.8\ M$$

Hence the costs are three times as great for a 25% acceleration. Correspondingly we would expect a cost reduction if more development time were allowed. Clearly time costs money.

The Norden-Rayleigh model provides a macroscale handle on a very important part of the software life cycle: the size and cost. Given the following parameters:

$$T = \text{state of technology}$$
$$K = \text{total effort}$$
$$t_d = \text{development time}$$

we can compute various quantities of enormous value using Putnam's formulas:

$$S_s = TK^{1/3}t_d^{4/3}$$
$$Kt_d^4 = \text{constant}$$
$$D = \frac{K}{t_d^2}$$
$$C = \frac{K}{t_d^3}$$

These formulas yield a first-order estimate of the effort, cost, and size of a software life cycle. The reader should be warned that the values of T, D, and C may be subject to change within an application area, among different programmers, and over time. Each project manager should determine these parameters from careful evaluation and/or time-motion studies.

The Brooks Model

An earlier productivity model was first proposed by Brooks. This model concentrates on the activities most familiar to programmers (see Figure 0-3).

Brooks observed that productivity decreased more than at a linear rate with any increase in the size of the software (where size is equal to number of lines of source code). However, he also noticed less difference in productivity due to the use of a programming language than due to the size of a program. For example, when he compared the development of OS/360 written in assembly language with MULTICS written in PL/I, the rate of code production was roughly equivalent for equivalent tasks.

OS/360 Assembler language projects

Control Program Teams: 600 to 800 Debugged Instructions per Programmer-Year

Compiler Construction Teams: 2000 to 3000 Debugged Instructions per Programmer-Year

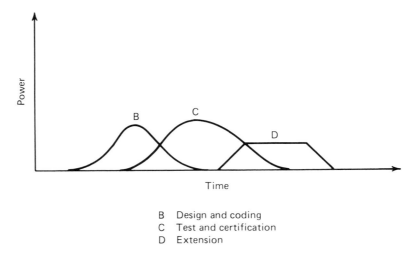

B   Design and coding
C   Test and certification
D   Extension

Figure 0-3. Phases addressed by the Brooks model.

Project MAC—MULTICS—PL/I

1200 Lines of Debugged PL/I Statements per Programmer-Year

This led Brooks to formulate a law of large programs based on the task and the number of lines of code regardless of the language used to implement the code.

Law of large programs

$$E = mS_s^{1.5}$$

where

E = programming effort

m = application constant

S_s = size of the program in machine instructions

The law of large programs relates the complexity of large programs to the amount of effort required to produce code. This fact is illustrated in the diagram of Figure 0-4.

The application constant, m, depends on the abilities of individual programmers and, more importantly, on the application. For example, the value of m for a business application is vastly different than for an operating system project.

Brooks observed that the effort *increased* whenever additional power was applied to speed up a failing software development project. In this

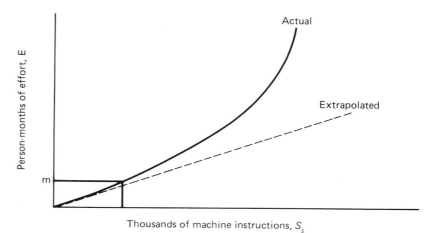

Figure 0-4. Linear extrapolation is meaningless.

respect, Brooks and Putnam agree in their observation of time versus people-power.

If we imagine a programmer group as a collection of n interacting parts (teams), then we must also account for the effort that goes into coordinating these parts. Suppose we call the interaction between the n parts the *communication effort*, E_c. A modified law of large programs can now include this effort:

$$E(n) = mS_s^{1.5} + E_c \left[\frac{n(n-1)}{2} \right]$$

In this version of the Brooks model, the number of interactions between any two members of a group of n parts is $n(n-1)/2$. The number of interactions is weighted by the group average comunication effort, E_c. Hence, in order to produce S_s lines of source code, the group must expand both coding and communication effort.

Whenever $n = 1$, the extended formula reduces to the law of large programs:

$$E(1) = mS_s^{1.5}$$

This formula assumes equal ability on the part of each programmer. Furthermore, it assumes some level of "divide and conquer" such that each group is responsible for producing S_j lines of code. Thus,

$$S_s = \sum_{j=1}^{n} S_j$$

If S_j lines of code are assigned to each group, then it is possible to lower the total effort [$E(1)$] by solving n subproblems instead of one large problem. That is, we may be able to beat the law of large programs. Each group is asked to spend E_j effort in developing S_j lines of code. Thus

$$E_j = mS_j^{1.5}$$

With this in mind, it is possible to optimize the total effort [minimize $E(n)$] by careful allocation of S_j to each of the groups. This is done by minimizing the cost function:

$$\text{Cost} = E(n) - \text{lambda} \left(S_s - \sum_{j=1}^{n} S_j \right)$$

where

$$E(n) = m \sum_{n=1}^{n} (S_j^{1.5}) + \frac{E_c n(n - 1)}{2}$$

The resulting allocation is as expected:

$$S_j = \frac{S_s}{n} \text{ for all } j = 1, \ldots n \text{ groups}$$

This value is substituted into the equation for total coding effort to obtain the following formula:

$$E^*(n) = \frac{E(1)}{\sqrt{n}} + \frac{E_c n(n - 1)}{2}$$

Thus, we conclude that there are diminishing returns in increasing the number of subparts (groups) of a software project. Since $\sqrt{n}$ increases only moderately with increasing values of n, the advantage of subdivision rapidly diminishes (see Figure 0-5).

The disappointing behavior of Figure 0-5 shows what can happen to a late software project. If additional programmers are added to a failing project, the effort required increases because the number of interacting parts increases (n is greater). This in turn may move the project upward along the relative effort curve, therefore increasing the effort needed.

$E^*(n)$ gives the total effort needed to simultaneously produce S_s lines of code by n interacting parts of a software development team. The idea is to shorten the development time by concurrently developing each of the S_j lines of code. But Putnam's model dictates an effort-time conservation law:

$$E^*(1)t_d^4(1) = E^*(n)t_d^4(n)$$

where

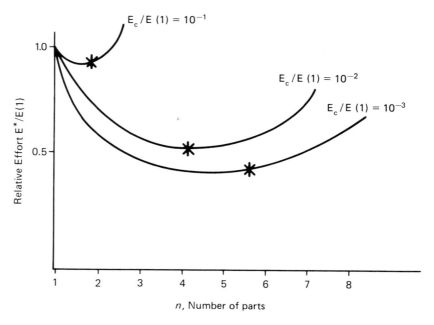

Figure 0-5. Team performance curve.

$E^*(1)$ = effort by a single programmer

$t_d(1)$ = development time of a single programmer

$E^*(n)$ = effort by n cooperating programmers, each with S_s/n lines of code

$t_d(n)$ = development time for the n concurrently working team members

To illustrate how these two models might interact, suppose we study the life-cycle envelope for a project with the following given parameters:

$$m = 2.14 \times 10^{-7} \quad \text{(see references)}$$
$$E_c = 0.05E^*(n) \quad \text{(assumed)}$$
$$S_s = 64,000 \text{ lines}$$

(a) What is the effort needed by one programmer?

$$E^*(1) = mS_s^{1.5} = 3.24MY$$

If the system is implemented by a single programmer, then we could expect 3.24 years of development. Thus,

$$t_d(1) = 3.24YR$$

(b) What is the effort needed by n programmers?

$$E^*(n) = \frac{E^*(1)}{\sqrt{n}} + E_c \left[\frac{n(n-1)}{2} \right]$$

and

$$E_c = 0.05E^*(n)$$

Therefore, rearranging the right-hand side:

$$E^*(n) = \frac{E^*(1)}{\sqrt{n} \left[1 - \dfrac{0.05n(n-1)}{2} \right]} \qquad (n < 7)$$

(c) What is the best value of n?

Suppose Putnam's conservation law is used with the formulas above to compute the following table. The last column of this table shows the ratio of cost per unit of time, $E^*(n)/t_d(n)$.

n	E^* (n)	t_d (n)	Cost/Year
1	3.24	3.24	1.00
2	2.41	3.49	0.69
3	2.20	3.57	0.62
4	2.31	3.53	0.65
5	2.90	3.33	0.87
6	5.29	2.87	1.87

If we select $n = 3$, we get the least expensive but longest development schedule. If we select $n = 6$ programmers to do the system, we get the software in the least time, but the cost is the greatest (by a factor of 3).

The Brooks model relates the coding effort to the size of software. It is a simplistic model that may be useful as another estimator, say, to compare with the Putnam model.

Given the following parameters:

m = application constant assumed uniform across all programmers

E_c = communications constant, assumed uniform across all applications and programmers

the two laws governing the Brooks curve are:

$$E = mS_s^{1.5}$$

$$E^*(n) = \frac{E(1)}{\sqrt{n}} + \frac{E_c n(n-1)}{2}$$

A Language-Dependent Model

The models studied so far have ignored potential differences in languages. Indeed, Brooks's results would lead us to believe that programming language differences are insignificant when compared to differences in task difficulty. There is, however, a group of software engineers who believe that programming *language level lambda* influences the productivity of programmers.

Halstead developed an information theory-based model of programs with the interesting property that every program can be analyzed by counting its operator and operand symbols. All other considerations, such as the number of executable paths, or the complexity of the problem being solved, are of little concern when using Halstead's model.

There are only four software parameters used by Halstead. These are called the *directly counted software parameters* because they are obtained directly from a program listing:

N_1 Total number of operators appearing in the module.
N_2 Total number of operands appearing in the module.
n_1 Number of distinct operators used in the module.
n_2 Number of distinct operands used in the module.

The small segment of program shown in Figure 0-6 will be used to illustrate the directly counted software parameters: N_1, N_2, n_1, and n_2. These values are derived in the following way.

First, we remove the formal parameters from consideration. This means the QUAD:**PROCEDURE** line and **DCL** line of code are not counted as part of the directly counted parameters.

Second, we ignore the control structure syntax; e.g., **IF, THEN, DO, END, RETURN,** and **ELSE** are not counted. (*Note:* This is one of several counting experiments suggested in the list of references. Other methods seem equally acceptable but may give different results.)

Next, we construct a list of operators and operands that are counted. We get, for example, the following list from Figure 0-6:

Operators	Count	Operands	Count
PUTLIST	2	A	6
GETLIST	1	B	4
=	1	C	2
SQRT	1	X	9
( )	5	2	2
–	4	4	1
=	7	0	3

*	3	Y	3
**	1	"NO REAL SOLN"	1
/	2		
Totals: 10	27	9	31
Parameter: n_1	N_1	n_2	N_2

This list includes the number of *distinct* operators and operands counted as well as the total number of operators and operands counted. Other rules for defining the directly counted parameters have been studied. See references to Elshoff. It was discovered that the method of counting has a dramatic effect on the actual numbers computed but that a consistent use of one counting method produces suitable measures.

The length of a program is the sum of its operators and operands. Thus,

$$N = N_1 + N_2 = 58$$

is the length of the program in Figure 0-6. Furthermore, we define the size of a program's vocabulary as the sum of its distinct operators and operands. Thus,

$$n = n_1 + n_2 = 19$$

is the size of the vocabulary used in Figure 0-6.

```
QUAD:   procedure (A, B, C) returns (X, Y);
        dcl A, B, C, X, Y;
        get list (A, B, C);
        X = B**2 − 4*A*C;
        A = 2*A;
        if X >= 0 then do;
                X = SQRT (X);
                Y = (X−B)−A;
                X = (−X−B)/A;
                put list (X, Y);
                    end;
            else do;
                put list ("NO REAL SOLUTION");
                X = 0; Y = 0
                end;
        return (X, Y);
        end QUAD;
```

Figure 0-6. Example of directly counted parameters.

A program is of the "right" size when the programmer has carefully used the vocabulary of operators and operands to construct the program. A sloppy programmer will produce a program that is too long.

If programming is viewed as a nondeterministic process of selecting operators and operands, then $\log_2 n_1$ mental discriminations (yes/no answers to the question, "Is this the one I need to use?") are needed to select each of the n_1 operators. This yields a total of $n_1(\log_2 n_1)$ mental discriminations.

Similarly, it takes $n_2(\log_2 n_2)$ total discriminations to select the operands used to construct a program. In other words, each of the n_1 operators is selected $\log_2 n_1$ times, and each of the n_2 operands is selected $\log_2 n_2$ times. This gives a total of $n_1 \log_2 n_1 + n_2 \log_2 n_2$ discriminations needed to construct a program.

Program length A program is well structured if its length is $\overline{N}$, where

$$\overline{N} = n_1 \log_2 n_1 + n_2 \log_2 n_2$$

This conjecture is difficult to accept at first glance, but we can test it with the data provided by Figure 0-6. The following length is computed from the table for the program of Figure 0-6:

$$N = N_1 + N_2 = 58 \quad \text{(directly counted)}$$
$$\begin{aligned}
\overline{N} &= n_1 \log_2 n_1 + n_2 \log_2 n_2 \\
&= 10 \log_2 10 + 9 \log_2 9 \\
&= 61.75 \quad \text{(expected)}
\end{aligned}$$

This agrees reasonably well with the directly counted value; hence the program is well structured. But the numbers do not explain why the metric works! Let's examine the program to see why the metric predicts the length of a well-structured module.

The example program is well structured because it uses psychological chunking in the proper places. The most obvious chunk is exhibited by the variable K. We use X to chunk together B, 2, 4, A, and C into a single expression. Additionally, X is modified into a "larger" chunk in the subsequent steps involving SQRT, and the final calculated value of X.

A second example of chunking is illustrated by operator chunking in the SQRT routine and in the replacement of $2*A$ with A (see the program listing).

"Impurities" in a program may be the cause of a poorly structured module (Fitzsimmons and Love, p. 5) due to the following:

1. Cancellation of operators, e.g., A/2+B/2 instead of (A+B)/2.
2. Overload operands: The same operand might be used to represent two or more quantities in a program.
3. Ambiguous operands: Two different operands represent the same quantity in a program.

4. Common subexpressions:

$$A(I+1) := A(I+1)+10$$

5. Unnecessary replacements.
6. Unfactored expressions.

A program is difficult or easy to write in a given programming language if its volume is large or small, respectively. The *volume* of a program is proportional to the number of decisions required to choose each of the directly counted operators or operands in the program.

Program volume The number of decisions needed to write the program is proportional to V, where

$$V = N(\log_2 n)$$

For the program of Figure 0-6,

$$V = 58(\log_2 19)$$
$$= 246.38 \text{ bits}$$

The problem with program volume, V, is that it does not take into consideration the programming language. A high-level language should require fewer decisions to implement a program than a low-level language. Is it possible to normalize V to a minimum volume for a given algorithm?

Suppose V^* is the volume of the most compact representation of an algorithm in some programming language. Then, a lower-level implementation of the same algorithm would require more operands and operators leading to a higher value of V relative to V^*. In short, an algorithm can be implemented in various levels, each level imposed by a programming language.

Program level The program level of an implemented algorithm depends on the representation of the algorithm in a language. The level L is the ratio of minimum program volume V^* to program volume, V. That is,

$$L = \frac{V^*}{V}$$

Others [Elshoff, Halstead] have studied a second measure of quality using L and the estimated minimum volume, V^*. The quality of a program is a function of its static characteristics; in particular, quality depends on the number of input/output variables and program volume.

Program quality A program (representation of a given algorithm) is of low quality, that is, it has impurities, if its level $\overline{L}$ is significantly lower than the directly counted level, L, where

$$\overline{L} = \frac{\overline{V}}{V}$$

$$\overline{V}* = (2 + p) \log_2(2 + p)$$

p = number of input/output parameters for the algorithm

Again, the example in Figure 0-6 with $p = 5$ input/output parameters gives

$$\overline{L} = \frac{(2 + 5)\log_2(2 + 5)}{246.38}$$

$$= 0.079$$

This means the representation of QUAD is not especially high level. We must keep in mind, however, that level is relative to a minimum encoding of the algorithm. The best we can do is obtain $L = 1.0$. The program of Figure 0-6 is of modest quality when compared with the level of other PL/I programs. Therefore, quality is judged relative to the volume of other programs written in the same programming language. If the quality is lowered, volume is increased in a kind of "conservation of agony." Halstead, in fact, discovered such a conservation law.

Conservation laws are useful static measures of program quality because they measure the quality of information encoding. A "good" program is one that has been compactly encoded in some representation. If impurities creep into the implementation, then the quality of such an implementation suffers. This loss in quality manifests itself as a violation of the conservation law.

Halstead's conservation of volume   Level and volume are conserved for a given algorithm. That is,

$$LV = \text{constant}$$

This conservation law holds for particular representations of a certain algorithm. If we compare the quality of an algorithm in FORTRAN with other FORTRAN representations of the same algorithm, the constant remains unchanged. However, if we switch to assembly language as a form of representation of the same algorithm, then the constant changes. The constant, then, is actually a quantitative measure of language level.

Programing language level

$$\text{Lambda} = LV*$$

It should take less volume to encode a program in a high-level language than in a low-level language. Thus, lambda should be larger for FORTRAN, say, than for an assembler language. This is indeed the case as shown by the table below.

Language	Level (avg. lambda)
English prose	2.16
PL/I	1.53
ALGOL 58	1.21
FORTRAN	1.14
Assembler (CDC)	0.88

Source: Fitzsimmons and Love, p. 9.

Since we defined V in terms of decisions (mental effort), the advantages of a high-level language must be to reduce mental effort. Let E be the effort expended to understand a program at some level, L. Then,

$$E = \frac{V}{L} \qquad \text{(programming effort)}$$

$$\text{Lambda} = L^2 V \qquad \text{(language level)}$$

Thus,

$$E = \frac{(V^*)^3}{\text{lambda}^2}$$

This result says that programming effort is defined in terms of the number of mental discriminations (decisions) needed to implement an algorithm in a programming language with level lambda. For example, using the table above, PL/I takes less effort to represent an algorithm than FORTRAN. In fact, PL/I requires about 1.8 times less effort than FORTRAN, and 3.0 times less effort than CDC Assembler. Conversely, we might be tempted to say that PL/I is three times as "high level" as CDC assembler language.

This formula was used by Schneider to derive a software life-cycle estimation formula. The model also contains an estimate of the defect count to be expected in a module, where

$$N = 2667I \qquad \text{(assembly language lambda} = 0.88),$$

$$N = 1900I \qquad \text{(FORTRAN lambda} = 1.14), \text{ and}$$

$$I = \text{number of 1000 lines of code.}$$

The constants in the formulas for N and lambda above reflect the increased difficulty in programming a system in a low-level language. Also, since the values of I are obtained by measuring the output of an assembler or FORTRAN compiler, the constants must account for the "work" performed by the translator.

Schneider assumed $I \times 1000$ instructions were developed from n modules, each module containing an estimated average of $(I/n) \times 1000$ lines of code. Using least squares estimators and data obtained from completed systems, Schneider obtained an estimate for the effort needed to develop a single module. He then used this estimate to yield an expression similar to Brooks's formula:

$$E_{mm}(n) = \left(\frac{41.8}{n^{0.83}}\right) I^{1.83}$$

This formula appears to be reasonably accurate for software ranging in size from $3 \leq I \leq 288$ thousand lines of source code with an average of 374 modules. Furthermore, assuming the modularity of FORTRAN programs and the language level of FORTRAN,

$$
\begin{aligned}
E_{mm} &= 28I^{1.83} &\text{(FORTRAN)}\\
&= 59.8I^{1.83} &\text{(Assembler)}
\end{aligned}
$$

In other words, assembly language programs were found to require twice the effort to produce the same amount of machine code as FORTRAN programs. Schneider verified these formulas for modules consisting of an average of 138 statements per module with a range of $22 \leq$ size ≤ 780 statements per module.

Using least squares curve fitting techniques, again, it is possible to estimate the project duration as a function of effort:

$$t_d = 2.47E_{mm}^{0.35} \quad \text{(months)}$$

So the estimators proposed by Schneider lead to a different model that incorporates a new parameter, lambda. The question naturally arises, "How does this new model compare with the previous ones?"

Comparisons

The formulas proposed by Schneider are closely related to the formulas derived in the preceding section. They are both of the same form:

$$\text{Effort} = \text{constant (size)}^{1.5}$$

The difference in constants is due to the language level parameter not included in the Brooks model.

These formulas do not, however, compare closely with the model given by Putnam. Recall that the Norden-Rayleigh envelope encloses the entire software life cycle, not merely the development phase. Therefore, it may not be appropriate to compare Schneider's or Brooks's results with Putnam's result.

In Putnam's model there is a theoretical limit to the size of a software system. Given a fixed length of development time, t_d, we cannot hope to produce more lines of code per effort than the conservation law states.

$$Kt_d{}^4 = \text{constant}$$

Accordingly there is a limited productivity rate set by technology. Once the technology constant is known, it is fixed, and we can only transfer effort to time and vice versa. Thus,

$$S_s = T \text{ (constant)}^{1/3} = TA^{1/3}$$

where $A = \text{constant}$

In Schneider's model, improvements in productivity can be made by choosing a "higher level" language. This increases lambda and in return reduces the development effort. However, the development time formula does not suggest a trade-off between time and effort.

This rule suggests a diminishing return on effort: the development time is cut in half for every tenfold increase in effort expended. Although Putnam's conservation law may be overly pessimistic, Schneider's development time rule is perhaps misleading in its optimism.

In summary, the models presented here offer software engineers a choice. Macroscale estimates are obtainable from Putnam's model, whereas programmer productivity may be deduced from Schneider's formulas. In the final analysis, none of the models can be used blindly. Each application of a formula must be preceded by careful study of the dynamics of the software life cycle.

REDUCING SOFTWARE LIFE-CYCLE COSTS

The success of a software project appears to be highly correlated with the structure of the software system. Furthermore, a cost-effective approach to software development appears to involve a discipline of structured design and implementation of large-scale software systems. Jones, for example, extensively studied many successful software projects ranging in size from 2K to over 512K lines of source code (see references). The objective of his study was to identify and "prove" or "disprove" commonly held beliefs about programming and software in general. Some of his findings are summarized below.

Effective Programming Techniques

Jones "proved" the following hypotheses by measuring a large set of software systems. These "proofs" are statistical in nature; no counterexamples were found to exist in his study.

1. Large programs cost more per unit of code than do small programs. This hypothesis is supported by the software life-cycle models studied in

Table 0-1. Programming Technique versus Effectiveness

Technique	Smallest <2K	Small 2–16K	Medium 16–64K	Large 64–512K	Super >512K
Planning-control	3	2	2	1	1
Defect prevention	1	1	1	1	1
Defect removal	2–1	2–1	2–1	1	1
Development aids	2–1	2–1	1	1	1

Notes:

1 = Technique is of great value.
2 = Moderate value.
3 = Low value.

the previous sections. Obviously, large programs require a greater amount of planning, coordinating, and communicating than do smaller programs. Large systems take an overhead toll that is reflected in the larger cost per program statement.

2. Individual human variances are extreme in programming. This hypothesis confirms a natural suspicion that some people are better programmers than others. The variances found by Jones suggest that the differences are often extreme enough to "wash out" other factors in programmer productivity.

3. Defect removal costs are a major cost factor in programming. Again, this hypothesis is in line with the models studied earlier. Only 40% of the cost of software is in development, whereas the other 60% is in maintenance, modification, and managing. Of the 40% indicated by the Norden-Rayleigh curve, perhaps 15% is dedicated to testing. Reducing the 60% cost remaining after a system is developed is the most pressing problem facing software engineers in the near future. This is why we will devote the remaining chapters of this book to the important issue of defect detection and removal.

Jones found additional evidence to strongly support the following conjectures. These beliefs were not always supported by the facts, but in most cases they were found to be true.

4. Design problems are the main source of large-system defects. In fact, there is a difference between "large" program behavior and "small" program behavior. For example, Table 0-1 shows how ineffective large-program development techniques are when applied to small programs.

5. Error-prone modules tend to exist in large systems. We will address this issue in great detail in a later chapter. It is a particularly severe problem in concurrent programs such as found in real-time software systems.

6. Early defect removal leads to high productivity. In the remainder of this book we will strive to develop methods for early defect removal. Such methods hold the greatest promise for defect removal at a reasonable cost.

7. Defect prevention leads to high productivity. We can go even further in the process of combating errors in software. The prevention of defects obviates a need to remove them, whether immediately or at some time in the software life cycle. We pursue this idea relentlessly in the remainder of this book.

Structured Testing

Structured testing is the term used to describe the process of top-down certification of software carried out by the software development team while the software is being developed. Defect prevention and early defect removal are part of structured testing. Indeed, in many cases the actual cost of traditional testing procedures (after coding is completed) is 10 to 100 times greater than the cost of structured testing (see Fagin).

In several controlled experiments conducted during the development of both systems and applications programs, it was shown that two-thirds and four-fifths of the coding errors were found *before* machine testing was started. Although such high returns from structured testing may not be the case every time, it is sufficient reason to advocate early testing procedures.

Structured test procedure

1. Define software development as a team process with *activities* and their corresponding *completion criteria*, which must be satisfied in steps called *levels of abstraction*.

2. Certify each completion criterion through a team activity called *inspection*. Each inspection consists of five well-defined procedures:
   (a) Get the big picture.
   (b) Prepare a brief.
   (c) Find errors.
   (d) Rework the module.
   (e) Follow up rework.

3. Classify errors by type, and rank frequency of occurrence of each type. Spend most of the time and effort on the "error-prone" modules.

4. Use software instruments (called *probes* or *meters*) and written forms to describe how to find future errors.

5. Improve the probes and forms of steps 2–4 by analyzing the results of previous structured tests. Use the improved methods in subsequent tests.

The heart of structured testing is the team activity called *inspection*. Inspection is used to communicate ideas to all team members, find errors, assure defect removal, and guarantee completion of each level in the design. Thus, an inspection *might* be performed at completion of each of the levels of abstraction shown below:

Levels of abstraction

Design	
1. Blueprint—0 level—module specifications	I_0
2. Blueprint—1 level—logic specifications	I_1

Coding	
1. Blueprint—2 level—source statement coding	I_2
2. Blueprint—3 level—object code testing	I_3

Testing (traditional)	
1. System testing	I_4
2. Production	maintenance

Notice we have included production phase maintenance as part of testing. In unstructured testing, some defects are delivered with the software. Maintenance is used as a means of removing the remaining bugs as well as making enhancements. This approach is very costly and reduces *net* programmer productivity. Instead, we suggest an early defect removal process whereby inspections I_0, I_1, I_2, and I_3 account for most of the defect removal.

The I_0 inspection is trivial; the designer and systems analyst must agree that the design objectives are satisfied by the software to be constructed. This inspection often constitutes a contract for the actual development work to be performed. Since this is not directly related to programmer productivity, we will not discuss it here.

Figure 0-7 shows how structured testing is applied to the design and coding levels of abstraction. Note the emphasis on inspections I_1, I_2, and I_3. It is important to identify the meaning of each of these inspections because they define the completion of each level of abstraction.

I_1 The design is finished and correct.

I_2 The source code is written and is correct. (This inspection is done after the *first* successful compilation of the source code.)

I_3 The object code for each module is written and is correct.

I_4 The complete software system is finished and runs correctly.

The interesting thing about these definitions is that most of the design and coding errors are found and removed before the program is actually

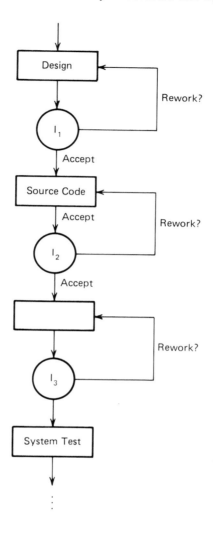

Figure 0-7. Structured test procedure.

run on a machine! That is, I_1 and I_2 account for over two-thirds of the errors found (see Fagin).

Furthermore, I_3 is a counterproductive test and should not be performed according to the IBM study done by Fagin. In a study performed within an operating system development group, the inspections produced the following results (HRS/K.NCSS means hours per 1000 lines of non-commented source code):

I_1 12% increase in productivity including 78 programmer HRS/K.NCSS of rework effort.

$I_1 + I_2$ 22% increase in productivity including 36 programmer HRS/K.NCSS above the rework due to I_1 and also adjusting for the Hawthorne effect.

I_3 decrease in productivity due to wasted time and effort (loss of 20 programmer HRS/K.NCSS).

This result suggests I_1 and I_2 are the most valuable production-increasing activities. What exactly is involved in I_1 and I_2 inspections?

The inspections conducted in the controlled experiments cited above consisted of five parts (as noted earlier):

Get the big picture (the whole team). The designer describes the overall problem and then the specific module to be inspected. The stage is set for the third part by noting whether this is a rework inspection or a new piece of code. Documentation is given to all members of the inspection team.

Prepare a brief (individual members). Using data provided beforehand, the team members study the design and/or source code to understand it. They are given a checklist to fill out and return when the whole team reconvenes.

Find errors (the whole team). The implementer describes how the design will be implemented (I_1) or how the coding was done (I_2). Each logic decision is discussed at least once, and if the inspection is I_2, then every branch in the program is discussed.

The discussion is opened up to the other members of the inspection team. The team tries to find errors. When errors are found, they are recorded. No solutions are discussed; only the errors are noted and recorded by the moderator for follow-up.

This part is *not* intended for redesign or evaluation of alternate solutions. This is important to remember since the team may be distracted by open discussion.

The inspection meeting must be limited to two hours in duration. The defect removal efficiency of the team declines after about two hours or if inspection is done more than twice a day.

Rework the module. The implementer removes the defects. If more than 5% of the design code is reworked, the inspection must be done again. If 5% or fewer errors are reworked, the moderator can approve the inspection without reconvening the team.

Follow up rework. The moderator must guarantee the correction of every error, resolution of every concern and settlement of every issue raised during the previous inspection meeting. If fewer than 5% errors, then the inspection is completed.

When structured testing was applied to eight modules of 4.5K statements written in COBOL for an application in the insurance industry, it resulted in a 25% increase in productivity (46.5 programmer-days rather than 62). Furthermore, the inspection rates for design and coding were four to six times greater than for systems programs:

		I_1	I_2
Get the big picture	:	898 K.NCSS/HR	709 K.NCSS/HR
Find the errors	:	652 K.NCSS/HR	539 K.NCSS/HR

The effectiveness of the inspections shows how important defect prevention is relative to the overall defect removal process.

$$I_1 + I_2 \quad 38 \text{ errors found/K.NCSS}—82\%$$
$$I_3 \quad 8 \text{ errors found/K.NCSS}—18\%$$

Of the errors that were located in these inspections, most of them were confined to a small subset of error types.

	Distribution of Design Errors
Logic	39.8%
Prologue/Prose	17.1%
Definitions/Usage	10.4%
	Distribution of Coding Errors
Logic	26.4%
Design	22.1%
Prologue/Prose	14.9%

It is also useful to know the form of errors signified by the types discovered during design inspections.

Missing item in the design	57%
Wrong item in the design	32%
Unneeded item in the design	11%

For example, a missing constant in the pseudocode design contributes to a "missing item" error; an incorrect comparison of two variables is part of a "wrong item" category; and an unneeded branch is an example of the last form of an error.

The concept of early defect removal and structured testing is an important one that we return to many times throughout this book.

The fundamental law of structured design   The design of reliable programs must include software inspection at the earliest stages of design, throughout the levels of refinement, and all the way down to final testing.

This law is often overlooked by software designers in their haste to implement code. We have shown that such haste leads to higher software costs when the resulting code is certified after the design and coding stages rather than in parallel with design and coding.

SUMMARY

This survey of software life-cycle models is intended to prepare the reader for the systematic software engineering techniques to be introduced in the remaining chapters. The central problem of software engineering is to produce high-quality software at the lowest possible cost. We have shown that this is done by attacking the most cost-intensive phases of the software life cycle. Furthermore, it appears that a disciplined approach using structured design and structured testing offers the greatest hope of reducing software life-cycle costs. Therefore, the remainder of this book is dedicated to the development of software engineering analysis techniques that a practicing programmer can successfully apply on a day-to-day basis.

PROBLEMS

1. Show that K is the area under the Norden-Rayleigh envelope by taking the limit:

$$\lim_{t \to \infty} y = k.$$

2. Suppose $\$U = 30,000$, and $K = 100$. What is the development cost of a software project if the Norden-Rayleigh model is used?

3. Plot the curve of S_s versus D. Plot S_s versus C. What can you say about code productivity as a function of difficulty or complexity?

4. Suppose a software project is estimated to require 50,000 lines of source code to complete. Also, the project is thought to be extremely complex, $C = 27$. What will be the total effort if the project develops the 50,000 lines of code in 3 years? Suppose the project succeeds; what level of technology, T, is expected?

5. Given a level of technology, $T = 10,000$, and development time $t_d = 2$ years, how much effort is needed to develop 28,000 lines of code?

6. In problem 5, above, what happens to K when t_d is changed to $t_d = 1.75$? 1.5? Draw a graph of K versus t_d.

7. Use Brooks' model and $m = 2 \times 10^{-7}$ to estimate the number of lines of source code that a single programmer can produce in one year.

8. Perform the following experiment. Study the effort in producing a program assigned in a computer science class and use your data to estimate m for yourself.

9. Construct a list of the rules given in this chapter. Can you add rules of your own?

10. Suppose $E(1) = 10$, $E_c = 0.05$. What is the best size for a team with these parameters?

11. Assume the Brooks model is used to evaluate a team of programmers of different abilities. Let m be replaced by m_i for $i = 1, 2, \ldots, n$. What becomes of the optimal model now?

12. Conduct an experiment. Divide your class into four teams. Let two teams implement a program in assembler language, and the other two teams implement the same program in a high-level language. How does programmer productivity vary?

13. Compute E_{mm} for a FORTRAN program that generates 35,000 lines of machine code.

14. How long will it take to develop the program in Problem 13?

15. Compute the development time, t_d, and efforts K, E_{mm}, $E^*(n)$ for a project involving 10,000 lines of FORTRAN code and a single programmer. How do the different models compare in their estimates?

16. Present a paper to your class on a structured design methodology. How does it compare with the methodologies in this chapter?

17. Write a short report comparing the structured testing method with the traditional (ad hoc) testing method.

18. Obtain a published program from the computing literature. Form an inspection team and attempt to find errors in the published program. Report your results to the class.

19. An application program is known to have 100 defects in its design and source code. How many bugs are expected to be found in $I_1 + I_2$ inspection?

REFERENCES

Brooks, F. P. *The Mythical Man-Month,* Addison-Wesley Pub. Co., Reading, MA, 1975.

Edwards, N. P., "The Effect of Certain Modular Design Principles on Testability," *IEEE Proceedings International Conference Reliable Software* (April 1975), pp. 401–410.

Elshoff, J. L. "An Investigation into the Effects of the Counting Method Used on Software Science Measurements," *ACM SIGPLAN Notices* (Feb. 1978), pp. 29–46.

Elshoff, J. L. "Measuring Commercial PL/I Programs Using Halstead's Criteria," *ACM SIGPLAN Notices* (May 1976), pp. 30–45.

Fagin, M. E., "Design and Code Inspections and Process Control in the Development of Programs," IBM TR 00.2763 (June 10, 1976). Poughkeepsie Laboratory, NY.

Fitzsimmons, A. and T. Love, "A Review and Evaluation of Software Science," *Computing Surveys,* Vol. 10, no. 1 (March 1978), pp. 3–18.

Halstead, M. H. *Elements of Software Science,* Elsevier North-Holland, Inc., NY, 197.

Jones, C., "Program Quality and Programmer Productivity," IBM TR 02.764 (January 1977). Santa Teresa Laboratory, San Jose, CA.

Mayer and Stalnaker, "Selection and Evaluation of Computer Personnel," *On the Management of Computer Programming,* G. F. Weinwurm (ed.), Auerbach (1970), pp. 133–157.

Moranda, P. B., "Software Quality Technology: (Sad) Status of; (Unapproached) Limits to; (Manifold) Alternatives to," IEEE Computer Society *Computer Magazine,* No. 11 (November 1978), pp. 72–78.

Putnam, L. H., "A General Empirical Solution to the Macrosoftware Sizing and Estimating Problem," *IEEE Transactions Software Engineering,* SE-4, no. 4 (July 1978), 345–361.

Schneider, V., "Prediction of Software Effort and Project Duration—Four New Formulas," *SIGPLAN Notices,* vol. 13, no. 6 (June 1978).

Scott and Simmons, "Predicting Programmer Group Productivity: A Communications Model," *IEEE Transactions Software Engineering,* SE-1, no. 4 (December 1975), 411.

Shell, D., "Work Measurement for Computer Program Operation," *Industrial Engineering* (October 1972), 32–36.

Wolverton, R. W., "The Cost of Developing Large-Scale Software," *IEEE Transactions Computers,* C-23, no. 6 (June 1974).

1

A Transform Theory of Software Performance

INTRODUCTION

Software engineering deals with the design, implementation, and documentation of correctly functioning computer programs. We might compare the design and implementation of computer software with the design and construction of a building by a civil engineer. First, functional requirements are stated that define the purpose and use of the new building. Then the building is designed to fulfill the stated requirements. An architectural rendition is sometimes drawn up to show the customer how the finished building will appear and how it might function.

The building is designed and implemented in stages. Each stage corresponds to a *level* of detail. The top level of detail is very superficial; for example, the architect's rendition shows the new building as it will appear on the exterior but tells nothing of its inner construction. The middle level of detail corresponds to the building plans. These plans may in turn be *refined* into greater details by *concrete specifications*. For instance, the plans may be refined into electrical wiring diagrams, mechanical structures, plumbing, and so forth. These additional plans show considerably more detail than the more *abstract* building plans initially prepared by the architect.

The lowest level of detail is the most *concrete* of all; it includes the actual building as constructed by carpenters, plumbers, electricians, and masons. This level is an exact duplicate of the imagined building, except it is the real thing. Hence, the stages of a newly designed and constructed building are stages in which the building is refined in levels. The top levels are abstractions, whereas the lowest level is real (concrete). The docu-

31

ments that describe these *levels of abstraction* are the lists of requirements, parts, supplies, and the plans that specify the construction steps.

New buildings are put together by teams of people. The architect and buyer decide upon the functional requirements, and they specify the highest level of abstraction. The construction engineer makes sure the building is (1) structurally sound, and (2) meets or exceeds its intended performance requirements. The construction workers make sure the building is constructed as it should be according to the plans.

This book is intended for the software construction engineer. That is, we disregard the other steps in constructing software in order to concentrate on the techniques that apply to the correct functioning of programs (structurally sound) and to estimating software performance (meet or exceed intended performance requirements). We want to analyze the software architect's rendition, the levels of abstraction, and sometimes the program code itself to see whether it is *correct* (does what it is supposed to do), and whether it is up to expected performance (runs fast enough).

These two areas of analysis (correctness and performance) are carried out in a number of ways by the practitioner. Principally, correct functioning is determined by thorough testing. We will examine a method of testing that is a blend of mathematical proof and program execution. The area of program performance, however, will be developed first so that it can be applied to all software analyzed in this book.

Performance estimates depend on the time delay imposed by machine operations and on the frequency of execution of the machine operations. Therefore, we first develop a model of time-delay behavior in computer programs, and then modify the model to incorporate execution frequencies. The time delays and execution frequencies form a *network* of interacting parts when used to model computer programs. These networks will be the subject of analysis in the final section of this chapter.

TIME-DELAY TRANSFORM OPERATION

We might imagine the execution of a program segment (statement, subprocedure) to be an action that imposes a delay on a control signal as it flows through the program. Such delays may be due to the time it takes the machine to add two numbers together, copy a value from one place in memory to another, or compare two values and decide which operation to execute next.

The total time elapsed between the beginning of a program and its termination will be the sum of the individual time delays in each segment of the program weighted by the number of times each segment is executed. Figure 1-1 shows how a typical program execution profile may appear. The frequency of execution of segments taking 1, 2, . . . , 6 time units is

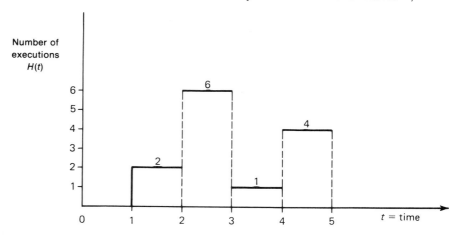

Figure 1-1. Execution profile of a program.

shown as $H(t)$. The elapsed time between beginning and termination of the program will be the area under the plot of Figure 1-1.

$$\text{Total time} = \sum_{t=0}^{4} H(t)$$

We can easily compute the performance of a computer program from an execution profile as shown in Figure 1-1. Unfortunately, we do not always have such a profile from which to estimate the total elapsed time. The execution frequencies may not be known, or if they are known for each program segment, we may not know in advance how they interact. For example, a program loop may or may not be executed a specified number of times.

Second, we may also be interested in the program's performance as a function of one or more parameters. We may not care so much about the measured speed of a program as about the relationship between memory space, say, and performance. To obtain such a quantitative measure of performance, we need to know the *performance formula* of a given program.

For these reasons we develop a mathematical means of deriving performance formulas for software given estimated frequency and time delay for each segment used to construct a program. These formulas are derived by applying a *time-delay operator* to the program. This operator is related to the classical *z*-transform of feedback control theory.

Let the *z-transform* of a time-delay function $f(t)$ be defined as follows:

$$f(z) = \sum_{t=0}^{\infty} f(t)z^{t} \qquad (|z| < 1)$$

The time-varying function $f(t)$ is said to be transformed from the t-domain into the z-domain by $f(z)$. The t-domain is the discrete-valued semi-infinite interval $[0,\infty)$ representing the time delays which occur during a program's execution. The z-domain is actually a complex valued interval $[0,1)$ that represents a *weighted* sum of the transformed function. We can see how the value of z weights the values of f by computing the transformed function for Figure 1-1. Suppose $z = \frac{1}{2}$ and we compute $f(\frac{1}{2})$:

$$f\left(\frac{1}{2}\right) = \sum_{t=0}^{4} H(t) \left(\frac{1}{2}\right)^{t}$$

$$= 0 \cdot 1 + 2 \cdot \left(\frac{1}{2}\right) + 6 \cdot \left(\frac{1}{2}\right)^{2} + 1 \cdot \left(\frac{1}{2}\right)^{3} + 4 \cdot \left(\frac{1}{2}\right)^{4}$$

$$= 2\tfrac{7}{8}$$

$$= 2.875$$

Compare this weighted sum with the sum of $f(t)$:

$$f(1) = \sum_{t=0}^{4} H(5) = 0 + 2 + 6 + 1 + 4$$

$$= 13$$

Table 1-1 shows the effect of the weights z^{t} on the value of $f(t)$.

The z-transform of a function is most useful when applied to arbitrary functions in order to study the behavior of the function without knowing everything about the function in advance. This will be the case in many applications of the transformed time-delay function when applied to program performance. For this reason, we study the z-transformation of several useful functions.

Some Useful Transformations

Let $N(t)$ be a constant for $t \geqslant 0$. Then the transformation of N_0 is derived as follows:

$$f(z) = \sum_{t=0}^{\infty} N_0 z^{t} = N_0 \sum_{t=0}^{\infty} z^{t}$$

Since $|z| < 1$, we can compute the geometric progression in closed form:

$$\sum_{t=0}^{\infty} z^{t} = \frac{1}{(1 - z)}$$

This equivalence is shown by noting that the infinite summation S is factorable. Thus,

Table 1-1.

z	f (z)
0.0	0.00
0.1	0.26
0.2	0.65
0.3	1.20
0.4	1.93
0.5	2.88
0.6	4.09
0.7	5.64
0.8	7.59
0.9	10.01
1.0	13.00

$$S = \sum_{t=0}^{\infty} z^t$$

$$= 1 + z + z^2 + \cdots$$
$$= 1 + z(1 + z + \cdots)$$
$$= 1 + zS$$

Therefore, solving for S:

$$S - zS = 1$$
$$(1 - z)S = 1$$
$$S = \frac{1}{(1 - z)}$$

So,

$$f(z) = \frac{N_0}{(1 - z)}$$

Figure 1-2 compares the transformed time-delay function from Figure 1-1 with the transform of $N_0 = 2.6$ derived above. Notice how $N(t) = N_0$ holds for unbounded t, and $f(z)$ is infinite at $z = 1$.

A second example illustrates how to transform polynomials into the z-domain. Let

$$N(t) = t \qquad (t \geq 0)$$

Then,

$$f(z) = \sum_{t=0}^{\infty} (tz^t)$$

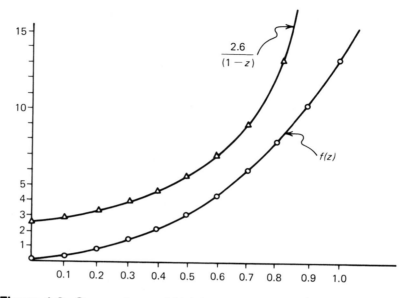

Figure 1-2. Comparison of $f(z)$ from Figure 1-1 with $2.6/(1 - z)$.

We can compute the summation in closed form as before by noting the derivative of z^t is tz^{t-1}. Thus,

$$\frac{d}{dz}\sum_{t=0}^{\infty} z^t = \sum_{t=0}^{\infty} (tz^{t-1})$$

Hence,

$$f(z) = z \cdot \frac{d}{dz}\sum z^t$$

$$= z\frac{d}{dz}\left[\frac{1}{(1 - z)}\right]$$

$$= z\left[\frac{1}{(1 - z)^2}\right]$$

$$= \frac{z}{(1 - z)^2}$$

A segment of program imposes a very simple *unit time delay*. This is shown in Figure 1-3(a) as a spike at t_0 in the time-domain. The transformation of a unit time delay is derived below.

Let

$$N(t) = N_0 \qquad \text{(at } t = t_0)$$
$$\text{(0 everywhere else)}$$

Then,

$$f(z) = \sum_{t=0}^{\infty} N(t)z^t = N_0 z^{t_0}$$

An ensemble of time delays is shown in Figure 1-3(b). The z-transformation of this ensemble is simply the sum of all unit time-delay transformations. Hence, we can think of t_0, t_1, t_2 as the time delays imposed by three program segments. The z-domain version of these time delays is as follows:

$$f(z) = N_0 z^{t_0} + N_1 z^{t_1} + N_2 z^{t_2}$$

This leads to the following observation:

> Multiplication by z in the z-domain corresponds with a time delay in the t-domain.

Hence, if $f(z) = N_0 z^{t_0}$, we get $N_0 z^{t_0+1}$ if we multiply by z. This causes the spike of height N_0 to move to time $t_0 + 1$ in the t-domain. But what inter-

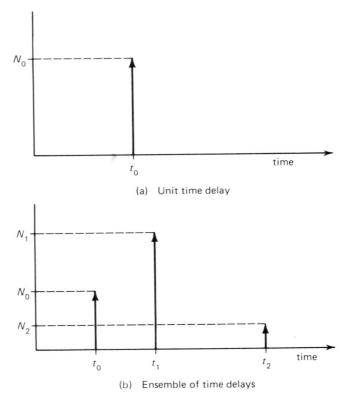

(a) Unit time delay

(b) Ensemble of time delays

Figure 1-3. Unit time delays.

pretation do we make of the coefficients N_0, N_1, N_2? The coefficients are magnitudes that, taken together, can be thought of as a *probability density function* defining the probability of time delay t.

Probabilistic Time Delays

Suppose $N(t)$ is defined as the *probability density function* (pdf) of the time-delay parameter t. That is, $N(t)$ is the instantaneous probability that a system (program) will incur a time delay of t units. Note:

$$\sum_{t=0}^{\infty} N(t) = 1$$

The *average time delay* is the expected delay of a system (program) computed by averaging over all values of t. Thus,

$$tau = \sum_{t=0}^{\infty} t N(t)$$

It may be difficult to obtain tau directly, as we mentioned earlier. This is where the z-transformation comes in. The average time delay, tau, is also computed from $f(z)$ by setting $z = 1$ in the first-order derivative of $f(z)$. That is,

$$f'(z) = \frac{d}{dz} \sum_{t=0}^{\infty} N(t)z^t$$

$$= \sum_{t=0}^{\infty} N(t) \frac{d}{dz} (z^t)$$

$$= \sum_{t=0}^{\infty} N(t) \cdot tz^{t-1}$$

Now, set $z = 1$ and we get tau once again.

$$f'(1) = tau = \sum_{t=0}^{\infty} t \cdot N(t)$$

This leads to an important observation:

The average time delay of a system with z-transform $f(z)$ is tau $= f'(1)$.

Let's illustrate the power of this observation by computing the average time delay of several common probability density functions. Let

$$N(t) = \frac{1}{(t_b - t_a + 1)} \qquad (t_a \leq t \leq t_b)$$

$$= 0 \qquad\qquad\qquad \text{(otherwise)}$$

This pdf is shown in Figure 1-4. Now let's derive tau from $f(z)$.

$N(t)$ is an ensemble of time delays. Each spike in the ensemble is located at a discrete value of t from $t = t_a$ to $t = t_b$. Hence,

$$f(z) = \sum_{t=t_a}^{t_b} \left[\frac{z^{t_a}}{(t_b - t_a + 1)} \right]$$

$$= \frac{z^{t_a} + z^{t_a+1} + \cdots + z^{t_b}}{(t_b - t_a + 1)}$$

Differentiating $f(z)$, we get

$$f'(z) = \frac{t_a z^{t_a-1} + (t_a + 1)z^{t_a} + \cdots + t_b z^{t_b-1}}{(t_b - t_a + 1)}$$

and then set $z = 1$:

$$f'(1) = \frac{t_a + (t_a + 1) + \cdots + t_b}{(t_b - t_a + 1)}$$

$$= \frac{\sum_{i=0}^{t_b-t_a} (t_a + i)}{(t_b - t_a + 1)}$$

The summation can be expressed in closed form as follows:

$$\sum_{i=0}^{t_b-t_a} (t_a + i) = (t_b - t_a + 1)t_a + \frac{(t_b - t_a + 1)(t_b - t_a)}{2}$$

$$= \frac{(t_b - t_a + 1)(t_a + t_b)}{2}$$

This leads to the final expression for the average time delay of a uniform pdf:

$$\text{tau} = f'(1) = \frac{t_a + t_b}{2}$$

Suppose $t_a = 3$, $t_b = 5$ as shown in Figure 1-4(b). The average time delay is

$$\text{tau} = \frac{3 + 5}{2} = 4 \text{ units}$$

This result can be checked by computing the average from the t-domain sum:

$$\sum_{t=t_a}^{t_b} \left[\frac{t}{(t_a - t_b + 1)} \right] = \frac{1}{3} \sum_{t=3}^{5} t = \frac{1}{3}(3 + 4 + 5) = 4$$

What is the purpose of the z-transform and calculation of the average

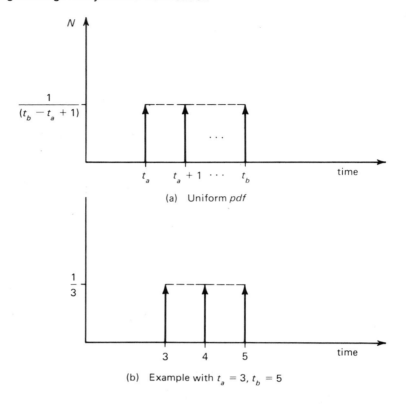

Figure 1-4. Time delays with uniform pdf.

time delay illustrated by the examples above? Before we can answer this question we must add one more piece to the performance model puzzle.

An ensemble of time delays is taken from a network model of a computer program that we want to analyze. In order to put the z-transform theory to work, we must develop a transform theory that works for a network of time delays.

DELAYS IN SOFTWARE NETWORKS

A *software network* is a graph G = {Nodes, Arcs, Map} containing a set of Nodes, a set of Arcs that connect nodes, and a Map function that defines the connection of nodes via the arcs. Furthermore, we assign a particular meaning to the software network of a given computer program. The arcs represent *execution* of program segments, and the nodes serve to designate the *state* of the program prior to the execution of a segment. The state of a program is loosely defined at present. In its simplest interpretation, we refer to the state of a program as the current point of control in the program's overall flow of control. A state is a place between two or more executable segments.

Let t_i be the time delay associated with a control signal propagating through arc i of a software network. Furthermore, let p_i be the probability of arc i being selected when the program is executed. Thus G is labeled (t_i, p_i) as shown in Figure 1-5(a).

We can transform a software network from its t-domain into its z-domain by replacing (t_i, p_i) on each arc with $p_i z^{t_i}$ as shown in Figure 1-5(b). Each arc of the graph in Figure 1-5(b) is executed with probability p and imposes a time delay t. Given these probabilities and time delays, what is the overall time delay in the graph? This question is answered by *reducing* the graph using a collection of *decomposition rules*.

Software Network Decomposition

A transformed software network is *reduced* if it is rewritten with fewer arcs and/or nodes. Reduction of a transformed network does not change

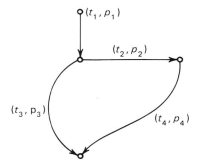

(a)   Software network in its t-domain

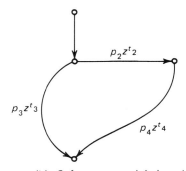

(b)   Software network in its z-domain

Figure 1-5. Transformation of software networks.

the essential time-delay model, however. The model merely becomes macroscopic and loses some of its detail. The purpose of network decomposition, of course, is to find a single function $f(z)$ that can be used to estimate the overall performance of the network.

It may not be possible to reduce a network to a single arc. Indeed, only *structured* networks can be reduced to a single arc. A structured network consists of subnetworks that are made of concatenated or nested structured networks. The simplest structured subnetworks are shown in Figure 1-6. They are: (1) succession, (2) alternation, and (3) looping.

These rules can be immediately applied to the simple network of Figure 1-5(b). The first reduction uses succession to combine two arcs into one; see Figure 1-7(a). The alternation reduction rule combines the parallel arcs into one as shown in Figure 1-7(b). Finally, we use succession again to obtain the resulting $f(z)$ for the network. The final formula in Figure 1-7(c) can be differentiated to compute the average time delay in the complete software network. Thus,

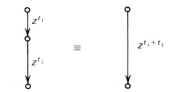

(a) Decomposition rule for succession network

(b) Decomposition rule for alternation network

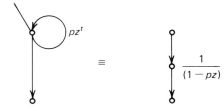

(c) Decomposition rule for loop network

Figure 1-6. Reduction rules for structured networks.

$$f(z) = (1 - p)z^{t_1+t_3} + pz^{t_1+t_2+t_4}$$

$$f'(1) = \text{tau} = (1 - p)(t_1+t_3) + p(t_1 + t_2 + t_4)$$

$$= t_1 + (1 - p)t_3 + p(t_2 + t_4)$$

If $p = \frac{1}{2}$ and $t_1 = t_2 = t_3 = t_4 = 1$, the performance of a computer program modeled by the network of Figure 1-7 would be

$$\text{tau} = 1 + \left(1 - \frac{1}{2}\right) \cdot 1 + \frac{1}{2}(1 + 1)$$

$$= 1 + \frac{1}{2} + 1 = 2.5$$

We applied two rules for the decomposition of the software network in Figure 1-7. The succession rule states that the total time delay of a series of time delays is equal to the sum of the delays. The alternation rule says the total time is the weighted average of the two delays. The loop rule requires an additional explanation because it is not altogether obvious how the rule of Figure 1-6(c) is obtained.

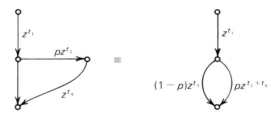

(a) Succession decomposition

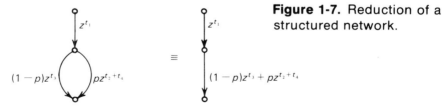

(b) Alternation decomposition

Figure 1-7. Reduction of a structured network.

(c) Succession decomposition

Feedback Networks

The decomposition rule of Figure 1-6(c) is an example of a *feedback loop*. Such networks are very important in software analysis because they model program loops. The time-delay formula shown in Figure 1-6(c) is nonintuitive, however, and requires a derivation to fully understand it.

The feedback loop is executed with probability p and not with probability $(1 - p)$. Each execution absorbs an amount of time given by t. We can show this as a series of alternation subnetworks as illustrated in Figure 1-8. At each stage in the execution of Figure 1-8(b), a choice is made: either exit or go back to the previous state. The overall time delay is the sum of each path through the feedback loop simulated by alternative subnetworks.

$$\text{Total delay} = (1 - p)z^0 + (1 - p)(pz^t) + (1 - p)(pz^t)^2 + \cdots$$

$$= (1 - p) \sum_{i=0}^{\infty} (pz^t)^i$$

$$= \frac{(1 - p)}{(1 - pz^t)}$$

The average time delay of a feedback loop is the value obtained in the usual way:

$$\text{tau} = f'(1)$$

$$= \left. \frac{tpz^{t-1}(1 - p)}{(1 - pz^t)^2} \right|_{z=1}$$

$$= \frac{pt}{(1 - p)}$$

The term $(1 - pz^t)^{-1}$ is often called the *loop difference* because we can apply the loop decomposition rule by merely substituting the loop difference in place of a unit time delay and treating the affected arc like a succession subnetwork. This is illustrated in the reductions of Figure 1-9.

The three network decomposition rules provide a tool for analyzing software networks for average time delay. In the next section we apply this tool to the analysis of two computer programs. The technique is quite straightforward as illustrated by these examples.

EXAMPLES USING THE TRANSFORM THEORY

The idea in using z-transforms and software networks is to model the program to be analyzed by drawing its software network. The network is labeled with estimated time delays and estimated probabilities of execution. The software network is transformed into an isomorphic (same

(a) Feedback loop with time delay t.

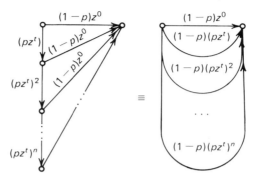

Figure 1-8. Feedback loop decomposition rule.

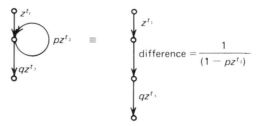

(a) Use the loop difference and create an additional node

(b) Treat the loop difference as if it were a succession reduction

Figure 1-9. Loop reduction.

shape) graph with z-domain labels. Finally, the z-domain graph is reduced to a single arc by applying decomposition rules. A structured network is always reducible to a single arc.

Example of *If-Then-Else* Program

Suppose we analyze a program for calculating the roots of a quadratic:

$$Ax^2 + Bx = C = 0$$

The solution to this problem depends on the values of A, B, C. If A equals zero, there is only one solution. If A and B are both zero, the problem is ill-defined. The pseudocode abstraction of this problem, including the possibilities that A and/or B are zero, is given in Figure 1-10.

Figure 1-10 is turned into code as shown in Figure 1-11. This program is next analyzed for performance by simply drawing a software network that we believe accurately models the flow of control through QUAD. Such a network is shown in Figure 1-12.

The software network is drawn by designating an arc for each segment of program that we wish to model. In Figure 1-12 we use an arc to designate each "arm" of each **if-then-else** statement; we have grouped together each segment of straight-line code, e.g.,

TERM   := − B/(2*A) ;
DISCRIM := SQR(B) − 4*A*C ;

The software network represents the flow of control structure of the program that it models.

The labeled network of Figure 1-12(a) consists of estimates based on the following assumptions:

Each arithmetic operator is assumed to impose a time delay of one unit (+, −, *, /, := etc.).

Each function or subprocedure invocation is assumed to impose ten time-delay units (WRITE, SQR, READ, SQRT, etc.).

Hence,

WRITELN(TERM,'+ −',SQRT(− DISCRIM)/(2*A),'Imaginary')

is estimated to impose 23 time units of delay:

Delay	Operation/Call
10	WRITELN
10	SQRT
1	−DSCRIM
1	/
1	2*A
23	Total count

Solution To $Ax^2 + Bx + C = 0$ Using $\dfrac{B \pm SQRT(B*B - 4*A*C)}{(2*A)}$

1. Input A,B,C
2. Compare A : 0?

$A = 0$ $\begin{cases} \text{Compare B : 0?} \\ \quad B = 0 \text{ \{Output 'Bad Inputs'} \\ \quad B \neq 0 \text{ \{Output } -C/B \end{cases}$

$A \neq 0$ $\begin{cases} \text{TERM} := -B/(2*A) \\ \text{DISCRIM} := SQR(B) - 4*A*C \\ \text{Compare DISCRIM : 0?} \\ \quad \text{DISCRIM} < 0 \text{ \{Output TERM,} \pm SQRT(-DISCRIM)/(2*A) \\ \quad \text{DISCRIM} \geqslant 0 \begin{cases} \text{FACTOR} := SQRT(DISCRIM)/(2*A) \\ \text{Output TERM+FACTOR, TERM-FACTOR} \end{cases} \end{cases}$

3. End.

Figure 1-10. Pseudocode abstraction of Program QUAD.

```
program QUAD;
  var
    A,B,C : real; (* inputs *)
    TERM,DISCRIM,FACTOR : real; (* working values *)
  begin
    WRITE('EnterA,B,C:');READLN(A,B,C);
    if A = 0
      then if B = 0 then WRITELN('Bad Inputs')
                    else  WRITELN(-C/B,'=Solution')
      else begin
        TERM := -B/(2*A);
        DISCRIM := SQR(B) - 4*A*C;
        if DISCRIM < 0
          then WRITELN(TERM,'+-',SQRT(-DISCRIM)/(2*A),'Imaginary')
          else begin
            FACTOR := SQRT(DISCRIM)/(2*A);
            WRITELN(TERM+FACTOR,'And',TERM-FACTOR,'=Solutions')
          end
      end
  end.
```

Figure 1-11. Program QUAD computes the roots of $Ax^2 + Bx + C = 0$.

These time estimates are quite arbitrary, of course, and more accurate estimates depend on the particular machine, quality of compiler, and so on. These estimates usually yield order-of-magnitude values, only. The resulting formula gives the software engineer a parameterized equation that can be used to make performance improvements, however.

The series of reductions shown in Figure 1-13 lead to the transformed delay equation:

$$f(z) = z^{20}(1 - p)z^{17}[(1 - r)z^{24} + rz^{23}] + z^{20}pz[(1 - q)z^{11} + qz^{13}]$$
$$= (1 - p)(1 - r)z^{61} + (1 - p)rz^{60} + p(1 - g)z^{32} + pqz^{34}$$

The average time delay is

$$\text{tau} = f'(1) = 61(1 - p)(1 - r) + 60(1 - p)r + 32(1 - q)p + 34pq$$
$$= (1 - p)(61 - r) + p(32 + 2q)$$

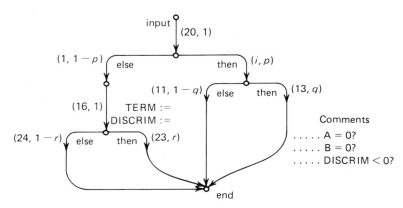

(a)   Software network of program QUAD shaving (time delay, probability) at each arc.

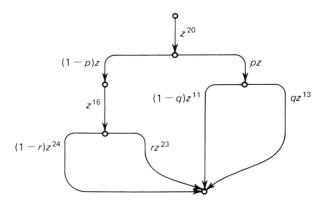

(b)   Transformed software network of program QUAD.

Figure 1-12. Software network model of Program QUAD.

$$= 61 - (1 - p)r + p(2q - 29)$$

where

$$p = \text{probability that } A = 0$$
$$q = \text{probability that } B = 0$$
$$r = \text{probability that DISCRIM} < 0$$

Suppose $p = q = r = 0$ (the typical case?), then tau = 61 time units.

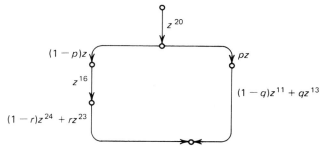

(a) Reduction using alternative decomposition rule (twice)

(b) Reduction using succession decomposition rule (twice on the left and once on the right side)

(c) Reduction using alternative decomposition rule

Figure 1-13. Reduction of transformed network model.

Alternatively, if $p = q = r = \frac{1}{2}$, the expected time is

$$\text{tau} = 61 - \frac{1}{4} + \frac{1}{2}(1 - 29)$$

$$= 46.75 \text{ time units}$$

This example illustrates the value of using the transformed software network. The resulting formula for tau is parameterized so we can study the effects of changing the parameters.

This example uses the succession and alternation transformations, but perhaps of greater interest is the loop transformation. We turn now to an example that uses the loop transformation to study the performance of a single looping program.

Example of a Looping Program

The time delay imposed by a program is a function of the execution probabilities and the individual time delays of the program segments. In programs containing loops, the individual time delays of each loop body segment are accumulated while the body is repeated. Each pass through the loop increases the expected execution time. Difficulty in estimating the total accumulated time spent in a loop is traceable to the uncertain number of passes through the loop. This problem is illustrated by the following example.

Suppose an array of information is stored in the following data structure:

```
type
    LIST = array [1 . . N] of record
                        INFO : string;
                        KEY : integer
                    end;
var
    A : LIST;
```

The following segment of program searches the list A for a matching key, K. The value of LOOKUP is zero if no match is found, and I, otherwise, where I is the location of the matching key.

```
I := 0;
repeat
  I := I + 1
until (A[I].KEY = K) or (I=N);
if A[I].KEY = K
  then LOOKUP := I
  else LOOKUP := 0;
```

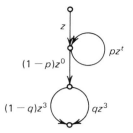

(a)   Transformed software network for LOOKUP

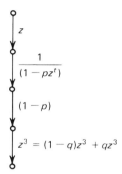

(b)   Reduction using loop difference

Figure 1-14. Reduction steps for LOOKUP.

Obviously, the performance of this program segment depends on the number of times the repeat loop is executed. But how many times must the loop body be repeated before a match is made?

Figure 1-14 shows how we apply the loop difference formula to reduce the software network model of the program segment LOOKUP. The transformed time delay is obtained by taking the product of the successive arcs in Figure 1-14(b). Thus,

$$f(z) = \frac{(1 - p)z^4}{(1 - pz^t)}$$

where

$$p = \text{probability repeat is executed again}$$
$$(1 - p) = \text{probability match is made}$$
$$t = \text{time delay of loop body}$$

The four units of time delay are estimates obtained by counting the number of operations in the loop body:

$$\text{tau} = f'(1) = \frac{4(1-p)(1-p) + pt(1-p)}{(1-p)^2}$$

$$= 4 + \frac{pt}{(1-p)}$$

This formula reveals the following properties of the looping program:

- If $p = 0$, the program takes four units of time.
- If $p = 1$, the program never terminates.
- The execution time is a nonlinear function of p.

The loop is repeated as long as the match fails, or as long as the list contains elements that have yet to be compared. Suppose we assume a uniform frequency of match between K and the list elements $A[I].KEY$. Then,

$$(1-p) = \frac{1}{N}$$

So,

$$\text{tau} = 4 + (N-1)t$$

This estimate depends on N, so we say the performance of LOOKUP is of *order* N. Thus, we can write the formula in an abbreviated notation using a large letter O:

$$\text{tau} \sim O(N)$$

This designates the performance of LOOKUP as a *linear algorithm* because it is linearly related to N.

Another way to evaluate tau in this example may also be acceptable. Each pass of the repeat component eliminates part of the list. Thus, on the ith pass through the loop, the probability of making a match depends on the number of passes already completed:

$$(1-p) = \frac{1}{(N-i+1)} \qquad (i\text{th pass})$$

The last pass terminates the loop whether a match is made or not. The value of tau becomes

$$\text{tau} = 4 + (N-i)t$$

The expected value of tau (averaged over all values of i) is obtained by averaging:

$$\overline{\text{tau}} = 4 + \frac{t}{N} \sum_{i=1}^{N} (N-i)$$

$$= 4 + \frac{t}{N} \left[N^2 - \frac{N(N + 1)}{2} \right]$$

$$= 4 + t \left(N - \frac{N + 1}{2} \right)$$

$$= 4 + t \left(\frac{N - 1}{2} \right)$$

This evaluation gives an improved performance estimate, but the program is still an O(N) algorithm. This last formula is the generally accepted time estimate for a linear search. It is derived from assuming the match is found at random in the list. On the average, one-half of the list is examined before the match occurs. The problem with this, however, is the assumption that the match always occurs. Clearly, it is possible that the key k is not to be found in A[I].

The technique of averaging tau will be useful in estimating the performance of more elaborate programs. Before we can apply the technique, however, we must develop a theory of software verification. This is the subject of Chapter 3.

SUMMARY

A software engineer is responsible for the construction of correctly functioning computer programs that perform within stated time requirements. In this chapter we have examined a technique for estimating the performance of a program given its software network. A software network is a graph model of a program with labeled arcs denoting the execution time and probability of execution of the corresponding program segment represented by the arc.

Execution time is estimated by transforming the original software network into a network defined in the z-domain. Multiplication by z in the z-domain corresponds to a unit time delay in the t-domain. Thus, we derived a collection of rules for reduction of any transformed network to a simple network consisting of one arc. In this chapter we used (1) succession, (2) alternation, and (3) looping rules to reduce transformed software networks. The reduced network yields a formula for overall time delay of the original network.

The value of the first derivative of the transformed time-delay function is equal to the average time delay tau when z is set to 1. This is a useful result for estimating average time performance of any computer program.

The estimate is obtained as follows:

1. Given a computer program, draw a software network model of the program.

2. Label the network with time and probability estimates.

3. Transform the network into the z-domain.

4. Reduce the transformed network to a single arc using the decomposition rules given in Figure 1-7.

5. Differentiate the resulting $f(z)$ obtained from step 4, and set $z = 1$. The average time delay is $f'(1)$.

This method of performance evaluation will be used throughout the remainder of this text. It provides a convenient method for comparing functionally equivalent algorithms.

Figure 1-15. Transformed network for Problem 2.

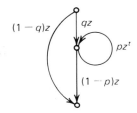

Figure 1-16. Transformed network for Problem 3.

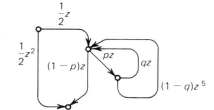

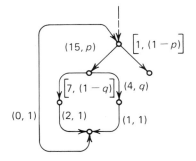

Figure 1-17. Software network for a program. Each arc is labeled (time, probability).

PROBLEMS

1. What is the z-transform of the following functions in the t-domain?

   (a) $N(t) = 1 \qquad (t = 0)$

          $= 0 \qquad$ (everywhere else)

   (b) $N(t) = t^2 \qquad (t \geqslant 0) \left[Hint: \text{Use } \dfrac{d^2}{dz}. \right]$

   (c) $N(t) = \dfrac{1}{5} \qquad (5 \leqslant t \leqslant 9)$

          $= 0 \qquad$ (otherwise)

    [*Hint:* Use the uniform pdf formula.]

   (d) $N(t + 1) = 10 - N(t) \qquad (t \geqslant 0)$

         $N(0) = 1$

    [*Hint:* Transform $N(t + 1)$ and $N(t)$; then solve for $N(z)$.]

2. Reduce the transformed network in Figure 1-15 to a single arc and find tau as a function of p, q, and t.

$$Solution: (1 - q) + 2q + \frac{pqt}{(1 - p)} = (1 + q) + \frac{pqt}{(1 - p)}$$

3. Reduce the transformed network of Figure 1-16 to a single arc and find tau as a function of the probabilities and time delays.

4. Assume all operations take one unit of time to perform in the program segment below. That is, $<>$, $<$, $:=$, $+$, $-$, each take one unit.

        while x $<>$ y **do**

          if x $<$ y **then** y $:=$ y $-$ x

              else x $:=$ x $-$ y

Draw a software network for the segment of program and use the network to derive tau. Assume probabilities p and q are parameters in your formula.

5. Find tau for the network of Figure 1-17.

6. Show the reduction steps of the transformed network given in Figure 1-17.

7. Why is the software network of Figure 1-17 considered a structured network?

8. Is the network of Figure 1-16 a structured network? Why?

2

A Network Model of Structured Programs

INTRODUCTION

A civil engineer designs buildings using standard components: beams, doors, windows, and so forth. A software engineer designs programs using standard components, also. A *structured program* is a program with single entry-single exit components. The simplest single entry-single exit components that are sufficiently powerful to construct *any* computer program are:

Basic actions. Control flows sequentially from one component to another (concatenation).

Choice. Control branches from a single point into two or more paths; then all paths merge into a single point of exit (**if-then-else**).

Iteration. Control repeatedly passes through one or more inner components and then exits to a single point (looping).

A *D-structured program* is a program implemented using the single entry-single exit control structures shown in Figure 2-1. We will employ the D-structures of Pascal in the examples throughout this book. Examples of each type of component are shown below.

Basic actions

```
READLN (A,B);
ANEW := A + B;
begin X := ANEW; Y := B end
```

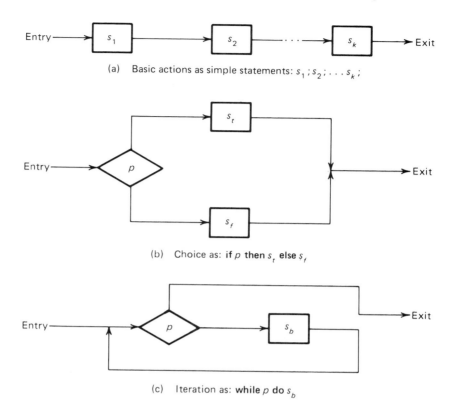

(a) Basic actions as simple statements: $s_1; s_2; \ldots s_k;$

(b) Choice as: **if** p **then** s_t **else** s_f

(c) Iteration as: **while** p **do** s_b

Figure 2-1. Components of D'-structure programs.

Choice

> **if** A = 0 **then** A := 1 **else** A := B

Iteration

> **while** A <> B **do** S := S + X;
> **while** B > A **do**
> > **begin**
> > > B := B − A;
> > > WRITELN (B)
> > **end**

For convenience we will frequently use the D'-structures of Pascal. The D'-structures are single entry-single exit components made up of the D-structures plus the following enhancements:

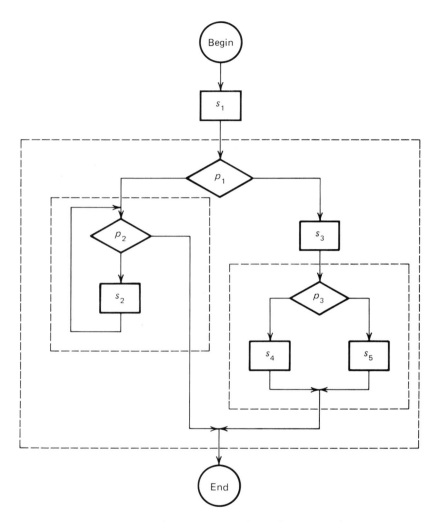

(a) A program made up of concatenated and nested D'structured components.

Figure 2-2. Single-entry–single-exit programs are structured, and structured programs are reducible.

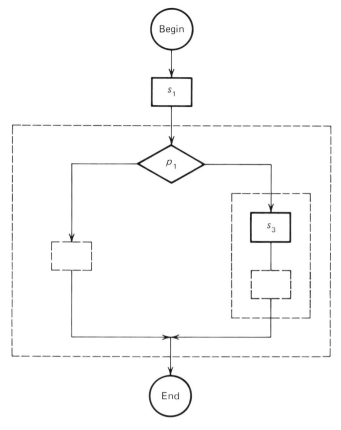

(b) Reduction of nested while-do and nested if-then-else.

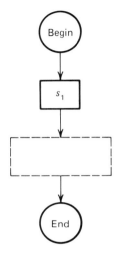

(c) Reduction of concatenated if-then-else component.

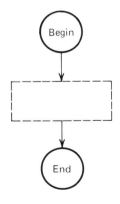

(d) Reduction of concatenated basic actions.

Figure 2-2. Continued.

Choice

> **if** p **then** s_t;
> **case** id **of** . . **end;**

Iteration

> **repeat** . . **until** p;
> **for** id := start **to** stop **do** s_b;
> **for** id := start **downto** stop **do** s_b;

These are for added convenience in structuring programs and do not alter the single entry-single exit property of structured programming. Instead, they make it easier to implement the three fundamental control structures: basic, actions, choice, and iteration.

A structured program is composed of *concatenated* and *nested* D'-structures. The concatenation of components is done by a *serial* connection; one component follows another. A nested structure is accomplished by inserting one component inside another component anywhere a statement is allowed. For example, the following **if-then-else** statement is nested inside an (outer) **while-do** component.

> **while** x <> y **do**
> **if** x > y
> **then** x := x − y
> **else** y := y − x

Concatenation and *nesting* are the only permitted composition rules of structured programming. These two rules guarantee programs that are *reducible* to a single entry-single exit flowchart as shown in Figure 2-2(a–d). A program flow chart is *not* reducible if it contains overlapping control structures as illustrated in Figure 2-3.

The flow chart of Figure 2-3 represents an unstructured program because it is impossible to partition all components into concatenated and nested single entry-single exit control structures. All attempts to reduce this flow chart fail because of the overlapping control paths shown as *knotted* paths in Figure 2-3. Therefore, a program is structured if it has zero knots. An unstructured program has one or more knots.

In this chapter we develop a network model of structured programs. Such programs are reducible; therefore the network model will also be reducible. This is an important feature of the network model because it will permit analysis of programs for both performance and correctness.

In the next section we develop network models of each fundamental D'-structured component. These components can be concatenated and/or nested without loss of the property of network reducibility. Hence, the model can be used in conjunction with the performance model of the previous chapter.

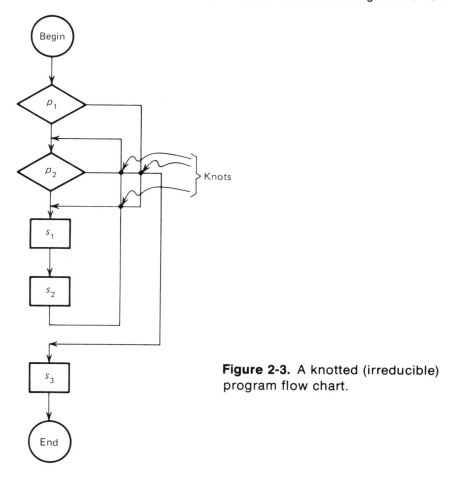

Figure 2-3. A knotted (irreducible) program flow chart.

PETRI NETWORK OF D'-STRUCTURED COMPONENTS

Petri Networks

A Petri network (simply "network") is a bipartite graph $G = \{$Places, Transitions, Arcs, Map$\}$:

Places. Set of program states representing the beginning or end of an action.

Transitions. Set of program actions representing operations, statements, program segments, modules, etc.

Arcs. Set of control paths representing the flow of control from places to transitions and from transitions to places.

Map. The topology of the graph is determined by connectivity of places and transitions. Arcs are permitted to connect places-to-transitions and transitions-to-places. Arcs are never allowed to connect places-to-places or transitions-to-transitions.

The network of Figure 2-4 illustrates the notation used to describe a Petri network. The circled nodes are places, the bars are transitions, and the arrows are connecting arcs. The topology (map) of a network is given by the drawing itself.

Notice that flow through a network can be split by a forked transition and merged by a place. These operations correspond to the flow of control in a program. Indeed, the places correspond to control statements of a

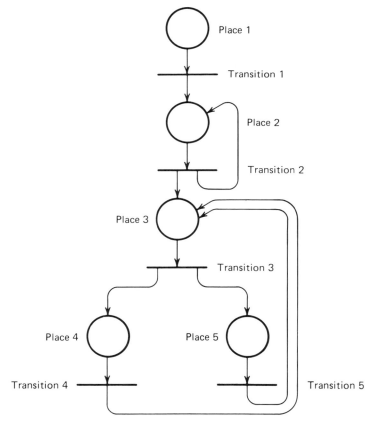

Figure 2-4. Petri networks are bipartite graphs consisting of places, transitions, arcs, and connectivity.

program, and the transitions correspond to executable operations performed by a program.

Application to Structured Programs

We can express the D'-structures in Petri network notation. The places are labeled with key words, and the transitions correspond to executable statements in the D'-structured component. The resulting network is one of the familiar networks we analyzed in Chapter 1, so we can also derive the corresponding z-domain formula for its performance.

Every D'-structured network is reducible; hence the network of concatenated and/or nested D'-structures is reducible. This leads to the possibility of analyzing any structured program using its network model and the z-transform developed earlier.

Figure 2-5 shows the network model of the D-structures. The "before" network corresponds to the appropriate structure, and the "after" network corresponds to the reduced component after application of a network reduction (decomposition) rule.

Basic action   The z-transform expression for the basic action network in Figure 2-5(a) is:

$$\tau_s(z) = z^{t_1 + t_2}$$

Thus, to obtain the average time delay for successive basic actions, we set z to 1 in the derivative:

$$\tau_s'(z) = (t_1 + t_2)z^{t_1 + t_2 - 1}$$
$$\tau_s'(1) = t_1 + t_2$$

This result is the expected time delay of the reduced "after" network for concatenation of two statements s_1, s_2.

Choice   The derivation of the time delay in Figure 2-5(b) uses the alternation reduction rules as follows:

$$\tau_a(z) = z^{t_1}[pz^{t_t} + (1 - p)z^{t_e}]$$
$$= pz^{t_t + t_1} + (1 - p)z^{t_e + t_1}$$

Then,
$$\tau_a'(1) = p(t_t + t_1) + (1 - p)(t_1 + t_e)$$
$$= t_1 + pt_t + (1 - p)t_e$$

Iteration   The derivation of time delay for the **while-do** structure of Figure 2-5(c) uses the loop difference formula derived in Chapter 1:

$$\tau_w(z) = \frac{(1 - p)z^{t_t}}{1 - pz^{t_t + t_b}}$$

Hence,

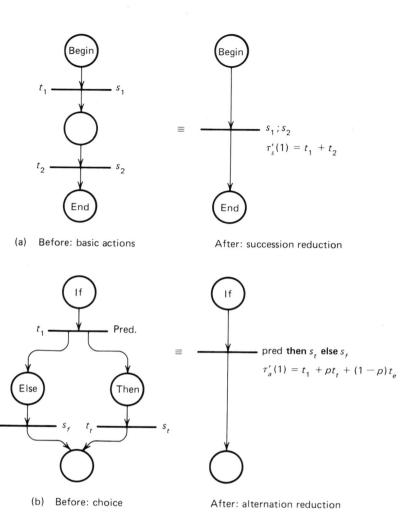

(a) Before: basic actions

After: succession reduction

$$\equiv \quad s_1 ; s_2$$
$$\tau_s'(1) = t_1 + t_2$$

(b) Before: choice

After: alternation reduction

$$\equiv \quad \text{pred } \textbf{then } s_t \textbf{ else } s_f$$
$$\tau_a'(1) = t_1 + p t_t + (1 - p) t_e$$

(c) Before: iteration

After: loop difference

$$\equiv \quad \textbf{while } \text{pred } \textbf{do } s_b$$
$$\tau_w'(1) = \frac{t_t + p t_b}{(1 - p)}$$

Figure 2-5. Structured networks.

$$\tau'_w(1) = \frac{(1-p)(1-p)t_t + (1-p)p(t_t + t_b)}{(1-p)^2}$$
$$= \frac{(1-p)t_t + p(t_t + t_b)}{1-p}$$
$$= \frac{t_t + pt_b}{1-p}$$

This time delay states the obvious: If the probability of repeating the loop is unity, the loop never terminates.

The reductions of Figure 2-6 show the remaining D'-structured networks and their performance. The **if-then** component yields the same performance as the **if-then-else** structure when t_e is set to zero. The **case-of** structure is a generalization of the **if-then-else** component. Note that Σp_j must sum to unity.

In Figure 2-7, the **for-do** loop structure repeats s_b a specified number of times. Hence the performance of **for-do** is a constant multiple of the time needed to test the loop counter plus the time to execute the loop body. The **repeat-until** component always executes the loop body at least once. Therefore, its best-case performance is $p = 0$, and $\tau'_r(1) = t_t + t_b$. It is interesting to compare the performance of **repeat-until** with **while-do.** Figure 2-8 shows the difference in performance between these two components for $t_t = 1$ and $t_b = 10$.

These fundamental components are used to construct reducible programs by concatenation and nesting. The reduction rules are used to decompose the corresponding network into a single transition and two places. This is shown in Figure 2-9. Each transition is labeled with its estimated time delay. Each forked transition is labeled with a time delay and a probability estimate.

Figures 2-10 and 2-11 further illustrate the technique of performance estimation using the network model and the z-domain formulas for time delay. Figure 2-10 illustrates the effect of nested looping. The performance estimate $\tau'(1)$ depends on p_1 and p_2 (the loop probabilities). Figure 2-11 illustrates the effect of a nested **if-then-else** statement within a loop. The performance of the loop is most critical to the overall performance of the program.

PERFORMANCE ANALYSIS OF PROGRAM QUAD

Let's apply the theory of D'-structure performance estimation to the quadratic formula program developed in Chapter 1 (see Figure 1-11, Chapter 1).

The network model associates a state of the program with each place in the network, and one or more statements with a transition in the network.

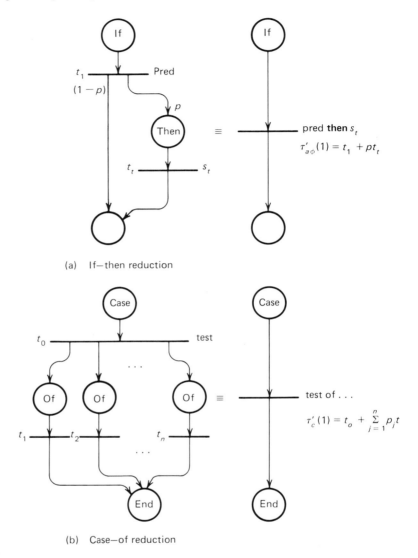

(a) If—then reduction

(b) Case—of reduction

Figure 2-6. Choice components for D'-structure enhancements.

Figure 2-12 shows the model and the estimated time delays (see Figure 1-12, Chapter 1).

Recall the assumption that each operation takes one unit of time, and each procedure takes ten units plus the time to calculate the value of all actual parameters. We have also estimated the probability of execution of each branch of the **if-then-else** components.

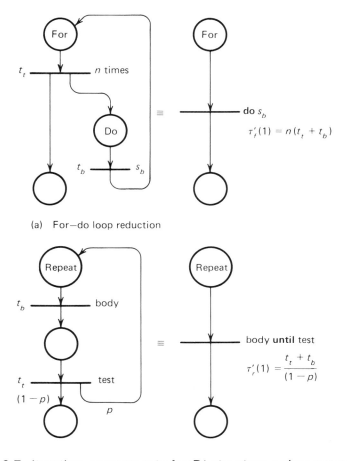

(a) For—do loop reduction

Figure 2-7. Iteration components for D'-structure enhancements.

Figure 2-13 shows the steps in the reduction of the network in Figure 2-12. The final estimated (average) time delay for QUAD is 58.7 time units. This estimate is compatible with the bounds derived in Chapter 1.

$$46.75 \le 58.7 \le 61.0$$

We made different assumptions about the probabilities to obtain these different estimates.

SUMMARY

In this chapter we developed a refinement to the software network model of Chapter 1. The Petri network refinement distinguishes program

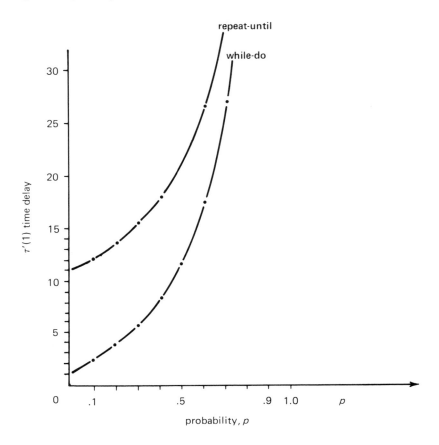

Figure 2-8. Comparison of **while-do** vs. **repeat-until** performance $t_t = 1, t_b = 10, p = (0 \ . \ . \ 1)$.

states called *places* from program operations called *transitions*. Furthermore, we showed how to model the fundamental components of D'-structured programs in Petri network form.

The performance estimation technique based on z-domain graph theory applies to the network model. We can use the reductions of Figures 2-5 to 2-8 to derive the performance estimate of any D'-structured program. These estimates depend on transition time-delay estimates and fork probabilities.

Here are the steps taken to evaluate a software system:

1. Construct the Petri network model of the software.
2. Label the network with time and probability estimates.

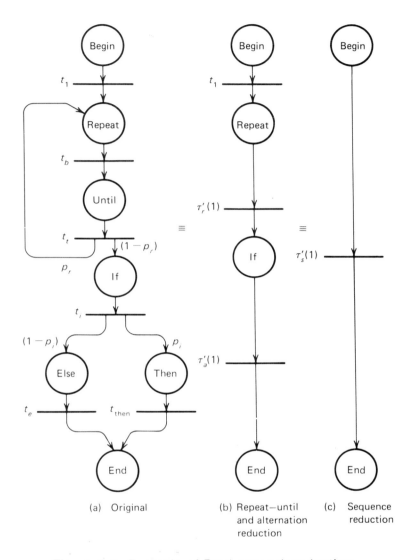

Figure 2-9. Example of Petri network reduction.

3. Apply the network reduction rules. If the software is knotted, the reduction will fail as soon as the knot is found. Otherwise the network will reduce to a single transition.

4. The performance formula for the resulting single transition in the reduced network will be the performance estimate for the entire system.

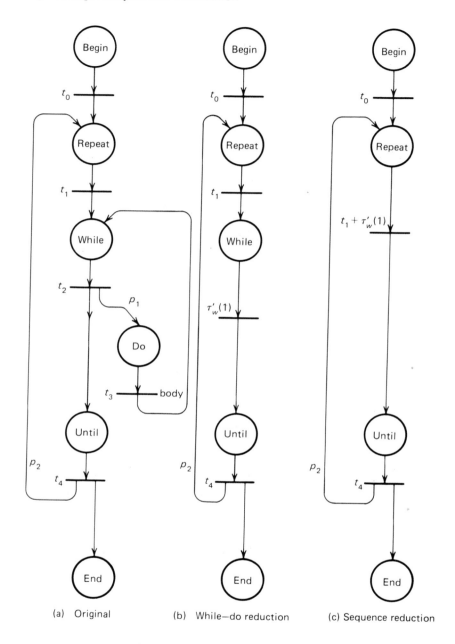

Figure 2-10. Example showing nested components.

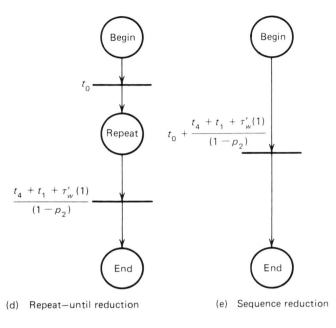

(d) Repeat—until reduction   (e) Sequence reduction

Thus,

$$\tau'(1) = t_0 + \frac{t_4 + t_1 + \dfrac{t_2 + p_1 t_3}{(1 - p_1)}}{(1 - p_2)} = t_0 + \frac{(1 - p_1)(t_1 + t_4) + (t_2 + p_1 t_3)}{(1 - p_1)(1 - p_2)}$$

Figure 2-10. Continued.

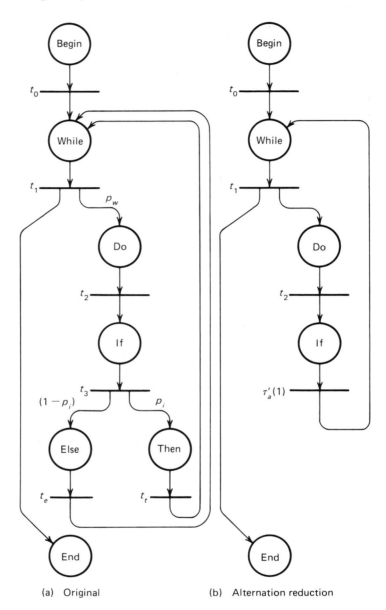

Figure 2-11. Example showing nested choice.

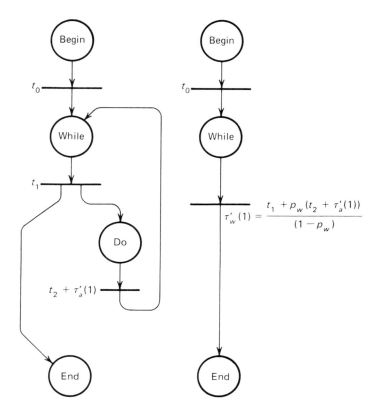

(c) Sequence reduction   (d) While–do reduction

$$\tau'(1) = t_0 + \frac{t_1 + (t_2 + \tau_a'(1))p_w}{(1 - p_w)} = t_0 + \frac{t_1 + (t_2 + t_e(1 - p_i) + t_t p_i + t_3)p_w}{(1 - p_w)}$$

Figure 2-11. Continued.

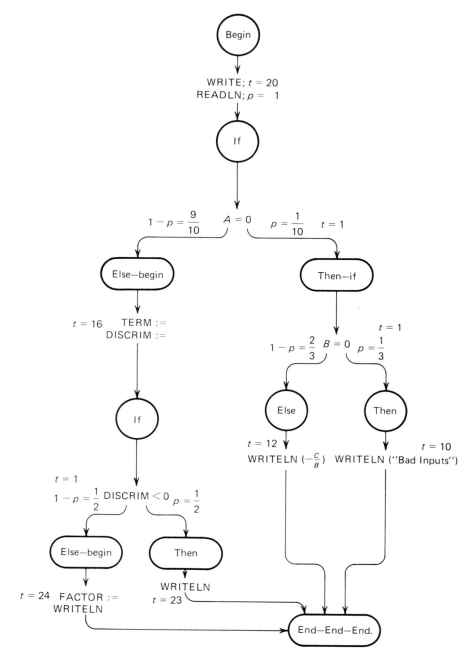

Figure 2-12. Network model of Program QUAD.

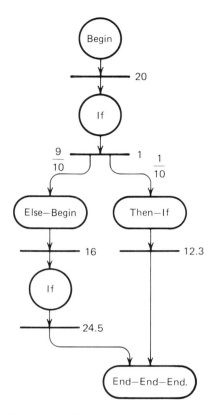

(a) Reduction of if–statements:

if DISCRIM < 0: $1 + \frac{1}{2} \cdot 24 + \frac{1}{2} \cdot 23 = 24.5$

then if $B = 0$: $1 + \frac{1}{3} \cdot 10 + \frac{2}{3} \cdot 12 = 12.3$

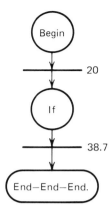

(b) Reduction of sequence and if–statement

Sequence: $16 + 24.5 = 40.5$

if $A = 0$: $1 + \frac{1}{10} \cdot 12.3 + \frac{9}{10} \cdot 40.5 = 38.7$

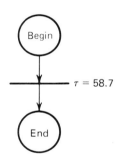

(c) Reduction of sequence and final value

Figure 2-13. Reduction of network for Program QUAD.

PROBLEMS

1. Is the following program structured, and if not, how many knots does it have?

```
program KNOTORNOT;
    label 1,2;
    var
        x,y : integer;
    begin
        READLN (x,y);
        if x = y then goto 1
        while x <> y do
            begin
                if x = y then goto 2;
                x := x div y;
            end;
        1: WRITELN (x,y);
        2: WRITELN (x,y)
    end.
```

2. Draw the Petri network of the program in Problem 1. Is it a reducible network?

3. Make a list of the D-structures. Make a list of the D'-structures.

4. The following function computes the location of character CH within string X.

```
function LOCATE(X:string; CH:char) : integer;
    var
        I,N : integer ; DONE : boolean ;
    begin
        I := 1 ; N := LENGTH(X) ;
            repeat
                DONE := X[I]=CH ;
                I := I+1 ;
            until (DONE) or (I>N) ;
            if DONE then LOCATE := I - 1
                        else LOCATE := 0
    end;
```

(a) Draw the Petri network for this function.
(b) Label the network with time estimates $t_i | i = 1, 2, 3, 4, 5, 6$ and execution probabilities $p_j | j = 1, 2$.
(c) Compute $T'(1)$ for the function using z-transforms and reduction rules for *repeat, sequence,* and *alternation*.
(d) What is the time-delay estimate for LOCATE?

(e) Let $(1 - p_1)^{-1} = (N - l)$ where l = loop counter. Average over $l|l = 0, 1, 2 \ldots, (N - 1)$ to estimate $\tau'(1)$.

5. Estimate the performance of the following program. State your assumption for the transition probabilities and time delays.

```
program DOESNOTHING;
var
    A,B,C : integer ;
    I     : 1 . . 4 ;
begin
    READLN (A,B,C) ;
    while A = B do
      begin
        if A = 0
          then for I := 1 to 4 do
                  C := C*I
          else B := 0;
          A := A + 1
      end ;
    if B = 0
      then WRITELN (B)
      else WRITELN (A)
end.
```

3

A Transform Theory
of Software
Verification

INTRODUCTION

In addition to performance analysis, the software engineer must be able to guarantee correctly functioning programs. A program is said to be *correct* if it produces the correct outputs anticipated for a given set of inputs. The anticipated inputs and outputs of a program are determined by software requirements and specifications. Therefore, program correctness is a *relative* measure of program quality.

In nearly all applications, *absolute correctness* of a program will be an unrealistic goal to attain. A program may not be required to function correctly for arbitrary inputs, for such a high standard of excellence is not usually required in practice. *Relative correctness* suffices in practical software development.

A program is said to be *certified* if it has passed an *acceptance test*. A variety of methods exist for certifying software. For example, mathematical proof techniques may be employed to rigorously analyze a program. Mathematical proofs *verify* the correctness of a program relative to an acceptance test given in advance. The disadvantage of using mathematical proof techniques is that they are labor-intensive and therefore slow to complete.

A second method of certifying a program is to execute it using selected test data as inputs and then analyzing the outputs. This is called *dynamic testing* and is used to verify the correctness of a program relative to the test data. The disadvantage of dynamic testing is the possibility that some unique combinations of inputs may have been overlooked that can cause the program to fail. Thus, a dynamic test may fail to completely test a program. Dynamic testing may not find all errors as shown in Table 3-1.

The "best" technique reported in Table 3-1 succeeded in finding fewer than two-thirds of the errors. When all test methods were used in combination, only 93% of the errors were revealed (Howden).

On the one hand, mathematical proof techniques are highly reliable in revealing program errors when performed by a reliable person (or by an effective theorem-proving program). But mathematical proving is slow, and it is often difficult to provide acceptance tests that are meaningful.

On the other hand, dynamic testing is unreliable because it cannot guarantee a complete "coverage" of the program using test data as inputs. Yet, dynamic testing is fast and easy to do.

Goodenough and Gerhard summarize this problem and suggest a way out:

> Neither testing nor program proving can in practice provide complete assurance of program correctness, but the techniques complement each other and together provide greater assurance of correctness than either, alone. (p. 172)

In this chapter we develop a verification technique based on both formal methods and less formal dynamic testing. We define a transformation for each D'-structure component and then use test data to "force" the resulting transformed program. Before presenting the theory of D'-structure transformations we discuss a simple convention for selecting test data. This convention will be used to *force* the transformed programs studied in the remainder of this book.

SOFTWARE TESTING

Error Analysis

Software verification by testing can be subdivided into dynamic testing and static analysis. We defined *dynamic testing* in the previous section as a method based on execution of the software using test data. The actual output is compared with the expected output, and if the two are in agreement, we say the acceptance test is true.

Static analysis can be applied to software *before* it is executed. Static analysis can reveal interface errors (wrong types, wrong number of parameters), undeclared or undefined variables (missing value), and anomalies in the flow of control (dead code, dead ends, improper structure). Many high-level language compilers perform static analysis during translation. Indeed, Table 3-2 suggests that finding syntax errors is an easy matter in many languages.

Modern programming languages attempt to shift the errors from

Table 3-1. Dynamic Testing Methods and Their Success Rate.

Method/Explanation	Percent Errors Detected
Path Testing: Every path through the program is executed once.	64
Branch Testing: Every **if-then-else** condition is executed once, but only one path or the other is taken.	21
Structured Composition: Program modules are constructed and tested using stubs (partially completed modules) in a top-down fashion.	43
Special Value Test Data: Limited test data are used based on boundary values, zeros, degenerate arrays, etc.	61
Symbolic Execution: Program is symbolically executed using symbol manipulation instead of actual test data.	61
Interface Consistency: I/O and parameter-passing values are tested.	7
Anomaly Analysis: Check undefined variables and anomalous control structure.	14
Standard Specifications: Check program against programming standards.	25

Source: Howden, pp. 293–298.

execution-time failures to compile-time failures because of the ease in detecting and correcting compile-time errors. Strong typing, range-checking, and simplified I/O are several advances in programming that have contributed to the shift from execution errors to compiler errors.

The most difficult errors to detect and correct are still execution errors, however, and dynamic testing is the most prevalent means of locating and correcting such errors. Little is known about the psychological causes of execution errors, but there are indications that some programming components are more error-prone than others. For example, the results of an experiment on relative-error-proneness (REP) are shown in Table 3-3.

$$\text{REP} = \frac{\text{number of faulty constructs found}}{\text{number of constructs, total}}$$

The REP number of Table 3-3 measures the error-proneness of a language construct by computing the ratio between the frequency of occurrence of faulty program statements and the total frequency of occurrence of a statement (averages were computed over many programs). The star-

Table 3-2. Syntax Error Rates Measured During Program
Translation for Four Languages.

Language	Percent of Programs		
	No Errors	One or More Errors	Translation Failed
FORTRAN	78%	15%	6%
Assembler	62%	12%	26%
PL/I	73%	17%	10%
Student FORTRAN	64%	36%	?

Source: Boies and Gould, p. 255.

Table 3-3. Relative Error Proneness in PL/I.

Construct	Percent Defects	Rep
Allocation (**dcl**)	16	0.9
Assignment	29	0.7
Iteration (**do**)	10	1.1
I/O Formats	6	1.5
Other I/O	8	1.1
Parameters/Subscripts	5	0.6
Conditional (**if**)	5	5.0
Delimiter (**end**)	4	3.3

Source: Young, E. A., p. 361–376.

tling observation in Table 3-3 is that **if-then-else** and **end** are highly
error-prone. Conversely, assignment statements are relatively "safe"
when compared with their occurrence in a "typical" program (Young).
The experiment with the REP number suggests our first convention for
forcing programs during dynamic testing, as follows:

> *Test Data Convention:* Use test data that exercise **if-then-else** compo-
> nents. In particular, select test data that exercise the predicate (condi-
> tion part) of **if-then-else** components on their boundary.

Suppose the following **if-then-else** is part of a program to be certified:

$$\textbf{if } A = B$$
$$\textbf{then } S := 2$$
$$\textbf{else } T := 3$$

The predicate $(A = B)$ has a boundary defined by B. Hence, we might select $A := B$, $A := B + 1$, or $A := B - 1$ as the set of test data values for A.

A more elaborate example, as shown here:

$$\textbf{if } (A - X) < (B + Y)$$
$$\textbf{then } S := 2$$
$$\textbf{else } T := 3$$

suggests even more boundary values. Assuming X, Y, and B are computed in the program and A is the only input value, the **if-then-else** predicate can be used to obtain the following values for A:

$$A < (B + Y + X)$$
$$A > (B + Y + X)$$
$$A = (B + Y + X)$$

This convention leads to path testing, which, according to Table 3-1, is not 100% reliable. Indeed, even if path testing was a flawless method of dynamic testing, the number of paths (and consequently the number of test data values) can be enormous. Therefore, we must devise a test method that reduces the number of cases considered when attempting to select test data for a program of moderate length. Fortunately, the coupling effect leads us to believe that we can get by with fewer test cases than blind application of the convention suggests.

The Coupling Effect

Several investigators have observed a kind of "error clustering" in practical software engineering that leads to a reduction in the number of test cases needed to certify a program. In short, the occurrence of complex errors is coupled to simple and easy-to-correct errors.

> *Coupling Effect:* Test data that distinguishes all programs differing from a correct one by only simple errors is so sensitive that it also implicitly distinguishes more complex errors. (DeMillo, Lipton, and Sayward, p. 35)

The coupling effect is a pragmatic convention that we can put to use in selecting test data that exercise **if-then-else** statements. It is also a useful convention for exercising programs containing structured data. For example, the coupling effect and the convention discussed earlier suggest the following rules for selecting *array data:*

Arrays as subscripts. Include cases in which array values are outside the range of the array.

Negative domain. Include cases in which array values are simple negative constants.

Nonunique domain. Include cases in which array values are repeated constants.

Degenerate domain. Include degenerate cases such as zeros and single element arrays.

Suppose we use these conventions to derive test data to force the following **if-then-else** component:

$$\textbf{if } A[I+J] < 0$$
$$\textbf{then } . \; .$$
$$\textbf{else } \; . \; .$$

We might use the following values for A[1 . . N]. (Each selection corresponds to one of the rules above.)

$$A[1 \; . \; . \; 1] = \{2\}$$
$$A[1 \; . \; . \; 2] = \{-1, -2\}$$
$$A[1 \; . \; . \; 2] = \{-1, -1\}$$
$$A[1 \; . \; . \; 5] = \{0,0,0,0,0\}$$

The **if-then-else** convention and the rules derived from the coupling effect suggest a place to begin a theory of software verification through dynamic testing. However, a complete theory of verification must take advantage of formal as well as informal techniques. Therefore, we turn to the formal aspects of verification in the next section.

FUNCTIONAL TRANSFORMATION OF SOFTWARE COMPONENTS

Test data selection rules and the simplifications they offer help to make software certification an easier task. However, they are not sufficiently powerful enough to constitute a theory of verification. Software verification is much too complex to do with a set of pragmatic rules and observations. What is needed is a set of rules for transforming complex programs into simpler (equivalent) programs.

A program component is transformed into an *equivalent* component if two components perform equivalent computations. For example, the two segments below compute the same results for variable *A*:

(a) B := 10; C := 5; A := B+C;

(b) A := 15;

The computation in (b) is equivalent to the computation in (a) as far as the resultant value of *A* is concerned. However, (b) is much simpler than (a).

A second example will illustrate the central issue of this section further. We could compute the final value of X below in two equivalent ways. One is more complex than the other, but the resultant value of X is identical.

(a) $X := 5; I := 0;$ **while** $I <= N$ **do**
$$\qquad\qquad\qquad \textbf{begin}$$
$$\qquad\qquad\qquad\qquad X := X + 1;$$
$$\qquad\qquad\qquad\qquad I \;:= I + 1;$$
$$\qquad\qquad \textbf{end}$$
(b) $X := N + 6;$

The idea underlying a transformational theory of software verification is demonstrated by these two examples. We seek a set of rules for transforming program components like those of example (a) into simpler program components like those of example (b). Thus, the transformed components are easier to verify; yet they perform the same computation as the more complex (original) components.

Assignment Statement Transformation

Let s_i be a concatenated sequence of assignment statements:

$$\{s_1; s_2; \ldots s_n\}$$

The braces are metasymbols used to indicate serial execution of statements s_i. The semicolon designates concatenation. Let T_s be an *assignment transform*. Thus,

$$T_s\{s_1; s_2; \ldots s_n\} \equiv \begin{bmatrix} s_1 \\ s_2 \\ \cdot\,\cdot \\ s_n \end{bmatrix}$$

The square brackets are metasymbols used to indicate parallel (concurrent) execution of the statements s_i. Actually, the parallel execution notation is strictly a notational device; we do not care about what order the assignment statements are executed, only that they *can be executed in any order*.

The T_s transform simplifies the original sequence of statements because it removes data dependencies from the original sequence. The *independent* version is easier to verify than the dependent version.

Examine the following (untransformed) sequence of concatenated assignment statements:

$$\text{(a)} \ \{A := 5; B := A + 3; C := A + B;\}$$

This sequence is *data-dependent* because the value of B depends on the value of A, and the value of C depends on both A and B.

The data dependencies of (a) can be removed by *forward substitution* of the *values* of A and B into the expressions used to compute B and C, respectively. Thus, the equivalent parallel version of (a) is derived by forward substitution as follows:

$$T_s\{A := 5; B := A + 3; C := A + B\} \equiv \begin{bmatrix} A := 5 \\ B := 5 + 3 \\ C := 5 + 8 \end{bmatrix}$$

The transformed sequence of assignment statements is simple to verify. If we carry out the expression evaluations, the resultant values of A, B, and C are immediately verified.

The sequence of assignment statements are transformable into parallel form by T_s because the data dependencies are simple. However, the sequence of assignment statements shown below are not easily transformed:

$$\{A := 5; B := B + 3\}$$

The definition of B is computed recursively. This leads to a problem when using T_s. The forward substitution transform applies to a *simple, single-assignment sequence* (SSA) only.

> SSA: A simple, single-assignment sequence is a sequence of assignment statements in which left-hand side variables are distinct (only appear once on the left-hand side), and the right-hand side expressions *do not* contain recursively defined variables.

The T_s transform applies to SSA segments of program code. All other segments must be transformed into SSA sequences before T_s can be used. The following counterexamples illustrate the difficulty of transforming non-SSA sequences.

$$\left\{ Y := Y + 1; I := \frac{I}{2} \right\}$$

We cannot simplify Y or I because they are both defined recursively. Recursive expressions are not always easy to detect. Consider the following:

$$\{X := 1 - B; B := 1 - X\}$$

This example reveals a recursive sequence of assignments when X := 1 − B is forward substituted into B := 1 − X.

$$\{X := 1 - B; B := B\}$$

Such recursion is typically found in program loops. Therefore, we discuss the loop transformation in the next section.

Iteration Transformations

Consider the following simple **while-do** component:

$$X := 0; \textbf{while } X < N \textbf{ do } X := X+C;$$

This loop repeatedly performs a test and a recursive assignment statement. We designate the tth pass through the loop by rewriting the body of the loop as follows. The first pass corresponds with $t = 1$, the second $t = 2$, and so forth.

$$X_0 := 0; \textbf{while } X_{t-1} < N \textbf{ do } X_t := X_{t-1} + C;$$

Therefore, X_0 is the initial value of X, and X_t is the value of X after the loop has executed t times. If the loop terminates after $(t' - 1)$ iterations, the value of X is $X_{(t'-1)}$.

We seek a transformation that reduces the segment above into a segment of program containing $X_{t'}$ but *no* loop component. In other words, the transform replaces the loop with the values computed by the loop. Thus,

$$T_w \left\{ X_0 := 0; \textbf{while } X_{t-1} < N \textbf{ do } X_t := X_{t-1} +C \right\} \equiv \left\{ X_{t'} := C \left\lceil \frac{N}{C} \right\rceil \right\}$$

How was $X_{t'}$ derived? The T_w transform computes a *loop functional* that terminates the loop. A loop functional is a series of computations that find t' such that the loop test is false. That is, we seek a functional that forces

$$(X_{t'-1} < N)$$

to become

$$(X_{t'-1} >= N)$$

and in the process makes the loop terminate. To find the loop functional, we ask, "What value of $(t' - 1)$ makes the loop stop?"

The recursive body of the **while-do** component must be converted into its iterative equivalent. This is done by solving the recurrence relation:

$$X_{t+1} - X_t = C \qquad (X_0 \text{ is given})$$

This is a first-order difference equation with solution

$$X_t = X_0 + Ct \qquad (t = 0, 1, 2, \ldots)$$

This iterative version of X_t is substituted into the loop:

$$X_0 := 0; \textbf{while } X_{t-1} < N \textbf{ do } X_t := X_0 + C*t;$$

The initial value of $X_0 := 0$ can be forward substituted into the body of the **while-do,** and the loop test can be rewritten. Thus,

$$\textbf{while } C*(t - 1) < N \textbf{ do } X_t := C*t;$$

Now, the loop terminates when

$$(C(t' - 1) >= N)$$

Hence,

$$t' - 1 \geqslant [N/C]$$
$$t' \geqslant [N/C] + 1$$

Finally, t' is the smallest integer that terminates the loop. Thus we can use the equals relation:

$$t' = [N/C] + 1$$

The resultant value of X_t after $t' - 1$ iterations is $X_{t'}$.

$$X_{t'-1} := C*(t')$$

Thus,

$$X_{t'-1} := C*[N/C]$$

Suppose $N = 10$ and $C = 3$. The loop terminates after 4 iterations.

$$t' - 1 = \lceil 10/3 \rceil 1 = 4$$

The terminal value of X is,

$$X_{t'-1} = X_4 = 3*(4) = 12.$$

Therefore, the transformation of the **while-do** computes t' and determines X *after* the loop terminates.

$$T_w\{X := 0; \textbf{ while } X < 10 \textbf{ do } X := X+3;\} \equiv \{X := 12\}$$

This leads to a formal definition of T_w.

T_w: Let LHS_0 and LHS_t be the initial and loop body segment of statements, respectively,

$$LHS_0; \textbf{ while } p \textbf{ do } LHS_t$$

where t is an artificially induced loop counter and p is the loop predicate.

If there exists a *loop functional* $LF(p)$ which determines the value of $t' = $ number of loop executions, then,

$$T_w\{LHS_0; \textbf{ while } p \textbf{ do } LHS_t\} \equiv \{LHS_{t'}\}$$

This transformation may not always be simple to find. The loop functional is usually a difference equation whose solution yields t'. The solution of the difference equation may be extremely complex, however.

Once the value of LHS_t is obtained through the solution of a recurrence equation, the value t' can be found by solving for a t such that the loop predicate is false. That is,

$$not\ p \text{ implies } t'$$

Let us illustrate the technique using the incorrect function in Figure 3-1. LOCATE is supposed to return the location of character CH in string X, but as the following test indicates, the program contains an error.

For convenience, we abbreviate **repeat-until** with a U and **if-then-else** with a horizontal bar separating **then** and **else** clauses. As before, t is an artificially induced loop counter.

The function of Figure 2-4 can be rewritten in abbreviated form as follows:

$$\begin{bmatrix} I_0 := 1 \\ N := \text{LENGTH(X)} \end{bmatrix} \{\text{DONE}:=X[I]_{t-1}=\text{CH};I_t:=I_{t-1}+1\} \underset{\substack{\text{DONE} \\ \text{or} \\ (I_t>N)}}{\mathbf{U}} ; \underset{\text{DONE}}{\mathbf{IF}} \left\{\frac{\text{LOCATE}:=I_t}{\text{LOCATE}:=0}\right\}$$

The U designates the **repeat-until** component, and the IF designates the **if-then-else** component. The U component terminates when (DONE) **or** $(I_t > N)$ is true. If IF component selects either the top or bottom statements separated by the horizontal bar. The values of I_t refer to the values of I on the tth pass through the **repeat-until** loop.

The loop body can be rewritten in iterative form as follows:

$$I_t := I_0 + t \ (t = 1, 2, \ . \ . \ .)$$

Hence, by forward substitution of $I_0 := 1$ into the loop, we get

$$I_t := t + 1;$$

Since $I_{t-1} = t$ and $N := \text{LENGTH}(X)$, we get (by forward substitution):

$$\{\text{DONE}:=X[t]=\text{CH};I_t:=t+1\} \underset{\substack{\text{DONE} \\ \text{or} \\ (t+1>\text{LENGTH}(X))}}{\mathbf{U}} ; \underset{\text{DONE}}{\mathbf{IF}} \left\{\frac{\text{LOCATE}:=t+1}{\text{LOCATE}:=0}\right\}$$

Further forward substitution of DONE yields

$$\{I_t:=t+1\} \underset{\substack{(X[t]=\text{CH}) \\ \text{or} \\ (t+1>\text{LENGTH}(X))}}{\mathbf{U}} ; \underset{(X[t]=\text{CH})}{\mathbf{IF}} \left\{\frac{\text{LOCATE}:=t+1}{\text{LOCATE}:=0}\right\}$$

Before we can go any further, we need test cases to force the transformed program. The test cases are selected with the advice of the conventions discussed in the previous section on testing. Table 3-4 shows a matrix of test cases and the corresponding results.

Notice the loop termination conditions:

$$t' = \text{LENGTH}(X)$$
$$X[t'] = \text{CH}$$

These two conditions give rise to the test cases in Table 3-4. The resulting

```
function LOCATE ( X : string ; CH : char ) : integer ;
  var
    I, N : integer ;
    DONE : boolean ;
  begin
    I := 1 ;
    N := LENGTH ( X ) ;
    repeat
      DONE := X[I] = CH ;
      I := I + 1 ;
    until ( DONE ) or ( I>N ) ;
    if DONE
      then LOCATE := I      (* correction : I−1 *)
      else  LOCATE := 0 ;
  end ;
```

Figure 3-1. LOCATE function containing an error.

value of t' is substituted into the expression for LOCATE. This substitution reveals an error in the program when a match is found: $(X[t'] = CH)$.

The LOCATE function can be corrected by replacing LOCATE := I with LOCATE := $I - 1$ as shown in Figure 3-1. The tth character is found in $X[t]$ in the corrected version, instead of $X[t + 1]$.

To summarize, loop transformations are carried out as follows:

Step 1. Introduce a loop counter, say t, in every recursive statement within the loop body.

Step 2. Convert all recursive statements to iterative form by solving the equivalent finite difference equations.

Step 3. Perform all forward substitution transformations permitted, and simplify the reduced program.

Step 4. Find a loop functional that terminates the loop. This is usually found by computing a final value of the loop counter, say t', such that the loop terminates. In the case of **while-do** loops the loop predicate is false; in **repeat-until** loops the predicate is true when the loop stops.

Table 3-4. Test Cases for Function LOCATE

	$X[t']=CH$	$X[t']\neq CH$
$X[t']=CH$	LOCATE := $t'+1$	not possible
$t'=\text{LENGTH}(X)$	LOCATE := LENGTH(X) + 1	LOCATE := 0

Step 5. Replace the loop with its equivalent computation. This is done by computing the final value (termination value) of the loop body using the functional of Step 4.

In the previous example we used a shorthand notation. This notation will be a convenience used throughout the remainder of the text. For loops, they are summarized as follows:

$$T_w \{\textbf{while } p \textbf{ do } s\} \equiv \underset{p}{\boldsymbol{W}} \{s\}$$

$$T_{for} \{\textbf{for } \langle \text{interval} \rangle \textbf{ do}\} \equiv \underset{\langle \text{interval} \rangle}{\boldsymbol{F}} \{s\}$$

$$T_r \{\textbf{repeat } s \textbf{ until } p\} \equiv \{s\} \underset{p}{\boldsymbol{\mathsf{U}}}$$

We next turn to the choice components in order to complete the basic testing theory for D′-structured programs. These transformations form the basis of a software verification method when combined with the test data conventions discussed earlier.

Choice Transformations

The choice transformation is the most difficult to use in the transformational theory of software testing. The reason is quite simple. Every **if-then-else** and **case-of** component creates two or more paths through the program in question. These paths tend to rapidly increase in number, leading to a large number of test cases to be examined.

The following transformation rules attempt to reduce the number of paths created by the **if-then-else** and **case-of** components. Unfortunately, they often do not succeed in reducing the number of paths. We must resort to careful selection of test data in order to simplify the majority of programs containing choice components.

The T_{if} transform divides the flow of control into two paths. The "upper" path is taken when the choice predicate is true. The "lower" path is taken when the predicate is false.

$$T_{if}\{\textbf{if } p \textbf{ then } s_t \textbf{ else } s_f\} \equiv \left\{ \frac{\{p\}s_t}{\{\textbf{not } p\}s_f} \right\}$$

We can sometimes use $\{p\}$ and $\{\textbf{not } p\}$ to simplify s_t and s_f, respectively. Forward substitution of the relation $\{p\}$ or $\{\textbf{not } p\}$ may lead to a simplification as illustrated by the absolute value function below:

function ABS (**var** X : **real**) : **real**;
  begin
    if X < 0
      then ABS := − X
      else ABS := X
  end;

The transformed function yields two paths:

$$T_{if}\{\text{if } X < 0 \text{ then ABS} := -X \text{ else ABS} := X\} \equiv \frac{\{X < 0\}\{\text{ABS} := -X\}}{\{X >= 0\}\{\text{ABS} := X\}}$$

Suppose we introduce an artificial variable S that is always positive; then the relations in the transformed **if-then-else** component are rewritten as follows:

$$\frac{\{X = -S\}\{\text{ABS} := -X\}}{\{X = S\}\{\text{ABS} := X\}} \qquad (\text{where } S > 0)$$

Forward substitution of the artificially introduced (equivalent) values of X give the simplification we seek:

$$\frac{\{\text{ABS} := S\}}{\{\text{ABS} := S\}} \equiv \text{ABS} := S \qquad (\text{where } S > 0)$$

Hence, the two paths have been reduced to a single path.

Unfortunately, this "trick" does not always work for **if-then-else** components. In general, we must use test data to force one path or another. This simplification weakens the test but greatly simplifies the analysis.

The **case-of** transformation is a generalization of the **if-then-else** transform.

$$T_{case}\{\text{case } s \text{ of}\} \equiv \frac{\frac{\{s = \#1\}s_1}{\{s = \#2\}s_2}}{\cdots}{\{s = \#n\}s_n}$$

Verification of MAXIMUM

A program for finding the maximum element of a list X[1 . . N] is shown in Figure 3-2. We can reveal an error in MAXIMUM by applying the transform theory.

The abbreviated version of MAXIMUM is annotated with loop counter t:

$$\{\text{BIG}_0 := X[I]\} \mathop{\mathbf{F}}_{(I:=1 \text{ to } N)} \left\{ \frac{\{\text{BIG}_{t-1} < X[I]\}\{\text{BIG}_t := X[I]; \text{LOC}_t := I\}}{\{\text{BIG}_{t-1} >= X[I]\}} \right\} \{\text{MAX} := \text{BIG}_N\}$$

```
procedure MAXIMUM ( X : array [1 . . N] of integer ;
                        var MAX, LOC : integer ) ;
  var
    BIG, I ; integer ;
  begin
    BIG := X[1] ;
    for I := 1 to N do
      if BIG < X[I]
        then begin BIG := X[I] ; LOC := I end ;
    MAX := BIG ;
  end ;
```

Figure 3-2. MAXIMUM procedure containing an error.

The **if-then-else** transform has been applied to the abbreviated program. The **for-do** loop counter I runs over the values $[1 . . N]$. When $I = 1$, the artificially introduced counter $t = 1$, and so on until $I = N$, $t = N$. The value of I becomes undefined outside the **for-do** loop, but t is defined $(t = N)$.

This program demonstrates the difficulty posed by **if-then-else** branches in a program. The only way out of this difficulty is to select test data that force the program to execute paths that can be examined to conjecture that the program works correctly.

We employ the coupling effect to obtain test data. Three cases are used:

Arrays as subscripts: This program does not use arrays as subscripts to (other) arrays. So we choose a simple "identity" function as test data. Let

$$X[I] = I \quad \text{where } I \text{ in } [1 . . N]$$

Negative domain: Include simple negative values; so let

$$X[I] = -I \quad \text{where } I \text{ in } [1 . . N]$$

Nonunique domain and degenerate domain: Include repeated values and degenerate values, e.g., zero. These two cases are combined:

$$X[I] = 0 \quad \text{when } I \text{ in } [1 . . M - 1] + [M + 1 . . N]$$
$$= 1 \quad \text{when } I \text{ is } M$$

First, we perform the transformation of MAXIMUM using $X[I] = I$ as test data.

TEST #1 $(X[I] = I)$

Notice that when $t = 1$, we get $BIG_0 >= 1$; so $BIG_1 = BIG_0 = 1$. Then when $t > 1$, we observe that $BIG_t = t$ and $BIG_{t-1} = t - 1$. These observations lead to a simplification in the transformed and abbreviated program:

$$\underset{(t\ \text{in}\ [2\ ..\ N])}{\mathbf{F}} \left\{ \frac{\{(t-1) < t\}\ \{BIG_t := t;\ LOC_t := t\}}{\{(t-1) >= t\}} \right\} \{MAX := BIG_N\}$$

Since $(t-1) < t$ is *always* true, the **if-then-else** expression reduces to the true-clause only. Thus,

$$\underset{(t\ \text{in}\ [2\ ..\ N])}{\mathbf{F}} \{BIG_t := t;\ LOC_t := t\} \{MAX := BIG_N\}$$

The **for-do** loop terminates with $(t' - 1) = N$ ($t' = N + 1$ fails) and $BIG_N = N$, $LOC_N = N$. Functional transformation of the **for-do** loop results in the following:

$$\{BIG_N := N:\ LOC_N := N\} \{MAX := BIG_N\}$$

and forward substitution yields the final result:

$$\{LOC_N := N\} \{MAX := N\} \equiv \begin{bmatrix} LOC_N := N \\ MAX := N \end{bmatrix}$$

We conclude that the first test case certifies a correct program. The largest element of $X[I] := I$ is N, and it is found in $LOC := N$.

TEST #2 $(X[I] := -I)$

The abbreviated version of MAXIMUM with this input is

$$\{BIG_0 := -1\} \underset{(I:=1\ \text{to}\ N)}{\mathbf{F}} \left\{ \frac{\{BIG_{t-1} < (-I)\}\ \{BIG_t := (-I); LOC_t := I\}}{\{BIG_{t-1} >= (-I)\}} \right\} \{MAX := BIG_N\}$$

Notice that when $t = 1$, $I = 1$,

$$BIG_0 < (-1) \equiv -1 < (-1)$$

which is false. Thus, $BIG_1 = BIG_0 = (-1)$. Furthermore, when $t > 1$, $I = t$,

$$BIG_{t-1} < (-t)$$

is also false.

$$BIG_{t-1} >= (-t)$$

is always true leading to execution of the false-clause of the **if-then-else** component. The loop transforms into

$$\{BIG_0 := (-1)\}\{BIG_N := BIG_0\}\{MAX := BIG_N\}$$

Finally, forward substitution yields

$$\{MAX := (-1)\} \equiv [MAX := (-1)]$$

The resulting value of MAX is correct, but the value of LOC is undefined. Hence, the program contains an error. This error is corrected by defining LOC as shown in Figure 3-3.

```
procedure MAXIMUM ( X : LIST; var MAX, LOC : integer ) ;
   var
      BIG, I : integer ;
   begin
      BIG := X[ 1 ] ;
      LOC := 1 ; (* correction *)
      for I := 1 to N do
        if BIG < X[ I ]
           then begin BIG := X[ I ] ; LOC := I end ;
      MAX := BIG ;
   end ; (* MAXIMUM *)
```

Figure 3-3. MAXIMUM procedure with correction.

Now, we perform a final test using repeated zeros and a single maximum of one.

TEST #3 $(X[I] = 0; I \neq M; X[M] = 1)$

When $M = 1$, we get

$$\begin{bmatrix} BIG_0 := 1 \\ LOC_0 := 1 \end{bmatrix} \underset{(I:=1 \text{ to } N)}{\mathbf{F}} \{BIG_t := BIG_{t-1}\} \{MAX := BIG_N\}$$

since $(BIG_{t-1} < X[I]) \equiv (1 < X[I])$ is always false. The resulting output values are

$$\begin{bmatrix} LOC := 1 \\ MAX := 1 \end{bmatrix}$$

When $M > 1$, we notice that every pass through the loop executes the false-clause of the **if-then-else** component until the $X[M]$ element is compared. Then the true-clause is executed once. BIG becomes 1 and subsequent passes through the loop execute the false-clause again. Thus, the abbreviated program transforms into:

$$\{BIG_N := 1;\ LOC_N := M\}\{MAX := BIG_N\}$$
$$\equiv \begin{bmatrix} LOC_N := M \\ MAX := 1 \end{bmatrix}$$

Therefore, the third test succeeds, and we are more confident in the correctness of the program.

In the next section we apply the transform theory to a complete program consisting of loops, arrays, and choice components.

A COMPLETE EXAMPLE: MERGE

Two ordered lists are *merged* into a single ordered list according to the following plan:

1. Let L1 and L2 be two ordered lists, and LOUT the output of MERGE.

2. Repeat the following until one or the other list is exhausted:

   (a) Compare elements of L1 and L2.
   (b) Copy the smallest element to LOUT.
   (c) Update list counters in L1 and L2.

3. Copy the trailing elements from the list that was not exhausted in Step 2 into the output list LOUT.

4. The output list LOUT is in order and of length equal to the sum of the lengths of L1 and L2.

This plan is implemented in procedure MERGE shown in Figure 3-4. The lists are of length N, M, and NPLUSM. The variables I and J keep track of the locations of elements to be copied into LOUT next. The MIN function returns the smallest value of its two arguments.

It is important to note that only one of the **for-do** loops is executed in the procedure of Figure 3-4. Either I exceeds N, or J exceeds M when this point is reached. The **for-do** loop that is executed simply copies the trailing elements into LOUT as specified in Step 3 of the plan.

The most challenging segment of procedure MERGE is the **while-do** loop. We can begin an analysis of MERGE by studying this most difficult loop segment and noting the following equivalent program segments. The ORD function returns 0 if its argument is false, and 1 if its argument is true.

$$\frac{\{L1[I] < L2[J]\}\{I := I + 1\}}{\{L1[I] >= L2[J]\}\{J := J + 1\}} \equiv \begin{bmatrix} I := I + ORD(L1[I] < L2[J]) \\ J := J + ORD(L1[I] >= L2[J]) \end{bmatrix}$$

That is, the successive value of I and J is determined by comparison of L1 and L2. In the case $L1[I] < L2[J]$, we add 1 to I. When $L1[I] >=$

```
procedure Merge ( L1, L2 : LIST ; var LOUT : LISTOUT ) ;
  var
    I, J : integer ;
  begin
    I := 1 ; J := 1 ;
    while ( I <= N ) and ( J <= M ) do
      begin
        LOUT[ I+J−1 ] := MIN( L1[ I ], L2[ J ] ) ;
        if L1[ I ] < L2[ J ]
          then I := I + 1
          else  J := J + 1
      end ;
    for I := I to N do LOUT[ I+J−1 ] := L1[ I ] ;
    for J := J to M do LOUT[ I+J−1 ] := L2[ J ] ;
end ; (* merge *)
```

Figure 3-4. MERGE two ordered lists.

L2[J], we add 1 to J instead. The two expressions are computationally equivalent, but the version that employs ORD simplifies verification because we do not have to deal with the **if-then-else** component. Now we can rewrite the **while-do** loop in transformed notation:

$$
\begin{bmatrix} I_0 := 1 \\ J_0 := 1 \end{bmatrix} \underset{\substack{(I_{t-1} <= N) \\ \textbf{and} \\ (J_{t-1} <= M)}}{\mathbf{W}} \left\{ \begin{array}{l} \text{LOUT } [I_{t-1} + J_{t-1} - 1] := \text{MIN}(\text{L1}[I_{t-1}], \text{L2}[J_{t-1}]) \\ I_t := I_{t-1} + \text{ORD}(\text{L1}[I_{t-1}] < \text{L2}[J_{t-1}]) \\ J_t := J_{t-1} + \text{ORD}(\text{L1}[I_{t-1}] >= \text{L2}[J_{t-1}]) \end{array} \right\}
$$

According to the loop transform theory, we must solve the recurrence formulas to obtain an equivalent iterative form for I_t and J_t. Since $I_0 = 1$ and $J_0 = 1$, we get a solution that depends on the value of ORD:

$$
I_t = 1 + \sum_{s=1}^{t} \text{ORD}(\text{L1}[I_{s-1}] < \text{L2}[J_{s-1}])
$$

$$
J_t = 1 + \sum_{s=1}^{t} \text{ORD}(\text{L1}[I_{s-1}] >= \text{L2}[J_{s-1}])
$$

The value of ORD(x) is either zero or one depending on the truth value of x. Hence the value of I_t is equal to one greater than the number of times L1[I_{s-1}] is less than L2[J_{s-1}]. A similar result is obtained for J_t.

Before we can go further, we must select test data L1 and L2 that force values for ORD.

TEST #1 (L1[1 . . N]=0; L2[1 . . M]=0)

This is a simple, repeated, and degenerate case that should work even if nothing else does! These values cause ORD to return zero in the formula for I_t, and one in the formula for J_t.

$$I_t = 1 + \sum_{s=1}^{t} 0 = 1$$

$$J_t = 1 + \sum_{s=1}^{t} 1 = t + 1$$

Since $I_0 = J_0 = 1$, we get an abbreviated version of MERGE:

$$\mathbf{W}_{\substack{(1 <= N) \\ \mathbf{and} \\ (t <= M)}} \begin{Bmatrix} \text{LOUT}[t] := 0 \\ I_t := 1 \\ J_t := t+1 \end{Bmatrix}$$

This loop terminates when $(t' <= M)$ is false:

$$t' > M \text{ implies } t' = M + 1$$

Therefore we can complete the transformation of the **while-do** loop:

$$\equiv \begin{bmatrix} \text{LOUT}[1 . . M] := 0 \\ I := 1 \\ J := M + 1 \end{bmatrix}$$

This result can be combined with the remainder of the program:

for I := 1 **to** N **do** LOUT[I+M] := L1[I];

which simply copies array L1 into the remaining elements of LOUT[$I + M . . N + M$].

This test shows that MERGE first copies M zeros from L2 into LOUT, and then copies N zeros from L1 into the remaining N elements of LOUT. Hence, we conclude that the procedure works for these degenerate lists.

TEST #2 (L1[I]=2*I; L2[J]:=2*J−1)

The purpose of this test is to study MERGE when the data values alternate back and forth. Thus,

$$\text{ORD}(L1[I_{s-1}] < L2[J_{s-1}])$$

becomes

$$\text{ORD}(\text{odd}(s))$$

and

$$ORD(L1[I_{s-1}] >= L2[J_{s-1}])$$

becomes

$$ORD(even(s))$$

where odd(s) is true if s is an odd integer, and even(s) is true if s is an even integer. Therefore,

$$I_t = 1 + \sum_{s=1}^{t} ORD(odd(s)) = 1 + [t/2]$$

$$J_t = 1 + \sum_{s=1}^{t} ORD(even(s)) = 1 + [(t + 1)/2]$$

where [x] means the integer part of x.

Then,

$$MIN(L1[I_{t-1}], L2[J_{t-1}]) = t$$
$$I_{t-1} + J_{t-1} - 1 = t$$

The transformed loop becomes

$$\mathop{\mathbf{W}}_{\substack{(1 + \lfloor(t-1)/2\rfloor <= N \\ \text{and} \\ (1 + \lfloor t/2\rfloor <= M)}} \left\{ \begin{array}{l} LOUT[t] := t \\ I_t := 1 + [t/2] \\ J_t := 1 + [(t+1)/2] \end{array} \right\}$$

The output list LOUT correctly copies the values in order for as long as the loop repeats. The remaining question is whether the loop terminates as expected. Two cases are considered.

CASE A: $1 + [(t' - 1)/2] > N$

Case A corresponds with termination of the loop because all elements of L1 are copied into LOUT. The smallest value of t' that satisfies this condition is

$$t' = 2N + 1$$

Therefore, the **while-do** loop is performed (t' − 1) times (it fails before the t'th pass). The values of I and J at (t' − 1) = 2N are

$$I_{(t'-1)} = 1 + \left[\frac{2N}{2}\right] = 1 + N$$

$$J_{(t'-1)} = 1 + \left[\frac{2N + 1}{2}\right] = 1 + N$$

The remaining elements of LOUT are obtained from the remainder of L2. Note

$$I + J - 1 = 1 + N + J - 1 = N + J$$

Thus, the **for-do** loop becomes

for $J := N+1$ **to** M **do** $LOUT[N+J] := L2[J]$;

For example, consider the two lists, $L1[1 \; . \; . \; 2]$ and $L2[1 \; . \; . \; 3]$:

	L1		L2
	2		1
L1[N] =	4	L2[M] =	3
			5

The output list LOUT contains the following merged items when the loop terminates:

LOUT
1
2
3
4

and $I = J = N+1 = 3$. Therefore, the remaining element of L2 is copied:

for $J := 3$ **to** 3 **do** $LOUT[2+J] := L2[J]$;

LOUT contains all items of both lists.

CASE B: $1 + [t'/2] > M$

Case B is the mirror image of Case A except it models the program when L2 is copied into LOUT first. The smallest value of t' that terminates the loop is

$$t' = 2M$$

Therefore, the **while-do** loop is performed $(t' - 1) = 2M - 1$ times. The termination values of I and J are

$$I_{(t'-1)} = 1 + \left\lceil \frac{2M-1}{2} \right\rceil = M$$

$$J_{(t'-1)} = 1 + \left\lceil \frac{2M}{2} \right\rceil = M + 1$$

This time, however,

$$I + J - 1 = I + M + 1 - 1 = I + M$$

and the **for-do** loop for copying the remainder of L1 is executed $(N - M + 1)$ times. Thus,

for $I := M$ **to** N **do** $LOUT[I + M] := L1[I]$;

Consider as an illustration the two lists, $L1[1 \ . \ . \ 3]$ and $L2[1 \ . \ . \ 2]$:

	L1	L2
	2	1
	4	$L2[M] = 3$
$L1[N] =$	6	

The final values of I and J when the **while-do** loop is terminated are

$$I = M = 2$$
$$J = M + 1 = 3$$

The **for-do** loop copies the remaining *two* elements of L1 into $LOUT[4 \ . \ . \ 5]$.

for $I := 2$ **to** 3 **do** $LOUT[I + 2] := L1[I]$;

We might continue to test MERGE using various test data to force a variety of combinations of statements to be executed. This example demonstrates our conventions for selecting test data and the use of functional transformations in simplifying program components.

SUMMARY

Testing software is not an easy or straightforward task. We need a theory that simplifies and formalizes the steps in testing. The theory presented here is based on a combination of formal mathematical proof technique and pragmatic test data selection.

We use test data to simplify the program to be tested. Although this approach simplifies the task, it also weakens the results because we cannot always be sure a program works simply because it works for a few test cases. The coupling effect is a pragmatic rule for test data selection that claims "good" results for the practitioner. We rely heavily on the coupling effect in this theory of testing.

We use the formalism of *functional transformation* of program components to simplify the control structure of a program. This approach is sufficiently strong to nearly constitute a proof of the program's correctness. Unfortunately, it does not always succeed in transforming the program in question into its simplest form. Therefore, we must frequently rely on test data to aid in the functional transformation.

The ideas underlying the transform theory are simple: (1) apply forward substitution wherever possible, (2) reduce loops to straight-line code segments wherever possible using the loop transformation, (3) remove branching choice components wherever possible using test data (in most cases), and (4) attempt to simplify the resulting transformed program to a parallel collection of simple, single-assignment statements. In the following chapters we will be given ample opportunity to apply this theory to a variety of software engineering situations.

PROBLEMS

1. Verify the following program fragment using the theory of transforms. Under what conditions on A and B will the program be guaranteed to terminate?

```
program WHIZ;
  var
    A,B : integer;
  begin
    READLN(A,B) ;
    while A < B do A := A+3 ;
end.
```

2. Verify the MERGE program of Figure 3-4 using the following test data to aid in transformation of MERGE:

$$L1[I] = I \; ; \; I = 1 \text{ to } N$$
$$L2[J] = J \; ; \; J = 1 \text{ to } N$$
$$M = N$$

3. List some problems encountered in attempting to verify the following code fragment for computing the greatest common divisor.

```
while X <> Y do
  if X > Y
    then X := X−Y
    else  Y := Y−X
```

4. Use $X = 1$ and $Y > 1$ to test the program fragment of Problem 3.

5. What is the final value of Y as a function of C and X in the following code fragment?

$$Y := C ;$$
$$\textbf{while } Y > X \textbf{ do } Y := Y/2 ;$$

[Hint: Solve the recurrence relation $Y_{t+1} - Y_t/2 = 0$]

6. Verify the MAXIMUM procedure of Figure 3-7 using the following test data,

$$N = 5, X[I] = I^2 - 3 ; I = 1 \text{ to } 5.$$

7. Verfiy the MERGE program of Figure 3-8 using the following test data,

$$L1[I] = 1 \quad ; N = 3$$
$$L2[J] = (-1) ; M = 4$$

8. How many iterations are carried out by the loops, below?

(a) $X := 0$; **repeat** $X := X + 5$ **until** $X > 20$;
(b) $X := 33$; **while** $X > 0$ **do** $X := X/3$;
(c) $X := N$; **repeat** $X := X + 5$ **until** $X > Y$;
(d) $X := N$; **while** $X > 0$ **do** $X := X/Y$;
(e) $X := N$; **while** $(X > Y)$ **and** $(X > Z)$ **do** $X := X/2$;

[Note: Under what conditions might each one of these loops fail to terminate?]

REFERENCES

Boies, S. J., and J. P. Gould, "Syntactic Errors in Computer Programming," *Human Factors,* 16, no. 3 (1974), 253–257.

DeMillo, R. A., R. J. Lipton, and F. G. Sayward, "Hints on Test Data Selection: Help for the Practicing Programmer," *IEEE Computer,* 11, no. 4 (April 1978), 34–41.

Goodenough, J. B., and S. L. Gerhart, "Toward a Theory of Test Data Selection," *IEEE Transactions on Software Engineering,* SE-1, no. 2 (June 1975), 156–173.

Howden, W. E., "Theoretical and Empirical Studies of Program Testing," *IEEE Transactions on Software Engineering,* SE-4, no. 4 (July 1978), 293–298.

Young, E. A., "Human Errors in Programming," *International Journal of Man-Machine Studies,* 6, no. 3 (1974), 361–376.

4

Application to Searching

INTRODUCTION

Programs that search a data structure are called *searching routines*. A searching routine uses a *search key* to compare against another key in the data structure. If the search key matches the data structure key, the searching routine either reports the match, returns the location within the data structure of the matching key, or both.

A *key* is any uniquely identifying value within a data structure. Keys may be strings of numerals, letters of the alphabet, numerical values, or combinations of strings and numbers. We will refer to the data structure being searched as the *list*.

A variety of searching routines are used in software engineering. They all work by scanning part or all of the list in order to compare the search key with the keys imbedded in the list. Broadly speaking, there are two types of search routines: *comparative* and *divide-and-conquer*.

The comparative methods search the list exhaustively until the key is found or until the end of the list is reached. Comparative routines exhibit a poor worst-case performance, but they are simple to understand and easy to program. Because of their simplicity, comparative search routines are in widespread use.

Divide-and-conquer methods attempt to eliminate part of the list from further consideration. In a divide-and-conquer search routine, only a small part of the complete list is examined even in the worst-case event that no match is made. Since these methods limit the amount of scanning, they are among the fastest methods of searching. Some, however, are difficult to understand and often complex to program.

In this chapter we study two comparative search routines and two simple divide-and-conquer routines called *binary search* and *tree search*. Other more sophisticated divide-and-conquer search routines are treated separately in the chapters on hashing and file structures.

We apply the theory of software performance and the theory of software verification to the search routines given in this chapter. First, the routines are presented in the form of a program and corresponding software network. Then each program listing is used to verify the program by transformation. Finally, the network is used to compute the performance of each program by z-domain analysis.

SEARCHING LINEAR LISTS

A *linear list* is a sequence of objects, $d_1, d_2, \ldots, d_n$ of length n containing information of interest to some application. Typically, the sequence is stored in an array or linked list of elements. Each element of the sequence contains a component called the *key*, which uniquely identifies the element.

Suppose we assume the sequence is stored in an array, as illustrated in the following search routines. In the linear search routine we compare every element in the array to find a match. In the binary search we use a divide-and-conquer method to reduce the search time.

Linear (Sequential) Search

Suppose a sequence of integers is stored in an array of length N. The linear or sequential search routine begins with the first array element and scans the array until a match occurs or the last array element is compared. In function LINEAR, the search key KEY is compared with each element in LIST until a match occurs (see Figure 4-1).

There is a nonzero probability that the search key is not found in the list. There is a chance that every element of LIST is compared with KEY and yet *no* match results. In this case, DONE will be false, and ORD(DONE) will be zero. Thus, when the search routine fails to find a match, the value returned is LINEAR = 0. Otherwise, the value returned is the subscript location of the matching value within LIST.

Does the search routine of Figure 4-1 correctly return the subscript value expected? Suppose we apply the transformation theory of verification to LINEAR. The abbreviated version of LINEAR is

$$\{I_0:=0\}\,\{DONE:=LIST[I_{t-1}+1]=KEY;I_t:=I_{t-1}+1\}\, \bigcup_{\substack{(DONE)\\ \text{or} \\ (I_t=N)}}\,\{LINEAR:=ORD(DONE)*I_{t'}\}$$

```
function LINEAR ( KEY : integer ; LIST : LISTS ) : integer ;
var
  I      : POINTERS ;
  DONE : boolean ;
begin
  I := 0 ; repeat
        DONE := ( LIST[ I+1 ] = KEY ) ;
        I       := I + 1 ;
        until ( DONE ) or ( I = N ) ;
  LINEAR := ORD( DONE ) * I ;
end ;              (* linear *)
```

(a) Pascal function for linear search

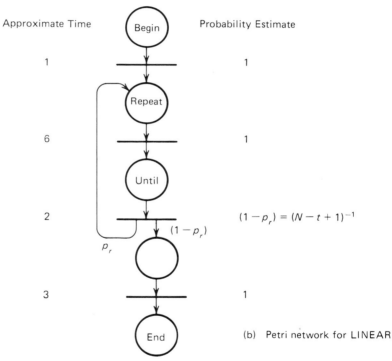

Figure 4-1. Linear (sequential) search routine.

The recurrence relation for I_t is easily reduced to an iterative form by solving the difference equation below and noting that $I_0 = 0$:

$$I_t = I_{t-1} + 1 \qquad (I_0 = 0)$$
$$I_t - I_{t-1} = 1$$

Thus,

$$I_t = t \qquad (t = 0, 1, 2, \ldots)$$

Now, $I_t = t$, $I_{t-1} + 1 = t$, and the loop functional computes a terminal value t' for t. This leads to the transformed version of LINEAR:

$$\{DONE:=LIST[t]=KEY; I_t=t\} \underset{\substack{(DONE) \\ or \\ (I_t=N)}}{U} \{LINEAR:=ORD(DONE)*I_{t'}\}$$

Forward substitution and noting the loop termination condition for t' gives

$$\{\ \} \underset{\substack{(LIST[t']=KEY) \\ or \\ (t'=N)}}{U} \{LINEAR:=ORD(LIST[t']=KEY)*t'\}$$

That is, the loop terminates because t' equals the location of KEY, t' equals N, or both occur simultaneously. These three possibilities are listed in the matrix below. The value returned by LINEAR is given for each case.

	$LIST[t']=KEY$	$LIST[t']<>KEY$
$t' = N$	$LINEAR:=N$	0
$t'<>N$	$LINEAR:=t'$	not possible

The value of t' can be computed by noting the loop functional:

$$LIST[t'] = KEY$$

Hence,

$$t' = \text{location of KEY in LIST}$$

This is the expected result, so we claim that this program is correct.

Performance of Linear

Figure 4-1(b) shows the network corresponding to function LINEAR. The approximation of each time delay is made by assuming each operation takes one time unit. The operations are:

:=	One time unit to assign a value
[ ]	Subscripting takes one time unit
+	One time unit to add
=	One time unit to compare

ORD   One time unit to return zero or one
*   One time unit to multiply

Therefore, the loop body takes six time units to compute:

DONE: = (LIST[I + 1] = KEY);
I := I + 1;

and two time units to perform the loop test.

The probability estimates of Figure 4-1(b) are unity in all transitions except the loop test transition. If we assume the KEY is matched at some time in the loop, then $(1 - p_r)$ is the probability that a match is made on the tth iteration through the **repeat-until** loop.

Actually, $(1 - p_r)$ is a *conditional* probability because it changes as a function of the number of array elements that have already been examined. In the first pass none of the elements have been compared with KEY so there is one chance in N that a match will occur (if we assume a uniformly random placement of the key in LIST). The second pass through LIST no longer needs to be concerned with N elements. Instead, $(N - 1)$ elements remain, so there is one chance in $(N - 1)$ that a match occurs. Subsequently, the tth pass eliminates t comparisons leaving $(N - t + 1)$ elements. Therefore, the probability of finding the matching key is $(N - t + 1)^{-1}$ on pass t.

This argument is based on several assumptions. First, we have assumed a uniformly random placement of an element in LIST, and second, the probability estimate assumes the match will always occur. However, the search may not always find the element because it may not be in the list.

Suppose we assume a probability q that the element with value equal to KEY is in the LIST. The probability of success (KEY = LIST[t']) is weighted by q. Therefore we must weight the result we obtain by q.

The network of Figure 4-1(b) is reduced to the final network of Figure 4-2. The z-domain reduction yields an average time delay:

$$\tau' = 2 + \frac{8}{(1 - p_r)}$$
$$= 2 + 8(N - t + 1)$$

Now, this is the time estimate we can use with probability q. But the loop will take $8N$ passes with probability $(1 - q)$. So,

$$\text{Time delay} = q\tau' + (1 - q)8N$$
$$= q(10 + 8N - 8t) + 8N - 8Nq$$
$$= (10 - 8t)q + 8N$$

This result depends on the loop counter t. Since each pass through the loop is equally likely to terminate the loop with a match, we can *average* this estimate over t. Thus,

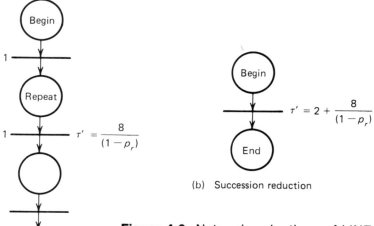

(b)   Succession reduction

Figure 4-2. Network reductions of LINEAR.

(a)   Repeat-until reduction

Average time delay over $t = \dfrac{1}{N} \sum\limits_{t=1}^{N} (10 - 8t)q + 8N$

Recalling that

$$\sum_{t=1}^{N} t = \frac{N(N + 1)}{2}$$

we get

Average time delay over $t = 6q + (8 - 4q)N$

Suppose, for example the probability that the LIST always contains the search key is $q = 0.1$, we would expect

$$.6 + 7.6N$$

units of time delay in LINEAR.

This search routine takes roughly twice as long when the list is doubled in size. We indicate this *linear increase* with respect to the size of the input data structure using the *order of performance notation*, $O(N)$. Hence, this routine is a linear routine because its time performance is linear in N. We say the algorithm is "oh-of-N."

The LINEAR program is simple, but because it is slow, we turn to other methods of searching. In particular, we can employ a divide-and-conquer method when the list is maintained in ascending order.

Binary Search

If the sequence of elements are in ascending (descending) order, we can use a divide-and-conquer method of searching called *binary search*. A binary search repeatedly eliminates roughly one-half of the list from further consideration in each step of the divide-and-conquer method. For this reason, BINARY is a rapid search routine (see Figure 4-3).

Before we show that BINARY is correct, suppose we study an example. Consider the list of six ordered elements:

LIST: 1 2 3 4 5 6

Suppose we use the binary search routine of Figure 4-3 to locate KEY=5 in the LIST. The values of Y and Z will be $Z=6$, $Y=-6$, initially. Each pass through the **while-do** component will increment Y and Z, accordingly.

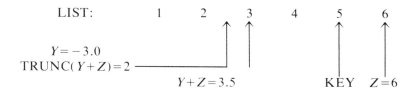

The next pass begins with $Y=-3.0$ and $Z=6$. After Y is divided by two and the second pass is completed, we have

The KEY is now bracketed between LIST[4] and LIST[6]. In two passes we have eliminated three-fourths of the list from further consideration. The next pass yields

because KEY$<=$LIST[5] is true and Z is incremented to $(Z+Y)$.

The loop terminates at this point because $(Y<-1)$ is false (so is LIST[TRUNC (Z)]$<>$KEY). The value returned through BINARY is the TRUNC(Z) = 5. Therefore, the routine correctly computes the location of KEY = 5. This example also illustrates the virtue of BINARY. We found the KEY value in only three comparisons out of a total of six values.

```
function BINARY ( KEY : integer ; LIST : LISTS ) : integer ;
var
    Y, Z : real ;
  begin
    if ( LIST[ 1 ] <= KEY ) and ( KEY <> LIST[ N ] )
      then
        begin
          Z := N ;
          Y := N ;
          while ( Y < - 1 ) and ( LIST[ TRUNC( Z ) ] <> KEY ) do
            begin
              Y := Y / 2 ;
              if KEY <= LIST[ TRUNC( Z + Y ) ] then Z := Z + Y ;
            end ;      (* while *)
          BINARY := TRUNC( Z ) * ORD( LIST[ TRUNC( Z ) ] = KEY ) ;
      end      (* if-then *)
    else BINARY := 0 (* not in list *)
end ;      (* BINARY *)
```

Figure 4-3. Binary search routine.

Certification The above example also raises several questions about the correctness of the program for other cases. What happens if the KEY is missing? This question and others are answered by considering the following test cases and their corresponding test data.

CASE A. The KEY is missing.

SUBCASE A.1. Outside the range of the LIST.

This case can be checked by considering any values of KEY that lie below the smallest element or above the largest element.

$$KEY > LIST[N] \text{ implies } BINARY = 0$$
$$KEY < LIST[1] \text{ implies } BINARY = 0$$

SUBCASE A.2. Between adjacent elements of LIST.

This case can be checked by selecting a value of KEY that lies between any two elements of LIST.

$$\text{LIST}[I] < \text{KEY} < \text{LIST}[I-1] \text{ implies BINARY} = 0$$

Notice that this corresponds to termination of the **while-do** loop because $(Y < -1)$ becomes false.

CASE B. The KEY is in the LIST.

This means that a t' exists such that

$$\text{LIST}[t'] = \text{KEY}$$

We can examine simple degenerate test data such as KEY = 0 and

$$\text{LIST}[I] = 0 \text{ for all } I = 1 \ . \ . \ N \text{ implies BINARY} = N$$

Also the boundary value KEY = 1 and

$$\text{LIST}[I] = I \text{ for all } I = 1 \ . \ . \ N \text{ implies BINARY} = 1$$

or the boundary value KEY = N using the same LIST above.

We begin by certifying Case A first since it is the easiest. The BINARY search routine is said to be correct if each case implies a correct value of BINARY.

TEST A.1

The first component of BINARY clearly guarantees BINARY = 0 when KEY lies outside the range of the ordered LIST:

if (LIST[1] <= KEY) **and** (KEY <= LIST[N])

    then . .
    else BINARY := 0 ;

Thus both cases below are satisfied:

$$\text{KEY} > \text{LIST}[N] \text{ implies BINARY} = 0$$
$$\text{KEY} < \text{LIST}[1] \text{ implies BINARY} = 0$$

TEST A.2

Test A.2 forces the **while-do** loop to either execute forever, or terminate because $(Y < -1)$ becomes false. Hence the loop functional of the transformed loop computes a final value of t, say t'.

$$T_w \left\{ \begin{array}{c} \textbf{while } (Y < -1) \textbf{ do} \\ Y := Y/2 \ ; \end{array} \right\} \equiv \left\{ \begin{array}{c} \textbf{while}(Y_{t-1} < -1) \textbf{ do} \\ Y_t := Y_0/2^t \ ; \end{array} \right\}$$

This result is obtained by solving the difference equation equivalent for Y:

$$Y_t - \tfrac{1}{2} Y_{t-1} = 0$$

Hence,

$$Y_t = Y_0 \left(\frac{1}{2}\right)^t \text{ for } t = 1, 2, \ldots, t'$$

The loop functional computes t' (final value of t):

$$not \ (Y_{t'-1} < -1) \text{ implies } Y_{t'-1} > = -1$$

Substituting the iterative form of Y into this inequality and solving for $(t' - 1)$:

$$Y_0 \left(\frac{1}{2}\right)^{t'-1} > = -1$$

So,

$$(t' - 1) > = [\log_2(-Y_0)]$$

But since $(t' - 1)$ must be an integer (integral number of passes through the loop),

$$(t' - 1) = \lceil \log_2(-Y_0) \rceil$$

where $\lceil x \rceil$ is the smallest integer greater or equal to x.
Now, notice the initial value of Y,

$$Y_0 = -N$$

Hence,

$$(t' - 1) = \lceil \log_2 N \rceil$$

The reader can verify that the loop terminates because the following are true for the final loop condition:

$$\frac{-N}{2^{\lceil \log_2 N \rceil}} > = -1 \ ; \ N \text{ is odd}$$

Since $(\text{LIST}[\text{TRUNC}(Z)] = \text{KEY})$ is false in this test case, we note that

$$\text{ORD}(\text{LIST}[\text{TRUNC}(Z)] = \text{KEY}) = 0$$

Hence,

$$\text{BINARY} = 0$$

and this case is verified.

TEST B

In this case we must show that t' exists such that LIST[t'] = KEY implies BINARY = TRUNC($Z_{t'}$). The test is based on two propositions. First, the **while-do** loop must terminate, and second, the value of BINARY (hence t') must be correct.

Suppose we examine a simple degenerate case first. Let LIST[I] = 0 for all I = 1 . . N and KEY = 0. Since the KEY is actually in the LIST, the routine attempts to execute the **while-do** loop. The loop functional computes a termination value t' on the first attempted pass:

$$T_w \{\textbf{while } (\text{LIST}[\text{TRUNC}(Z_{t'-1})] <> \text{KEY}) \text{ do}\}$$
$$\equiv \text{LIST}[\text{TRUNC}(Z_{t'-1})] = \text{KEY}$$

In other words, the loop terminates for $(t' - 1) = 0$, leaving

$$\text{TRUNC}(Z_0) = \text{location of KEY in LIST}$$

Since Z_0 = N, we get

$$\text{BINARY} = \text{TRUNC}(Z_0) = N$$

This means that the location of KEY returned by BINARY is always N when all list elements are identical to the KEY. This degenerate case suggests that a final value t' exists, but we turn to a more challenging case to see if the loop *converges* properly.

Let LIST[I] = I for I = 1 . . N, and test the convergence of TRUNC($Z_{t'-1}$) at the boundaries KEY = 1 and KEY = N. First examine the lower boundary.

TEST B.1: KEY = 1

The inner **if-then** component will be true every time the **while-do** iterates; hence

$$T_w \{\textbf{while } (Y_{t-1} < -1) \text{ and } (\text{LIST}[\text{TRUNC}(Z_{t-1})] <> \text{KEY do};$$
$$Y_t := Y_0 \left(\frac{1}{2}\right)^t ; Z_t := Z_{t-1} + Y_t\}$$

We can solve for Z_t by noting

$$Z_t = Z_{t-1} + \frac{Y_0}{2^t} \qquad (t = 1, 2, . . .)$$

which has solution

$$Z_t = \frac{-Y_0}{2^t} \qquad (t = 1, 2, . . .)$$

Now, since KEY = 1, the loop functional computes

$$Y_{t'-1} >= -1$$

or

$$\text{LIST[TRUNC}(Z_{t'-1})] = 1$$

or both. Hopefully the loop terminates for $\text{TRUNC}(Z_{t'-1}) = 1$. This means

$$Z_{t'-1} < 2$$

and to make sure the loop does not stop too early, we must check Y to assure

$$Y_{t-1} < -1$$

until KEY is located (at which time both terminating conditions may become false).

First, check the termination condition for $Z_{t'-1} < 2$:

$$\frac{-Y_0}{2^{t'-1}} < 2$$

Thus,

$$t' > \log_2(-Y_0)$$

and

$$(t' - 1) > \lceil \log_2(-Y_0) - 1 \rceil$$

but since $(t' - 1)$ must be an integer,

$$(t' - 1)_z = \lceil \log_2(-Y_0) - 1 \rceil$$

where $(\cdot)_z$ denotes the final value computed for Z.

Next, we check the termination condition on Y (derived earlier in Test A.2):

$$(t' - 1)_y = \lceil \log_2(-Y_0) \rceil$$

where $(\cdot)_y$ denotes the final value computed for Y.

Since

$$(t' - 1)_z <= (t' - 1)_y$$

we are correct in claiming that Z_t converges to its final value before the loop stops. Therefore, the loop functional computes a final value $(t' - 1)_z$ such that

$$\text{LIST[TRUNC}(Z_{t'-1})] = 1$$

$$\text{TRUNC}(z_{t'-1}) = \text{location of 1 in LIST}$$

By forward substitution into

$$BINARY := TRUNC(Z_{t'-1}) * ORD(LIST[TRUNC(Z_{t'-1})] = KEY)$$

we get

$$BINARY := 1 * 1 = 1$$

Therefore, for this test data, the routine is correct. Next, we look at the upper boundary value.

TEST B.2 : KEY = N

This case is easier to verify than it might appear to be at first. The match occurs immediately because the loop functional computes $(t' - 1) = 0$ since $(LIST[TRUNC(Z_0)] <> KEY)$ is false, leading to

$$TRUNC(Z_0) = N = \text{location of KEY} = N$$

Suppose, however, that the value of KEY = $(N - 1)$. The loop would be repeated many times until $TRUNC(Z_{t'-1}) = (N - 1)$ or $(Y_{t'-1} >= -1)$. Notice that the innermost **if-then** is *always* false until the very last pass. Hence, $Z_t = N$ until the last pass when $Z_{t'-1} = (N - 1)$ because $(-Y_{t'-1}) <= 1$. In this case, both conditions terminate the loop.

We have shown that BINARY is correct for the most demanding cases of input values. The reader can also verify other cases, such as $N = 1$, or $LIST[I] = (N - I)$, etc.

In many test cases we used the abbreviated model below:

$$\begin{bmatrix} Z_0 := N \\ Y_0 := -N \end{bmatrix} \quad \underset{\substack{(Y_{t-1} < -1) \\ \textbf{and} \\ (LIST[TRUNC(Z_{t-1})] <> KEY)}}{\mathbf{W}} \quad \left\{ \begin{aligned} & Y_t := Y_0/2^t \\ & Z_t := \begin{cases} Z_{t-1} \\ \text{or} \\ Z_{t-1} + Y_t \end{cases} \end{aligned} \right\}$$

$$\{BINARY := (Z_{t'-1}) * ORD(LIST[TRUNC(Z_{t'-1})] = KEY)\}$$

Performance   The next study analyzes the network model of BINARY in order to estimate its performance. Figure 4-4 contains a partially simplified network model of BINARY with approximate time estimates labeling each transition and variables q and p representing the probability of branching and looping, respectively.

The network is simplified: the inner body of the loop is represented by a single transition (no **if-then** component is shown). Segments of straight-line code have been grouped together in several transitions. We are interested in only the most significant features of BINARY.

Figure 4-5 shows the sequence of reductions leading to a single transition. The overall average time delay function depends on the loop probability p and the range probability q. Thus,

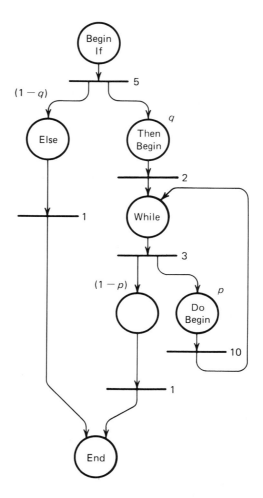

Figure 4-4. Network of BINARY routine.

$$\tau' = 5 + (1 - q) + q \left[3 + \frac{3 + 10p}{(1 - p)} \right]$$

We can only guess at the value of q, but a more detailed analysis will yield an approximation to $(1 - p)$.

The probability of a match is $(1 - p)$. This probability estimate is conditional and depends on the number of passes through the loop. We can use the worst-case value t' derived in the verification analysis earlier, and note that the loop test is performed t_f times:

$$t_f = (t' - 1) = \lceil \log_2 N + 1 \rceil$$

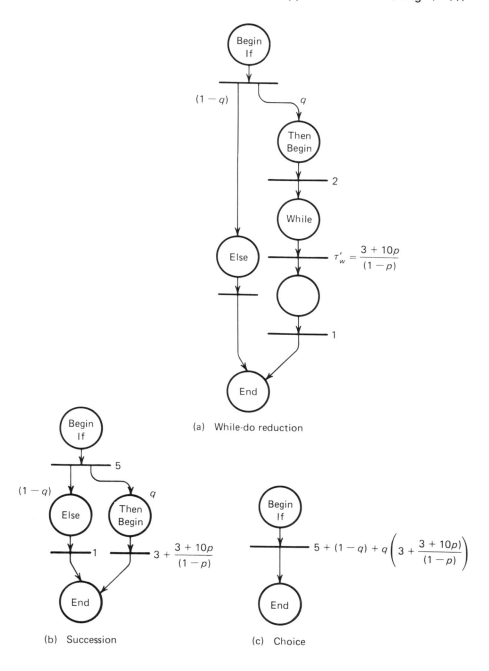

(a) While-do reduction

(b) Succession

(c) Choice

Figure 4-5. Performance of BINARY.

The conditional probability is

$$(1 - p) = \frac{1}{t_f - t + 1} \qquad (t = 1, 2, \ldots, t')$$

Thus,

$$p = \frac{t_f - t}{t_f - t + 1}$$

These expressions can be substituted into the formula for average time delay to obtain

$$\text{Average time delay} = 6 + 2q + [13(t_f - t) + 3]q$$
$$= 6 + 5q + 13t_f q - 13tq$$

The expected value of t is

$$\left(\frac{1}{t_f}\right) \sum_{t=1}^{t_f} t = \frac{t_f + 1}{2}$$

So we can compute the expected value over all t for the average time-delay formula by averaging:

$$\text{Expected average time delay} = 6 + 5q + 13t_f q - 13q \left(\frac{t_f + 1}{2}\right)$$
$$= 6 - \frac{3q}{2} + \frac{13q}{2} t_f$$

This routine is $O(\log_2 N)$ because of the t_f term. In fact, if $q = 1$,

$$\text{Average for } q = 1 = \frac{13}{2} \lceil \log_2 N \rceil - \frac{3}{2}$$

We conclude that binary search is faster than linear search because $O(N) > O(\log_2 N)$. Note that the worst-case performance of the two methods is also $O(N) > O(\log_2 N)$. Of course BINARY only works on ordered lists whereas LINEAR works equally well on ordered or unordered lists.

Is there any way to combine the speed of BINARY with the generality of LINEAR? We must maintain an order on the LIST when using BINARY, but how do we obtain an ordered list in the first place? Furthermore, what happens when we insert a new element into an ordered sequence? These questions are answered (in part) by analyzing a nonlinear list structure called the *tree*.

TREE SEARCHING

A *binary tree* is a data structure consisting of an empty list, or a list containing a special storage cell called a *root*, with zero, one, or two subtrees linked to the root. That is, the root maintains a left and right link, each of which points to nothing or else points to another tree structure. Each subtree is also a tree; hence a binary tree is recursively defined in terms of zero or more triads as shown in Figure 4-6.

Each triad has zero, one, or two descendants linked to it by LEFT or RIGHT pointers, as shown in Figure 4-6. The terminating triads (zero descendants) are called the *leaves* of the tree. Hence, there is a single path from the root of the binary tree to each leaf.

The binary tree structure exactly mirrors the divide-and-conquer feature of the binary search routine discussed in the previous section. Notice that each triad divides the list into two sublists. Each sublist contains (roughly) one-half of the remaining elements. This is the property used in designing the *binary search tree*.

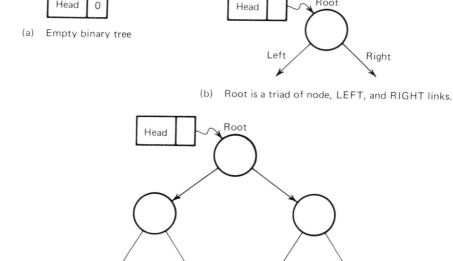

(a) Empty binary tree

(b) Root is a triad of node, LEFT, and RIGHT links.

(c) A complete binary tree is a collection of triads

Figure 4-6. Binary tree is (a) empty, (b) a triad, or (c) a collection of triads.

Binary Search Tree

Suppose we use the binary tree to store the elements of a list in order. The binary search tree search routine must take advantage of the tree structure to equal the performance of the binary search method, $O(\log_2 N)$. Recall that BINARY requires an ordering such that one-half of the remaining list is eliminated after each comparison of the search key. The binary tree provides these advantages:

1. The binary tree stores the list in order at all times, thus yielding high-speed searching.

2. The binary tree can be rapidly extended while maintaining its order property.

Figure 4-7 illustrates the application of the binary tree structure to searching. The tree is empty, initially. When key 'G' is inserted into the tree, the list HEAD is made to point to a newly designated root triad; see Figure 4-7(a). The root triad consists of the key 'G' and LEFT = RIGHT = 0 links.

Figure 4-7(b) illustrates what happens when keys 'D' and 'L' are added to the list. The key of the root is compared:

$$\text{'D'} < \text{'G'}$$

Hence the LEFT link is set to "point to" the newly created triad containing 'D'. Similarly,

$$\text{'L'} > \text{'G'}$$

Hence the triad containing 'L' is inserted into the binary tree at the location pointed to by the RIGHT link of the root triad.

Continuing, Figure 4-7(d) shows how key 'K' is inserted into the tree by following the path established by comparisons:

$$\text{'K'} > \text{'G'}$$
$$\text{'K'} < \text{'L'}$$
$$\text{'K'} > \text{'J'}$$

A *binary search tree* is a binary tree in which the keys of each triad are ordered as follows:

Keys of LEFT subtree < key of parent ≤ keys of RIGHT subtree

Every triad's LEFT pointer points to all the keys less then itself, and the triad's RIGHT pointer points to all the keys greater than (or equal to) itself.

Suppose we use an array of triads to construct a binary search tree. Each triad contans KEY, INFO, and left and right links, LEFT and RITE. Triads are designated as NODES in the Pascal data structure below:

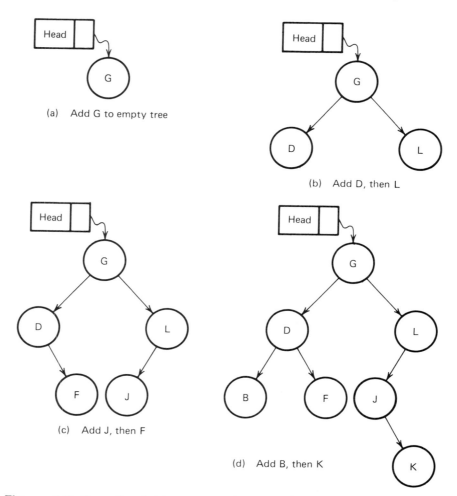

Head

G

(a) Add G to empty tree

Head

G

D   L

(b) Add D, then L

Head

G

D   L

F   J

(c) Add J, then F

Head

G

D   L

B   F   J

K

(d) Add B, then K

Figure 4-7. Growth of binary search tree with entries G, D, L, J, F, B, K (order of insert).

```
type
  POINTER = 0 . . N ;
  STRING  = array [1 . . 20] of char ;
  NODES   = record
                    KEY :STRING ;
                    INFO:real;
                    LEFT,RITE : POINTER
                    end;
  TREE    = array [POINTER] of NODES;
```

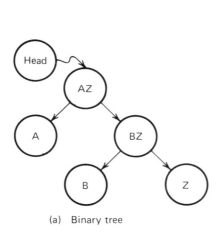

(a) Binary tree

Figure 4-8. Binary search tree representation.

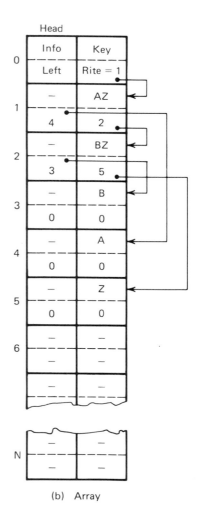

(b) Array

Furthermore, suppose element zero of the array of NODES is used to maintain a HEAD for the structure, and elements [1 . . N] are used to store the list to be searched. This allocation scheme is illustrated in Figure 4-8. The root of the binary search tree is accessed by first accessing the HEAD (element zero), using pointer RITE to access the root, and then following the correct path leading to the desired key.

TREESEARCH

Function TREESEARCH in Figure 4-9 looks for a match between search key *K* and the KEY components of T:TREE. The root of *T* is lo-

```
function TREESEARCH ( K : string ; var T : TREE ) : POINTER ;
  var
    PROBE : POINTER ;
  begin
    T[ 0 ].KEY := K ; PROBE := T[ 0 ].RITE ;
    while T[ PROBE ].KEY <> K do
      with T[ PROBE ] do
        if K < KEY
          then PROBE := LEFT
          else  PROBE := RITE ;
  TREESEARCH := PROBE
end ;        (* treesearch *)
```

Figure 4-9. TREESEARCH search routine.

cated by copying $T[0] \cdot$ RITE into PROBE, and then successively se-lecting LEFT or RITE links "hand-over-fist" until either

1. The matching key is found, KEY = K; or

2. A leaf is reached that contains LEFT or RITE set equal to zero. At this time, $T[0] \cdot$ KEY is accessed and matched with K. The routine re-turns zero.

Case (1) above is a clever trick. The search key is stored in $T[0] \cdot$ KEY $:= K$, initially. This means the search *always finds a match*. If the match is made by returning to the HEAD element, TREESEARCH is set to zero, indicating a "not found" condition. In order for this trick to work, all leaf triads must be linked to HEAD. Thus LEFT = 0, RITE = 0, for all leaves in the tree. Indeed, all null links must be set to zero as il-lustrated in Figure 4-10.

Verification of TREESEARCH   The heart of TREESEARCH is the loop

$$\text{while } T[PROBE] \cdot \text{KEY} <> \text{K do}$$

which terminates with functional

$$T[PROBE_{t'}] \cdot \text{KEY} = K$$

or

$$PROBE_{t'} = \text{location of } K \text{ in } T$$

Thus, the routine computes the desired result:

$$\text{TREESEARCH} := PROBE_{t'} = \text{location of } K \text{ in } T$$

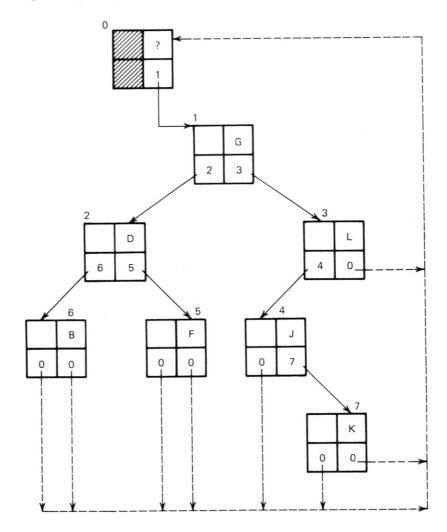

Figure 4-10. Every path through a binary search tree leads back to the head element.

if and only if the loop terminates. But we must prove that the loop converges. Two cases exist.

CASE 'Found'

If no element exists such that KEY = K, then it must be in a path from the root to some leaf. Since every root-to-leaf path is uniquely defined by a search key, K, the loop converges to KEY = K.

CASE 'Not Found'

If no element exists such that KEY = K, then the loop converges to the HEAD element because of Figure 4-10. This is guaranteed by the fact that every path from root-to-leaf is connected to HEAD by way of the zero stored in each triad. In this case,

$$\text{PROBE}_{t'} = 0$$

and

$$T[0] \cdot \text{KEY} = K$$

So the loop terminates.

Performance of TREESEARCH   The performance of TREESEARCH is claimed to equal that of BINARY. Figure 4-11 may be used to derive the average time delay of TREESEARCH assuming unit time delay per operation and loop probability p:

$$\text{Average time delay} = 7 + \frac{3 + p}{(1 - p)}$$

This formula is indeed reminiscent of the formula obtained for BINARY.

The value of p is a function of the number of previous passes through the loop. In fact, each pass corresponds to a level in the binary search tree. If we assume a *balanced* search tree as shown in Figure 4-12(a), then the tree has $\lceil \log_2 N \rceil$ levels. Therefore,

$$t' = \lceil \log_2 N \rceil$$

and

$$(1 - p) = \frac{1}{t' - t + 1} \qquad (t = 1, 2, \ldots, t')$$

yielding a result very similar to the performance of BINARY:

$$\text{Expected time delay} = 8 + 2t'$$

This result is $O(\log_2 N)$ as is the estimate for BINARY. The trouble with the derivation, however, is it assumes a balanced binary search tree, and as shown in Figure 4-12(b), it is possible to construct unbalanced search trees. The performance of TREESEARCH is $O(N)$ when searching the linear (degenerate) structure of Figure 4-12(b).

Wirth has shown that the average value of t' over all possible random trees is bounded by 1.39 times the case for a balanced tree. Hence, we can be conservative and use

$$t' = 1.39 \lceil \log_2 N \rceil$$

in the performance formula. The result is still $O(\log_2 N)$ as before. How-

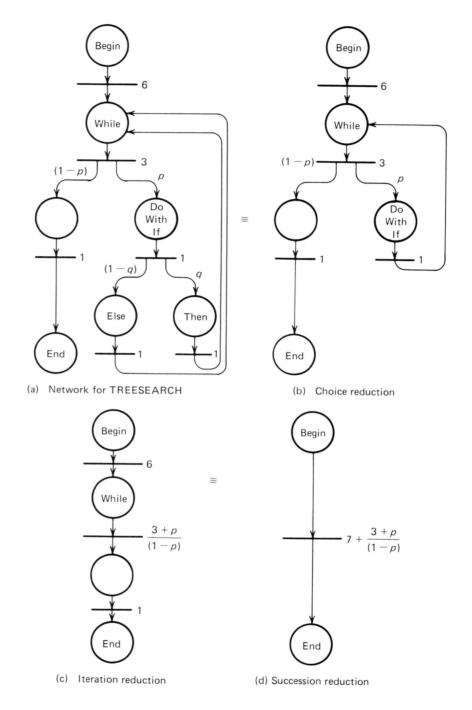

(a) Network for TREESEARCH

(b) Choice reduction

(c) Iteration reduction

(d) Succession reduction

Figure 4-11. Network reductions for TREESEARCH.

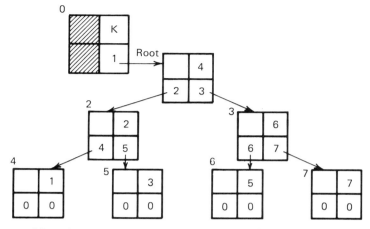

(a)   Balanced tree containing 4, 2, 6, 1, 3, 5, 7 (order of insertion)

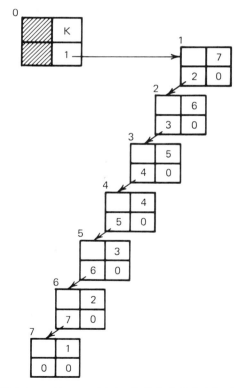

(b)   Unbalanced tree containing 7, 6, 5, 4, 3, 2, 1 (order inserted)

Figure 4-12. Balanced and unbalanced search trees.

ever, it does suggest that a worst-case binary search tree routine is no better than a linear search routine. This (rare) possibility must be guarded against in certain applications. These applications are discussed more fully in the chapter on file structures.

The performance of TREESEARCH is equal to the performance of BINARY. In addition, we can insert new elements into a binary search tree without disrupting its order, in time proportional to $\log_2 N$. A binary search tree search routine is fast and flexible. The penalty for using TREESEARCH, however, is the need for additional memory space to hold the KEY and the LEFT and RITE pointers. This is usually an acceptable penalty.

There are still applications of computing where the binary search tree search routine is not suitable. In the next section we analyze a more general data structure and its search routine.

GRAPH SEARCHING

Suppose we want to search an arbitrary data structure like the structure illustrated in Figure 4-13. We call such arbitrary data structures *graphs* because they are made of nodes, links, and a mapping rule for connecting nodes using the links. The nodes in Figure 4-13(a) are labeled A, B, C, D, and E. The links are simply pointers connecting the nodes.

The search routine we seek must be able to scan the entire graph without being trapped in a loop or cycle. In Figure 4-13(b), for instance, the scan must look at nodes X, Y, and Z without repeating scans on any of the nodes. Without checking which nodes have already been scanned, the search routine might repeat X forever, or be trapped by the loop on node Y.

Additionally, the graph search routine must be able to detect when it has traced a cycle in the graph only to return to a previously searched node. The cycles in Figure 4-13(a) are:

(A,B,A)
(A,C,B,A)
(A,C,D,E,B,A)

The graph search routine must be able to search all nodes without becoming trapped in any one of these cycles.

The graph search routine has one additional complexity we must note. Which link do we select next when scanning a node? We can search the graph of Figure 4-13(a) in one of several different orders:

(A,B, back up to A and then C,D,E)
(A,C,B, back up to C and then D,E)
(A,C,D,E,B)

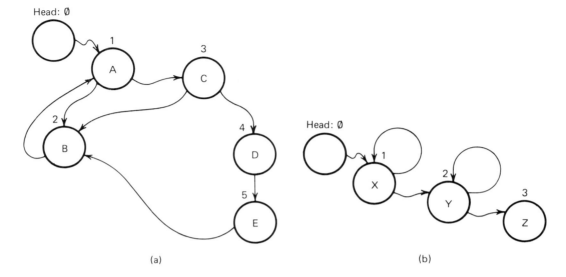

Figure 4-13. Arbitrary data structures containing loops, cycles, and multiple links.

The graph search routine must select one link from among many choices, follow the link, and eventually back up to the earlier node in order to select the next link and follow it, and so on. In short, the routine must be able to "remember" where it came from and then back up to take an unexplored path through the graph.

In summary, the graph search routine must:

1. Mark the nodes as VISITed so they are scanned only once, and

2. Back up to a previous node so that alternate links can be used to scan the remaining parts of the graph structure.

GRAPHSEARCH

The features above are incorporated into the routine we will design now. First we define a graph data structure with nodes containing a key, KEY, information, INFO, a flag indicating whether the node has been visited or not, VISIT, and an array of links that point to other nodes in the graph, POINTER[1 . . NPTS].

Second, we will use a push-down stack to remember the nodes we must visit and another stack to remember the nodes we have already visited. The first stack provides a way to back up and select alternate paths through the graph. The second stack is used to reset the VISIT flags in all scanned nodes. VISIT must be reset to FALSE so that subsequent searches will be allowed to scan those nodes.

The graph search routine uses the following data and stack-processing modules:

```
type
  POINTERS = 0 . . N ;
  DATA      = real ;
  STRING    = packed array [1 . . 20] of char ;
  STACKS    = record
                FRAME : array [POINTERS] of POINTERS ;
                TOP    : POINTERS ;
              end;
  PLEXES    = record
                KEY      : STRING ;
                INFO     : DATA ;
                VISIT    : boolean ;
                POINTER : array [1 . . NPTS] of POINTERS ;
              end;
  GRAPH     = array [POINTERS] of PLEXES ;
```

The permissible operations on stacks are defined by the following routines:

```
procedure PUSH (P:POINTERS ; var S : STACKS);
  begin
    S.TOP := S.TOP+1 ;
    S.FRAME[S.TOP] := P ;
  end ;
function POP (var S:STACKS) : POINTERS ;
  begin
    POP := S.FRAME[S.TOP] ;
    S.TOP := S.TOP−1 ;
  end ;
function SIZE(S:STACKS) : POINTERS ;
  begin
    SIZE := S.TOP ;
  end
procedure INITSTACK (var S:STACKS) ;
  begin
    S.TOP := 0
  end ;
```

The basic idea of the GRAPHSEARCH routine shown in Figure 4-14 is similar to the TREESEARCH routine, as noted below:

1. Store the search key K in the zero-th element of G, initially. Since all

```
function GRAPHSEARCH (K:STRING ;
                     var G : GRAPH) : POINTERS;
var
  NEXT, I : POINTERS;
  BKUP, STK : STACKS;
begin
  G[0].KEY:=K ; G[0].VISIT := TRUE;
  INITSTACK (STK) ; INITSTACK (BKUP);
  PUSH (0, STK) ; PUSH (0, BKUP);
  NEXT := G[0].POINTER[1];
  while G[NEXT].KEY <> K do
    begin if not G[NEXT].VISIT
        then with G[NEXT] do
          begin
            VISIT := TRUE ; PUSH(NEXT, BKUP);
            for I:=1 to NPTS do
              if POINTER[I] <> 0 then PUSH(POINTER[I],STK)
          end; (* with *)
      NEXT := POP(STK);
    end; (* while *)
  GRAPHSEARCH := NEXT;
  for I:=1 to SIZE (BKUP) do G[POP(BKUP)].VISIT:=FALSE;
end; (* GRAPHSEARCH *)
```

Figure 4-14. GRAPHSEARCH routine.

null pointers are set to zero, the search will always return to this element if the search key is not matched. The value returned (0) will indicate a "no match."

2. Repeat the scan by popping a pointer off the STK stack. This stack is pushed with all successive pointers found in each node as the nodes are searched. Thus, when a new pointer is needed, we get it by backing up to a previous pointer. Since the stack is popped in reverse order from a push, the next pointer traversed is the last one pushed onto STK.

3. Remember which nodes were visited by pushing the links that point to them onto stack BKUP. This stack is emptied after the search is finished. As each point is removed from BKUP, the VISIT flag of the corresponding node is reset to FALSE.

The reader may want to verify that GRAPHSEARCH scans the graph of Figure 4-13(a) in the order

(A,C,D,E,B)

If we assume the following values for the pointers:

$$G[0] \cdot POINTER[1] = 1$$
$$G[1] \cdot POINTER[1] = 2$$
$$POINTER[2] = 3$$
$$G[2] \cdot POINTER[1] = 1$$
$$POINTER[2] = 0$$
$$G[3] \cdot POINTER[1] = 2$$
$$POINTER[2] = 4$$
$$G[4] \cdot POINTER[1] = 0$$
$$POINTER[2] = 5$$
$$G[5] \cdot POINTER[1] = 2$$
$$POINTER[2] = 0$$

Keep in mind that the push and pop operations on STK reverse the order of access to the links stored in POINTER[1 . . 2].

Let's turn now to a more formal verification of GRAPHSEARCH. We examine three test cases.

Verification of GRAPHSEARCH

We use the coupling effect to aid in selecting test data. The following data are designed to test three conditions:

Boundary conditions: The list is empty.
Simple condition: A linear linked list.
Cyclic condition: The VISIT flags are used.

Each test case is selected to simplify the function. In each case we transform the code into a trivial program that can be readily verified.

TEST #1: Empty List [see Figure 4-15(a)]

Suppose we examine the most degenerate case first. Let NPTS = 1, $K =$ anything, and the graph G be empty. This means NEXT := 0, and the **while-do** loop is not entered because

$$G[NEXT] \cdot KEY = K$$

immediately. The transformed function is written in abbreviated notation below:

$$\begin{bmatrix} G[0].KEY := K \\ G[0].VISIT := TRUE \end{bmatrix} \{INITSTACK(STK); PUSH(0,STK); INITSTACK(BKUP) ;$$
PUSH $(0,BKUP); NEXT_0 := G[0].POINTER[1]\} \{GRAPHSEARCH := NEXT_0\}$
$\{G[POP(BKUP)].VISIT := FALSE\}$

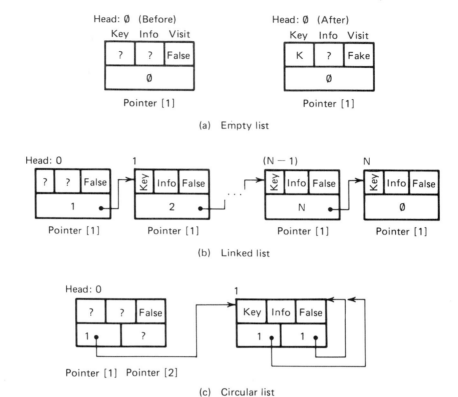

Figure 4-15. Test data for GRAPHSEARCH.

Since $G[0].POINTER[1] = 0$, and we can forward substitute PUSH $(0,BKUP)$ into POP(BKUP) to get

$$\{INITSTACK(BKUP);POP(PUSH(0,BKUP))\} \equiv \{0\}$$

the transformed function is rewritten as

$$\begin{bmatrix} G[0].KEY:=K \\ G[0].VISIT:=TRUE \end{bmatrix} \{INITSTACK(STK); PUSH(0,STK); GRAPHSEARCH:= 0;$$

$$G[0].VISIT:=FALSE\}$$

Finally, $G[0].VISIT$ is redefined by $G[0].VISIT:=FALSE$, so we can simplify the abbreviated form above by removing the statement $G[0].VISIT:=TRUE$ without changing the computational equivalence of this particular version. Also,

$$\{INITSTACK(STK); PUSH(0,STK)\} \equiv \{STK[1] = 0\}$$

leading to the simple concurrent version below:

$$\begin{bmatrix} G[0].\mathrm{KEY}:=K \\ \mathrm{STK}[1] = 0 \\ \mathrm{GRAPHSEARCH}:=0 \\ G[0].\mathrm{VISIT}:=\mathrm{FALSE} \end{bmatrix}$$

Therefore, when the graph is empty, the value returned for any key K is GRAPHSEARCH = 0. The visit flag $G[0].\mathrm{VISIT}$ is reset to FALSE as it should be, and the push-down stack STK retains the index of the HEAD node. We can be reasonably sure that function GRAPHSEARCH works correctly for this simple case.

TEST #2: Linked List [see Figure 4-15(b)]

Next we verify GRAPHSEARCH by showing correctness when G is a linear-linked list as shown in Figure 4-15(b). It is obvious that the **while-do** component terminates when a match is encountered somewhere in the list. Thus,

$$G[\mathrm{NEXT}_{t'-1}].\mathrm{KEY} = K$$

And

$$\mathrm{NEXT}_{t'-1} = \text{location of } K \text{ in } G$$

The terminal value $\mathrm{NEXT}_{t'-1}$ is returned by noting

$$\mathrm{GRAPHSEARCH}:=\mathrm{NEXT}_{t'-1}$$

in the function.

We are more concerned that the loop converge to a termination loop functional:

$$\mathrm{NEXT}_{t'-1} = \text{location of } K \text{ in } G$$

than we are concerned about the final value. Therefore, we must show that every element in G is examined until either a match occurs within G, or zero is returned indicating a "no-match" condition.

Since $G[0].\mathrm{KEY}$ is set to K, initially, all we need to do is show that the entire graph is searched before returning to $G[0]$ when K is not stored in G. Thus, we must show that GRAPHSEARCH correctly scans the entire list and returns to $G[0]$. We also want to make sure that all the VISIT flags are restored to FALSE, so subsequent searches will be fully performed.

In this test we note that

$$G[\mathrm{NEXT}_t].\mathrm{POINTER}[1] = t + 1; t = 0, 1, \ldots (N - 1)$$
$$= 0; t = N$$

and

$$NEXT_0 = 1$$
$$NEXT_t = t + 1 \; ; \; t = 1, \; . \; . \; (N - 1)$$
$$= 0 \qquad ; \; t = N$$

As before, we will use STK[1] = 0 and BKUP[1] = 0 in place of

$$INITSTACK(STK) \; ; \; PUSH(0,STK)$$
$$INITSTACK(BKUP) \; ; \; PUSH(0,BKUP)$$

Furthermore, because the test data are a linear-linked list, all VISIT flags will be FALSE while executing the loop that scans the list. Hence, the **if-then** component is always TRUE. These facts lead to the following abbreviated form of GRAPHSEARCH: ($t=1$ first time through the loop, $t=2$ second time, etc.)

$$
\begin{bmatrix}
G[0].KEY := K \\
G[0].VISIT. := TRUE \\
STK[1] := 0 \\
BKUP[1] := 0 \\
NEXT_0 := 1
\end{bmatrix}
\underset{G[t].KEY<>K}{\mathbf{W}}
\{VISIT := TRUE; PUSH(t, BKUP); PUSH(t+1, STK); \\
NEXT_t := POP(STK)\}
$$

$$\{GRAPHSEARCH := NEXT_{t'-1}\} \underset{I = 1 \text{ to SIZE(BKUP)}}{\mathbf{F}} \{G[POP(BKUP)].VISIT := FALSE\}$$

Forward substitution reduces

$$\{PUSH(t+1, STK); NEXT_t := POP(STK)\} \equiv \{NEXT_t := t+1\}$$

except when $t = N$, in which case the loop terminates because

$$G[N].POINTER[1] = 0$$

So,

$$G[0].KEY = K$$

is a match, leading to

$$NEXT_{t'-1} = 0$$

Now, the transformed loop is

$$\underset{t = 1 \text{ to } N}{\mathbf{W}} \{G[t].VISIT := TRUE; BKUP[t+1] := t\}$$

and GRAPHSEARCH := 0 as expected. The **for-do** loop is transformed into

$$\underset{t = N + 1 \text{ downto } 1}{\mathbf{F}} \{G[BKUP[t]].VISIT := FALSE\}$$

because the push-down stack reverses the order of its contents when frames are deleted.

$$G[0].\text{KEY} := K$$
$$G[0].\text{VISIT} := \text{TRUE}$$
$$\text{STK}[1] := 0$$
$$\text{BKUP}[1] := 0$$
$$\text{NEXT}_0 := 1$$

$$\underset{G[\text{NEXT}_{t-1}].\text{KEY} <> K}{\mathbf{W}}$$

$$\left\{ \begin{array}{l} \{\textbf{not}\ G[\text{NEXT}_{t-1}].\text{VISIT}\}\ \{\text{VISIT}:=\text{TRUE};\text{PUSH}(1,\text{BKUP});\ \underset{I=1\ \text{to}\ 2}{\mathbf{F}}\ \{\text{PUSH}(1,\text{STK})\} \\ \hline \{G[\text{NEXT}_{t-1}].\text{VISIT}\} \end{array} \right. ;\ \text{NEXT}_t:=\text{POP}(\text{STK})$$

$$\underset{I=1\ \text{to size (BKUP)}}{\mathbf{F}}\ \{G[\text{POP}(\text{BKUP})].\text{VISIT}:=\text{FALSE}\}$$

$$\{\text{GRAPHSEARCH}:=\text{NEXT}_{t'-1}\}$$

Therefore, forward substitution of the results obtained from the **while-do** component into the **for-do** component yields

$$G[t-1].\text{VISIT}:=\text{FALSE} \; ; \; t = N + 1 \textbf{ downto } 1$$

The transformed test for a linear linked list is

$$\begin{bmatrix} G[0].\text{KEY} = K \\ \text{GRAPHSEARCH} := 0 \\ G[t-1].\text{VISIT} := \text{FALSE} \end{bmatrix} \; ; \; t = N + 1 \textbf{ downto } 1$$

The function correctly searches the linked list and returns zero when no match is made. Furthermore, this test shows that the loop converges by exhaustively scanning the entire list before terminating with the zero-th element (HEAD).

TEST #3: Circular List [see Figure 4-15(c)]

The final test case attempts to verify the ability of GRAPHSEARCH to scan a circular list as shown in Figure 4-15(c). This list has two pointer components, POINTER[1], POINTER[2], which are set to 1. Hence we want to verify that the VISIT flags do their job properly, and prevent perpetual cycling within the **while-do** loop. As before, we assume key K is not in the list, so a complete search is performed before returning to the HEAD element.

We transform the function by noting

$$G[0].\text{POINTER}[1] = 1$$
$$G[1].\text{POINTER}[1] = 1$$
$$G[1].\text{POINTER}[2] = 1$$

and simplifying the stack operations as we have done before, we get the equation shown on the previous page.

The **while-do** loop can be transformed into separate loops: one pass for the case that finds VISIT to be false, and then subsequent passes for the case VISIT is true. The first pass produces

$$\text{BKUP}[2] = 1$$
$$\text{STK}[2] = 1$$
$$\text{STK}[3] = 1 \; ; \; \text{NEXT}_t := \text{POP(STK)}$$

leading to

$$\text{BKUP}[2] = 1$$
$$\text{STK}[2] = 1$$
$$\text{NEXT}_1 = 1$$

Thus, we can rewrite the abbreviated function using these values in place of the first pass through the **while-do** loop. Combining terms, we have

$$
\begin{bmatrix}
G[0].\text{KEY}:=K \\
G[0].\text{VISIT}:=\text{TRUE} \\
\text{STK}[1]=0 \\
\text{STK}[2]=1 \\
\text{BKUP}[1]=0 \\
\text{BKUP}[2]=1 \\
\text{NEXT}_0=1 \\
\text{NEXT}_1=1 \\
G[1].\text{VISIT}:=\text{TRUE}
\end{bmatrix}
\underset{G[\text{NEXT}_{t-1}].\text{KEY}<>K}{\mathbf{W}}
\{\text{NEXT}_t:=\text{POP(STK)}\}
$$

$$
\{\text{GRAPHSEARCH}:=\text{NEXT}_{t'-1}\}
\underset{I=1 \text{ to SIZE(BKUP)}}{\mathbf{F}}
\{G[\text{POP(BKUP)}].\text{VISIT}:=\text{FALSE}\}
$$

The loop functional

$$\text{NEXT}_{t-1} = 0$$

terminates the loop because

$$G[0].\text{KEY} = K$$

leaving

$$\text{GRAPHSEARCH} := 0$$

as desired. The transformed function is now

$$
\begin{bmatrix}
G[0].\text{KEY}:=K \\
G[0].\text{VISIT}:=\text{TRUE} \\
\text{BKUP}[1]:=0 \\
\text{BKUP}[2]:=1 \\
G[1].\text{VISIT}:=\text{TRUE} \\
\text{GRAPHSEARCH}:=0
\end{bmatrix}
\underset{I=1 \text{ to } 2}{\mathbf{F}}
\{G[\text{POP(BKUP)}].\text{VISIT}:=\text{FALSE}\}
$$

Hence, all flags in the elements visited are reset to VISIT:=FALSE.

The function is apparently correct for a simple circular list. This case does not provide a totally convincing proof for all circular lists, however. Further testing (dynamic execution) would have to be performed to increase our confidence in the function. However, the *coupling effect* prompts us to believe that these simple tests are indicative of a correctly functioning GRAPHSEARCH program. Indeed, the program has proven to be reliable when used in practice.

Performance of GRAPHSEARCH

The network of Figure 4-16 models GRAPHSEARCH performance. The formula for average time delay of the network is

$$\tau' = t_0 + \tau'_w + \tau'_s$$

$$= t_0 + \frac{t_1 + p\tau'_a}{(1 - p)} + t_2 + s(t_5 + t_6)$$

where

p = probability key K is not found on a pass through the **while-do** loop.

$(1 - p)$ = probability key K is found on a pass through the **while-do** loop.

s = number of iterations of the **for-do** loop. This is equal to the number of graph elements visited in order to locate key K.

t_i = estimated time delay associated with each transition of the network.

and

$$\tau'_a = t_3 + t_4 q$$

q = probability of **not** $G[\text{NEXT}].\text{VISIT}$

Suppose we assume the following values for each of the parameters above. Let

$$(1 - p) = \frac{1}{N_e - t + 1}$$

where N_e = number of nonzero POINTERS in G

t = pass number of loop, 1, 2, . . N_e

The **while-do** body is executed once for each link in the graph. If N_e is the number of links (nonzero POINTERS), then the first link points to the matching key with probability $(1/N_e)$; the second link examined points to the desired key with probability $(1/(N_e - 1))$; and so on until all N_e links have been examined. The **while-do** loop terminates when most N_e links have been examined.

Let $s = q$ (expected number of loop iterations)

where $q = \dfrac{N_n}{N_e}$ (N_n = number of elements in G)

This expression is derived by assuming s PUSH (NEXT,BKUP) operations are performed inside the **while-do-if** component. To estimate s, we count the number of times the **while-do** is expected to execute and multi-

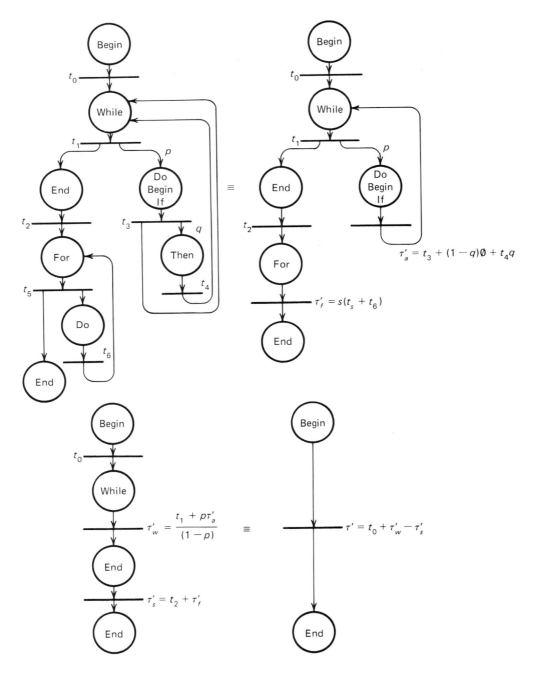

Figure 4-16. Network and transformation for performances of function GRAPHSEARCH.

ply by the probability that the **if-then** component is also entered. Since s is SIZE(BKUP), we simply count the number of push operations that exactly equal the size of BKUP.

We estimate q by claiming that only N_n codes can be visited in N_e attempts since there are only N_n nodes in the graph. For example, the linked list of Figure 4-15(b) has $N_n = N$ nodes and $N_e = N$ links. Thus, $q = 1$ in this case (as expected). But the graph structure of Figure 4-15(c) has $N_n = 1$ node, $N_e = 3$ links for a resulting value of $q = \frac{1}{3}$ (again as intuition might suggest).

So,

$$s = \frac{N_n}{N_e} \quad \text{(expected number of loop iterations)}$$

Now, the number of loop iterations is given by the z-transform of the **while-do** component with zero time to perform the loop test, and a unit time delay for each pass through the loop body. In short,

$$\text{Number of loop iterations} = \frac{p}{(1 - p)}$$

Since

$$p = \frac{N_e - t}{N_e - t + 1}$$

and

$$(1 - p) = \frac{1}{N_e - t + 1}$$

we get

$$\text{Number of loop iterations} = N_e - t$$

Averaging this value gives the expected number of loop iterations:

$$\text{Expected number of loop iterations} = \left(\frac{1}{N_e}\right) \sum_{t=1}^{N_e} (N_e - t)$$

Hence,

$$s = \left(\frac{q}{N_e}\right) \sum_{t=1}^{N_e} (N_e - t)$$

$$= q \left(\frac{N_e - 1}{2}\right)$$

$$= \left(\frac{N_n}{N_e}\right) \frac{(N_e - 1)}{2}$$

$$= \left(\frac{N_e - 1}{N_e}\right) \frac{N_n}{2}$$

Now we can turn our attention to the problem of estimating the overall performance of GRAPHSEARCH. Substituting $(1 - p)$ and s into the formula derived by network reduction, we get

$$\tau' = t_0 + t_2 + (t_5 + t_6) \left(\frac{N_e - 1}{N_e}\right) \frac{N_n}{2} + \frac{t_1 + p(t_3 + t_4 q)}{(1 - p)}$$

Suppose (based on unit time delay per operation)

$$t_0 = 50 \qquad \text{(subprocedure calls take ten units)}$$
$$t_1 = 3$$
$$t_2 = 11$$
$$t_3 = 3$$
$$t_4 = 13 \,(\text{NPTS} + 1) \qquad \text{(approximately)}$$
$$t_5 = 11$$
$$t_6 = 13$$

Furthermore, assume

$$\frac{N_e - 1}{N_e} \sim 1$$

Then

$$\tau' = 61 + 12 N_n + \frac{3 + p(3 + 13q(\text{NPTS} + 1)}{(1 - p)}$$

Recall the average of $3/(1 - p)$ and $p/(1 - p)$ over all values of p is $3(N_e + 1)/2$ and $(N_e - 1)/2$, respectively. Therefore,

$$\text{Avg} \,(\tau') = 61 + 12 N_n + \frac{3(N_e + 1)}{2} + (N_e - 1) \frac{[3 + 13q(\text{NPTS} + 1)]}{2}$$
$$\doteq 67.5 + 3 N_e + 6.5 \text{NPTS} + 12 N_n$$

assuming $[(N_e - 1)/Ne] \sim 1$.

We can conclude that GRAPHSEARCH is a linear algorithm, $O(N_e + N_n + \text{NPTS})$, where it depends on the number of links, the number of nodes in G, and the maximum number of POINTER components allowed in each node.

This evaluation has been lengthy but simple except for the assumptions about s, q, and $(1 - p)$. Different assumptions lead to different performance formulas. We believe the analysis given here is a reasonable one. It is based on the following arguments:

1. The probability of each pass of the loop is conditionally dependent on the number of links that *may* remain to be followed.

2. The expected length of BKUP is approximated by the average

number of times PUSH(NEXT,BKUP) is executed. This average is equal to the average number of loop passes times the probability, q.

3. The value of q is approximately equal to the ratio of the number of nodes in G and the number of links in G.

SUMMARY

We have analyzed four fundamental search routines for correctness and performance. The linear search routine is simple to program, but as the name implies, its performance is linear in N (the length of the list).

The binary search routine uses an a priori ordering of the list to speed its execution. Hence, binary search uses $O(\log N)$ time to locate an element in a list of length N. It is a relatively simple method, but if the list is constantly being changed, it is difficult to keep in order. Hence, the binary search tree may be better.

The binary search tree uses links to maintain a search list in order so it can be searched in $O(\log N)$ time. Furthermore, TREESEARCH searches a list that can be both updated and kept in order. Programming TREE-SEARCH is relatively simple, but we have not discussed methods of updating the binary search tree data structure.

The graph search routine is a generalized routine for searching any (arbitrary) data structure. If each element of the list is linked to no more than NPTS links, and the graph consists of N_n nodes and N_e links, then the GRAPHSEARCH program performs searching in $O(N_n + N_e + \text{NPTS})$ time. This routine is not particularly fast, but it is extremely versatile and can be used in many practical applications.

In the next chapter we study extremely high-speed search routines. These routines use sophisticated divide-and-conquer techniques called *hash coding*. Consequently, their operation is more complex and difficult to analyze.

PROBLEMS

1. List the four search routines analyzed in this chapter and tell whether they are comparative or divide-and-conquer routines.

2. Verify the following version of the linear search routine using the methods illustrated in this chapter:

```
I:=N ; repeat
        DONE:=(LIST[I]=KEY) ;
        I:=I-1;
        until (DONE) or (I=0) ;
LINEAR:=I ;
```
[*Hint:* The segment contains a slight error.]

3. Use the BINARY function of Figure 4-3 to search the following list for KEY = 5. Show the value of variables Y and Z after each pass through the **while-do** loop.

$$LIST = \{0, 0, 0, 1, 1, 1, 2, 5, 35\}$$

4. Verify BINARY using $LIST[I] = I - N$ for $I = 1, 2, . . N$ and $KEY = (1 - N)$. How does your verification compare with Tests A.1 and A.2 in the text?

5. What is the worst-case and average-case expected time delay for BINARY?

6. Construct a binary search tree by adding the following list of elements in the order they appear below (left to right):

$$\{10, 8, 20, 9, 5, 0, 15, 12, 18\}$$

7. Verify TREESEARCH of Figure 4-9 using the tree of Figure 4-10 as test data and search key $K = 1$.

8. Use GRAPHSEARCH of Figure 4-14 to search the entire structure of Figure 4-13(a). After each pass through the **while-do** loop, show the contents of STK, BKUP, and NEXT.

9. Can GRAPHSEARCH be used to search a binary search tree? Use the binary search tree of Figure 4-10 as test data. Explain the difference between TREESEARCH and GRAPHSEARCH when scanning the entire tree.

10. What is N_e, N_n, and NPTS for the graph structure in Figure 4-13(a)? Use these values to estimate the average time delay in searching this graph using GRAPHSEARCH.

REFERENCES

Wirth, N., *Algorithms + Data Structures = Programs*. Englewood Cliffs, N.J.: Prentice-Hall, Inc., 1976.

5

Application to Hash Coding

INTRODUCTION

The goal of all search routines is to be fast and efficient. For this reason a large amount of time and effort has been devoted to the study of a special class of divide-and-conquer techniques that rapidly discard most of the list, leaving a small portion containing the search key. These techniques are called *key-to-address transforms* or sometimes *hashing* functions because they compute a correspondence between each search key and a table address ("address" refers to the location of the search key in the table). The table is a list containing keys and their corresponding information. In the contemporary literature on hashing functions, the table is called a *scatter table* because, as we will demonstrate, the information stored in a scatter table is located at scattered places throughout the table.

The idea underlying hashing functions is to find a mapping function H that transforms each key W_i from a list $W = \{W_1, W_2, \ldots, W_n\}$ into a location $[0 \ldots (n - 1)]$. That is,

$$H(W_i) = j$$

where j is in $[0 \ldots (n - 1)]$ and i is in $[1 \ldots n]$. For example, a list of squares

$$W = \{1,4,9,16,25\}$$

can be transformed into $[0 \ldots 4]$ by the function

$$H = (W_i + 3) \textbf{ div } 6$$

In this example, the correspondence between the keys and the location assigned to each key is shown below.

i	W_i	$H(W_i)$
1	1	0
2	4	1
3	9	2
4	16	3
5	25	4

A Pascal program that computes the function is simple and fast:

function HASH1 (W:KEY) : **integer** ;
begin HASH := (W + 3) **div** 6 **end** ;

We use this transformation to *insert* new keys into the scatter table as well as to locate (search) keys in the table. One of the main advantages of hash coding is the elegant solution it provides to list maintenance. The same transformation is used to rapidly insert and look up search keys whenever needed.

The simple transformation HASH1 is called a *perfect hashing function* because it produces a perfect fit between the set of keys and the set of table locations. In general, we must know the set of search keys in advance in order to derive a perfect hashing function. This requirement may not be possible in many applications, however. Instead, it may be necessary to estimate the function used to map from an arbitrary (not known in advance) key into a scatter table location. Such less-than-perfect hashing functions are known as *general hashing functions*.

In this chapter we study both perfect and general hashing functions. Both of these functions are used widely in software engineering to speed retrieval of information from tables stored in main memory and secondary storage devices. We might use a perfect hashing function to organize a static membership list (names), telephone numbers, zip codes, dictionary words, and so on. The general hashing function technique is used when the keys are not known in advance, for example, in mapping social security numbers, license numbers, personal names, etc., into a table.

In a perfect hashing function we are guaranteed access in an exceptionally short time since only one table access is needed. A general hashing function, on the other hand, may require more than one access because the general hashing technique only narrows down the search to a subset of table locations. Thus,

$$H(W_i) = H_1$$

where H_1 is a subset of the table locations. Typically, we locate a key in a general hashing function routine by successive hashes:

$$H_0(W_i) = H_1$$
$$H_2 = H(H_1)$$
$$H_3 = H(H_2)$$
$$\vdots$$
$$H_k = H(H_{k-1})$$

Therefore, after k accesses, the location containing W_i is examined, and a match occurs. In our study of the general hashing function, we will attempt to minimize k in order to derive a fast routine.

PERFECT HASHING

A perfect hashing function guarantees a successful search in one access (comparison, retrieval, copy, etc.) to the table containing all elements of a list. Given a key $W[I]$, we perform a hash $H(W[I])$ to obtain the location of $W[I]$ within LIST:

$$H(W[I]) = \text{location of } W[I] \text{ in LIST}$$

In the best of all circumstances, we find a LIST of size N to hold N keys. But in practice we are usually not so lucky. Usually more than N table locations are needed to store N elements because H serves as a compression transformation. Suppose we attempt to compress the set of keys below into a LIST of length $N = 6$ locations:

I	LIST[I]	$H = (\text{LIST[I]}-1) \text{ div } 2$
1	1	0
2	2	0
3	3	1
4	5	2
5	8	3
6	13	6

This compression leads to two problems:

1. Duplicate assignments to location zero are made by H. These duplicates are called *synonyms,* and when they are assigned to the same location, we say they *collide.*

2. This transformation requires a table of length seven to store six elements thus leaving one unused. The remaining entry is called an *empty* lo-

cation because it is never used by this transformation. Actually, because of the synonym problem in #1 above, we see that two locations (4,5) are wasted.

The perfect hashing problem can be defined as follows: Find a function H such that every key $W[I]$ is assigned a *unique location* in a scatter table, and furthermore, H must compress the locations such that the *smallest* scatter table possible is required to store the keys (and their associated information). In a sense, we are attempting to find the "best" perfect hashing function given a set of keys W.

Heuristic for PERFECT

Many proposals for an "ideal" perfect hashing function have been studied. In this section we study the *quotient function* defined by two constants S and M:

$$H(W) = (W + S) \text{ div } M$$

where W is a key and S and M are parameters.

The two parameters S and M are called the *translation* and *compression constants*, respectively. S shifts the set of keys, and M expands or contracts the set.

Clearly, $S = 0$ and $M = 1$ yield a working perfect hash function because every key is assigned a location identical to its value. This assignment may be the best we can do for a given list of keys. Hopefully a more compact assignment is possible, however.

As an example, the list of powers-of-two {1,4,9,16} can be translated and compressed into a list without empty locations by the perfect hashing function:

$$H = (W + 1) \text{ div } 5$$

The assignment is

I	$W[I]$	$H(W[I])$
1	1	0
2	4	1
3	9	2
4	16	3

In general, we are not so fortunate when attempting to find the appropriate values of S and M. Consider the following illustration where 50% of the table is wasted due to empty locations; that is,

$$H = (W - 52) \textbf{ div } 49$$

I	$W[I]$	$H(W[I])$
1	100	0
2	120	1
3	150	2
4	210	3
5	500	9

Let alpha be the *loading factor* of a scatter table:

$$\text{Alpha} = \frac{\text{number of used locations}}{\text{length of table}}$$

$$= \frac{N}{L}$$

In the example above,

$$\text{Alpha} = \frac{5}{10} = 0.50$$

The best perfect hashing function yields an alpha = 1.0; and the lower alpha becomes, the more memory we waste. The perfect hashing function trades memory space for speed because it always guarantees access to the desired table location in one retrieval. But how do we obtain S and M?

Figure 5-1 shows how we go about finding an S and M that map the set of keys into unique locations. Since translation of each key by more than $(M - 1)$ contributes nothing to the search, we note that

$$-W[1] \leqslant S \leqslant M - 1$$

Furthermore, the smallest table possible fits N elements of a list into N locations; or, in other words,

$$M \leqslant \left\lceil \frac{W[N] - W[1]}{(N - 1)} \right\rceil$$

where M is an integer. We also note that if everything else fails, the list can be stored in locations identical to the values of the search keys. Thus,

$$1 \leqslant M$$

These bounds define a region containing the best possible M and S; see Figure 5-1(a). The heuristic of Figure 5-2 searches the region of Figure 5-1(a) when it computes S and M for the keys shown in Figure 5-1(b). The pair (S,M) is initially $(-3,6)$ as shown by START. The heuristic performs trial hashes at the following locations:

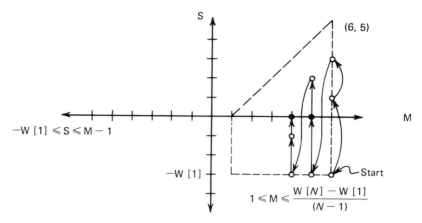

(a) Search heuristic for perfect hash

I	W [I]	H(W [I])
1	3	0
2	5	1
3	8	2
4	13	3
5	21	5
6	34	8

(b) Perfect hash $S = 0$, $M = 4$, for Fibonacci sequence, $N = 6$

Figure 5-1. Perfect hash heuristic.

$$(S,M)$$
$$(-3,6)$$
$$(1,6)$$
$$(3,6)$$
$$(-3,5)$$
$$(0,5)$$
$$(2,5)$$
$$(-3,4)$$
$$(-1,4)$$
$$(0,4)$$

and stops at $S = 0$, $M = 4$. Thus the heuristic yields a perfect hashing function:

$$H = (W[I] \text{ div } 4)$$

This function maps $N = 6$ elements into nine locations for a loading factor of

$$\text{Alpha} = \frac{6}{9} = 67\%$$

The perfect hashing function heuristic of Figure 5-2 sometimes fails to find the best (most compact) mapping values (S,M). This is unfortunate since determination of a nonoptimal pair (S,M) means wasted memory. However, PERFECT yields the best pair (S,M) *most of the time*, as we will show. More important, however, is determining if PERFECT works correctly.

Certification of PERFECT   What does procedure PERFECT compute? Since this program sometimes fails to find the best values of (S,M), we cannot certify it by showing that the best values are always obtained. Instead, we will show that PERFECT returns (S,M) such that the mapping produces unique locations for each W[I], and the program will terminate.

```
procedure PERFECT( W : LIST ; var S, M : integer ) ;
  var
    I, DEL, MIN, NEXTH, NEXTM, H : integer ;
  begin
      S := − W[ 1 ] ; M := ( W[ N ] − W[ 1 ] ) div ( N−1 ) ;
    repeat
      I := 1 ; NEXTH := HASH( W[ 1 ], S, M ) ;
      DEL := ( NEXTH + 1 ) * M − W[ 1 ] − S ;
      MIN := DEL ;
    repeat
       I := I+1 ; H := NEXTH ; NEXTH := HASH( W[ I ], S, M ) ;
       DEL := ( NEXTH + 1 ) * M − W[ I ] − S ;
       MIN := MINIMUM( MIN, DEL ) ;
      until ( H = NEXTH ) or ( I = N );
      if H = NEXTH then
        begin
          S := S + MIN ;
          NEXTM := ( W[ I ] + S ) div ( NEXTH + 1 ) ;
          I := 1 ;
          if S >= M then
            begin
              S := − W[ 1 ] ; M := NEXTM − ORD( M = NEXTM ) ;
            end ; (* if S >= M then *)
        end ; (* if H = NEXTH then *)
    until ( I = N − or ( M = 1 ) ;
  end ;      (* PERFECT *)
```

Figure 5-2. A heuristic for finding S and M.

Two **repeat-until** loops govern the behavior of PERFECT. Thus,

> **repeat**
>   . . .
>   **repeat**
>   . . .
>   **until** (H = NEXTH) **or** (I = N)
> **until** (I = N) **or** (M = 1)

The inner loop repeats until every trial hash (NEXTH) is unique, or until the first instance of a collision (H = NEXTH) occurs. If no collision occurs, then the loop terminates with loop functional

$$I_{t'} = N$$

which also terminates the second loop. Therefore, either the procedure terminates because it succeeds in finding the *first* perfect hashing function it encounters, or because $M = 1$. When $M = 1$, the identity mapping results, and the procedure terminates anyway.

The procedure terminates with $(I = N)$ or $(M = 1)$. The worst-case situation occurs when $(M = 1)$, but how do we know $M = 1$?

The largest possible value of M is given by

$$M := (W[N] - W[1]) \text{ div } (N-1)$$

and M takes on monotonically decreasing values:

if S >= M **then**
  begin S := -W[1] ; M := NEXTM - ORD(M = NEXTM) **end**

while S ranges between $-W[1]$ and $(M-1)$. In the case $(M = NEXTM)$, we see that

$$M := NEXTM - ORD(M = NEXTM)$$

decrements M by one. Hence, the heuristic will always terminate, possibly with $M = 1$.

PERFECT finds the first values for S and M that yield a perfect hashing function. It begins with

$$S := -W[1]$$

and

$$M := (W[N] - W[1]) \text{ div } (N-1)$$

The search selects a new value of S by a local adjustment. That is, S is increased by an amount equal to the smallest possible shift needed to avoid a collision. If H and NEXTH collide, then the smallest DEL,

$$DEL := (NEXTH + 1) * M - W[I] - S$$

is added to S to remove the collision. This expression is obtained by noting that a collision at NEXTH is removed by hashing into table location (NEXTH+1):

$$(NEXTH+1) = (W[I]+(S+DEL)) \textbf{ div } M$$

But we must use the smallest DEL here (MIN) because a larger value may cause a collision between another hash value and its adjacent neighbor. So,

$$(NEXTH+1) = (W[I]+(S+MIN)) \textbf{ div } M$$

The value of M remains constant as long as we can remove a collision by adjusting S. However, if S exceeds $(M-1)$, no further improvement will be possible. Therefore we adjust M by computing a NEXTM that removes the collision. Thus,

$$NEXTM := (W[I]+S) \textbf{ div } (NEXTH+1)$$

This is arrived at by noting

$$(NEXTH+1) = \left\lceil \frac{W[I]+S+MIN}{NEXTM} \right\rceil$$

as before.

Figure 5-1(a) illustrates how PERFECT converges to the first pair (S,M) that yields a perfect hashing function. Adjustments to S move the search vertically, as shown by the arrows, until the maximum value of S is reached. A NEXTM is selected that removes a collision, and we search for another S. Finally, a "perfect" (S,M) is reached, and the heuristic terminates. In the worst-case situation, $M = 1$, and the hashing function maps each key $W[I]$ into location $W[I]+S$.

Suppose we test PERFECT using very simple test data. Let $W[I] = I$, and $N > 1$. Initially, $S = -1$, $M = 1$. The procedure can be rewritten in abbreviated form:

$$\begin{bmatrix} S := -1 \\ M := 1 \\ \\ \end{bmatrix} \begin{cases} I_0 := 1 \\ NEXTH_0 := 0 \\ DEL_0 := 1 \\ MIN_0 := 1 \end{cases} \begin{cases} I_t := t+1; H_t := NEXTH_{t-1} \\ NEXTH_t := t; DEL_t := 1 \\ MIN_t := 1 \end{cases} \left. \right\} \bigcup_{\substack{(H_t=NEXTH_t) \\ \text{or } (I_t=N)}} \left. \right\} \bigcup_{\substack{(I_t=N) \\ \text{or } (M=1)}}$$

because $(H_t=NEXTH_t)$ is never ture. Thus, both loops terminate for $I_t=N$.

$$\begin{bmatrix} S := -1 \\ M := 1 \\ NEXT_t := t \end{bmatrix} \quad \text{(for } t=1,2,...,N)$$

Hence the hashing function for the test data $W[I] = I$ is

$$H = (W[I]-1)$$

If PERFECT fails to find a perfect hash for initial values of (S,M), it computes new trial values by first adjusting S and then adjusting M. If (S,M) are adjusted by too much, the heuristic skips over the best values. Therefore, PERFECT may not always return the best perfect hashing function. Now we examine the performance of PERFECT.

Performance Evaluation The performance of PERFECT depends on the good fortune of finding (S,M) on a given pass through its inner loop. This could happen at any time while searching the region of Figure 5-1(a).

Suppose every point in the acceptable region of Figure 5-1(a) is examined one at a time. There are R points in this region:

$$R = (M_0 - 1)\left(\frac{M_0 - 1}{2} + W[1]\right)$$

where

$$M_0 = (W[N] - W[1]) \textbf{ div } (N - 1)$$

The number of pairs (S,M) that PERFECT might have to search is $O(M_0{}^2)$. Since M_0 depends on the set of keys and the length of the list of keys, we might expect PERFECT to compute (S,M) in time proportional to the number and magnitude of the keys.

The execution time of PERFECT is shown in Figure 5-3 for randomly generated sets of keys. In Figure 5-3(a) the keys were randomly selected from the interval [1 . . 100,000]; in Figure 5-3(b) from interval [1 . . 10,000]; and in Figure 5-3(c) from interval [1 . . 1000]. Clearly, the performance of PERFECT depends on both the size of the keys and their number, N.

The value of PERFECT also depends on how much memory the perfect hashing function uses to store keys (and empties). A "good" perfect hashing function compresses the keys into a small table so that alpha is close to 1.0. A poor function yields a low value of alpha.

Figure 5-4 shows the results of an experiment where the loading factor is plotted against the number of keys, N, for the intervals sampled in Figure 5-3. Notice how low the loading factors became for "large" lists!

We conclude that the perfect hashing function, $H = (W + S) \textbf{ div } M$, is suitable for short lists of static keys. Thus,

$$\textbf{function HASH } (W,S,M) : \textbf{integer} ;$$
$$\textbf{begin } HASH := (W + S) \textbf{ div } M \textbf{ end} ;$$

When the list becomes long and the loading factor drops, the perfect hashing function technique should be replaced by a more general hash coding routine. We discuss general algorithms in the next section. However, before dropping the subject of perfect hashing, we study application of perfect hashing to secondary storage retrieval.

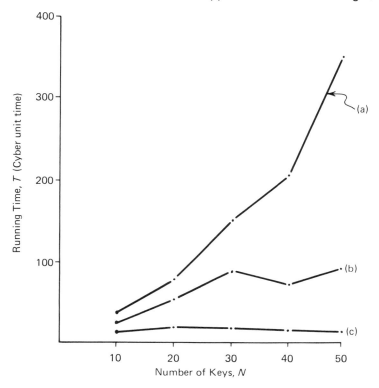

Figure 5-3. Running time (CDC Cyber) versus number of keys. (a) [1 . . 100,000], (b) [1 . . 10,000], (c) [1 . . 1000].

Heuristic for BUCKET

Hashing functions are used to compute the *bucket number* of a key. A *bucket* is any unit of storage that can be directly accessed in one probe. For example, secondary storage devices are usually accessed by performing a *seek* to find the appropriate bucket, followed by a read/write operation that moves the data from/to memory at high speed. Typical buckets are disk sectors or cylinders.

Any secondary storage device can be considered a sequence of buckets if the time to perform a seek (bucket selection) is relatively high compared with read/write transfers. Usually, a bucket corresponds to a disk sector.

In most applications several search keys can be stored in each bucket. This means that the keyed elements of a list can be grouped together and can be retrieved by reading the entire group into main memory in one seek. All but the desired element is discarded after the group has been examined in main memory.

The dominant time delay in bucket access is in performing the seeks.

Therefore, we can minimize the delay due to seek by purposely grouping the keyed elements together using a bucket hash code that is multiple-valued. Thus,

$$\text{Bucket number} = \text{HASH (set of keys)}$$

This function purposely returns the same bucket number for a group of unique keys in order to cluster the set of keys together in one bucket.

Consider, for example, the keys defined by the power-of-two relation:

$$W[I] = 2^{I-1} \text{ ; for } I = 1, 2 \ldots (N-1)$$

If we used procedure PERFECT from the previous section to compute a perfect hash function for these values ($N = 10$), we would get a low loading factor:

$$H_{\text{perfect}} = W[I] \textbf{ div } 2$$

$$\text{Alpha} = \frac{10}{257} = 0.039$$

and a poor key-to-address transformation.

If we attempt to compute a perfect hashing function for a disk file with bucket capacity $B = 5$ keys, we get the following pleasant transformation.

$$H_{\text{bucket}} = (W[I] + 479) \textbf{ div } 511$$

$$\text{Alpha} = 10/((2 \text{ buckets}) * (5 \text{ keys per bucket}))$$

$$= 1.0$$

The result of this transformation maps one-half of the list into bucket zero, and the other one-half into bucket one. For $B=5$, $S=479$, and $M=511$,

I	$W[I]$	H_{bucket}
1	1	0
2	2	0
3	4	0
4	8	0
5	16	0
6	32	1
7	64	1
8	128	1
9	256	1
10	512	1

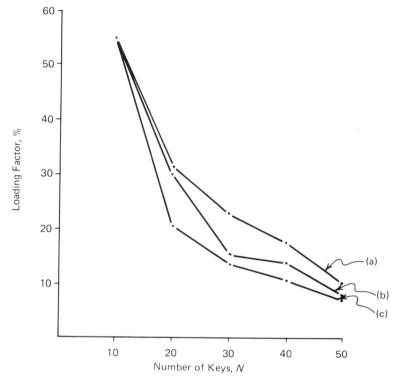

Figure 5-4. Loading factor versus number of keys. (a) [1 . . 100,000], (b) [1 . . 10,000], (c) [1 . . 1000].

This example naturally raises a question about modifying procedure PERFECT to make it find (S,M) such that B keys are transformed into a single bucket. Indeed, this can be done as shown in Figure 5-5.

Procedure BUCKET is actually procedure PERFECT with the following minor modifications. We let BCOUNT be a counter which counts the number of colliding trial hashes. As long as the number of trial hashes that collide is less than or equal to B (bucket size), no adjustments in S or M are needed. The test, ($H=$NEXTH), is changed to (BCOUNT $> B$) as Figure 5-5 shows.

We initially set M to the largest value it could be:

$(N-1)$ **div** B = number of unique bucket numbers we need in the best of circumstances

$$M := (W[N] - W[1]) \textbf{ div } ((N-1) \textbf{ div } B)$$

This calculation sets an upper bound on M. Any decrease in M will mean some wasted space in the file of buckets.

The number of trial hashes that are part of a run of identical hash values are computed by properly incrementing BCOUNT:

if   H = NEXTH
    then   BCOUNT := BCOUNT + 1 (* run of matches *)
    else   BCOUNT := 1   (* end of run *)

Procedure BUCKET computes exactly the same values of (S,M) as PER-FECT when $B = 1$. When $B > 1$, however, we get a dramatic improvement in the loading factor (see Table 5-1).

Table 5-1. Fibonacci Keys:
$$W[I] = W[I-1] + W[I-2]$$

I	$W[I]$	HASH				
1	1	0	0	0	0	0
2	2	1	0	0	0	0
3	3	2	1	0	0	0
4	5	4	1	1	0	0
5	8	7	2	1	1	0
6	13	12	3	1	1	1
7	21	20	4	2	1	1
S =		−1	2	5	12	7
M =		1	5	10	20	20
B =		1	2	3	4	5

The loading factor for $B = 1$ (alpha = 33%) is one-half the value obtained for $B = 5$ (alpha = 70%). In experiments using random keys, it was observed that the loading factor steadily improves with increasing bucket size B until about $B = 8$ (Wilson and Lewis). Since these experiments are based on averages over uniformly random keys, we can conclude that further research is needed before the benefits of large bucket hashing can be determined.

The BUCKET heuristic performs about the same as the PERFECT routine because it is basically identical to PERFECT. The region containing feasible values of (S,M) is larger due to the increased size of M_0, initially. The number of adjustments is reduced, however, because BUCKET purposely causes collisions in the trial hashes in order to group keys together into buckets.

The advantages and disadvantages of the two perfect hashing functions discussed here are listed before we leave this subject.

Advantages

1. A perfect hash locates the desired element of a list (stored in a scatter table on a disk file of buckets) in a single retrieval probe.

2. The perfect hashing function studied in this chapter is simple and fast once S and M are known.

Disadvantages

1. The heuristic for computing (S,M) is time-consuming and does not guarantee the best (largest loading factor) transformation.

2. The list of search keys must be known in advance, or else PER-FECT and BUCKET cannot find (S,M).

3. The best perfect hashing function may waste memory because the loading factor seems to decrease dramatically as the size of the list of keys increases; see Figure 5-4.

The most damaging disadvantage of this class of hashing functions is the need to know the list of keys in advance. If we are willing to give up the single-probe advantage, we can remove the need to know the keys beforehand. This is the subject of the next section, which deals with general hashing functions.

QUOTIENT HASHING

A general hashing function is a key-to-address transformation $H_g(\text{KEY})$, which computes the location of a search key KEY by the divide-and-conquer technique:

$$H_g(\text{KEY}) = H_0(\text{KEY}) + H_{\text{off}}(\text{KEY})$$

where H_0 is the home address of KEY, and $H_{\text{off}}(\text{KEY})$ is the offset location of KEY.

The home address is the location of the first probe of the scatter table. Since the home address of two or more keys may be identical, we use the offset H_{off} to locate KEY. That is, given a subset of synonyms $\{K_1, K_2, \ldots, K_m\}$,

$$\text{home address} = H_g(K_i) \text{ for } K_i \text{ in } \{K_1 \ldots K_m\}$$

The central problem we must solve in order to find a general hashing function is to find H_0 and H_{off} such that H_0 elminates as many keys as possible from further consideration, and H_{off} eliminates all but one remaining key from the set selected by H_0.

Many proposals have been put forth for H_0 and H_{off}, but the most durable and frequently used functions are:

```
procedure BUCKET( W : LIST ; B : integer ; var S, M : integer ) ;
  var
    BCOUNT, I, DEL, MIN, NEXTH, NEXTM, H : integer ;
  begin
    S := - W[ 1 ] ; M := ( W[ N ] - W[ 1 ] ) div ( ( N-1 ) div B );
    repeat
      I := 1 ; NEXTH := HASH( W[ 1 ], S, M ) ;
      DEL := ( NEXTH + 1 ) * M - W[ 1 ] - S ;
      MIN := DEL ;
      BCOUNT := 1 ;
      repeat
        I := I+1 ; H := NEXTH ; NEXTH := HASH( W[ I ], S, M ) ;
        if H = NEXTH
          then BCOUNT := BCOUNT + 1
          else  BCOUNT := 1 ;
        DEL := ( NEXTH + 1 ) * M - W[ I ] - S ;
        MIN := MINIMUM( MIN, DEL );
      until ( BCOUNT > B ) or ( I = N ) ;
      if BCOUNT > B then
        begin
          S := S + MIN ;
          NEXTM := ( W[ I ] + S ) div ( NEXTH + 1 ) ;
          I := 1 ;
          if S >= M then
            begin
              S := - W[ 1 ] ; M := NEXTM - ORD( M = NEXTM ) ;
            end ;   (* if S >= M then *)
        end ;       (* if H = NEXTH then *)
    until ( I = N ) or ( M = 1 ) ;
  end ;     (* BUCKET *)
```

Figure 5-5. Bucket heuristic.

$$H_0 (KEY) = KEY \bmod N$$
$$H_{off} (KEY) = i * (KEY \operatorname{div} N)$$

where N = length of the scatter storage table, and i is determined by a linear search routine. We also must guarantee $H_{off} > 0$. Thus,

if $H_{off} = 0$, then $H_{off} := 1$

because the offset must force the hashing function to search another scatter table location if the home address does not contain the desired key.

Function H_0 is called a *prime-division* hash because, as we will show, N must be a prime number in order for the function to guarantee a full search of the scatter table. The function H_{off} is called a *quotient* hash because it uses the quotient of (KEY $\div$ N) as the offset from H_0 in case of a synonym collision at location H_0.

These two functions are combined to give a simple, yet powerful, general hashing function that is used to insert elements into TABLE $[0 . . N-1]$ and then retrieve them again.

The *pseudocode for general hash code insert* is:

1. Compute $H_0(\text{KEY})$ and $H_{off}(\text{KEY})$.

2. Loop while TABLE $[H_0]$ is already occupied and the search does not cycle back to the home address: Replace H_0 with $(H_0 + H_{off})$ modulo N.

3. If TABLE $[H_0]$ is unoccupied (empty), then insert KEY into the table at location H_0; otherwise the table is full and the insertion fails.

The *pseudocode for general hash code lookup* is:

1. Compute $H_0(\text{KEY})$ and $H_{off}(\text{KEY})$.

2. Loop while TABLE $[H_0]$ is occupied and not equal to KEY, and the search does not cycle back to the home address: Replace H_0 with $(H_0 + H_{off})$ modulo N.

3. If TABLE $[H_0]$ = KEY, then return H_0 as the location of KEY; otherwise return zero (not found).

The two routines are almost identical. To insert a new element with key KEY, we look for an unoccupied TABLE element and write the new element into location H_0. To retrieve an element with key equal to KEY, we search for TABLE $[H_0]$ = KEY, or until the first unoccupied TABLE element is encountered, or until the search returns to the home address.

Consider the following example using the table and keys shown in Figure 5-6. The set of keys {77,51,33,10} are inserted immediately at their home addresses because they are *not* synonyms and do not collide:

$$H_g(77) = H_0(77) = 77 \bmod 5 = 2$$
$$H_g(51) = H_0(51) = 51 \bmod 5 = 1$$
$$H_g(33) = H_0(33) = 33 \bmod 5 = 3$$
$$H_g(10) = H_0(10) = 10 \bmod 5 = 0$$

After these keys are inserted (in any order), the table is nearly full as shown in Figure 5-6(a). Now, suppose we use the offset H_{off} to insert KEY = 13 into the table:

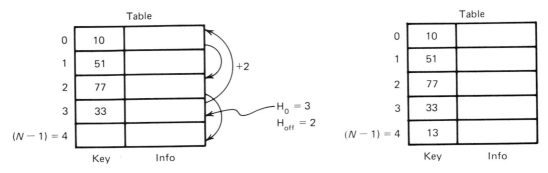

(a) Path taken to insert key = 13

(b) After key = 13 is inserted

Figure 5-6. Insert operation: Quotient-offset hash.

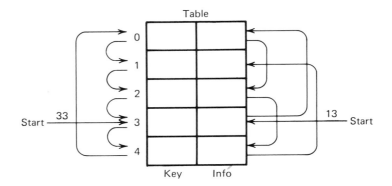

H(13)⟶ 3 ⟶ ∅ ⟶ 2 ⟶ 4 ⟶ 1 ⟶ 3 (back home)

H(33)⟶ 3 ⟶ 4 ⟶ ∅ ⟶ 1 ⟶ 2 ⟶ 3 (back home)

Figure 5-7. Quotient offset avoids secondary collisions.

$$H_0(13) = 13 \text{ mod } 5 = 3$$
$$H_{off}(13) = 13 \text{ div } 5 = 2$$

Since TABLE[3] is occupied, we must add the offset to arrive at another (trial) location:

$$H_0 := (3 + 2) \text{ mod } 5 = 0$$

Again, TABLE [0] is occupied, so we must probe the table at location

$$H_0 := (0 + 2) \text{ mod } 5 = 2$$

Figure 5-6(a) shows the path of probes into the TABLE as we compare each TABLE [H_0] key component. Finally,

$$H_0 := (2 + 2) \bmod 5 = 4$$

turns up empty, and we can insert KEY = 13 into TABLE[4].

The example for KEY = 13 demonstrates two phenomena of scatter table searching. First, TABLE[3] was already occupied by 33 because it is the home address of synonyms 13 and 33. We call a collision at the home address a *primary collision*. Second, after adding the quotient offset H_{off} to the home address, we still encountered a series of collisions. These subsequent conflicts are called *secondary collisions*. A general hashing function should provide a means of minimizing both primary and secondary collisions.

A good general hashing function is designed so that H_0 scrambles the location of keys in order to avoid primary collisions. The H_{off} hash attempts to avoid secondary collisions by choosing a different search path for each synonym. For example, the search paths for synonyms 13 and 33 are different:

For 13, search locations: 3,0,2,4,1,3
For 33, search locations: 3,4,0,1,2,3

Figure 5-7 shows the two *different* paths taken by 13 and 33, even though they collide at their home address. This is why the quotient-offset hashing function is such an excellent general hashing function.

The quotient-offset hashing function searches the entire table before it returns subsequently to the home address. This is a very important feature of any general hashing function because without this feature we might think the table is full when in fact it is not. More importantly, the algorithm may never return to the home address as prescribed by the pseudocode. This important feature of the quotient-offset hashing function is explored in detail in the next section.

The QHASH Algorithm

The quotient-offset algorithm is (incorrectly) implemented as function QHASH in Figure 5-8. This routine computes the location of KEY in table *T*.

```
type
  TABLE = array[0 . . N − 1] of record
                      KEY: integer;
                      occupied: boolean;
                      INFO: string
                      end;
```

```
function QHASH ( K :integer) : integer ;
  const
    NULL = −1 ;
  var
    H, Q, Y : integer ;
  begin
    H := K mod N ; Q := K div N ; Y := H ;
    while ( T[Y].KEY <> K)
              and
          ( T[Y].OCCUPIED)
              and
          ( (Y+Q) mod N <> H)
      do Y := (Y+Q) mod N ;
    if T[Y].KEY = K
      then QHASH := Y
      else  QHASH := NULL
  end;      (* QHASH *)
```

Figure 5-8. Look-up using quotient-offset hashing.

We assume an initial state of the table defined by

```
var
  T : TABLE;
begin
  for I := 0 to (N−1) do
    begin
      T[I] .KEY := NULL;
      T[I] .OCCUPIED := FALSE;
      T[I] .INFO := EMPTY
    end;
end;
```

where NULL = (−1) and EMPTY is the empty string containing zero characters. The flag OCCUPIED is FALSE if the table element is unoccupied, and TRUE when it is occupied.

Suppose we use QHASH to build the table of Figure 5-6, and then search for KEY = 13. Figure 5-9 shows T and the search path taken by QHASH in order to look up KEY = 13.

Before we place too much confidence in QHASH, we need to certify its correctness. This is the subject of the next section on testing.

Correctness of QHASH

The correctness of QHASH depends on two fundamental facts that we

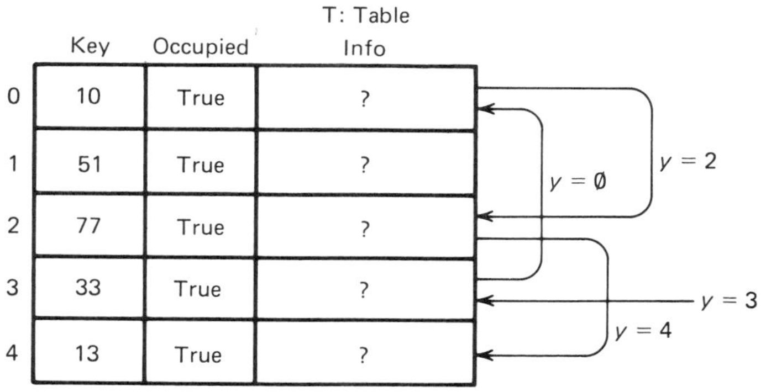

Figure 5-9. Search path to find QHASH (13).

must show. First, we must show that QHASH returns the location of a
search key if it does indeed exist in the table. Second, we must show that
the **while-do** loop terminates (convergence), and when it does (if it does),
the correct value is returned.

Obtaining the final value of Y is an easy problem because if the loop
converges to $Y_{t'}$ (final value of Y), it is due to one of the following conditions: Either

$$T[Y_{t'}].\text{KEY} = K$$

or

$$T[Y_{t'}].\text{OCCUPIED} <> \text{TRUE}$$

or

$$(Y_{t'} + Q) \textbf{ mod } N = H$$

or all of the conditions are true. In the first condition we get

$$Y_{t'} = \text{location of } K \text{ in } T$$

which is a desirable result.

Suppose no match occurs, and instead one of the other conditions
holds. In this case,

$$Y_{t'} = \text{location of some other key}$$

and

$$T[Y_{t'}].\text{KEY} <> K$$

If we forward substitute this condition into the **if-then-else** component
following the loop, we get the desired result:

$$\text{QHASH} := \text{NULL}$$

Now, suppose the matching condition never occurs because K is not in the table. In fact, suppose we test QHASH using the following degenerate case:

TEST #1. $T[I].\text{KEY} = \text{NULL}$, $T[I].\text{OCCUPIED} = \text{FALSE}$, $T[I].\text{INFO} = ?$, for $I = 0 \ldots (N-1)$.

In this case the loop will terminate under only one condition; that is,

$$(Y_{t'} + Q) \bmod N = H$$

The success of this test is based on showing that this *always* happens when no matching key is found. In abbreviated form, QHASH becomes

$$\begin{bmatrix} H := K \bmod N \\ Q := K \textbf{ div } N \\ Y_0 := H \end{bmatrix} \underset{(Y_{t-1} + Q) \bmod N <> H}{\mathbf{W}} \{Y_t := (Y_{t-1} + Q) \bmod N\}$$

This recursive form can be transformed into an equivalent iterative form by solving

$$\{Y_{t+1} - Y_t = Q \quad \bmod N\}$$

The solution is

$$Y_t = (Y_0 + Qt) \bmod N$$

And since $Y_0 = H$,

$$Y_t = (H + Qt) \bmod N$$

where $t = 0, 1, \ldots$

Substitution of this iterative form into QHASH, and noting the loop functional that terminates the loop, gives

$$\underset{(t-1)Q \bmod N <> 0}{\mathbf{W}} \{Y_t := (H + Q * t) \bmod N\}$$

The loop converges when

$$(t - 1)Q \bmod N = 0$$

There are two cases to consider, as shown below.

CASE $Q \bmod N = 0$

It is possible that $Q = 0 = (K \textbf{ div } N) \bmod N$. Unfortunately, this corresponds to an error in the design of QHASH. To correct this error we insert the following patch:

if $Q \bmod N = 0$ **then** $Q := 1$

Actually, we can set Q to any nonzero integer such that $Q \bmod N <> 0$, and the algorithm will work correctly. Note in Figure 5-10 we insert the correction before the **while-do** loop.

$$\text{CASE } (t - 1) \bmod N = 0$$

Since t starts at 1 and increments by 1 for each pass through the loop, we are interested only in the smallest value of $(t - 1)$ such that $(t - 1) \bmod N = 0$. The first time $(t - 1) \bmod N = 0$ is for

$$(t - 1) = N$$

Therefore,

$$t' - 1 = N$$
$$t' = N + 1$$

The loop terminates when the $(N + 1)$th pass is attempted. The terminal value of Y is $Y_N = (H + QN) \bmod N = H$.

The **while-do** loop terminates by returning to the home address. But these two cases overlook a subtle possibility. There is another case to consider.

```
function QHASH ( K : integer ) : integer ;
  const
    NULL = -1 ;
  var
    H, Q, Y : integer ;
  begin
    H := K mod N ; Q := K div N ; Y := H ;
    if Q mod N = 0 then Q := 1 ;
    if GCD( N, Q ) <> 1 then WRITELN( 'Warning ! Error in QHASH' ) ;
    while ( T[ Y ].KEY <> K )
            and
        ( T[ Y ].OCCUPIED = TRUE )
            and
        ( ( Y + Q ) mod N <> H )
      do Y := ( Y + Q ) mod N ;
    if T[ Y ].KEY = K
      then QHASH := Y
      else  QHASH := NULL
  end ;      (* QHASH *)
```

Figure 5.10. Correct version of QHASH.

CASE Partial Table Search

We must check QHASH to make sure that *every* element of T is searched before returning to location H. To do this we compute the length of a path L from home address back to home address again. If the length is equal to the size of the table N, then every element is searched. On the contrary, if $L < N$, then some of the elements must have been skipped.

From number theory we know that the number of numbers in the interval $[0 \ . \ . \ N-1]$ generated by $Y_t := (Y_{t-1} + Q)$ **Mod** N is

$$L = \frac{N}{\gcd(N,Q)}$$

where gcd is the greatest common divisor function. That is, $\gcd(N,Q) = 1$ if N and Q are relatively prime.

The largest value of L is obtained when $\gcd(N,Q) = 1$. Thus,

$$L = N \qquad \text{as needed, when } \gcd(N,Q) = 1$$

The only way we can guarantee this condition for arbitrary $Q > 0$, is by forcing N to be a prime number. Therefore, the final "correction" is to guarantee a table of prime number length; see Figure 5-10.

As a simple counter example, suppose we increase the length of the scatter table of Figure 5-9 to $N=6$, and hash $K=13$. The number of numbers generated is

$$L = \frac{6}{\gcd(6,2)} = \frac{6}{2} = 3$$

$$\text{because} \qquad H = 13 \textbf{ mod } 6 = 1$$

$$Q = 13 \textbf{ div } 6 = 2$$

Therefore, the QHASH routine searches $L = 3$ of the $N = 6$ locations before repeating:

$$Y = 1,3,5,1,3,5 \ . \ .$$

In this case, only $T[1]$, $T[3]$, and $T[5]$ are examined. The remaining elements of T are ignored.

The only way we can guarantee $L = N$ for every possible $Q >= 1$ is to force N to be a prime number. For this reason, QHASH is sometimes called a *prime-division hash* with quotient offset.

Other hashing functions have been used with equal success. The algorithm in QHASH yields good results for a variety of keys, and since it is fast and simple, it is also widely used.

Figure 5-11 gives a slightly modified QHASH routine which inserts new keys into the scatter storage table, T. This routine is identical to QHASH except for the final segment:

```
procedure INSERT ( K : integer;KINFO : string);
  const
    NULL = -1;
  var
    H, Q, Y : integer;
  begin
    H := K mod N ; Q := K div N ; Y := H ;
    if Q mod N = 0 then Q := 1 ;
    if GCD(N, Q) <> 1 then WRITELN('Error in INSERT');
    while (T[Y].KEY <> K)
              and
          (T[Y].OCCUPIED)
              and
          ( ( Y+Q ) mod N <> H)
      do Y := (Y+Q) mod N ;
    if T[Y].OCCUPIED
      then WRITELN ('INSERT Failed')
      else begin with T[Y] do
        begin
          KEY := K ; OCCUPIED := TRUE ; INFO := KINFO
        end;
      end;
  end;   (* INSERT *)
```

Figure 5-11. INSERT adds new items to a scatter table.

```
if T[Y].OCCUPIED
  then WRITELN ('INSERT FAILED')
  else begin with T[Y] do
    begin
      KEY := K; OCCUPIED := TRUE; INFO := KINFO
    end;
  end;
```

This segment reports an error if the search fails to find an unoccupied table location. Otherwise, the new key K and its information KINFO are inserted into $T[Y]$.

Let's summarize the facts we have learned by certifying QHASH:

1. The length of T must be a prime number.

2. The quotient Q can be any positive number except a multiple of N.

3. QHASH always stops: either key K is found in T at location Y, or else no match is made and QHASH returns NULL.

4. QHASH returns NULL when no match is made. This can occur because: (1) the entire table is searched, or (2) the search encounters an unoccupied element in T. Hence, most of the time the search stops as soon as the first unoccupied element is found.

The next question we need to examine is the performance of QHASH. This is the subject of the next section.

Performance of QHASH

Figure 5-12 shows the network to be analyzed for performance of QHASH. We have combined the three initial statements into a single transition with time delay t_1. The time delay of the **if-then-else** component that assigns a value to QHASH is assumed to be t_5 in either branch of the component. This simplifies the delay of the entire **if-then-else** component to $(t_4 + t_5)$.

Reduction of Figure 5-12 gives a time delay formula that depends on the **while-do** loop probability p and the time delays:

$$\tau = (t_1 + t_4 + t_5) + \frac{t_2 + t_3 p}{(1 - p)}$$

For example, if we assume the following approximations for delays:

$$t_1 = 30$$
$$t_2 = 10$$
$$t_3 = 2$$
$$t_4 = 3$$
$$t_5 = 1$$

the estimated performance depends only on the probability of repeated passes through the loop. Thus,

$$\tau = 34 + \frac{10 + 2p}{(1 - p)}$$

Clearly, this time estimate depends on p, and small changes in p lead to varied estimates. Let's examine the case where time delays for the loop are equal:

$$t_2 = t_3 = 1$$

Then,

$$\frac{1 + p}{(1 - p)} = \text{number of passes through the loop}$$

This expression is a measure of the number of probes (comparisons of

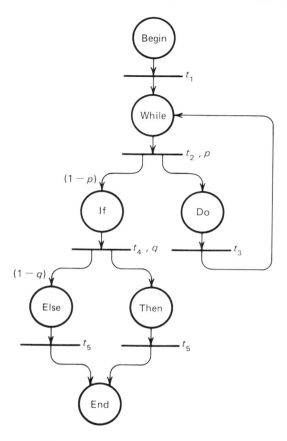

Figure 5-12. Network of QHASH.

K with KEY) made to find a key in the table. We might expect at least one probe for each key retrieved by QHASH. Furthermore, we terminate the search when the home address is reached again; so

$$1 <= \frac{1 + p}{1 - p} <= N$$

We must model the loop test before an estimate of p is obtained. Suppose we let α be the loading factor of T; then

$$\alpha = \frac{\text{number of occupied elements in } T}{\text{length of } T}$$

Furthermore, let S be the average number of synonyms per key. That is, every key K collides with an average of S synonyms before the search in QHASH locates the matching key $T[Y].\text{KEY}$.

The performance of QHASH depends on the loading factor and the likelihood of collisions. In fact, the probability of a subsequent pass through the loop depends on the probability of *not* hitting a synonym. Let p = (probability of occupied) (probability of *not* a match) where

$$(\text{probability of occupied}) = \alpha$$

$$(\text{probability of match}) = \left(\frac{1}{S}\right)^t$$

$$(\text{probability of } not \text{ a match}) = 1 - \left(\frac{1}{S}\right)^t$$

and t = loop counter. When $t = 1$, the first probe compares K with KEY. Hence,

$$p = \alpha \left[1 - \left(\frac{1}{S}\right)^t\right] (t = 1,2,\ldots)$$

The number of probes are equal to the average of $(1 + p)/(1 - p)$ over the loop counter values, $t = 1, 2, \ldots$. That is,

$$\frac{(1 + p)}{(1 - p)} = \frac{1}{t'} \sum_{t=1}^{t'} \left[\frac{S^t(1 + \alpha) - \alpha}{S^t(1 - \alpha) + \alpha}\right]$$

But t' is the number of probes made in order to find a matching key! That is,

$$\frac{(1 + p)}{(1 - p)} = t' = \frac{1}{t'} \sum_{t=1}^{t'} \left[\frac{S^t(1 + \alpha) - \alpha}{S^t(1 - \alpha) + \alpha}\right]$$

This circular derivation can be simplified by taking the first two terms of the expansion as an approximation to $(1 + p)/(1 - p)$. Thus, we set $t' = 2$, and compute an approximation to the average number of probes as follows:

$$t' = \frac{1}{2} \left[\frac{S(1 + \alpha) - \alpha}{S(1 - \alpha) + \alpha} + \frac{S^2(1 + \alpha) - \alpha}{S^2(1 - \alpha) + \alpha}\right]$$

This approximation becomes worse as the incidence of collisions increases, leading to a larger value of S. In asymptotic form,

$$t'_\infty \sim \frac{1 + \alpha}{1 - \alpha}$$

but the quotient-offset hash is much better than this "worst-case." Indeed, we anticipate a match in one or two probes; so as both S and α approach their "practical" limits, we get acceptable performance from QHASH. Let

$$\alpha = 1$$
$$S = 2$$

Then,

$$t' = S^2 + S - 1 = 5 \text{ probes per retrieval}$$

instead of an infinite number of probes as suggested by the asymptotic formula.

This result can be demonstrated by simulation of QHASH. The following tabulation (Table 5-2) was obtained by hashing random keys sampled uniformly from the range $[1 \ . \ . \ 32767]$ into a table of size $N = 11$. Each simulation result was averaged over 25 experimental cases using various loading factors. The number of probes and the number of synonyms were then tabulated and averaged over the 25 experiments. The approximate value computed from the formula used the experimental value of S to obtain the calculated number of passes through the loop.

Table 5-2. $N = 11$ Random Keys

Loading Factor α	Experimental Probes, t'	Experimental Collisions, S	Calculated Probes (Formula)
0.09	1.00	1.00	1.00
0.18	1.02	1.02	1.01
0.27	1.08	1.08	1.06
0.36	1.22	1.19	1.18
0.45	1.22	1.18	1.22
0.55	1.31	1.22	1.33
0.64	1.37	1.23	1.41
0.73	1.51	1.29	1.61
0.82	1.74	1.30	1.74
0.91	2.08	1.40	2.16

Table 5-2 shows how close the approximate solution is to the experimental results. The unfortunate aspect of the formula is its dependence on S. We cannot predict the average number of synonyms in advance. In fact, the value of S depends on the quality of the hashing function and on the nature of the keys. We therefore conjecture a pragmatic estimate for S in the formula

$$S \sim 1 + \frac{\alpha}{2}$$

But to caution the reader that this is a very experimental result, consider the results of another experiment that studied the performance of

QHASH when the search key K *is never found* in the table (see Table 5-3). This experiment was performed with random keys generated from [1 . . 32767] also, but then the lookup was performed using keys that were missing from the table. Thus, every search is a worst-case result because the loop in QHASH terminates only when $T[Y]$.OCCUPIED is false.

Table 5-3. $N = 11$, No Match Occurs.

Loading Factor, α	Experimental Probes, t'	Experimental Collisions, S	Calculated Probes (Formula)	$S = 1 + \frac{\alpha}{2}$
.09	1.04	1.04	1.01	1.05
.18	1.28	1.28	1.12	1.09
.27	1.12	1.12	1.09	1.14
.36	1.56	1.32	1.28	1.18
.45	1.84	1.56	1.55	1.23
.55	2.16	1.36	1.51	1.28
.64	2.64	1.60	1.96	1.32
.73	2.56	1.56	2.11	1.37
.82	3.16	1.52	2.26	1.41

The QHASH routine seems to be very good because it locates K in a few probes (passes through the loop). However, the actual performance of QHASH depends on the number of synonyms encountered in the table and on the loading factor. The difficulty in analyzing QHASH stems from the fact that S and α are related in a complex way. The approximate formula was shown here to give reasonable estimates for a set of uniformly random keys.

SUMMARY

In this chapter we have studied the class of divide-and-conquer search routines known as *hashing functions*. A perfect hashing function retrieves a search key in a single probe of the scatter table. A general hashing routine retrieves a search key in several probes.

A perfect hashing function can be optimized for memory space by finding the smallest scatter table that will deliver a single-probe lookup. We developed a heuristic for finding (S,M) that minimizes the size of the table (most of the time):

$$H = (W + S) \textbf{ div } M$$

This heuristic was shown to be rather slow, but once the values (S, M) are known, the retrieval time is small.

The problem with a perfect hashing function is that the set of keys must be known in advance. If the keys are not known, then we must resort to a general hashing function.

Perhaps the best general hashing function is the prime-division, quotient-offset hash. The quotient-offset technique reduces secondary collisions to a minimum, and the prime division reduces primary collisions and guarantees a full-table search.

Hashing functions are used in many applications to speed retrieval of information. The rudimentary methods presented here can be extended to include secondary storage hashing and dynamic information storage allowing inserts, deletes, and so on. A brief note on deletion of elements is worthwhile, as an example.

An element of a scatter table is deleted by one of two methods. Recall that a chain of synonyms is established whenever secondary collisions occur. This chain must not be broken whenever an element is deleted because subsequent lookups may depend on it. Hence, we must either mark the deleted element as such ($T[Y].$DELETED is true), or else we must fill in the deleted element with one of its synonyms.

For instance, if we delete KEY = 10 from the table of Figure 5-9, we can no longer find KEY = 13. The search for QHASH(13) terminates at location $T[0]$ because $T[0].$OCCUPIED is false.

If we use the method of deletion that fills in the deleted element with a synonym, the problem is solved; but the deletion routine runs slower than the lookup routine. In Figure 5-9, deletion of KEY = 10 from $T[0]$ could be done by searching for the last synonym in the search path established by the synonyms.

The last synonym for 10 is 13; so we mark $T[4].$OCCUPIED = FALSE, and copy 13 into $T[0]$. The scatter table becomes

I	Key	Occupied
0	13	TRUE
1	51	TRUE
2	77	TRUE
3	33	TRUE
4	—	FALSE

This deletion method avoids ending up with a table containing deleted elements. The lookup speed is preserved, but at the expense of deletion speed.

PROBLEMS

1. Implement a deletion procedure for the QHASH routine. Did you use the fill-in technique or the deletion flag method?

2. Perform an experiment on QHASH using random keys as described in the text. Let $N=29$ and compare your results for t' and S with the results obtained here.

3. Find a minimal perfect hashing function $H = (W+S)$ *div* M for the set of keys: $\{38,50,101,189,201,311,510,666,875,915,999\}$. What is the loading factor?

4. How do we know program PERFECT in Figure 5-2 always terminates?

5. Does program BUCKET in Figure 5-5 work when $B = N$? Prove it.

6. Find the best perfect hashing function (S,M) for the first 20 prime numbers.

7. Use $N = 11$ and QHASH to store and retrieve information indexed according to keys which are equal to,

   (a) $KEY_i = Ni$; $i = 1,2,..N$
   (b) $KEY_i = N+i$; $i = 1,2,..N$
   (c) $KEY_i = 2^i$; $i = 1,2,..N$

What conclusions can be made about the performance of QHASH when $\alpha = 1$ and these keys are used?

8. Compare the results obtained for Problem 7 if a minimal perfect hashing function is used instead. What does each set of keys do to the size of the scatter table?

9. Certify procedure INSERT of Figure 5-11.

10. Derive performance estimates for procedure INSERT of Figure 5-11.

11. What is the approximate number of probes for a lookup when $\alpha = 0.5$ and $S = 1.75$ using the QHASH routine?

REFERENCE

Wilson, J., and T. G. Lewis, "Simulation of Perfect Hashing Functions for Secondary Storage," Computer Science Technical Report, Oregon State University, Corvallis, Oregon, 1981.

6

Application to
File Structures

INTRODUCTION

The relatively small address space of most computers and the relatively large address space requirements of most computer applications have forced designers to consider hierarchies of memory as a solution to information storage. The working registers of a processor constitute the fastest but most expensive level of storage. The main memory is next in performance, relatively modest in cost and easily accessed by the processor. However, most programs and data will not fit within these two levels of memory. Consequently, low speed but inexpensive *mass memories* have been added to the hierarchy.

A *bubble memory* offers intermediate cost and performance advantages as a secondary mass storage media. But for removable (''infinite'' size) volumes, the magnetic rotating disk device offers storage at a very low cost.

A disk memory can be viewed as a collection of storage units called *buckets* (see Chapter 5 on hash coding). Each bucket occupies a physical space on a disk that can be accessed in a single operation called a SEEK. The SEEK operation typically requires a relatively long time to perform as compared with the transfer of information from the disk bucket into main memory. Therefore it will be very important to minimize the number of SEEKs whenever designing file access software.

The main issue in designing and implementing file structures is reduction or elimination of disk accesses because of the relatively high cost to perform a SEEK. For this reason, we will study various access methods suitable for secondary storage devices like disks. Such devices are characterized by:

1. Units of storage that can be accessed in a single SEEK. These units are called *buckets, sectors, tracks,* etc.

2. Long time delays associated with a SEEK operation. Therefore we attempt to minimize the number of accesses to different buckets.

3. Due to the discretization of storage into buckets, we typically store many elements of data in each bucket.

The last point deserves additional comment. A bucket may be large enough to contain many *records* of information. A file record (not to be confused with a Pascal record), is a collection of list elements defined by a record-type definition (format). For example, in Pascal we could equate a character and a file record as follows:

var
F : **file of char**;

Or a more elaborate example might equate a file F with inhomogeneous list elements such as shown below:

var
F : **file of record**
X : **real** ;
Y : **integer**
end ;

The storage requirements of file F may permit many records of *F* to be stored in a single disk bucket. For example, the second illustration of F above requires two words per file record (a word to hold *X* and another word to hold *Y*). The disk bucket may hold 128 words, say; hence 64 file records might be stored in each disk bucket.

File structure designs must therefore consider the time delay required to access each bucket, the number of file records per bucket, and the manner in which data are accessed (keys). These and other details are discussed in this chapter, beginning with simple organization of sequential and direct access and ending with a complete analysis of elaborate index file structures.

ACCESS METHODS

We will examine two fundamental file structures: a *sequential access method* and a *direct access method*. We further assume that every file has a name (fname) and an associated file pointer (f ↑). The name is used to identify the collection of buckets used to store all file records in fname. The file pointer (f ↑) is used to keep track of the location of the most recently accessed record (or sometimes the location of the next record to be accessed).

We *open* a file in order to prepare it for input and output. There are two ways to open a file in Pascal. In the first method we create a new file *and* prepare it for output. Here is an example:

```
           var
     F : file of record
                 X : integer ;
                 Y : char
           end ;
```

This declares F ↑ as the location of a record image in main memory. This image must be of type X : **integer** and Y : **char** as shown. Every input from the disk is placed in this image, and every output to the disk is taken from this image. In Pascal we call the storage space at F ↑ the *file window*.

The file named FNAME (any string) is created by rewriting:

$$REWRITE (F,FNAME) ;$$

and it is closed by

$$CLOSE(F) ;$$

The file can be subsequently opened, if it already exists, by using the reset intrinsic

$$RESET (F,FNAME) ;$$

and subsequently closed by

$$CLOSE(F) ;$$

as before.

Every file must be opened before it can be accessed, and every file should be closed after it is used. The CLOSE intrinsic serves to flush the last record in the window to the disk. Failure to close a file may result in loss of the final record.

Sequential Access

Perhaps the simplest file structure is the sequential access structure. Each record is stored on a disk in a manner quite similar to the elements of an array. Figure 6-1(a) illustrates the sequential file and the sequential file access path. Note that two records are stored in each bucket of the disk in the example of Figure 6-1(a).

Initially, F ↑ contains the first (zero-th) record of a newly reset input file. Each record is stored (transferred) in F ↑ , beginning with record zero and progressing to the next record after each GET intrinsic. Therefore, the console display statement,

WRITELN(F ↑ .X , F ↑ .Y) ;

outputs the zero-th record following a reset. The next record is fetched using a GET statement, and is displayed as follows:

GET(F) ;
WRITELN(F ↑ .X , F ↑ .Y) ;

A general model of sequential input from a file record to a file window is shown below:

```
RESET(F,FNAME) ;        (* open and GET first one *)
repeat
  if not EOF(F)         (* EOF reached ? *)
    then
      begin
      (* access record via F ↑ window *)
        GET(F) ;        (* fetch next one *)
      end ;
  until EOF(F) ;        (* stop when end-of-file *)
  CLOSE(F) ;            (* flush it *)
```

The EOF(F) intrinsic returns TRUE if the file window contains an EOF (end-of-file) marker instead of a record of data.

A general model of sequential file output to a newly created file is shown below:

```
REWRITE(F,FNAME) ;      (* create new file *)
repeat
  (* input data from user *)
    PUT(F)              (* copy from F ↑ to file *)
  until (* done *) ;    (* continue until done *)
  CLOSE(F) ;
```

This model uses the variable F ↑ to point to the window. Hence, a user might enter data into F ↑ by filling F ↑ .X and F ↑ .Y. For example,

READLN (F ↑ .X , F ↑ .Y) ;

puts a value of F ↑ .X and F ↑ .Y into the window prior to a PUT(F).

Each PUT/GET intrinsic causes the file pointer to advance to the next record. Since records are numbered from zero to N, the sequential file models given above cause the file pointer to advance from zero to some N.

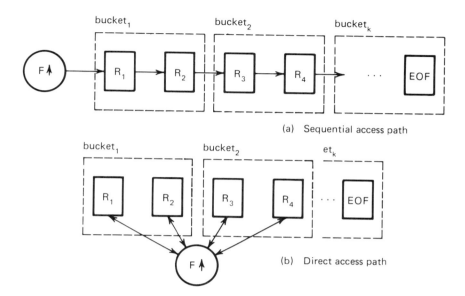

Figure 6-1. Access paths and buckets in sequential and direct access files.

We must close a sequential file and reset it in order to read a previously accessed record. This means it is impossible to access record K, for example, without passing over records 0, 1, . . . ($K - 1$), first. This leads to the major disadvantage of sequential access.

Disadvantage of sequential access   A sequential access file is slow because the number of disk accesses (SEEK operations) to access bucket K are equal to K.

There are reasons to use this method in spite of its limitation, however. First, a sequential access file is simple to understand and simple to implement in a program. We can perform file merges on ordered sequential files; for example, see Chapter 3 on theory of software verification. And we can apply searching algorithms to sequential files as shown before, using linear lists.

Perhaps the major advantage (and use) of sequential file access is to store *variable length records*. Suppose the size of each record varies (according to a variant in Pascal) so that we cannot determine the location of record K without knowing the sizes of all records, zero through ($K - 1$). In this case, we have no choice but to scan the entire file from beginning to end until we reach the desired record.

Advantage of sequential access   A sequential access file is able to store variable length records, one after the other, without knowing their lengths in advance.

As a final example of a sequential file containing records of integer, real, and character data, consider the following:

```
type
  INFO = record
              I : integer ;
              R : real ;
              C : char
            end ;
  var
    DISK : file of INFO ;
```

This defines a window at DISK ↑ that contains an integer, real, and character. Each access to the file will cause a transfer of information between the window and a file record. For instance, we can store N records in file records zero through $(N - 1)$:

```
REWRITE(DISK, 'MYDATA') ;     (* create 'MYDATA' *)
  for J := 1 to N do
    begin
      READLN (DISK ↑ .I , DISK ↑ .R , DISK ↑ .C) ;
      PUT(DISK) ;
    end ;
  CLOSE(DISK) ;
```

One of the biggest advantages of disk over tape storage is its ability to access any bucket with equal speed (almost). In other words, disk storage can support direct access as well as sequential access. This is the next step up in file organization.

Direct Access

A direct access file is stored exactly the same way as a sequential access file except it can be accessed directly, as shown in the access path diagram of Figure 6-1(b). Any record is directly accessed by specifying the file window variable, F, and the record number (zero to N).

The SEEK intrinsic is used to position the file record pointer to the correct record. Thus,

```
SEEK(F,5) ;
GET(F) ;
```

This illustrates how we obtain record number five directly. The disk record is copied into the window without additional accesses.

A general model of input from a direct access file uses RECNO as the record number. Thus,

```
    RESET(F,FNAME) ;          (* open FNAME *)
repeat
    (* access as many as wanted *)
    READLN(RECNO) ;      (* which one ? *)
    SEEK(F,RECNO) ;      (* position pointer *)
    GET(G) ;             (* transfer to window *)
    (* other things *)
until (* done *)
    CLOSE(F) ;                 (* flush it *)
```

Each GET or PUT must be preceded by a SEEK. The contents of record number RECNO are transferred into $F\uparrow$. The previous contents are lost. Thus, only one record is available in main memory unless copies of $F\uparrow$ are made.

The direct access file is faster than the sequential access file because it requires a single access. However, direct access presumes a collection of fixed-length records. Thus, we trade performance for flexibility when choosing one over the other.

A second problem occurs when using direct access. The RECNO of any desired record is needed before a SEEK can be performed. Unfortunately, most applications require records to be uniquely identified by some alphanumeric key rather than by a record number. Therefore we need some way to map the application-oriented key into a record number. This is the subject of the next section on index file structure.

FILE INDEXING

A file record is stored by record number in a direct access file; yet it is typically referenced by a unique key value. One way to overcome this difficulty might be to search the direct access file using one of the search routines discussed in Chapter 4 on searching, or a hash coding routine discussed in Chapter 5 on hash coding.

A binary search routine could be used to search an ordered direct access file. The list becomes a file instead of an array; thus,

```
    type
    ELEMENT = record
                    KEY : STRING ;
                    INFO : STRING
              end ;
    var
    DISK : file of ELEMENT ;
```

Instead of searching a LIST, we must seek and get each record of DISK $\uparrow$, one at a time. Modifications to the binary search routine lead to a relatively fast program. But the file must be kept in order to work with the search routine.

Another idea is to use the hashing functions discussed in Chapter 5. We transform each unique key into the corresponding record number. Thus, for key K and hashing function H, we can directly access the desired record in only a few accesses to the disk:

```
SEEK(F,H(K)) ;
GET(F) ;
```

The trouble with both of these methods is that they either require an ordering, or they work for single keys. If we try to use them on files with nonunique keys, unordered elements, or more than a single identifier key, we run into limitations. Instead, we are forced to sacrifice disk space and some processing time for greater flexibility.

An index file is a (direct access) file that contains the key values of all records stored in another file, plus the record numbers of each record containing the key value—as illustrated below:

```
type
    INDEXES = record
                IKEY : STRING ;
                RECNO : integer ;
                end;
    DATUM   = record
                DKEY : STRING ;
                INFO : STRING ;
                end ;
var
    MASTER : file of DATUM ;
    INDEX  : file of INDEXES ;
```

We call the information-containing file the *master file*. and the indexing file the *index file*. Thus, to access a MASTER file record with key K, we must first access INDEX in order to get INDEX ↑ .RECNO. We use RECNO to access MASTER ↑ .INFO. What is gained by increasing the number of accesses in this manner?

The main advantage of indexing is that we can index the MASTER file in as many ways as needed. For example, suppose each MASTER file record is indexed three ways: (1) by driver's license number, LICNO, (2) by social security number, SOC, and (3) by last name, NAME. We need three index files to hold this information as defined in Pascal, on the next page, and shown in the structure of Figure 6-2.

This data structure is used to access the file structure shown in Figure 6-2. If we desire a record from MASTER keyed by last name, then we use index NAME to locate the corresponding MASTER file record. Similarly,

```
type
    LICNOS = record
                    LIC : NUMBER ;
                    LR   : integer ;
             end ;
    SOC     = record
                    SS : NUMBER ;
                    SR : integer ;
             end;
    NAMES = record
                    N   : STRING ;
                    NR : integer ;
             end ;
    DATUM = record
                    MLIC  : NUMBER ;
                    MSOC : NUMBER ;
                    MN    : STRING ;
                    INFO  : STRING ;
             end ;
var
    MASTER : file of DATUM ;
    LICNO   : file of LICNOS ;
    SOC      : file of SOCS ;
    NAME    : file of NAMES ;
```

we use either index file LICNO or SOC to access a MASTER record keyed by driver's license number or social security number, respectively.

An immediate advantage of the system of index files is the ease with which we can rearrange the order of MASTER file records. For example, if we want the MASTER file to be printed in order by last name, we sort the NAME index only. The MASTER file remains as it was originally.

An immediate disadvantage of the system of index files is the difficulty of searching the index files themselves. Since every record of each index file is stored by record number and not by key value, how do we perform a key-to-record number transformation to find the appropriate entry in one of the index files? Another problem arises when we attempt to delete a MASTER file record. All index file entries must be deleted, not just the index record used to find the MASTER file record to be deleted.

These and other problems can be (partially) overcome by careful design of the index file structure. We want a file structure that is easy to search using a minimum number of SEEKs, easy to maintain (insert, delete), and not too costly in terms of file space. Furthermore, we want an index structure that allows direct access to keyed records in some prescribed order so that we rarely have to sort the index file.

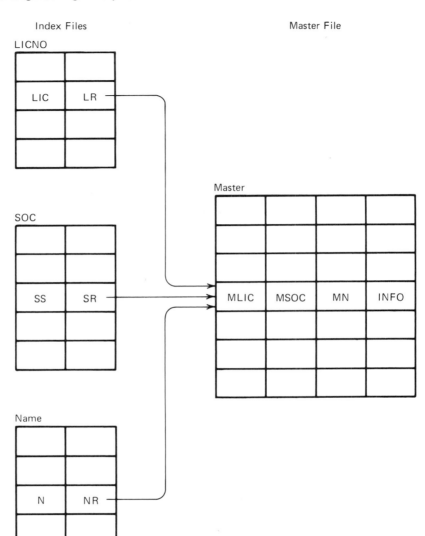

Figure 6-2. One MASTER file and three INDEX files.

In the next section we develop the concepts of *B*-trees. A *B*-tree structure satisfies most of the high demands listed above, yet it is relatively simple to program and understand.

B-TREE STRUCTURE

A *B-tree* is an *N*-ary tree containing the following three types of nodes:

1. *Root node:* A node used to begin a search for a leaf node containing the desired key.

2. *Internal node:* A node containing up to *N* record numbers that point to other *B*-tree nodes, and up to $(N - 1)$ redundant ordered keys used to guide a search routine from the root node to a leaf node.

3. *Leaf node:* A node containing up to $(N - 1)$ ordered MASTER keys along with record numbers that point to their corresponding MASTER file records.

A *B*-tree maintains order in a manner similar to a binary search tree. That is, all entries in a left-most subtree are less than all entries in a right subtree. The use of "left-most" and "right" are relative because each node of a *B*-tree may contain up to *N* subtrees. Hence, a subtree is left of another subtree if it appears anywhere to the left.

We use a *B*-tree to store index file information because it provides:

1. Divide-and-conquer performance during searching.

2. Ease of inserting new keys.

3. Balancing: A *B*-tree can never become unbalanced like a binary search tree.

4. Adaptability: We can tailor a *B*-tree so that each node fits one bucket. This optimizes the number of SEEKs by matching the size of each node to the capacity of each bucket.

How does a *B*-tree work? And how is it implemented in software? These and other questions are answered in the following detailed analysis of *B*-tree structure.

B-Tree Concepts

A *B*-tree appears to be a binary tree that has been broadened into an *N*-ary tree, but this is *not* the case. A binary tree begins with a root node and grows by adding leaf nodes as needed. This is exactly why a binary tree may become unbalanced. On the contrary, a *B*-tree begins with a leaf node and grows by adding new leaf nodes *and new root nodes* as needed. This is why a *B*-tree maintains its balance and preserves its high-speed search advantage.

Furthermore, a *B*-tree is designed to use all of the available space of a bucket, if possible. This reduces the number of seek operations by making the B-tree wide instead of tall. Each node corresponds to a bucket, and so most of the searching takes place in the file window rather than in the disk file.

Suppose we grow a B-tree of order $N = 3$. Each node is either a leaf or an internal node, and each node contains space for N keys along with their associated record number pointers. Furthermore, we want to be able to access the next key in order from the current key, so we will include a link that points to the next node in order (see the following program).

```
type
  NODES = record
            FLAG : boolean ; (* TRUE if a leaf *)
            SUBKEY : array[1 . . N] of KEYS ; (* MASTER keys *)
            POINTER : array [1 . . N] of integer ; (* record no.s *)
            LINK : integer ; (* order link *)
          end ;
var
  BTREE : file of NODES ; (* stored on disk *)
```

The sequence of "snapshots" in Figure 6-3 shows how this B-tree grows as we insert the following list of keys:

KEY	Pointer to Master File Record
Z	1.
Y	2.
X	3.
W	4.
V	5.

First, we insert 'Z' into an empty B-tree. This causes the first root node to be created. It is also the first leaf node; hence its flag is set to TRUE. Then we insert 'Y' into the B-tree, and this causes the previously inserted 'Z' to be moved over to the next SUBKEY entry in the root. The entries in a B-tree must always be in order from left to right. This means we always insert a new key in its proper place to keep order in the B-tree. The result is shown in Figure 6-3(b).

The next key is 'X'; and since it is "smaller" than all other keys in the B-tree, we insert it into the left-most entry of the node shown in Figure 6-3(b). The node "overflows" when 'X' is inserted because each node is allowed a maximum of $(N - 1)$ keys. Therefore, we must *split* this node into a left "child" and a right "child." We copy approximately one-half of the entries into the right child and leave approximately one-half in the (original) left child. Figure 6-3(c) shows the two offspring nodes and their contents.

A leaf is split each time it overflows as shown in Figure 6-3(c). The largest (middle) key of the left child is copied into a new root node and is linked to the left child via its POINTER component. The right child contains all keys greater than 'Y'; and so we link the new root to the right child also.

Notice the LINK component in Figure 6-3(c). It always points to the next node in sequence. This feature is exploited by the search routine to find the next key in order, without searching from root to leaf. We call this the *read-key-sequential link* because it provides read-key-sequential access to the MASTER file.

Additional insertions may or may not cause a leaf node to split. Leaf nodes split whenever SUBKEY[N] becomes occupied, but this only occurs when we insert a new key into a nearly full leaf. The leaf containing 'Z' will accommodate one more key without splitting; see Figure 6-3(c). However, we cause a split to occur if we insert the next key in descending order: 'W.'

Figure 6-3(d) shows the result of splitting a leaf and adding the new child to the root node. Again, the B-tree is in order (from left to right), and all leaf nodes are linked together in read-key-sequential order. The root node contains a list of ordered keys that direct the search routine to the proper subtree depending on the value of a search key.

We have seen how the insertion of a new key can lead to splitting of a leaf node, but internal nodes can be split also. If we split one of the leaf nodes in Figure 6-3(d), this will cause the root node to overflow. This, in turn, causes the root node to split into two internal nodes. A new root node is created to hold the keys needed to perform a tree search. This is shown in Figure 6-3(e), after insertion of the 'V' key.

This last example shows how a split leaf node may cause an internal node to split. In fact, it is possible to split all nodes from leaf to root, ending in a new root node being added to the tree. Therefore, the B-tree grows from its leaf nodes to its (new) root node.

We summarize the steps needed to grow a B-tree of order N:

STEP #1. Suppose we insert a new KEY with record number I into a B-tree of order N. We are given the location of the ROOT node.

STEP #2. Find the leaf node that should contain the new KEY and I value. This is done by searching from the ROOT down to the leaf node using a modified tree-search routine. We also use a push-down stack to remember the path taken to locate the appropriate leaf.

STEP #3. Add the new KEY and I values (SUBKEY and POINTER) to the leaf node. If there is enough room in the leaf, no splitting is needed, and we can update the disk file. In this case, insertion is completed and we exit the insertion routine.

STEP #4. If insertion in Step #3 causes the node to overflow (SUBKEY [N] is filled), we must subdivide the overflowed node into two nodes containing roughly one-half of the keys, each. The remaining "middle" key is moved up to the parent node of the two (split) nodes.

STEP #5. Now we must find a place to insert the new "middle" key and its corresponding pointer. The pointer will be the address of the new child node created by a split. These values are inserted into the parent

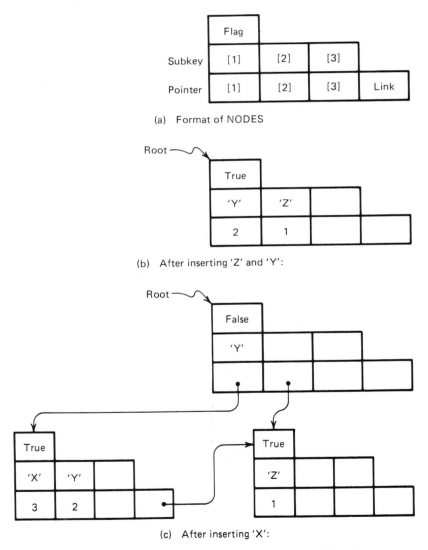

(a) Format of NODES

(b) After inserting 'Z' and 'Y':

(c) After inserting 'X':

Figure 6-3. Growth of a *B*-tree of order $N = 3$.

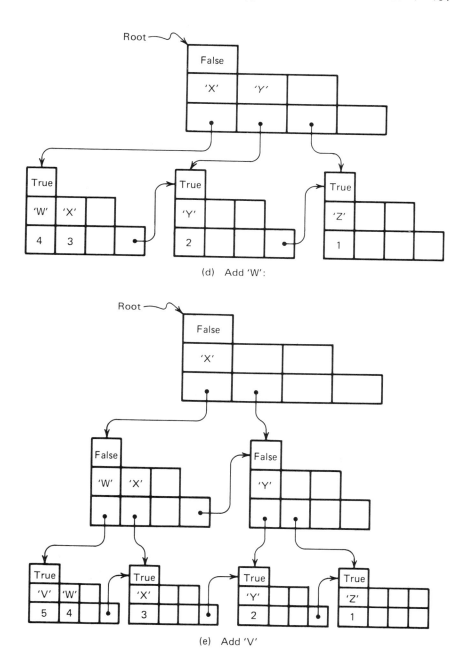

(d) Add 'W':

(e) Add 'V'

Figure 6-3. Continued.

node. The parent node is found by popping the stack containing the "remembered" node record numbers.

STEP #6. If the stack is empty, we must have overflowed the old root node. This means the root is split and a new root is needed. The new root is created and a left-most pointer and a right pointer are inserted.

This step-by-step design of a B-tree insert routine can be summarized as consisting of one of three actions: (1) a new key and record number are inserted into a leaf node; or (2) a new key and record number are inserted into a leaf node and the node is split; hence, we repeat the insert steps on the parent of the split nodes; or (3) we continue to split internal nodes after an insertion until a new root node is created. These actions are implemented in the program discussed next.

B-Tree Programs

To implement the B-tree search and insert software, we need to know the order of the B-tree, N, the length of keys, STRLEN, and the special values used to mark nodes (NULL pointer, EMPTY keys, etc.). These constants are defined below for program BTREE0:

```
const
   N = 3 ;              (* BTREE order      *)
   MAX = 10 ;           (* stack size       *)
   STRLEN = 20 ;        (* length of keys   *)
   NULL = -1 ;          (* null pointer valued *)
   EMPTY = '                    ' ; (* null key *)
```

We also need a data structure for working variables, file formats, and node formats. These are defined as the following types:

```
type
   STRING    = packed array [1 . . STRLEN] of char ;
   KEYS      = STRING ; (* keys are strings *)
   PAIRS     = record
                  BNODE : integer ; (* pointer to node *)
                  BITEM : integer ; (* pointer to item *)
               end ;
   NODES     = record
                  FLAG : boolean ; (* leaf or internal? *)
                  SUBKEY : array [1 . . N] of KEYS ;
                  POINTER : array [1 . . N] of integer;
                  LINK    : integer ;
               end ;
```

```
PDSTACK = record                          (* pushdown stack *)
            TOP : 1 . . MAX ;             (* stack pointer   *)
            FRAME : array [1 . . MAX] of PAIRS ; (* elements *)
          end ;
```

The B-tree programs also use a disk file called AVAIL to hold the record number of the current root node, and a counter that keeps track of the number of nodes (sectors) used. These variables, and others, are used by the B-tree processing programs.

Data structures for B-tree program

```
var
  BTREE : file of NODES ;              (* direct access *)
  AVAIL : file of record               (* header file *)
            ROOT : integer ;           (* current root node *)
            NUMBER : integer ;         (* number used up *)
          end ;
  STACK : PDSTACK ;                    (* remember search path *)
  NODE  : PAIRS ;                      (* working pointer *)
  KEY   : KEYS ;                       (* working search key *)
  ITEM  : integer ;                    (* working subscript *)
  NEWNODE : integer ;                  (* working record number *)
```

The push-down stack operations are defined as follows:

```
procedure POP (var NODE : PAIRS ;
                var STACK : PDSTACK) ;
  begin
    NODE := STACK.FRAME [STACK.TOP] ;
    STACK.TOP := STACK.TOP + 1 ;
  end ;
procedure PUSH (NODE : PAIRS ;
                var STACK : PDSTACK) ;
  begin
    STACK.TOP := STACK.TOP + 1 ;
    STACK.FRAME [STACK.TOP] := NODE ;
  end ;
procedure INITSTACK ;
  begin
    STACK.TOP := 1 ;
    STACK.FRAME [1] BNODE := NULL ;
    STACK.FRAME [1]. BITEM := NULL ;
  end ;
```

We also need a disk sector allocation routine that gives record numbers each time it is called. The simplest allocation routine increments the current value of NUMBER and returns the next available sector number (see below):

```
function ALLOCATE : integer ;
  begin
    AVAIL ↑ .NUMBER := AVAIL ↑ .NUMBER + 1 ;
    ALLOCATE := AVAIL ↑ .NUMBER ;
  end ;
```

Finally, we must open the *B*-tree file and its AVAIL header file at the start of the insertion operation, and close these files after updating them.

```
procedure STARTUP ;
  begin
    RESET (AVAIL , 'AVAIL') ;
    RESET (BTREE , 'BTREE') ;
  end ;
```

Of course, we have assumed these files already exist. If they are being created for the first time, then we would initialize AVAIL as follows:

```
begin          (* create files *)
  REWRITE (AVAIL , 'AVAIL') ;      (* create header *)
  AVAIL ↑ .NUMBER := 0 ;          (* root is zero . . *)
  AVAIL ↑ .ROOT := 0 ;            (* . . . record  *)
  PUT (AVAIL) ;
  CLOSE (AVAIL) ;
  REWRITE (BTREE , 'BTREE') ;
  CLOSE (BTREE)
end ;
```

At the end of each processing cycle (batch of inserts), we must close the files. If a new root has been added, we must record this fact in AVAIL, as shown here:

```
procedure SHUTDOWN ;
  begin
    SEEK (AVAIL , 0) ; PUT (AVAIL) ;
    CLOSE(AVAIL) ;
    CLOSE(BTREE) ;
  end ;
```

Now we are prepared to implement the insertion procedure ADB-TREE. This procedure uses the following subprocedures as modules:

NEWROOT This procedure creates a new root and stores pointers to the left subtree and right subtree, respectively.

```
procedure NEWROOT( KEY : KEYS ; ITEM : integer ; NEWNODE : integer ) ;
  var
    I : 1 . . N ;
  begin
    with BTREE ↑ do              (* BUILD ROOT NODE *)
      begin
        FLAG := FALSE ;              (* NOT A LEAF NODE *)
        POINTER[ 1 ] := ITEM;      (* INSERT KEYS AND POINTERS *)
        SUBKEY[ 1 ] := KEY ;
        POINTER[ 2 ] := NEWNODE ;
        SUBKEY [ 2 ] := EMPTY ;
        for I := 3 to N do
          begin POINTER[ I ] := NULL ; SUBKEY[ I ] := EMPTY end ;
      end ;     (* with *)
    with AVAIL^ do
      begin
        ROOT := ALLOCATE ;
        (* ALLOCATE NEXT SECTOR FOR NEW ROOT *)
        SEEK( BTREE, ROOT ) ;
      end ;     (* with *)
    PUT( BTREE ) ;
  end ;     (* NEWROOT *)
```

Figure 6-4. Add a new root node.

SPLIT This procedure splits a node into two adjacent child nodes. The LINK pointer is updated so that the next key in read-key-sequential order can be accessed.

INSERT This procedure moves keys to one side in order to make room for a new insertion. The new key and its associated pointer are inserted into SUBKEY and POINTER, respectively.

LOOKUP This function searches the *B*-tree from root to leaf node. It locates the correct place to insert the new key and its record number.

These routines are implemented as shown in Figures 6-4 through 6-7. The ADBTREE procedure is shown in Figure 6-8. The NEWROOT routine creates a new node and fills it with a left pointer and a right pointer. It also updates the current ROOT pointer in AVAIL. The SPLIT routine subdivides a node into two equal halves: the left child and the right child. The returned KEY and NEWNODE values are used by ADBTREE to update the parent of the two children nodes. The INSERT routine shifts POINTER and SUBKEY elements in order to make room for a new pair. The result of this shift could be an overflowed node. Thus, the overflow

```
procedure SPLIT( NODE : PAIRS ; ITEM : integer ;
                 var NEWNODE : integer ;
                 var KEY : KEYS          ) ;
  var
    NEW : NODES ;   (* WORKING NODE *)
    LAST, K : 1 . . N; (* WORKING COUNTERS *)
  begin
    LAST := ( N+1 ) div 2      ;        (* MIDDLE ITEM *)
    NEWNODE := ALLOCATE ;              (* CREATE RT. SON *)
    K := 1 ;
    with BTREE ↑ do                    (* COPY TO RT. SON  *)
      begin
        KEY := SUBKEY[ LAST ] ;                (* RETURN MID KEY *)
        while LAST + K <= N do
          begin
            NEW.POINTER[ K ] := POINTER[ LAST+K ];
            POINTER[ LAST+K ] := NULL;
            NEW.SUBKEY[ K ] := SUBKEY[ LAST+K ];
            SUBKEY[ LAST+K ] := EMPTY;
            K := K + 1 ;
          end ; (* while *)
        NEW.LINK := LINK ; LINK := NEWNODE ;
        (* UPDATE SEQUENTIAL LINKS *)
        NEW.FLAG := FLAG ;            (* LEAF OR INTERNAL NODE ? *)
      end ; (* with *)
    NEW.POINTER[ K ] := ITEM ; NEW.SUBKEY[ K ] := EMPTY ;
    for K := K+1 to N do
      with NEW do
        begin
          POINTER[ K ] := NULL ;
          SUBKEY[ K ] := EMPTY ;
        end ; (* for with *)
    SEEK( BTREE, NODE.BNODE ) ; PUT( BTREE ) ;
    (* REWRITE LEFT SON *)
    BTREE ↑ := NEW ;
    SEEK( BTREE, NEWNODE ) ; PUT( BTREE ) ; (* WRITE RT. SON *)
  end ;(* split *)
```

Figure 6-5. Split a node.

KEY and ITEM (record number) are returned. Finally, LOOKUP searches from root to leaf looking for a place to insert KEY. If LOOKUP finds a match, it means the key already exists. Thus, LOOKUP returns TRUE if no match occurs and FALSE if the key already exists in the *B*-tree.

Figure 6-8 implements the design described in the previous section. The information to be inserted is stored in the variables KEY and ITEM. Initially, these variables are set equal to DKEY and DITEM. If the leaf node overflows, then KEY and ITEM take on the values needed to update the parent of a split pair of nodes.

```
procedure INSERT( var KEY : KEYS ;
                      var ITEM : integer ;
                      LOC : integer ;
                      SPLITFLAG : boolean ) ;
  var
    K : 1 . . N ;
    TEMPTR : integer ;
  begin
    with BTREE ↑ do
      begin
        if LOC < N
        then begin
        TEMPTR := POINTER[ N ] ;      (* OVERFLOW ?? *)
        for K := N downto LOC + 1 do    (* INSERT AT LOC *)
          begin
            POINTER[ K ] := POINTER[ K − 1 ] ;
            SUBKEY[ K ] := SUBKEY[ K − 1 ] ;
          end ; (* for *)
        POINTER[ LOC + ORD( SPLITFLAG ) ] := ITEM ;
        SUBKEY[ LOC ] := KEY ;
        ITEM := TEMPTR ;      (* JUST IN CASE OF OVERFLOW *)
          end (* then *)
          else begin
            SUBKEY[ N ] := KEY ;
            if not SPLITFLAG
            then POINTER[ N ] := ITEM
          end ; (* else *)
        KEY := SUBKEY[ N ] ;
      end ; (* with *)
  end ; (* INSERT *)
```

Figure 6-6. Insert a new key into a node.

```
function LOOKUP( KEY : KEYS ; var STACK : PDSTACK ) : boolean ;
begin
    INITSTACK ;
    NODE.BITEM  := 1 ;
    NODE.BNODE := AVAIL↑.ROOT ; (* START AT ROOT NODE *)
    repeat
      SEEK( BTREE, NODE.BNODE ) ; GET( BTREE ) ;
      with BTREE ↑ do
        begin
          while ( SUBKEY[ NODE.BITEM ] < KEY )
                          and
                ( SUBKEY[ NODE.BITEM ] <> EMPTY )
            do NODE.BITEM := NODE.BITEM + 1 ;
          PUSH( NODE, STACK ) ;
          LOOKUP := SUBKEY[ NODE.BITEM ] <> KEY ;
          NODE.BNODE := POINTER[ NODE.BITEM ] ;
          NODE.BITEM  := 1 ;
        end ; (* with *)
      until BTREE↑.FLAG ;
  end ; (* LOOKUP *)
```

Figure 6-7. B-tree search routine.

SPLITFLAG is used to distinguish between an insertion into a leaf node (SPLITFLAG = FALSE) and one into an internal node (SPLITFLAG = TRUE). When inserting into an internal node, the NEWNODE pointer is skewed to the right. This is shown in Figure 6-6 as

POINTER[LOC+ORD(SPLITFLAG)] := ITEM ;

and is set up in Figure 6-8 as follows:

ITEM := NEWNODE ;

This is the only subtle "trick" in ADBTREE.

These programs are explored in greater detail in the next section. We are most concerned with "Does it work?" The anxious reader can perform a dynamic test of the system of programs by running sample cases using the following test harness:

```
begin                (* main test harness *)
    STARTUP ;
    repeat
      WRITE('Enter more?') ; READLN(CH) ;
      if CH <> 'N'
```

```
procedure ADBTREE( DKEY  : KEYS ;
                   DITEM : integer ) ;
  var
    KEY  : KEYS ;
    ITEM : integer ;
    SPLITFLAG : boolean ; (* true if node has been split *)
  begin
    KEY  := DKEY;
    ITEM := DITEM ;
    SPLITFLAG := FALSE ;
    if LOOKUP( KEY, STACK )
      then begin
        POP( NODE, STACK ) ;
        repeat
          INSERT( KEY, ITEM, NODE.BITEM, SPLITFLAG ) ;
          if KEY = EMPTY
            then begin SEEK( BTREE, NODE.BNODE ) ; PUT( BTREE ) end
            else begin
              SPLIT( NODE, ITEM, NEWNODE, KEY ) ; SPLITFLAG := TRUE ;
              ITEM := NODE.BNODE ;
              POP( NODE, STACK )    ;
              if NODE.BNODE = NULL
                then NEWROOT( KEY, ITEM, NEWNODE ) (* then *)
                else begin
                  SEEK( BTREE, NODE.BNODE ) ;
                  GET( BTREE ) ;
                  ITEM := NEWNODE ;
                end ; (* else *)
            end ; (* else *)
        until ( KEY = EMPTY ) or ( NODE.BNODE = NULL ) ;
      end (* then *)
      else WRITELN( KEY, ' Already in Btree' ) ;
  end ; (* ADBTREE *)
```

Figure 6-8. Add key and item to *B*-tree.

```
        then begin
          WRITE('Enter KEY=') ; READLN(KEY) ;
          WRITE('Enter ITEM=') ; READLN(ITEM) ;
          ADBTREE(KEY,ITEM) ;
        repeat     (* look at the B-tree *)
          WRITE('Enter sector number=') ; READ(NEWNODE) ;
          SEEK(BTREE,NEWNODE) ;
          GET(BTREE) ;
          for ITEM := 1 to N do
        begin
          WRITELN(BTREE ↑ .SUBKEY[ITEM]) ;
          WRITELN(BTREE ↑ .POINTER[ITEM]) ;
        end ;
          WRITELN(BTREE ↑ .LINK) ;
      until NEWNODE < 0 ;
      end (* then *)
      else SHUTDOWN ;
    until CH = 'N' ;
    end.
```

VERIFICATION AND PERFORMANCE

Testing *B*-Tree Programs

We show that the programs in Figures 6-4 through 6-8 work correctly by using the transform theory and special test data. A program is correct if it accepts its specified input values and produces its specified output values. Hence, if we show that every function or procedure does what it is supposed to do, then the program that uses these functions and procedures can be checked by assuming all subordinate parts are correct. Procedure ADBTREE (Figure 6-8) is certified by checking the subordinate parts; NEWROOT, SPLIT, INSERT, LOOKUP, and then the code for ADBTREE, itself.

Certification of NEWROOT   The purpose of NEWROOT is to create a new *B*-tree node on disk and store a single key and two pointers as shown in Figure 6-9. The inputs to NEWROOT are:

INPUTS

KEY	: middle key from left child.
ITEM	: pointer to left child.
NEWNODE	: pointer to right child.

The results (outputs) are:

FLAG = FALSE : internal node.
POINTER[1] = ITEM : left child.
SUBKEY[1] = KEY : left child largest key.
POINTER[2] = NEWNODE : right child.
SUBKEY[2 . . N] = EMPTY : all others are empty.
POINTER[3 . . N] = NULL : all others are null.
LINK   = NULL : no links.

plus a new root, ROOT = ALLOCATE, is created and output to disk:

SEEK(BTREE,ROOT) ; PUT(BTREE) ;

The code for NEWROOT is nearly in agreement with these INPUT/OUTPUT values. The only weakness in NEWROOT is a missing assignment statement that defines LINK—that is,

LINK := NULL ;

Although this oversight does not lead to failure in the executing program, it is a minor flaw that should be corrected.

Certification of SPLIT   The purpose of SPLIT is to divide the contents of a node at record number NODE.BNODE into approximately two equal parts; then store one-half in BNODE and create another node at NEW-NODE for the other half.

NODE : the location NODE.BNODE of the node to be split into two nodes.

ITEM : the overflow item to be inserted into the right child node overflow from NODE.BNODE. This is used when splitting an internal node.

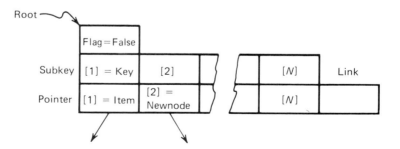

Figure 6-9. NEWROOT creates a new root node.

OUTPUTS

NEWNODE : pointer to the right child created by SPLIT.

KEY   : middle key to be elevated to the split node parent.

Further, we require the following outputs to the two children nodes; see Figure 6-10. $[x]$ means the least integer part of x.

Outputs to NODE.BNODE (left child):

FLAG : same as before

$$POINTER[1 \ . \ . \ \left\lfloor \frac{N+1}{2} \right\rfloor \ ] : \text{same as before}$$

$$SUBKEY[1 \ . \ . \ \left\lfloor \frac{N+1}{2} \right\rfloor \ ] : \text{same as before}$$

$$POINTER[\ \left\lfloor \frac{N+1}{2} \right\rfloor + 1 \ . \ . \ N] := NULL$$

$$SUBKEY[\ \left\lfloor \frac{N+1}{2} \right\rfloor + 1 \ . \ . \ N] := EMPTY$$

LINK := NEWMODE

Outputs to NEWMODE (right child):

FLAG : from NODE.BNODE,

$$POINTER[1 \ . \ . \ \left\lfloor \frac{N}{2} \right\rfloor \ ] := POINTER[\ \left\lfloor \frac{N+1}{2} \right\rfloor + 1 \ . \ . \ N]$$

$$SUBKEY[1 \ . \ . \ \left\lfloor \frac{N}{2} \right\rfloor \ ] := SUBKEY[\ \left\lfloor \frac{N+1}{2} \right\rfloor + 1 \ . \ . \ N]$$

All other POINTER values are NULL except

$$POINTER[\ \left\lfloor \frac{N}{2} \right\rfloor + 1] := ITEM$$

All other SUBKEY values are EMPTY and

NEWNODE : newly allocated node.

KEY   : same as $SUBKEY[\ \left\lfloor \frac{N+1}{2} \right\rfloor \ ]$ of NODE.BNODE.

These values are obtained from SPLIT by simple forward substitution and by application of the loop functional transform. In particular, we note that LAST = $(N + 1)$ **div** 2:

$$LAST = \left\lfloor \frac{N+1}{2} \right\rfloor$$

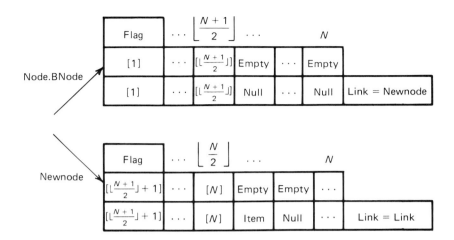

Figure 6-10. Result of SPLIT.

The **while-do** functional

$$LAST + K_{t-1} > N$$

results in

$$K_{t'-1} = N - LAST + 1$$

and since

$$K_t = K_{t-1} + 1 = K_0 + t = t + 1$$

we get

$$t' = N - LAST + 1$$
$$t' - 1 = N - LAST$$

Therefore, the terminal value of K is

$$K_{t'-1} = K_{N-LAST} = N - LAST + 1$$
$$K_{t'-1} = \left\lfloor \frac{N}{2} \right\rfloor + 1$$

because of the identity relation

$$\left\lfloor \frac{N+1}{2} \right\rfloor + \left\lfloor \frac{N}{2} \right\rfloor = N$$

This leads to transformations involving the range of values taken on by subscripts:

$$\text{Range of } LAST + K \text{ is } \left\lfloor \frac{N+1}{2} \right\rfloor + 1 \,..\, N$$

$$\text{Range of } K \text{ in } \textbf{while-do} \text{ is } 1 \,..\, \left\lfloor \frac{N}{2} \right\rfloor$$

We apply the loop functional values for K and LAST $+ K$ in procedure SPLIT, make the tedious forward substitutions, and the expected results are obtained. These results mean we can accept SPLIT as a correct procedure.

Certification of INSERT The purpose of INSERT is to shift the SUBKEY and POINTER arrays to one side in order to make room for a single entry at location LOC. This routine is complicated by the fact that shifts differ for leaf nodes and internal nodes. When an internal node is shifted, SPLITFLAG = TRUE, and we dislocate POINTER[LOC + 1] with the value of ITEM. The difference between a leaf split and an internal node split is shown in Figure 6-11. The reason for this is that internal nodes always hold $(m + 1)$ pointers for m keys, whereas leaf nodes hold m pointers for m keys.

Test-data

INPUTS

KEY	: new key to be inserted in SUBKEY.
ITEM	: new pointer for POINTER.
LOC	: location of insert.
SPLITFLAG	: TRUE if an internal node.
Implied BTREE file containing NODE.BNODE.	

OUTPUTS

If the insertion causes NODE.BNODE to overflow, then we must return the key and record number so that the overflow can be detected. Hence,

KEY = SUBKEY[N] , if overflowed.
ITEM = overflowed pointer.

Furthermore, INSERT modifies the node so that it contains the newly inserted values as shown in Figure 6-11.

We can easily obtain the returned values of KEY and ITEM in the event of an overflow. By forward substitution, the sequence

TEMPTR := POINTER[N].
ITEM   := TEMPTR.

implies

ITEM := POINTER[N] before the shift.

Then,

KEY := SUBKEY[N] after the shift.

The remaining verification arguments stem from the following asser-

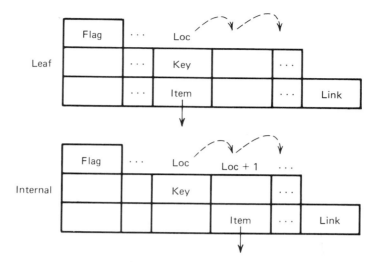

Figure 6-11. Different INSERT for leaf and internal nodes.

tions that the reader can show by examination of the program in Figure 6-6.

First, we have

for $K := N$ **downto** $LOC + 1$ **do**

This component moves all entries in the current node so that a new entry can be made at LOC. This is the "shift" operation.

Second, there is no loss of information in the shift because POINTER[N] is saved in TEMPTR, and SUBKEY[N] is used to detect an overflow. The "gap" at LOC is used to hold the newly inserted KEY and ITEM. However, when SPLITFLAG is true, the value at POINTER[LOC + 1] is lost. This is as it should be, however, because POINTER[LOC + 1] should point to NEWNODE instead of to the left child (previously POINTER[LOC]). This "skewing" guarantees the proper order for internal nodes. Recall that internal node pointers point to all keys "less than" the keys found in the internal node. The largest key within an internal node is greater than all keys in its left subtree, but the right subtree contains all keys greater than the largest key in the internal node.

Certification of LOOKUP The purpose of LOOKUP is to search every node from the root node to the proper leaf node and leave a stack containing the path from root to leaf. This search routine must locate the exact place within the B-tree where the new KEY and ITEM must be inserted in order to keep the B-tree ordered.

The stack is used to back up to parents of split nodes. The routine always searches until it finds a leaf node. Thus,

---
INPUTS

KEY   : search key.
STACK : empty pushdown stack.

OUTPUTS

LOOKUP : TRUE if no match (not in tree).
STACK   : trace (path) of the nodes scanned in order to locate the proper leaf node.

The outer **repeat-until** loop determines whether LOOKUP will find a *B*-tree leaf. Since the loop functional terminates the loop on leaf nodes (only a leaf contains BTREE ↑ .FLAG equal to TRUE), we know that LOOKUP finds a leaf (if it terminates). Thus,

    repeat
        NODE.BNODE := POINTER[NODE.BNODE]
    until BTREE ↑ .FLAG ;

The successor NODE.BNODE is a *B*-tree pointer. The *B*-tree has no cycles; hence every path leads to a leaf. Therefore the repeat loop terminates.

The successor to NODE.BNODE is computed by finding the correct NODE.BITEM. This is done within the **while-do** loop. The **while-do** always terminates because its loop functional is

$$SUBKEY[NODE.BITEM] >= KEY$$
or
$$SUBKEY[NODE.BITEM] = EMPTY$$

The first case here can occur at any time when the node contains a SUBKEY larger than the search KEY. The second case occurs as soon as an EMPTY is encountered. Since

$$SUBKEY[N] = EMPTY$$

in every node, the loop always terminates. Therefore,

$$NODE.BITEM_{t'-1} = \begin{cases} \text{location of SUBKEY} >= KEY \\ \textbf{or} \\ \text{location of SUBKEY} = EMPTY \end{cases}$$

The combination of the loop termination conditions for both loops in LOOKUP leads to a transformed program with the following sequence:

SEEK(BTREE,NODE.BNODE) ; GET(BTREE) ; (* get leaf *)

$$\text{NODE.BITEM}_{t'-1} = \begin{Bmatrix} \text{location of SUBKEY} >= \text{KEY} \\ \textbf{or} \\ \text{location of SUBKEY} = \text{EMPTY} \end{Bmatrix}$$

PUSH(NODE$_{t'-1}$,STACK) ;

$$\text{LOOKUP} := \begin{Bmatrix} \text{SUBKEY} <> \text{KEY} \\ \textbf{or} \\ \text{EMPTY} \quad <> \text{KEY} \end{Bmatrix} ;$$

NODE.BNODE$_{t'}$:= POINTER[NODE.BITEM$_{t'-1}$] ;

NODE.BITEM$_{t'}$:= 1 ;

The desired NODE is returned via the STACK that contains NODE$_{t'-1}$ and all nodes visited along the path from root to leaf.

Certification of ADBTREE   The (simplified) software network of Figure 6-12 will be used to discover test cases and to evaluate the performance of ADBTREE. We have eliminated all detail of ADBTREE except the modules, disk access, and predicate evaluations which control the flow through ADBTREE.

The decision table (Table 6-1) is derived from the software network and the flow predicates. Four paths (without looping) exist.

Table 6-1 leads to four cases we must consider.

CASE LOOKUP = FALSE

The first example corresponds to the case of a match between a SUBKEY and the search key. The output KEY 'Already in B-tree' alerts the user to this anomalie.

CASE SIMPLE LEAF INSERT

LOOKUP locates the correct leaf node in order, and POP returns the record number (NODE.BNODE) and item subscript (NODE.BITEM) of the leaf. The INSERT routine performs a shift and insert on a leaf, and SEEK/PUT stores the updated leaf. Hence,

```
LOOKUP ;
POP ;
INSERT ;
SEEK ; PUT ;
END.
```

These operations perform the anticipated update to the B-tree structure.

Table 6-1. Decision Table for ADBTREE

LOOKUP	KEY	NODE.BNODE	Action or Comment
FALSE	—	—	(1) 'Already in tree'
TRUE	EMPTY	don't care	(2) simple leaf insert
TRUE	*not* EMPTY	NULL	(3) SPLIT; NEWROOT
TRUE	*not* EMPTY	*not* NULL	(4) SPLIT; insert parent node(s)

CASE SPLIT ; NEWROOT

The third case corresponds to splitting a node after an insert and then finding the stack empty. Hence, a new root node is needed.

This example does not consider how many splits may be needed before the new root node is created. It only examines the last split and the consequences of a new root being added to the *B*-tree. The sequence is as follows:

```
LOOKUP ;
POP ;
INSERT ;
SPLIT (NODE,ITEM,NEWNODE,KEY) ; SPLITFLAG := TRUE ;
ITEM := NODE.BNODE ; POP ;
NEWROOT (KEY,ITEM, NEWNODE)
END.
```

The new root properly contains pointers to the left and right child nodes as shown earlier. Forward substitution of the values returned by SPLIT into the parameters used by NEWROOT shows what is inserted into the new root node. Thus,

NEWROOT (middle KEY from left child,
pointer to left child node,
pointer to right child node) ;

CASE SPLIT ; INSERT PARENT NODE(S)

The fourth case corresponds to the repeated splitting of parent nodes. The parent of a split node is itself split. This continues until either a new root is created or a partially empty parent node is encountered. The loop terminates with

$$\begin{cases} \text{KEY} = \text{EMPTY} \ (* \text{ parent is partially empty } *) \\ \quad \textbf{or} \\ \text{NODE.BNODE} = \text{NULL} \ (* \text{ new root created } *) \end{cases}$$

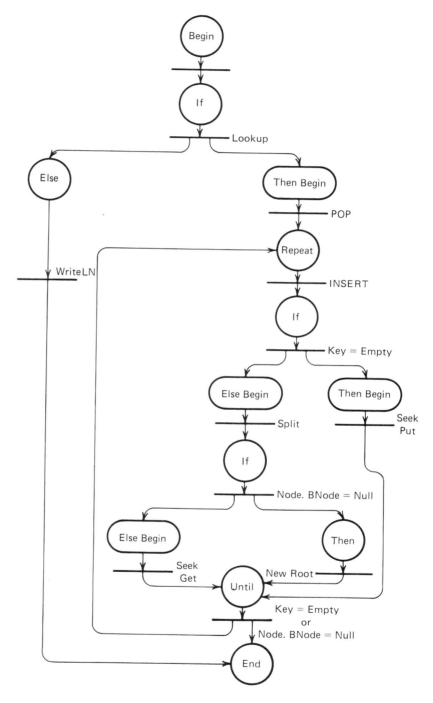

Figure 6-12. Software network for ADBTREE.

Both of these alternatives have already been considered. We need only show that the repeated splitting of parent nodes correctly inserts the left and right child nodes and that the middle key is properly elevated to the parent node.

The abbreviated ADBTREE code for this case is shown below:

$$\begin{bmatrix} \text{SPLITFLAG}_0 := \text{FALSE} \\ \text{KEY}_0 := \text{DKEY} \\ \text{ITEM}_0 := \text{DITEM} \end{bmatrix} ;$$

$$\mathbf{R} \begin{cases} \text{INSERT(KEY}_{t-1}, \text{ITEM}_{t-1}, \text{NODE.BITEM}_{t-1}, \text{SPLITFLAG}_{t-1}) ; \\ \text{SPLIT(NODE}_{t-1}, \text{ITEM}_{t-1}, \text{NEWNODE}_t, \text{KEY}_t) ; \\ \text{SPLITFLAG}_t := \text{TRUE} ; \\ \text{ITEM}_t := \text{NODE.BNODE}_{t-1} ; \\ \text{POP(NODE}_t, \text{STACK}) ; \\ \text{SEEK ; GET ;} \\ \text{ITEM}_t := \text{NEWNODE}_t ; \end{cases}$$

$$\left. \begin{matrix} \\ \end{matrix} \right\} \quad \mathbf{U}_{\substack{\text{KEY}_t = \text{EMPTY} \\ \textbf{or} \\ \text{NODE.BNODE}_t = \text{NULL}}}$$

As we have stated earlier, this case degenerates to one of the other cases as soon as the loop functional is satisfied. The question is whether the proper key and item are inserted when splitting is repeated. This can be studied by concentrating on the statements that modify KEY and ITEM.

$$\text{INSERT(KEY}_{t-1}, \text{ITEM}_{t-1}, \text{NODE.BITEM}_{t-1}, \text{SPLITFLAG}_{t-1}) ;$$
$$\text{SPLIT(NODE}_{t-1}, \text{ITEM}_{t-1}, \text{NEWNODE}_t, \text{KEY}_t) ;$$
$$\text{POP(NODE}_t, \text{STACK}) ;$$
$$\text{SEEK ; GET ;}$$
$$\text{ITEM}_t := \text{NEWNODE}_t ;$$

Therefore, using forward substitution and the fact that INSERT is repeated (the parameters at INSERT), we have

$$\text{KEY}_{t-1} = \text{KEY}_t \text{ from SPLIT}$$
$$\text{ITEM}_{t-1} = \text{NEWNODE}_t \text{ from SPLIT}$$
$$\text{NODE.BITEM}_{t-1} = \text{NODE.BITEM}_t \text{ from POP}$$
$$\text{SPLITFLAG}_{t-1} = \text{TRUE for } t > 1$$

We conclude from this that the split nodes are inserted into the parent node each time the loop is executed for $t = 2, \ldots, t'$. Of course, when $t = 1$, the INSERT routine properly adds the new key to the correct leaf node.

Performance Analysis

The B-tree structure is designed to minimize the most time-consuming part of disk accessing, that is, the number of seek operations. All other operations are insignificant compared to the time delay of a disk seek. Therefore, we can rewrite the software network of Figure 6-12 into a simplified network that represents only the most time-consuming seeks; see Figure 6-13.

Suppose we assume that LOOKUP always returns TRUE, and that

$$p_s = \text{probability of a split}$$
$$(1 - p_s) = \text{probability of no split}$$

Furthermore, let p_s be the probability of a subsequent pass through the repeat loop. Then, the estimated performance of ADBTREE is given by

$$\text{Avg. ADBTREE time} = t_L + \frac{2p_s + 1}{(1 - p_s)}$$

where t_L = time delay of LOOKUP.

We can estimate t_L by considering the following facts about the performance of LOOKUP. First, assume the B-tree holds K entries at the time of an ADBTREE execution. We also assume that each node is approximately one-half full; e.g., each contains $N/2$ entries. Since B-trees are always balanced, LOOKUP executes

$$\log_{[N/2]} K$$

SEEK operations (equivalent to the number of loops). $[x]$ is the greatest integer part of x ; $[x] >= x$. We see from Table 6-2 that the number of keys searched or eliminated after each disk seek rapidly decreases.

The lowest level of the B-tree holds all K entries (all entries are stored in the leaves). So

$$\frac{2K}{N} = \left[\frac{N}{2}\right]^{L-1}$$

which means there are L levels (root node is at level zero).

$$L = \log_{[N/2]} \frac{2K}{N} + 1$$
$$= \log_{[N/2]} K - \log_{[N/2]} (N/2) + 1$$

Since $\log_{[N/2]} (N/2)$ is approximately one,

$$L \doteq \log_{[N/2]} K$$

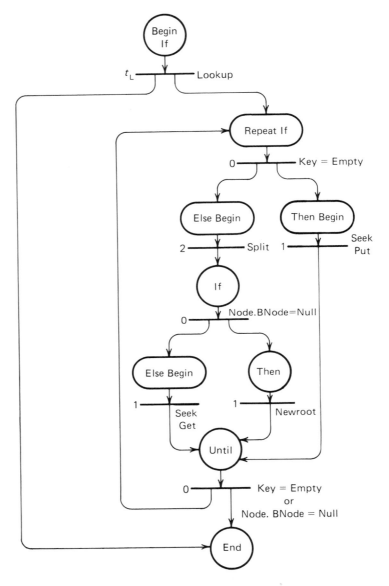

Figure 6-13. Performance model of ADBTREE.

Therefore,

$$\text{Avg. ADBTREE time} = \log_{\lceil N/2 \rceil} K + \frac{2p_s + 1}{(1 - p_s)}$$

Table 6-2. Number Entries
Searched or Eliminated

Level i	Number
1 (root)	1
2	$\left[\dfrac{N}{2}\right]$
3	$\left[\dfrac{N}{2}\right]^{2}$
.	.
.	.
.	.
L	$\left[\dfrac{N}{2}\right]^{L-1}$

For example, if 10% of the nodes are split during a typical ADBTREE operation, we estimate the performance as follows:

$$p_s = 0.1$$

Avg. ADBTREE time $\doteq \log_{\lceil N/2 \rceil} K + 1.33$

Suppose the tree contains $K = 2^{20}$ keys and the order of the B-tree is $N = 64$. The performance is $O(\log_{\lceil N/2 \rceil})$:

$$\doteq \log_{32} 2^{20} + 1.33 = 5.33$$

In other words, we can retrieve a single key among a million keys in less than six disk accesses!

SUMMARY

Disk files are organized according to the manner in which we access them. A sequential access disk file is accessed in strictly sequential fashion, one record after another. The advantage of this method is the ability to store and retrieve variable-length records. The disadvantage is that this method is extremely slow.

A direct access file is much faster because any record can be retrieved in a single disk access given its record number. Unfortunately, we often do not know the record number of a record containing a certain key. Thus, more sophisticated keyed-access methods are required. A common keyed-access method uses index files.

An index access file is actually a pair of files. The index file contains a list of keys and pointers to a second file. The second file is typically a direct access file holding the remaining information.

Access to the second file (MASTER) is made by finding the record number in the index file. The index file is organized to be very efficient because it is accessed many times.

The B-tree structure has been chosen as an excellent index file structure because it optimizes access to secondary storage devices like disk. A disk "bucket" is used to hold an entire B-tree node of order N. A single access to disk retrieves N keys. The keys are searched in high-speed main memory, and if not found, the appropriate subtree pointer is used to retrieve another node. This continues until the desired key is located (in a leaf).

B-trees are always balanced, and so they guarantee an optimal worst-case performance. The ADBTREE program, for example, was $O(\log_{\lceil N/2 \rceil} K)$ complex where N = order of the B-tree and K = number of keys in the B-tree.

The disadvantage of B-tree storage is obvious: it takes space. The B-tree requires approximately $2K$ nodes, and each node is approximately $2N$ elements long. Therefore, $4KN - K$ elements are redundant. Furthermore, each node is only partially filled at any time. For example, Figure 6-3(e) takes 42 elements of storage to store $K = 5$ keys. This is because redundant SUBKEY and POINTER information must be kept to maintain the B-tree structure.

However, the speed and flexibility advantages of B-tree indexing far outweigh the storage disadvantages. Notice how the B-tree index facilitates keyed-access in sequential order. The LINK field allows the next key in order to be retrieved with at most one additional disk access.

Furthermore, each record of a MASTER file may be indexed separately by a B-tree file. These separate index files maintain separate order relations for the MASTER file. Therefore, access can be made in a variety of ways without modification or file sorting.

PROBLEMS

1. Redesign the general model of sequential input from a file record to a window using the **while-do** structure instead of the **repeat-until** structure shown in the chapter.

2. Give a general model for creating and inputting data into a direct access file.

3. Modify the BINARY search program in Chapter 4 so that it searches a direct access file.

4. Modify one of the hashing functions developed in Chapter 5 so that it searches a direct access file.

5. Devise a file structure for a MASTER file containing three keys:

K_1, K_2, and K_3. How can this file structure be used to access any record in order, using K_1, K_2, or K_3?

6. List advantages and disadvantages of the following:
   (a) Sequential access file
   (b) Direct access file
   (c) Indexed access file
   (d) *B*-tree index

7. Draw the *B*-tree structure resulting from insertion of 'A' and 'C' into the *B*-tree of Figure 6-3(e).

8. Compile and execute the *B*-tree system. Use the input data shown in Figure 6-3. Do you obtain the same results?

9. How many iterations are performed by the following **while-do** component?

$$K := 1 ;$$
$$\textbf{while } LAST + K <= N \textbf{ do } K := K+1 ;$$

10. How can we modify ADBTREE so that duplicate keys are allowed?

7

Application to Sorting

INTRODUCTION

A list of length N is said to be in ascending order according to its LIST.KEY values if

$$\text{LIST[1].KEY} <= \text{LIST[2].KEY} <= \cdots <= \text{LIST[N].KEY}$$

and in descending order if

$$\text{LIST[1].KEY} >= \text{LIST[2].KEY} >= \cdots >= \text{LIST[N].KEY}$$

We call such lists *ordered lists*. The purpose of *sorting routines,* then, is to rearrange unordered lists to make them into ordered lists.

A sorting routine rearranges numerical lists into ascending or descending order according to one of the relations above. However, an alphabetical list may also be sorted according to a *lexicographical order*. We can define a lexical relation,

$$\text{LIST[1].KEY} <= \text{LIST[2].KEY} <= \cdots <= \text{LIST[N].KEY}$$

in many ways, but the most obvious is an alphabetical ordering as shown below:

$$\text{'A'} <= \text{'B'} <= \text{'C'} <= \cdots \text{'Z'} <= 0 <= 1 <= \cdots <= 9$$

Thus, for example,

$$\text{'MOON'} <= \text{'MU'}$$
$$\text{'AND'} \quad <= \text{'ANDY'}$$
$$\text{'AO'} \quad\quad <= \text{'Al'}$$

In many applications of computing, the need to sort a LIST can be avoided by careful design and implementation of the application software. *B*-tree index files, for example, define an ordering on a MASTER file. Thus, sorting can be avoided when using index files; see the previous chapter.

However, sometimes sorting is unavoidable. In such cases we must evaluate the problem at hand and determine what kind of sorting routine is the best to use. Basically, we must choose between internal and external sorting techniques.

An *internal sorting routine* is used to sort lists that are small enough to fit entirely within the main memory of the computer. If the list is too large to fit entirely inside main memory, then we must resort to an *external sorting routine*. In external sorting, we store the list on a secondary storage device, e.g., disk. Pieces of the disk file are transferred into main memory and sorted using an internal sort routine. The ordered pieces are written back onto disk and merged with other pieces during a later phase of the external sort.

Both internal and external sorting methods have their own unique problems to be overcome. For example, internal sorting is limited by main memory size (space) and by the time taken to perform the rearrangement of the original list (performance). We will be primarily concerned here with the performance estimates of various internal sorting routines.

Comparative Sorting

Most internal sorting routines perform rearrangements of the original list by comparing and exchanging keys when appropriate. Such routines are called *comparative sorts*.

Comparative sorting is theoretically limited by the time complexity formula:

$$\text{Average time delay} = CN \log_2 N$$

where

C = constant of proportionality

N = length of the list

Therefore, we always strive to find an internal comparative sort routine that performs as close to this lower bound as possible. This will be one of the goals of the section on internal sorting.

Distributive Sorting

Another philosophy of sorting is called *distributed sorting* because it leads to sort routines that (theoretically) are much faster than comparative sorting. A distributed sorting routine works by distributing the original list into buckets and then collecting the keys in order.

An example of a distributed sorting routine will help to demonstrate its potential. Suppose we devise a hashing function H that preserves the order relation:

$$\text{If Key}_1 <= \text{Key}_2$$
$$\text{then } H(\text{Key}_1) <= H(\text{Key}_2)$$

Therefore,

$$H(\text{Key}_1) <= H(\text{Key}_2) <= \cdots <= H(\text{Key}_N)$$

For example,

$$H(\text{Key}) = \text{KEY}$$

is an order-preserving hashing function.

We can use H to rapidly sort a set of keys. Here is the pseudocode for a distributed sorting routine based on $H(\text{KEY})$:

1. For all N keys in LIST (from 1 to N), store LIST[I] in memory cell H (LIST[I]).

2. For all M memory cells (from location zero to $M - 1$), collect the keys and store them back into LIST.

Obviously, this method of sorting depends on the availability of a huge memory. Each key is distributed to a memory cell and then collected back (in order by memory cell address) at high speed. Most of the memory will be empty, but the cells that are full contain an element of LIST.

The theoretical lower bound for distributed sorting is

$$\text{Average time delay} = C$$

where

C = a constant that depends on the speed of the machine and not on the size of the list

Unfortunately, this approach takes too much memory, so distributed sorting routines are usually modified to take more time in exchange for using less memory.

A Pragmatic Approach

In the remainder of the chapter we examine two internal sorting routines and two external sorting routines. We make no attempt to discuss all known algorithms for sorting. In fact, there are only a very small number of sorting routines that are worth knowing. Therefore we choose to study only the most useful sorting routines and to ignore all the others.

The selection sort is studied because it is a simple program that can be quickly written and used to sort very short lists. The major emphasis in the section on internal sorting is on the fastest known internal sorting routine—QUICKERSORT. This routine comes very close to the theoretical lower bound for comparative sorting routines and requires very little additional main memory space.

The external sorting section develops two approaches to sorting that consider practical issues such as (1) the size of main memory, (2) the access time and size of the secondary storage device, and (3) the complexity of programming optimized merging strategies. This approach ignores a vast body of literature on external sorting in favor of developing the "best" possible approach.

In each case studied, we apply the tools of software engineering that have been used in earlier chapters. Correctness and performance are constantly evaluated so that we can be sure of the sorting routines we design and implement.

INTERNAL SORTING

Internal sorting routines are applicable for lists of length $N <= M$, where M is the size of available main memory (we disregard the space used for the program itself). The speed of internal sorting routines is governed by the processing speed of the computer. This is usually related to the time it takes to compare, move, or manipulate the sort keys. In the case of comparative routines, we measure performance in terms of the number of comparisons expected.

We will study two sorting routines: (1) The *selection sort* is simple to understand, easy to program, and suitable for sorting lists of length $N <= 50$. (2) The ultimate sorting routine is the QUICKERSORT routine. It is especially good for large lists, and once understood, of moderate complexity. In fact, it is worthwhile spending considerable time and effort on Quickersort because it has been shown (experimentally) to be the best all-around comparative sorting technique to use for internal sorting.

Simple Sorting: Selection Sort

Selection sort is best known for its simplicity. Given a list of keys as shown below,

```
type
    DATA = record KEY : integer; INFO: string end;
    LISTS = array [1 . . N] of DATA;
var
    LIST : LISTS
```

we perform a selection sort by first exchanging the smallest key element in LIST[1] . . LIST[N] with LIST[1]. Next, we exchange the smallest key element in LIST[2] . . LIST[N] with LIST[2]. Continuing in this fashion, we exchange the smallest key element in LIST[I] . . LIST[N] with LIST[I] for I equal to 1, 2, 3, . . $(N - 1)$.

A procedure for selection sort is given in Figure 7-1. We can illustrate the procedure by example. Suppose $N = 5$ and the values stored in LIST[I].KEY are

8,3,1,5,2

The first pass of the outer loop of SELECT computes

$$K := 3$$

$$MIN.KEY := 1$$

The EXCHANGE (LIST[I], LIST[K]) (see Figure 7-2) swaps 8 and 1 to give

①,3,⑧,5,2

Continuing, we see that the exchanges lead to an ordered list:

1,②, 8 , 5 ,③
1, 2 ,③, 5 , 8
1, 2 , 3 ,⑤, 8   (swap with self)
1, 2 , 3 , 5 ,⑧   (swap with self)

We can test SELECT more thoroughly by carefully selecting test data to force the execution of SELECT as shown in the following certification exercises.

Certification of SELECT   We will use two sets of test data to test SELECT. The first set is a degenerate, trivial case. The second set is a descending list and shows that SELECT correctly reverses a descending list to give an ascending list.

Although these two tests are rather limited, they provide evidence that this simple sorting routine works correctly.

Test Data #1 LIST[1]·KEY = 1, LIST[2]·KEY = 0 ; N = 2

The abbreviated version of SELECT is

$$\mathbf{F}_{I:=1..1} \quad \mathbf{F}_{J:=2..2} \left\{ \begin{matrix} K:=J \\ MIN:=LIST[K] \end{matrix} \right\} \left. \begin{matrix} K:=I; \ MIN:=LIST[I] \quad ; \\ \\ \\ \end{matrix} \right\}$$

EXCHANGE(LIST[I],LIST[K])

```
    procedure SELECT (var LIST : LISTS);
      var I, J, K : integer;
         MIN : DATA;
      begin
        for I := 1 to N − 1 do
          begin
            K := I; MIN := LIST[I];
            for J := I + 1 to N do
              if LIST[J].KEY < MIN.KEY
                then begin K := J; MIN := LIST[K] end ;
            EXCHANGE ( LIST[I], LIST[K] );
          end
      end   (* SELECT *)
```

Figure 7-1. SELECT program performs a selection sort.

```
    procedure EXCHANGE (var LEFT : DATA;
                        var RITE  : DATA);
      var TEMP : DATA;
      begin
        TEMP := LEFT;
        LEFT := RITE;
        RITE := TEMP
      end;   (* EXCHANGE *)
```

Figure 7-2. EXCHANGE procedure.

Now, by forward substitution of I and J,

$$\equiv \left\{ \begin{array}{l} I := 1; \\ MIN := 1 \\ J := 2 \qquad \left\{ \begin{array}{l} K := 2 \\ MIN := 0 \end{array} \right. \\ EXCHANGE(LIST[1], LIST[2]) \end{array} \right\}$$

$$\equiv \left\{ \begin{array}{l} I := 1 \\ J := 2 \\ K := 2 \\ MIN := 0 \\ EXCHANGE(1, 0) \end{array} \right\}$$

Therefore, SELECT properly sorts this trivial list.

Test Data #2 LIST[1]·KEY $= N-I+1$; $N>1$.

The test data in this case are a descending list of integers, for example, 5,4,3,2,1; $N = 5$. The idea here is to test whether SELECT can "reverse" this list into ascending order. Hence, if SELECT is correct, it will exchange keys such that

$$\text{EXCHANGE(LIST}[I], \text{LIST}[N-I+1])$$

occurs for all values of I in $[1 \, . \, . \, \lfloor N/2\rfloor]$. For example, $N = 5$, $\lfloor N/2\rfloor = 2$, so

$$\text{EXCHANGE(LIST}[1], \text{LIST}[5])$$
$$\text{EXCHANGE(LIST}[2], \text{LIST}[4])$$

results in

$$①, 4 ,3, 2 ,⑤$$
$$1 ,②,3,④, 5$$

which is sorted into ascending order.

The test data in this case force the inner loop to locate the smallest key by scanning the LIST until the *first instance of a larger key* is encountered. Since the list is originally in descending order, the first time the inner loop is executed with $I = 1$, we encounter LIST[N]·KEY before any larger key is found. Hence, $K:=N$ when the inner loop terminates, and

$$\text{EXCHANGE(LIST}[1], \text{LIST}[N])$$

occurs as desired. Subsequent passes for $I:=2,3, \, . \, . \, \lfloor N/2\rfloor$ result in locating the $(N-I+1)$-th key in LIST. Thus,

$$K:=(N-I+1)$$

when the inner loop terminates for the I-th time. This means MIN:=LIST[$N-I+1$], and the abbreviated program becomes

$$\mathbf{F}_{I:=1 \, . \, . \, \left[\frac{N}{2}\right]} \left\{ \begin{array}{l} K:=I; \text{MIN}:=\text{LIST}[I]; \\ \left\{ \begin{array}{l} K:=N-I+1; \\ \text{MIN}:=\text{LIST}[N-I+1] \end{array} \right\} \\ \text{EXCHANGE(LIST}[I], \text{LIST}[N-I+1]) \end{array} \right\}$$

This results in

$$\text{EXCHANGE(LIST}[1], \text{LIST}[N])$$
$$\text{EXCHANGE(LIST}[2], \text{LIST}[N-1])$$
$$. \, . \, .$$
$$\text{EXCHANGE(LIST}[N \text{ div } 2], \text{LIST}[N \text{ div } 2+1])$$

This explains only part of the program's execution (for $I=1$ to $\lfloor N/2 \rfloor$). But what about the remaining values of I (for $I = \lfloor N/2 \rfloor + 1$ to $N-1$)? For the test data that we used to force the execution of SELECT, the remaining values of LIST[I] are sorted. The value of K is I, and the inner loop has no effect on K. Therefore, the algorithm performs wasteful exchanges.

$$\mathop{\mathbf{F}}_{I:=\left[\frac{N}{2}\right] + 1 \,\ldots\, (N-1)} \left\{ \begin{array}{l} K:=I;\ \text{MIN}:=\text{LIST}[I]; \\ J:=N; \\ \text{EXCHANGE}(\text{LIST}[I],\ \text{LIST}[K]) \end{array} \right\}$$

This leads to

$$\mathop{\mathbf{F}}_{I:=\left[\frac{N}{2}\right] + 1 \,\ldots\, (N-1)} \left\{ \text{EXCHANGE}(\text{LIST}[I],\ \text{LIST}[I]) \right\}$$

which does not alter the remaining LIST elements.

In summary, the SELECT procedure reverses LIST such that

$$\mathop{\mathbf{F}}_{I:=1 \,\ldots\, \left[\frac{N}{2}\right]} \left\{ \text{EXCHANGE}(\text{LIST}[I],\ \text{LIST}[N-I+1]) \right\}$$

or

EXCHANGE(LIST[1], LIST[N])

. . .

EXCHANGE(LIST[N **div** 2], LIST[N **div** 2+1])

Where we have noted that

$$N - \left\lfloor \frac{N}{2} \right\rfloor + 1 = \left\lfloor \frac{N}{2} \right\rfloor + 1.$$

Therefore, SELECT works for descending lists.

We can easily see why SELECT correctly sorts a list of unordered keys. If we accept the conjecture that the inner loop always finds the smallest key in the "tail" of the list, then SMALLEST returns the value to be exchanged. Thus,

SMALLEST(LIST,J);

This simplification allows us to rewrite SELECT in pseudocode form:

SELECT: **for** $I:=1$ **to** $N-1$ **do**
      EXCHANGE(LIST[I], SMALLEST(LIST,I+1))

Therefore, on each pass (each value of I), SELECT guarantees that the smallest value in the tail of the list is placed in location I.

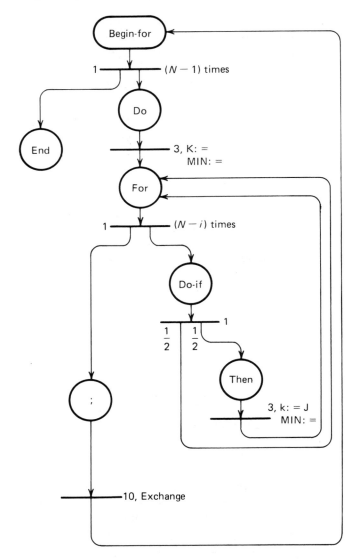

Figure 7-3. Software network for SELECT.

Performance evaluation SELECT *seems* to be a "good" sort routine, but is it fast enough? The software network for SELECT is shown in Figure 7-3. It contains estimates of the time needed to perform each transition. We have assumed a unit time delay for each arithmetic operation, and ten units delay for EXCHANGE. Each loop takes a fixed length of time, but the inner loop takes $(N - i)$ passes, where i changes with the number of passes through the outer loop. Therefore, to obtain the overall time delay estimate we must vary i from one to $(N - 1)$.

Figure 7-4 shows the derivation of the time delay formula. It assumes equal probabilities of branching in the **if-then** component. Thus,

$$\text{Average time delay} = \frac{52(N - 1) + 7N(N - 1)}{4}$$

$$= \frac{7N^2 + 45N}{4} - 13$$

Therefore,

$$\text{Average time delay} \sim O(N^2)$$

The selection sort routine performs in $O(N^2)$ time, so we can expect rapidly diminishing performance as the length of the LIST increases. For example, a list of length $2N$ takes nearly four times as long to sort than a list of length N. For this reason we must find a better way to sort a list when N is "large."

A "small" list of $N = 10$ keys takes

$$\text{Time}_{10} = 274.5 \text{ units}$$

and a "large" list of $N = 50$ keys takes

$$\text{Time}_{50} = 4,924.5 \text{ units}$$

Or in other words, the time expended per key is

$$\frac{\text{Time}_{10}}{10} = 27.45$$

$$\frac{\text{Time}_{50}}{50} = 98.51$$

The effort per key increases by a factor of 4 or 5. Therefore we should avoid SELECT when sorting "large" lists.

Fast Sorting: Quickersort

The reason SELECT is such a slow sorting routine is because it wastes exchanges on keys that do not need to be exchanged. We saw these wasted exchanges being performed in Test Data #2 of the previous section.

As a further illustration, observe the loss in efficiency in the following example (exchanges are in circles):

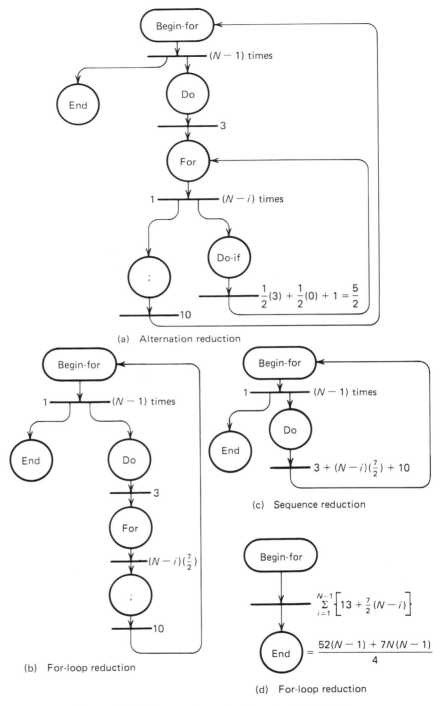

(a) Alternation reduction

(b) For-loop reduction

(c) Sequence reduction

(d) For-loop reduction

Figure 7-4. Network reduction for SELECT.

$$N = 5; \ 8 \ , \ 3 \ , \ 1 \ , \ 5 \ , \ 2$$

①	3	⑧	5	2	
1	②	8	5	③	
1	2	③	5	⑧	
1	2	3	⑤	8	(wasted)
1	2	3	5	⑧	(wasted)

In fact, we might consider any exchange that moves a key in the "wrong" direction to be wasted effort. That is, small keys should be moved to the left (beginning part of the list), and large keys should migrate toward the right end of the list. Let's look at the example, again.

①	3	⑧	5	2	(good move)
1	②	8	5	③	(3 in wrong direction)
1	2	③	5	⑧	(good move)
1	2	3	⑤	8	(wasted)
1	2	3	5	⑧	(wasted)

Only about one-half of the moves were productive in this example, and the other half were counterproductive.

We could improve selection sort by eliminating the counterproductive exchange operations. Suppose we attempt to improve the example by partitioning the list into roughly equal parts and then exchanging only those keys that are in the "wrong" partition. For example,

1	3

8	5	2

Now, the "small" keys should be moved to the left-most box and the "large" keys should be moved to the right-most box. But which keys are "small"? And which are "large"?

Suppose we make a rule that establishes the following:

1. Any key less than 4 is "small."
2. Any key greater than 4 is "large."

This rule means we must partition the original list into boxes as shown below:

"small"

1	3	2

"large"

8	5

Notice that we have moved only one list element at this point, but we have greatly improved the order of the list because all keys less than 4 are to the left and all keys greater than 4 are to the right.

We apply the same logic to each of the boxes. First the "small" box.

Let the rule be

1. Any key less than 2 is "small" and should be moved into the "small" box.
2. Any key greater than or equal to 2 is "large" and should be moved into the "large" box.

So,   "small"   "large"

| 1 | | 3   2 | | 8   5 |

Again, we apply the same steps to the boxes containing two or more keys. Thus,

| 1 | | 2 | | 3 | | 5 | | 8 |

The sorted list was obtained in nearly a minimum number of exchanges. The only additional information we need before this method can be automated is a rule for selecting a "middle" key such that

1. Any key less than "middle" is "small."
2. Any key greater than or equal to "middle" is "large."

Many proposals have been made for selecting "middle." The one that seems to work best is also the simplest. Thus let "middle" be the key near the midpoint of the sublist (box) being sorted. If the "box" is defined by L (left end) and R (right end), then

$$\text{MID} = \text{LIST}[(L+R) \textbf{ div } 2]$$

The example above assumed that boxes can be stretched to insert keys and can be squeezed when a key is removed. However, in practice, we cannot easily stretch and contract sublists because of the contiguous nature of the list. Therefore we must find candidate "small" and "large" keys to exchange. We do this by searching from the left end for a "large" key, and then searching from the right end for a "small" key. When they are found, we swap them.

For example, suppose we start with the following list (with MID = LIST[4] = 9).

8, 12, 3, 9, 16, 5, 7, 2

Searching from the left we get "large" equals 12, and searching from the right we get "small" equals 2. Therefore, we can exchange these two and obtain a "better" list:

8, ②, 3, 9, 16, 5, 7, ⑫

Continuing, we find "large" equal to 16 and "small" equal to 7:

$$8, 2, 3, 9, \textcircled{7}, 5, \textcircled{16}, 12$$

We cannot continue further because the two searches have met one another. Therefore we divide the list into sublists and repeat the entire process again on each sublist.

| 8, 2, 3, 9, 7, 5 | | 6, 12 |

Notice that all keys smaller than or equal to MID = 9 are in the left sublist, and all keys greater than 9 are in the right sublist. Therefore, no further exchanges need to take place between these two sublists.

The algorithm we have just described by way of example is Quickersort. It is a high-speed comparative sorting routine because it wastes very few exchanges (see Table 7-1).

Table 7-1. Average Number of
Exchanges per Key in Quickersort

Length, N	Avg. Exchanges
10	1.007
50	1.595
100	1.836
150	1.946
200	2.013
400	2.281

Procedure SWAP shown in Figure 7-5 performs the left and right search and exchange operations just described. SWAP returns a modified list with a left sublist beginning at location NewL and a right sublist terminating at location NewR. Note also that (NewL > NewR) terminates the SWAP routine.

A program for Quickersort (QSORT) is given in Figure 7-6. The stack operations STACKSIZE, INITSTACK, and PUSH and POP perform the obvious operations of returning the size of the stack, initializing the stack, and push/pop operations, respectively. We have not included these operations here.

Analysis of QSORT Procedure QSORT uses the divide-and-conquer technique to sort a list. The idea is simple:

1. Start with the original list.

2. Select a ''middle element'' that can be used to define ''large'' and ''small.''

```
procedure SWAP( L, R : integer ;
                var NewL : integer ;
                var NewR : integer ) ;
  var MID : DATA ;
  begin
    NewL := L ; NewR := R ; MID := LIST[( L+R ) div 2 ] ;
    repeat
      while LIST[ NewL ].KEY < MID.KEY do NewL := NewL + 1 ;
      while LIST[ NewR ].KEY > MID.KEY do NewR := NewR − 1 ;
      if NewL <= NewR
        then begin
             EXCHANGE( LIST[ NewL ], LIST[ NewR ] ) ;
             NewL := NewL + 1 ; NewR := NewR − 1 ;
           end ;
    until NewL > NewR ;
  end ; (* SWAP *)
```

Figure 7-5. Procedure SWAP partitions a list.

```
procedure QSORT( var LIST : LISTS ) ;
  var L, R, NewL, NewR : POINTERS ;
  begin
    INITSTACK ; PUSH( 1, M ) ;
    repeat
      POP( L, R ) ;
      repeat
        SWAP( L, R, NewL, NewR ) ;
        if NewL < R then PUSH( NewL, R ) ;
        R := NewR ;
      until L >= R ;
    until STACKSIZE = 0 ;
  end ; (* QSORT *)
```

Figure 7-6. Quickersort sorting routine.

3. Exchange elements so that all "small" keys are in the "left half" of the list, and all "large" keys are in the "right half" of the list.

4. Partition the list into left and right halves.

5. Remember the location of the right half sublist (push its beginning and ending subscripts onto a push-down stack).

6. Repeat the above exchange-partition steps on the sublist that remains.

7. When a left sublist is sorted, pop the stack to get a right sublist; repeat the exchange-partition steps on this sublist.

These steps are implemented in QSORT shown in Figure 7-6. The routine is initialized by clearing the stack (INITSTACK), and then placing the initial subscripts onto the stack PUSH(1,N). These are immediately removed from the stack by the first POP(L,R) operation.

The outer **repeat-until** STACKSIZE=0 loop simply terminates the sorting routine as soon as no sublists remain to be sorted. The inner **repeat-until** L>=R loop performs the exchange-partition step. Additionally, the inner loop pushes the subscripts of the right half sublist onto the stack whenever a nonempty sublist is generated by the exchange-partition operation.

Figure 7-7 shows the divide-and-conquer tree for QSORTing the list:

$$N = 8;\ 8,12,3,1,16,5,7,2$$

Each node of this tree contains a sublist of the original list, and each branch shows the result of an exchange-partition step. Thus, for example, SWAP(1,8,?,?) computes NewL=2 and NewR=1, leading to the two boxes containing

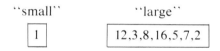

This occurred because MID.KEY = 1; so all "small" keys had to be less than (or equal to) MID.KEY = 1 and all "large" keys had to be greater than 1.

The leaf nodes of the tree in Figure 7-7 yield the final result of QSORT. Piecing them together gives

Certification of QSORT The essential operations of QSORT are contained within the inner loop (the stack operations are merely bookkeeping details).

```
repeat
    SWAP (L,R,NewL,NewR);
    if NewL < R then PUSH (NewL,R) ;
    R := NewR;
until L >= R;
```

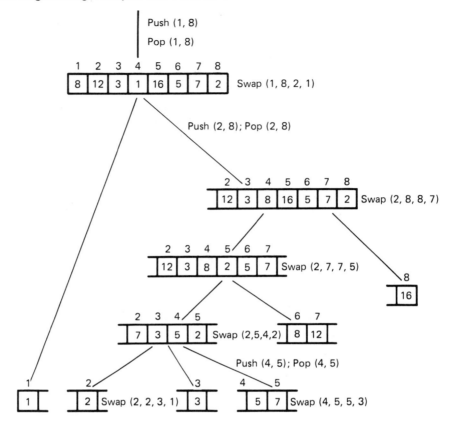

Figure 7-7. QSORT test showing tree-structured partitioning.

We can simplify even further by ignoring the inner **if-then** component (for the purposes of this test, at least). Thus,

```
repeat
    SWAP (L,R,NewL,NewR) ;
    R := NewR
until L >= R;
```

The resulting loop simply computes the exchange-partitions, which result in two (sometimes three) sublists as shown in the following diagram.

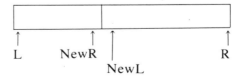

Note that the right sublist is pushed onto the stack if it is not empty, and the left sublist is once again partitioned. Noting R := NewR, we have the following:

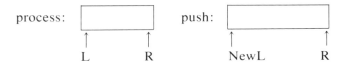

process:

push:

L   R   NewL   R

Eventually the right sublist becomes exhausted because L >= R. Thus,

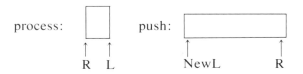

process:

push:

R   L   NewL   R

What we must now show is that each partition correctly places all "small" keys in the left sublist and all "large" keys into the right sublist each time SWAP is executed (see Figure 7-5). Therefore, we must show that

NewL > NewR **implies**((LIST[L].KEY . . LIST[NewL].KEY < MID.KEY) **and** (LIST[NewR].KEY . . LIST[R].KEY > MID.KEY))

The **while-do** loops in SWAP compute the location of keys to be exchanged (if necessary):

> **while** LIST[NewL].KEY < MID.KEY **do** NewL := NewL + 1;
> **implies** NewL = Location of a key >= MID.KEY

and

> **while** LIST[NewR].KEY > MID.KEY **do** NewR := NewR − 1;
> **implies** NewR = Location of a key <= MID.KEY

Then SWAP has either satisfied the termination condition (NewL > NewR), or else

> **if** NewL <= NewR
> **then begin**
> EXCHANGE(LIST[NewL], LIST[NewR]);
> NewL := NewL + 1 ; NewR := NewR − 1;
> **end;**

results in an exchange such that

$$(LIST[L].KEY . . LIST[NewL].KEY) < MID.KEY$$
$$(LIST[NewR].KEY . . LIST[R].KEY) > MID.KEY$$

Then SWAP has either satisfied the termination condition (NewL > NewR), or else it repeats the search process again. Upon termination, the exchange-partition gives the desired result:

NewL > NewR **implies** ((LIST[L].KEY . . LIST[NewL].KEY < MID.KEY)
and (LIST[NewR].KEY . . LIST[R].KEY > MID.KEY))

SWAP thus performs the desired partition of a sublist into two (or three) sublists that are ordered relative to MID.KEY. The example in Figure 7-7 illustrates the case of three partitions. For example,

$$\boxed{7,3,5,2}$$

is partitioned into

$$\boxed{2} \quad \boxed{3} \quad \boxed{5,7}$$

where MID.KEY = 3, and LIST[L].KEY = 2.

Performance evaluation We have claimed that Quickersort is the fastest internal sorting technique known. Actually, this fact is determined pragmatically by simulation of various sorting routines using randomly selected keys (Wirth, pp. 85–86). Since several other sorting routines perform near the theoretical lower bound for comparative sorts, we must be careful in evaluating the constant term in the formula

$$\text{Average time delay} = CN \log_2 N$$

where

$$C = \text{constant of proportionality}$$
$$N = \text{length of the list}$$

This term can be estimated from experimental data taken from simulation results performed on particular machines. For example, $C = 0.03$ on the CDC 6400 computer. This value will vary for different computers.

We can estimate the performance formula for QSORT by observing the (almost) binary tree structure of the exchange-partition operations (see Figure 7-7 for an example). Suppose we let α be a constant of proportionality, and p be the probability of a PUSH operation being performed in Figure 7-6. Then the innermost **repeat-until** loop is executed approximately $\alpha \log_2 N$ times (once each time the list is partitioned). The outer loop of QSORT is executed approximately $p\alpha \log_2 N$ (once for each time the list is partitioned *and* a sublist is pushed onto the stack—to be popped off, later).

A rough estimate of the time to execute the innermost loop body is

$$(p\alpha \log_2 N)(\alpha \log_2 N)T_{inner}$$

where T_{inner} is the time to execute the SWAP routine plus the POP, plus the other statements, e.g., R:=NewR.

Suppose we estimate T_{inner} as follows:

$$T_{inner} = t_{swap} + t_{pop} + 1$$

And since $t_{pop} + 1$ is only a small delay, let

$$T_{inner} = t_{swap}$$

Estimation of time to do SWAP Let each pass through the **while-do** loops take W time units, and the **if-then** take I time units to execute. The number of **while** loops executed equals $(L - R)$ because each pass of a **while** loop brings NewL closer to NewR (or NewR closer to NewL, or both converge) until the **repeat** loop terminates due to NewL > NewR.

Further, assume the **if-then** component is executed half of the time, so we get an approximation:

$$(L - R)\, W + \frac{1}{2}\, (L - R)I = \left(W + \frac{I}{2} \right) (L - R)$$

Again, assuming a binary tree structure, there are approximately $\alpha \cdot \log_2 N$ levels in the QSORT tree. Thus, the N keys are partitioned into $\alpha \log_2 N$ sublists of an average size of

$$\frac{N}{\alpha \log_2 N}$$

So the expected size $(L - R)$ is

$$(L - R) \approx \frac{N}{\alpha \cdot \log_2 N}$$

giving
$$T_{inner} = t_{swap} = \left(W + \frac{I}{2} \right)\left(\frac{N}{\alpha \log_2 N} \right)$$

We combine terms to obtain an estimated time delay for an "average" QSORT.

$$\text{Approx. avg. QSORT time delay} = \alpha \cdot p \left(W + \frac{I}{2} \right) N \cdot \log_2 N$$

This estimate is $Q(N \log_2 N)$ and therefore very close to the theoretical lower bound for comparative sort routines. In fact, the constant of proportionality depends on the speed of the machine and on the nature of the original list. Thus,

$$C = \alpha p \left(W + \frac{I}{2} \right)$$

The performance of QSORT depends on the nature of the original list in much the same way the binary search tree method of searching depends on the nature of the search list. A balanced QSORT performs faster than an unbalanced QSORT as shown in Figure 7-8. The pathological case in Figure 7-8(b) slows QSORT to the pace of a selection sort. Thus, in this case, QSORT is a cumbersome selection sort routine. Fortunately, this situation is rare (one out of $N!$ possible lists of length N).

Summary

A simple program for sorting lists is selection sort, which takes time proportional to N squared:

$$t_{select} = C_{select}N^2$$

A fast sort program like QSORT takes time proportional to $N \log_2 N$:

$$t_{Qsort} = C_{Qsort}N \log_2 N$$

SELECT can be used for short lists, where

$$t_{select} < t_{Qsort}$$
$$C_{select\,N} < C_{Qsort} \log_2 N$$

For example, QSORT is about ten times faster than SELECT for $N = 50$, but the two sorting techniques are roughly equivalent for $N = 12$. Indeed, a combination of these two techniques is often used to improve the performance of QSORT. QSORT may be improved by using SELECT to sort sublists of $N <= 12$ keys within QSORT. This strategy reduces the excessive PUSH and POP operations that often accompany QSORT when the original list is fragmented into many short sublists. The unbalanced QSORT tree of Figure 7-8(b) could be pruned by augmenting QSORT with SELECT such that SELECT sorts all sublists of fewer than K keys. If $K = 4$, for example, the list is sorted in only four push and pop operations instead of six.

EXTERNAL SORTING

We must resort to external sorting whenever the list to be sorted is too large to fit into main memory. If M is the size of main memory available for storing a list of length N, then $N > M$ means we must store part or all of the list in a secondary storage file.

External sorting routines differ from internal sorting routines because of the different nature of the storage devices. The time required to access and read a key stored in a secondary file is much greater than the time required to compare two (or more) keys in main memory. For this reason,

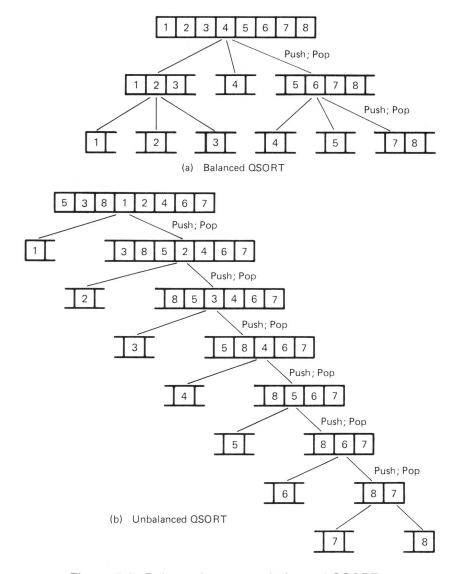

Figure 7-8. Balanced versus unbalanced QSORT.

most external sorting routines try to minimize the number of times each key is examined.

A Quickersort routine, for example, would be a very poor choice for an external sorting routine because it repeatedly scans sublists of the original list. Each time Quickersort performs a comparison such as

while LIST[NewL].KEY < MID.KEY **do** NewL := NewL + 1;

and

while LIST[NewR].KEY > MID.KEY **do** NewR := NewR - 1;

we would access the file containing list elements at record location NewL and NewR. Furthermore, the EXCHANGE operation must directly access the file in order to exchange two LIST elements.

A better strategy for external sorting uses the smallest number of accesses possible, even if it means performing more comparisons or moves within main memory. One way to minimize disk access is to merge subfiles (sublists stored in a file) using a sequential merge routine much like the one studied in Chapter 3. But before we can merge two subfiles, we must be certain they are ordered.

The basic idea in external sorting is this:

1. Break the file of length N into subfiles of length $K_i <= M$, where M is the amount of available storage in main memory and K_i is the length of the ith subfile.

2. Use an internal sorting routine to sort each subfile of length K_i, and write these subfiles back into their subfiles.

3. Use a merge routine to merge the subfiles together—resulting in an ordered file of length N.

This approach seems to be rather straightforward, but upon closer inspection it is not altogether obvious how to select K_i and then do step 3 in the fewest number of accesses. We will now study some of the problems and solutions raised by external sorting in this fashion.

Merge Strategies

We are faced with the following problem relative to external sorting: Given s subfiles of length $K_1, K_2 \ldots, K_s$, find the "best" merge strategy for combining them into one ordered file. By "best" we mean one that minimizes the activity of the disk.

One of the complicating factors in this problem is the possibility that the merging subfiles will overwrite one another during merging. Therefore we will need an auxillary file large enough to hold the entire input file. The subfiles are merged into this auxillary file, and then the (larger) subfiles that result are merged back into the input file. This is shown in Figure 7-9(c).

A simple merge strategy is illustrated in Figure 7-9(a–c). We assume $M = 4$ and select the *natural* subfiles defined by naturally occurring ascending-order sublists. A *natural* subfile is already ordered (by coinci-

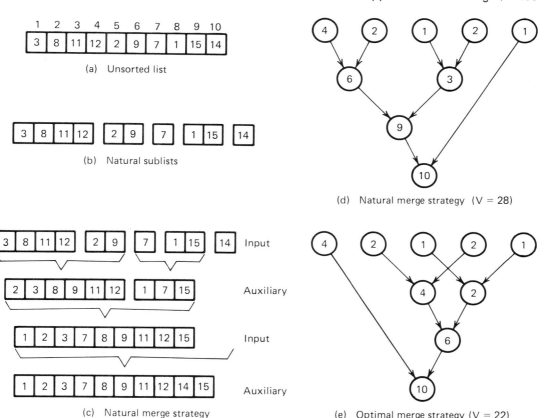

Figure 7-9. Merge sort strategies for $M = 4$.

dence), and so it does not need to be sorted by an internal sorting routine. In Figure 7-9(b) there are $s = 5$ natural sublists of length

$$K_1 = 4$$
$$K_2 = 2$$
$$K_3 = 1$$
$$K_4 = 2$$
$$K_5 = 1$$

We can take advantage of the natural order by merging pairs of subfiles from beginning to end. This results in larger subfiles as shown in Figure 7-9(c). Continued merging of pairs of subfiles yields an ordered file.

The merge strategy for natural merging of this list is shown in Figure 7-9(d). We can compute the value V of this merge tree as follows. Let each leaf of the tree be assigned a value equal to the number of keys in the subfile represented by the leaf. Thus, the values of the leaf nodes in Figure 7-9(d) are: $K_1 = 4$, $K_2 = 2$, $K_3 = 1$, $K_4 = 2$, $K_5 = 1$. Next, assign each leaf node a weight equal to the level of the leaf: the root node is at level zero, the next level is one, etc. The weights of the leaf nodes in Figure 7-9(d) are: $L_1 = 3$, $L_2 = 3$, $L_3 = 3$, $L_4 = 3$, $L_5 = 1$.

The level number of a leaf node measures the number of times each element of the original list is accessed in order to merge it into the final (ordered) file. The value of a merge tree is simply the total number of disk accesses needed to sort a collection of ordered subfiles. Therefore, V is a measure of the *effort* needed to do an external sort. That is,

$$V = \sum_{\text{all leaf nodes}} L_i K_i$$

where

$$L_i = \text{level of leaf node } i$$
$$K_i = \text{size of leaf node } i$$

The value of the natural merge tree of Figure 7-9(d) is

$$V = 3(4) + 3(2) + 3(1) + 3(2) + 1(1) = 28$$

Figure 7-9(e) shows that a better merge strategy exists for this example. The value of the optimal merge tree is $V = 22$. Six fewer disk accesses are needed using this strategy. It would appear that improvements are possible if we pay careful attention to the pattern of merging. This is true, and it raises the problem of finding optimal merge strategies.

Optimal Merge Sort

How can we obtain an optimal merge strategy given a collection of subfiles of length K_i for i in $[l \ . \ . \ s]$? An algorithm for finding optimal merge trees called *Huffman's algorithm* is simple to use:

1. Select the order of the merge (the order of the merge tree).

2. Repeat until a root is obtained. Merge together the smallest subfiles first, and assign their sum to the resulting node in the merge tree.

We will use a binary merge strategy in the external sorting method described next. However, the Huffman algorithm may require a slight modification when used to find ternary (and higher order) trees (Lewis and Smith). Also note that step 2 applies to both leaf nodes and internal nodes. The merge tree of Figure 7-9(e) was obtained from Huffman's algorithm. The tree means to:

1. Merge subfiles 3 and 5 to get another subfile of length 2.

2. Merge subfiles 2 and 4 to get another subfile of length 4.

3. Merge the subfile of length 2 with one of the subfiles of length 4 to get a subfile of length 6.

4. Merge the remaining subfile of length 4 with the subfile of length 6 to get the final file of length 10.

The reason Huffman trees are minimal is that they always access the largest subfiles the fewest number of times. For example, the largest subfile in Figure 7-9(e) is accessed only once—on the final merge step. The small files are accessed more often, but because they are small, the total number of accesses is held to a minimum.

Unnatural merging The natural merge strategy does not fully exploit the potential of external sorting. It is likely that the length of subfiles will be much shorter than the size of available main memory M. This means we are not fully using the merge operations because the subfiles are not as long as they could be if we sorted them first.

Suppose we use $M = 4$ to sort the original list in Figure 7-9(a) into three subfiles as shown in Figure 7-10. The value of the optimal merge tree in this case is $V = 16$; see Figure 7-10(b). We have greatly improved the performance of this external sorting routine by reducing the number of disk accesses needed to merge the subfiles into the final (ordered) file.

The merge pattern of Figure 7-10(b) is not as simple to implement in a program as it appears, however. Two problems get in the way:

1. *Ragged Edge Problem.* Given a memory of size M and a file of size $N \gg M$, one subfile of size $X = N$ **mod** M may result in an unbalanced merge tree. This leads to the second problem.

2. *Unbalanced Merge Tree Problem.* The optimal merge pattern may

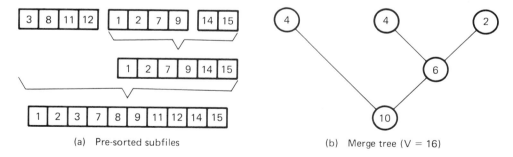

(a) Pre-sorted subfiles

(b) Merge tree (V = 16)

Figure 7-10. Optimal merge for $M = 4$, $N = 10$.

dictate merging two subfiles taken out of sequence. This means added bookkeeping to keep track of the subfiles that have already been merged.

We can avoid both of these problems by careful placement and subfile selection as described next in the optimal merge sort.

Algorithm for optimal merge sort   Let the ragged edge subfile of length $\chi = N \bmod M > 0$ be sorted by an internal sort routine and written to the auxiliary file first. The other subfiles will be of equal size, M. Next, expand the value $\lceil N/M \rceil = b_n \ . \ . \ b_1 b_0$ into a binary string, where b_i is the ith significant bit in $\lceil N/M \rceil$. The value of b_i determines the order of the optimal merge subtrees at stage i of the optimal merge sort. This is used to keep the number of accesses to a minimum by balancing the merge tree.

Step 1. Sort the first $\chi = N \bmod M > 0$ keys internally and write them into the first subfile. (Skip this step if $\chi = 0$.)

Step 2. Sort the remaining subfiles of length M internally and write them to the remaining subfiles.

Step 3. Set the bit counter: $i = 0$.

Step 4. Repeat until all subfiles have been merged:

(a) Merge the first $b_i + 2$ subfiles into one (larger) subfile.
(b) Repeat until the remaining pairs of subfiles have been merged into (larger) subfiles:
    Merge pairs of subfiles.
(c) Increment the bit counter: $i := i + 1$.

Step 5. Report which file (original or auxiliary) contains the ordered list.

This algorithm is illustrated in Figure 7-11 with a file of $N = 103$ keys and available main memory of $M = 5$ keys. The ragged edge subfile is $\chi = 3$ keys long. The binary expansion of $21 = 10101_2$ is shown also.

Notice how the optimal merge sort conveniently keeps the tree balanced by merging three subfiles whenever necessary. The value of this tree is $4(103) = 412$ (because all leaf nodes are at level 4). The value obtained using a straight binary (Huffman) merge tree pattern is $V = 460$. In addition, the straight binary merge tree involves messy accounting to keep track of the smallest sublist, the placement of output subfiles, and so on; whereas the optimal merge sort is simple and fast.

One reason why the optimal merge sort is superior to the straight binary merge tree is that it uses ternary merging once in awhile to keep the tree balanced. Any ternary merge will excel over a binary merge because fewer phases are needed ($\log_3 N$ instead of $\log_2 N$). This suggests another improvement over the optimal merge sort by increasing the order of the

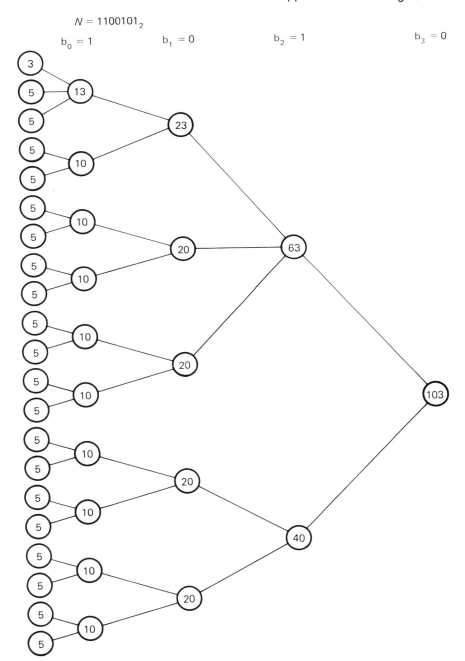

Figure 7-11. Optimal merge sort for $M = 5$, $N = 103$, $x = 3$.

merge tree. In fact, since we have M main memory cells, why not use an M-way merge tree? This is the next topic in our discussion.

Replacement-Selection Technique

An alternative method of external sorting called *replacement-selection* uses the M locations of main memory to hold M keys, one each from M subfiles. Each subfile is part of an M-way merge operation, which always selects the smallest key (MIN) to be output.

The internal list is kept in order by constructing a binary search tree (bst). The value of MIN is always the smallest key in the bst. The pseudocode for replacement-selection is given below.

Step 1. Obtain M ordered subfiles by some means (natural, sorting, etc.).

Step 2. Initially read M keys into main memory, taking the smallest key from each of the M subfiles.

Step 3. Construct a binary search tree (bst) with the M keys and their associated record number pointers (pointing to their location on disk).

Step 4. Repeat until bst is empty:

(a) Remove the smallest key (MIN) from the bst and write it out to the output file.

(b) If not end-of-file, then increment the record number pointer of MIN and read the next key from the subfile corresponding to MIN. Call this new key X.

(c) Insert X into the bst along with its associated record number pointer.

Step 5. M subfiles have been merged into one subfile.

We illustrate the replacement-selection technique using the example of Figure 7-9(b). Figure 7-12(a) shows the original subfiles and the initial contents of the bst (steps 1–3). Figure 7-12(b) shows the bst only for step 4. Notice how each input is taken from the subfile containing the smallest key (MIN). The bst decreases in size each time an end-of-file marker is reached.

The optimal merge tree for a five-way replacement-selection sort of the 21 subfiles of Figure 7-13 takes $V = 206$ accesses to sort $N = 103$ keys. The complete file is sorted in two passes ($\lfloor \log_5 103 \rfloor = 2$). Note how the ragged edge subfile is simply copied without being part of a merge on the first pass.

Replacement-selection sorting uses the full capacity of main memory while minimizing the number of disk accesses. Proper selection of the merge pattern and efficient implementation of the bst in main memory can result in a very high-speed external sorting routine.

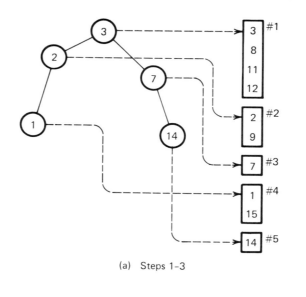

(a) Steps 1–3

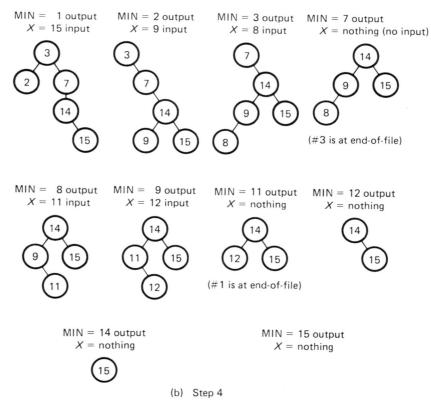

(b) Step 4

Figure 7-12. Five-way replacement-selection sort.

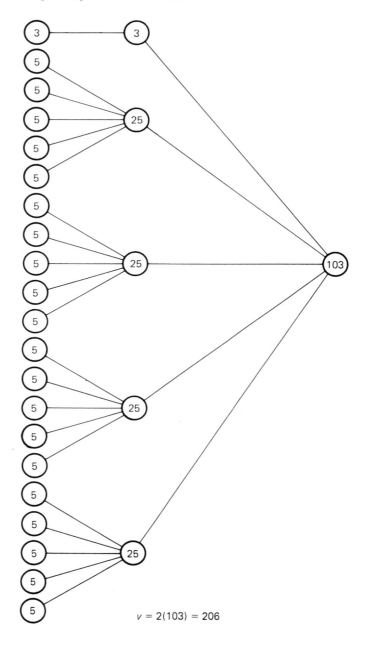

Figure 7-13. Replacement-selection sort for $M = 5$, $N = 103$.

SUMMARY

Sorting routines can be classified into internal and external methods. Internal sorting attempts to minimize the number of operations performed in main memory, whereas external sorting attempts to minimize the number of disk accesses.

Most internal sorting routines are comparative sorts. The fastest known comparative sort is Quickersort. A program for Quickersort (QSORT) is given in Figure 7-6. We showed how QSORT minimizes the number of times each key is moved by exchanging ''large'' and ''small'' keys. The exchange-partition method tends to move keys to ''their right place'' in the list.

Most external sorting routines are based on repetitive merging of previously ordered sublists. We use an internal sorting routine to obtain a collection of ordered sublists, and then we merge them into a final (ordered) list.

The pattern of merging is critical to the performance of external sorting routines. An optimal merge sort is a routine that minimizes the total number of disk accesses by merging the smallest subfiles first.

The optimal merge sort merges two (or three) subfiles into larger subfiles. The replacement-selection sort merges M subfiles at a time by maintaining an internal binary search tree containing pointers to the next input value. The smallest key in the bst is replaced by the next key selected from one of the M subfiles.

The performance of replacement-selection is approximately

$$M \lfloor \log_M N \rfloor$$

where M = size of available memory or the order of the merge

N = size of the original file

This formula does not include the time to sort the subfiles of size M. If Quickersort is used, then M subfiles of size M (approximate) are sorted beforehand, and the total delay is

$$T = M \lfloor \log_M N \rfloor T_a + C_{\text{Qsort}} M^2 \log_2 M$$

where T_a = access time

This formula depends on the characteristics of the specific machine doing the sorting.

PROBLEMS

1. Implement a program to do the optimal external sort routine. Test it using $M = 5$, $N = 103$.

2. Implement a program to do the replacement-selection sort routine. Test it using $M = 5$, $N = 210$.

3. Implement QSORT on your computer. Perform a series of simulation experiments designed to estimate the constant of proportionality for the QSORT performance formula.

4. Certify QSORT using a reverse list, $N = 9$, and LIST $= 9, 8, 7, 6, 5, 4, 3, 2, 1$.

5. When is SELECT a better sorting routine than QSORT?

6. Modify QSORT so that it uses the average value of the first two keys in each sub bst as the value of MID.KEY. Implement your modified algorithm and perform simulation experiments to study the effect of this change. Report your comparison results.

7. Repeat the example shown in Figure 7-7 using the LIST $= 8, 12, 15, 9, 16, 5, 9, 2$.

8. Repeat the example shown in Figure 7-9 (including the optimal merge tree) using the LIST $3, 4, 5, 1, 2, 3, 5, 4, 0, 16, 14, 15$.

9. Repeat the example shown in Figure 7-11 using an original unordered file of $N = 108$ and assuming $M = 5$.

10. Repeat the example of Figure 7-11 using a list of length $N = 49$ and $M = 5$.

11. Repeat the example of Figure 7-12 using the list below (already partitioned into subfiles).

$$\boxed{10, 23, 25, 31}$$

$$\boxed{8, 28, 45}$$

$$\boxed{16}$$

$$\boxed{5, 6, 7, 8}$$

12. Repeat the example of Figure 7-13 using $N = 37$ and $M = 4$.

REFERENCES

Lewis, T. G., and M. Z. Smith, *Applying Data Structures*. Boston: Houghton-Mifflin Company, 1976.

Wirth, Niklaus, *Algorithms + Data Structures = Programs*. Englewood Cliffs, N.J.: Prentice-Hall, Inc., 1976.

8

A Theory of Process

INTRODUCTION

The previous chapters were concerned with the execution of single programs on a single computer. In this chapter we introduce the concept of a *process,* and then extend the ideas of software network, correctness checking, and performance to processes. We go even further by studying the interactions that are possible in multiple-process computer systems.

An important class of software falls into the category of "multiple-process" computer. The most obvious example is any operating system, but perhaps the greatest number of applications is in the areas of real-time control, process control, and other time-critical applications. All of these applications are characterized by time-dependencies that make the job of software engineer much more difficult than do single-process applications.

Before we develop a model of multiple-process software, we must define what we mean by *process,* and then more importantly, what we mean by *concurrent process.* This chapter introduces the reader to concurrent programming, parallel processing concepts, and the rudiments of distributed processing. We will show how software can be encapsulated using special structures. We will also show how the problems of timing lead to synchronization policies in interprocess communication. But first, What *is* a "process"?

Definitions of Process

Perhaps the oldest definition is also the most succinct: "A process is a locus of control within an instruction sequence" (Dennis and Van Horn, p. 145). This definition abstracts the idea of a "control point" moving through some sequence of instructions much like a program counter moves through machine instructions during execution of a program. The definition does *not,* however, directly refer to a program or data.

Clearly, we must associate a process with executable instructions stored somewhere within a computer system. We will also be interested in the effects of a process on data stored somewhere within a computer system. Finally, we will find it difficult to "execute a process" without access to a machine of some sort. That is, in order to give a process some substance, we need the following:

- Executable code.
- Access to data.
- Access to a machine.

Therefore we will define a *process* as the locus of control that results from the execution of an instruction sequence while processing a segment of data within a given machine environment. We will *represent a process* as a 3-tuple as shown in Figure 8-1(a). The process of Figure 8-1(a) executes a sequence of operations as dictated by the code segment, modifies the values stored in its associated data segment, and modifies the environment of the machine that is carrying out the operations performed by the process.

The network model of Figure 8-1(b) is an abstraction of the concept of "locus of control." We imagine a process as shown in Figure 8-1(b) as a "control point" moving from the begin place, through a transition, to another place; see S_1 of Figure 8-1(b). After some elapsed time, the "control point" moves through another transition into the place marked S_2 in Figure 8-1(b), and so on.

Another definition of process includes the notion of multiple processes all of which are executing during various intervals of time: "Two processes are said to be concurrent if their operations can either overlap or interleave arbitrarily in time" (Tausworthe, p. 11). In fact, the possibility of interleaving processes gives rise to the Interleave Principle of design discussed in a later section of this chapter.

We define concurrent processes A and B as follows:

Process A, P_A is concurrent to process B, P_B if no *a priori* order is placed on the locus of control in P_A and P_B. P_B is concurrent to P_A if P_A is concurrent to P_B.

This definition allows for parallelism among processes, but concurrent pro-

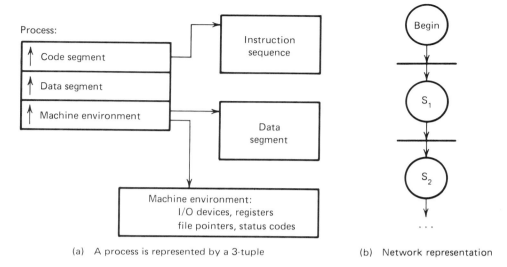

(a) A process is represented by a 3-tuple

(b) Network representation

Figure 8-1. Process models.

cesses are not necessarily parallel. In fact, we must provide multiple machine environments to get parallel execution of two or more processes.

Process P_A is parallel to process P_B if instructions from P_A and P_B are executed in the same time interval. The software networks shown in Figure 8-2 illustrate the subtle difference between concurrent processes and parallel processes.

In Figure 8-2(a) concurrent processes take turns making transitions (performing operations). That is, P_A executes a transition while P_B is idle (in a place), and P_B executes a transition while P_A is idle. Although we have shown P_A and P_B alternating between idle and active, this is not necessary in a system of concurrent processes. We could, for instance, perform several (all) transitions of P_A while P_B is idle. The important thing about concurrent processes is that only one process transition can be executed at a time while all other processes remain idle. This is because all processes must share a single machine environment. This is called *time-multiplexed sharing* of the machine environment.

A system of parallel processes, on the other hand, can simultaneously execute as many transitions as there are machine environments to support parallel execution. Figure 8-2(b) illustrates one possible way to execute two parallel processes. We could also have two or more transitions carried out by P_B while P_A is executing only one transition. The important feature of parallel processes is that they truly execute more than one transition at a time.

Concurrent processes can be time-multiplexed on single-instruction,

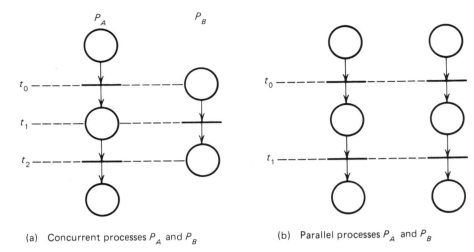

(a) Concurrent processes P_A and P_B

(b) Parallel processes P_A and P_B

Figure 8-2. Concurrent and parallel processes.

single-data stream machines. These are usually referred to as *SISD* systems. We could also design *SIMD* (single-instruction, multiple-data stream) machines, which execute concurrent processes whereby each process transforms multiple-data segments simultaneously. These machines do not increase the parallelism of process execution, but instead increase the parallelism of data that are modified by a single process.

Parallel processes must be executed on machines with multiple-instruction stream capability. An *MIMD* machine (multiple-instruction, multiple-data stream) may be constructed by combining processors into a network, or perhaps by adding processing elements to a common data bus. However, we will not be concerned here with the underlying physical structure of the machine environment.

Process Configurations

The definition of concurrent process does not restrict code or data segments to a single process. On the contrary, we can obtain a locus of control for processes P_A and P_B using identical code segments if we are careful how segments are implemented. In fact, P_A and P_B can safely share the same program if the program is reentrant.

A program is *reentrant* if it executes from a read-only memory and can be executed without dependence on (any) data segment. Reentrant code is code that can be easily separated from the data that it manipulates. If we prohibit modification of code within a program (put it in read-only memory), and if we separate one data segment from another, then many processes can share the same code segment.

There may be cases where it is desirable for the data segments of separate processes to be shared. For example, two processes may have common access to the same file within a filing system. In fact, one way in which two or more processes *communicate* is by sharing data segments or subsets of data segments.

However, there are certain risks involved in sharing data segments. We will study some of the problems of process synchronization that arise because of interprocess communication. Before we delve into these questions further, we will illustrate the variety of process configurations possible through sharing of code and/or data.

Figure 8-3(a) illustrates a process configuration often called *multiprogramming* because several independent programs are time-multiplexed on a single machine. Each process executes its own program and modifies its own data. The only sharing is done by time-multiplexing P_A and P_B on the shared host computer.

Figure 8-3(b) illustrates a process configuration often called an *operating system* or *database system* because processes communicate by overlapping their data segments. The overlapping data segments allow a common area containing data that are accessed by either P_A or P_B, or a message-passing scheme where P_A sends a message to P_B, or vice versa. Actually, the message-passing and common data modes of interprocess communication are distinct styles that lead to a duality principle discussed in detail in a subsequent chapter.

The process configuration of Figure 8-3(c) illustrates what is called *timesharing*. In a timesharing configuration, P_A and P_B share a code segment that must be reentrant. The data, however, are independent, and no communication is allowed. An example of a pure timesharing system is a BASIC language interpreter operating system. The shared code is the interpreter, itself, and the separate data segments contain each user's BASIC source statements. Additional input may be added to the data segments during execution of a user processes; that is the user's input to the BASIC program.

Notice that one consequence of the timesharing configuration is the need for reentrance. Actually, reentrance is simply an economy consideration because we can avoid the reentrant requirement by simply duplicating the code segment for use by each process. This would lead to the same configuration as shown in Figure 8-3(a). Indeed, some operating systems use this approach to accomplish timesharing.

Parts (d) and (e) of Figure 8-3 illustrate two MIMD configurations that support parallel processes P_A and P_B. The tightly coupled configuration refers to the high-speed connection made possible by sharing a main memory or high-speed bus between processors. The loosely coupled configuration refers to the relatively low-speed connection between processes executing on separate processors. In Figure 8-3(e), interprocess

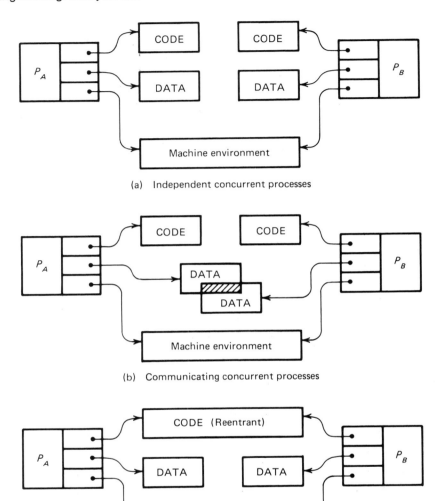

(a) Independent concurrent processes

(b) Communicating concurrent processes

(c) Independent concurrent processes sharing code

Figure 8-3. Process configurations.

communication must be done by message-passing through some sort of network. We will discuss this problem in greater detail.

The variety of configurations illustrated in this section tend to obscure the essential differences in software systems. This need not be the case,

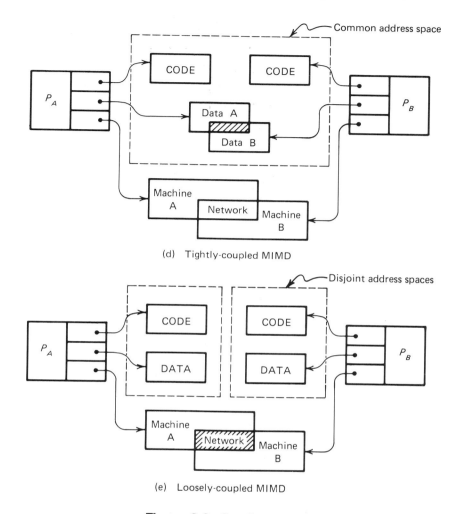

(d) Tightly-coupled MIMD

(e) Loosely-coupled MIMD

Figure 8-3. Continued.

however, if we realize that the key to an understanding of multiple-process systems is an understanding of concurrent versus parallel processes. Furthermore, software is implemented in layers using abstraction at each level to simplify the task of implementation. In the case of concurrent processes, the levels of abstraction simplify implementation by controlling concurrency. We see this most vividly in the design and implementation of a machine environment control program called the *system kernel*.

MACHINE VIRTUALIZATION

A computer system (or subsystem) is said to be *virtualized* if it is somehow extended via an abstract representation that separates the extended system from its real machine resources. Virtualization is a mapping from an abstract level onto a concrete level within a multilevel interpretive system. Actually, the "real" machine refers to a lower level of abstraction (more concrete), and the "virtual" system refers to a higher level of abstraction.

A common example of virtualization is provided by a high-level language. The abstract or virtual system of Pascal, for example, is the syntax and semantics of Pascal. The "real" machine is the code produced by the Pascal compiler. Thus,

$$X := (A + B) \textbf{ div } 3 \text{ ;}$$

is a statement in the virtual level, and the following instructions

```
PUSH A   ; put A on a stack
PUSH B   ; put B on a stack
ADD      ; A + B
PUSH #3  ; put #3 on the stack
DIV      ; (A + B) div 3
POP X    ; store result in X
```

are the corresponding statements in the real machine level. The *P*-code interpreter executes these instructions by performing real machine operations PUSH, POP, DIV, ADD, etc.

The *P*-code interpreter may itself be a virtual system for some lower-level interpreter. Hence, the real machine that interprets *P*-code may actually be a (software) program. This is the idea in multilevel interpretive systems.

Multilevel interpretation plays a significant role in the design of (correct) multiple-process systems. We will use abstraction as a means of encapsulating concurrent processes in order to structure them. This structure will be a big help in guaranteeing correctly implemented concurrent programs.

Levels of Abstraction

We use the following levels of abstraction to control concurrency in a system of communicating processes:

I. Machine environment-to-Pseudodata
Example: I/O registers-to-memory variables
II. Pseudodata-to-encapsulation
Example: **type** X = **record** A,B : **integer end** ;

III. Encapsulation-to-objects
   Example: **type** X = **object**

Level I virtualization   The first step in virtualization of a "real" machine is to absorb the machine environment into the data segment. This is done by memory-mapped I/O, naming, or other means, as shown in Figure 8-4. The machine environment includes working registers, program counter, I/O registers, and miscellaneous run-time resources typically used to execute a program (stack, pointers, etc.). These resources are virtualized by naming them and in many cases making copies of them so that each process "owns" its own copy of pseudodata. The result of this level of virtualization is that the machine environment can be treated as part of a data segment like any other data segment.

A machine environment is shared by sharing its pseudodata abstraction. Thus, working registers, I/O devices, and the like are shared by giving them pseudodata names like GPR (general purpose register), and CONSOLE, DISK, PRINTER, etc.

Level II virtualization   The second level of virtualization attempts to extend the pseudodata level to the encapsulation level. An encapsulated pseudodata resource is an *abstract data type* defined as follows:

1. An abstract data type is a storage region (address space) along with the permissible operations performed on the storage region.

2. Encapsulation of pseudodata is done by enclosing data or pseudodata within an abstract data type.

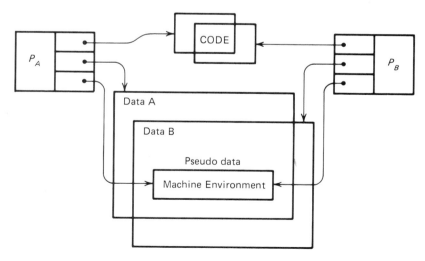

Figure 8-4. Machine environment virtualization.

The notion of encapsulation can be applied to a variety of resources in a computer system. For example, we might view a processor as a single encapsulated level. The main memory is the storage region, and the permissible operations are equated with the instruction set of the processor.

We will use encapsulation as a means of controlling the interrupt structure of a processor. The interrupt structure is a natural focal point because processes are time-multiplexed by way of the interrupt structure of a processor. Processes may even by activated by interrupts in an interrupt-driven software system.

The *kernel* of a processor is an encapsulation of the interrupt structure that

1. Defines the interrupt service routines as the permissible operations on the storage region encapsulated by the kernel.

2. Defines the pseudodata (machine resources) commonly associated with the privileged mode of operation as the storage region encapsulated by the kernel.

Combining levels of virtualization   Combining pseudodata and abstract data type virtualization leads to an extended machine that removes the interrupt structure from view. Therefore, it is the duty of the kernel to multiplex concurrent processes by scheduling them when they are ready to run, and preempting them when they are blocked (or need to be blocked for the purpose of synchronization). This leads to levels of interaction between the kernel and communicating processes as shown in Figure 8-5.

In Figure 8-5 three processes are time-multiplexed by the system kernel. The three processes have access to the kernel through the interrupt structure. A processs "calls" the kernel by causing an interrupt to occur. The kernel "fields" the interrupt by performing the desired operation on its pseudodata and then returning control to one of the processes.

The three processes of Figure 8-5 communicate by sharing access to data segments. The outer rims of the process wheel indicate the sharing of data between P_A and P_C, for example.

The kernel is a *monolithic abstract data type* because one and only one process is allowed to execute a kernel operation at a time. This is an important feature of the kernel and is the "handle" to process synchronization.

We have discussed two levels of virtualization that serve to structure concurrency so that we can correctly implement communicating processes. A very special level of virtualization encapsulates a machine's interrupt structure and is called the kernel. Only the service routines of the kernel are allowed as abstract data type operations. Hence, the kernel is a small collection of access routines that separate all other pro-

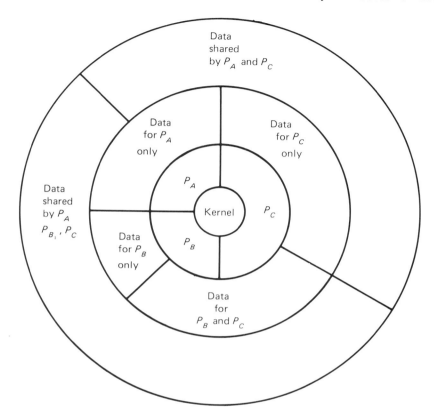

Figure 8-5. Encapsulation "wheel" for P_A, P_B, and P_C.

cesses from one another. An example of combined levels of virtualization is given below to illustrate one use of these concepts.

Example of virtualization Suppose we study a simple system with a single processor, main memory, and two I/O devices (we will call them *terminals*) that must communicate with one another through a buffer. We further assume the I/O subsystem is interrupt-driven; i.e., the terminals generate interrupts when ready to transmit data to the buffer.

Figure 8-6 illustrates the simple system containing terminals T1 and T2 along with the required I/O registers (STATUS and DATA), buffer, and user processes P_1 and P_2. The interrupt service routines are encapsulated inside the kernel that encloses all pseudodata for this system.

Figure 8-7 shows more detail of the encapsulation for the simple system. The pseudodata (level I virtualization) variables include all data that are under the exclusive control of the kernel. Only the operations defined by the kernel are allowed access to the pseudodata variables. There-

EXAMPLE: Simple Machine

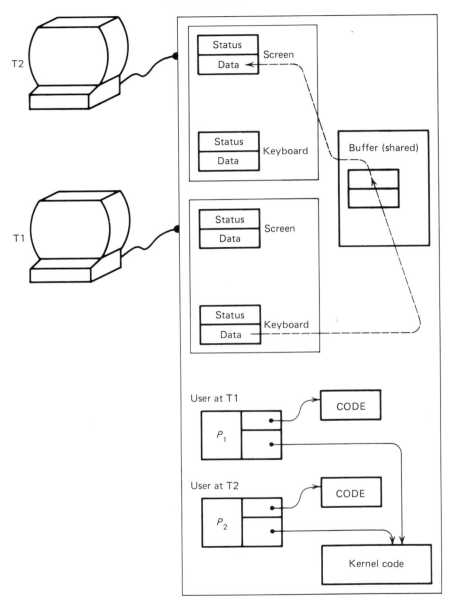

Figure 8-6. Two users communicate via a shared buffer.

Kernel Code and Pseudodata

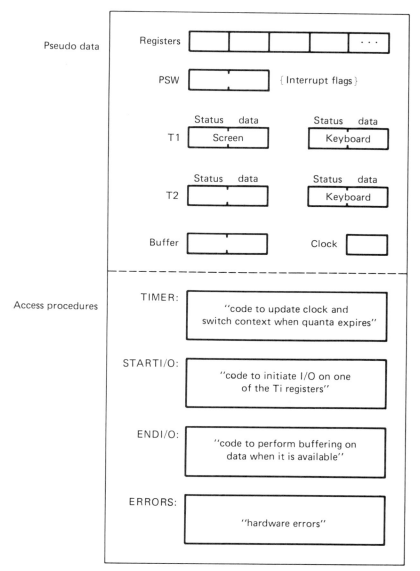

Figure 8-7. Encapsulation for example in Figure 8-6.

fore, users P_1 and P_2 must invoke the kernel on their behalf in order to access (indirectly) the terminal I/O registers or the shared buffer.

In Figure 8-7, note the TIMER service routine and the CLOCK pseudodata variable. They are part of the interrupt structure that the kernel encapsulates to time-multiplex multiple processes on a single (virtualized) processor.

Suppose terminal T1 desires to send a message to terminal T2. Process P_1 initiates an I/O operation by calling kernel routine STARTIO. When a character from T1's keyboard is generated (the user depresses a key), it enters the pseudodata variable T1.KEYBOARD.DATA, sets T1.KEYBOARD.STATUS to 'ready,' and generates an interrupt (ENDIO) that is fielded by the kernel. The ENDIO operation copies the character into the BUFFER and signals to T1 so that P_1 can produce another character (T1.KEYBOARD,STATUS = 'done').

Meanwhile, process P_2 may be waiting for the buffer to fill so that it can copy the message from the buffer onto the screen of T2. But what prevents P_2 from reading the buffer *before* the character from T1 is placed in the buffer? To solve this problem we must add two *synchronization* operations to the kernel.

Let kernel operations WAITFOR and GOAHEAD be blocking and unblocking operations, respectively. The WAITFOR(C) operation suspends any process that executes it unless C signals to continue. If C allows continuation, the WAITFOR operation has no effect on the process. The GOAHEAD(C) operation has no effect on a process as long as no other process is waiting for C. However, if a previously executed WAITFOR(C) operation has suspended a process, then GOAHEAD(C) causes the waiting process to execute before the process that called GOAHEAD is allowed to continue. In other words, GOAHEAD(C) suspends the process that called it whenever another process is waiting for C.

The additions necessary for implementing WAITFOR and GOAHEAD in the kernel of the example might appear as follows:

```
const
  N = 80 ; (* size of buffer *)
var
  IN, OUT, COUNT : O . . N ; (* counters *)
  NONEMPTY, NONFUL : signals ; (* condition C *)
  BUFFER : array [1 . . N] of char ; (* the buffer *)
kernel operation RECEIVE (var CH : char) ;
  begin
    if COUNT = 0 then WAITFOR (NONEMPTY) ;
    CH := BUFFER [OUT];
    OUT := (OUT mod N) + 1;
    COUNT := COUNT − 1;
    GOAHEAD(NONFULL) ;
  end
```

```
kernel operation ENDIO ;
  begin
    if COUNT = N then WAITFOR (NONFULL) ;
    BUFFER[IN] := T1.KEYBOARD.DATA ;
    IN := (IN mod N) + 1;
    COUNT := COUNT + 1;
    GOAHEAD(NONEMPTY);
  end
```

The variables IN, OUT, and COUNT must be initially set to:

$$IN := 1 ; OUT := 1$$
$$COUNT := 0$$

before the encapsulated system is used. Now we can continue with the example.

The ENDIO operation causes process P_1 (the sender) to wait for signal NONFULL whenever the buffer is full (COUNT=N). The RECEIVE operation causes process P_2 to wait for signal NONEMPTY whenever the buffer is empty. P_2 eventually works its way to the GOAHEAD operation, which signals NONFULL and permits the blocking of WAITFOR(NONFULL) to become unblocking. In this way the kernel has enforced correct access of the BUFFER by two processes P_1 and P_2. Recall that only one process can execute a kernel operation at any instant in time; so we need not be concerned with possible "race" conditions that might arise if these routines were shared (reentrant).

The RECEIVE/ENDIO example is an illustration of a *producer-consumer* problem commonly encountered in real-time software. We will devote subsequent chapters to futher examination of various producer-consumer problems. Before we do so, however, we must expand the theory of processes to include the notion of *state*.

Process State Diagram

The earlier definition of a process serves well when used in the abstract sense, but we have shown several examples where the defintion becomes obscured by levels of virtualization, kernels, and kernel operations like WAITFOR and GOAHEAD. It is not clear, for example, how a process progresses through time when waylaid by a WAITFOR. Indeed, we have not shown the effect of a WAITFOR operation on a process. To do this, we need a greater understanding of processes and a new concept called the *state of a process*.

Process state A process may interact with other processes by communicating through shared (pseudo) data. In order to do so, communicating processes must slow or stop one another in order to synchronize their access to shared data with respect to one another. Therefore, a model of processes must include time variations as well as code and data variations. In short, a process model must include the *state* of (1) a code segment, (2) a data segment, and (3) time—in order to be a viable tool in analyzing concurrent processes.

The *state of a process* P is the combined state of its code segment, data segment, and *timing relative to the kernel* that manages the process. We define each one of these states in the following equation:

$$\text{STATE}(P) = \text{Union of } \{\text{STATE(C), STATE(D), and STATE(T)}\}$$

where

STATE(C) = state of code segment. This is defined in the software network for the code executed by process P. The states of the code C are its *places* in the software network.

STATE(D) = state of data segment. This is defined by the values of each (all) variable in the data segment. We will abbreviate this state by concentrating on the shared variables only.

STATE(T) = timing relative to the kernel. This is defined in terms of the places in the state diagram shown in Figure 8-8. The value of this function is either RUNNING, READY, BLOCKED, KERNEL, BEGIN, or END.

The state diagram of Figure 8-8 shows how process P moves through time relative to the encapsulated kernel. First, P enters the system from the BEGIN state by making the START transition. It stays in the READY state until the kernel moves it into the RUNNING state. It may remain in the READY state for an arbitrary period of time.

The process continues to execute while in the RUNNING state. During this time, P moves through states defined by STATE(C) (its code segment), and STATE(D) (its data segment). The software network of code segment C defines these states (more on this later).

Eventually P is interrupted by a clock or other interrupt, and P enters the kernel state. While in the kernel state, P executes one or more kernel operations. For example, if the interrupt was due to a clock TIMER trap, the kernel operation called TIMER would be executed by P. This causes P to be put back in the READY state, and some other process is selected to enter the RUNNING state (begin executing).

The process may also be interrupted because it executes a WAITFOR or GOAHEAD operation. In this case, P is blocked as shown in Figure 8-8. Alternatively, the process may enter the BLOCKED state because of an interrupt that causes P to be preempted.

Finally, P may terminate; in which case it enters the END state and then leaves the system.

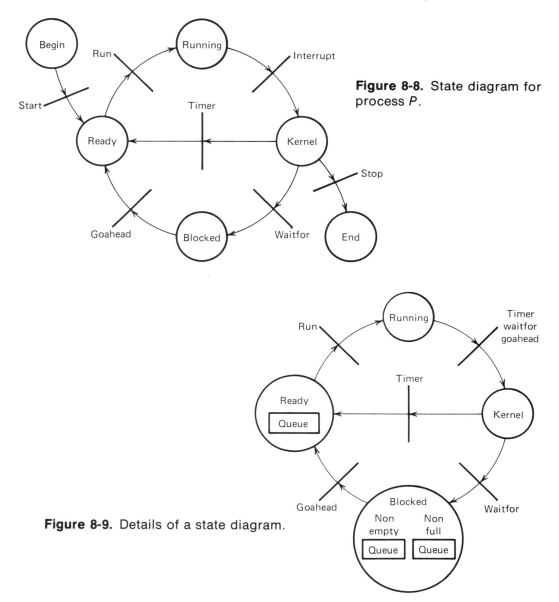

Figure 8-8. State diagram for process *P*.

Figure 8-9. Details of a state diagram.

The states of Figure 8-8 correspond to data structures for holding processes. For example, the state diagram of Figure 8-9 shows how the sample system discussed in Figures 8-6 and 8-7 might appear in process state diagram form. The blocking queues corresponding to the conditions NONEMPTY and NONFULL hold either P_1 or P_2 while awaiting a liberating GOAHEAD.

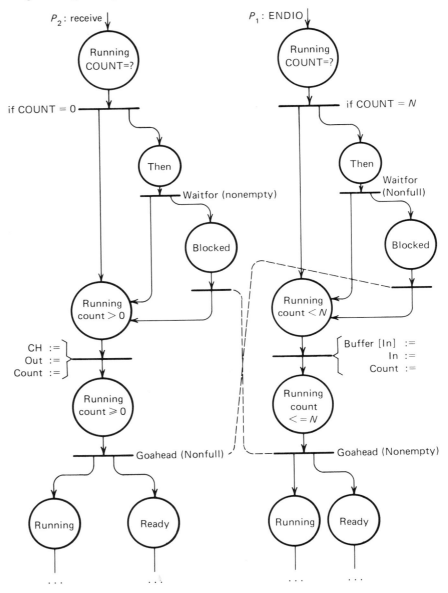

Figure 8-10. Software network for Figures 8-6 and 8-7.

Each time a process enters a state it is enqueued and moves toward the head of its queue until it is dequeued. The example of Figure 8-9 shows two blocking queues that hold processes P_1 and P_2. The WAITFOR (NONEMPTY) operation causes the RUNNING process to be enqueued on the NONEMPTY queue. The GOAHEAD (NONEMPTY) operation causes the first process at the head of the queue labeled NONEMPTY to be removed and put in the READY queue. Finally, a process waiting in the READY queue works its way to the head of the READY queue and then is dequeued and put in the RUNNING state.

The interaction between the processes P_1 and P_2 and the encapsulation studied in Figures 8-6 and 8-7 is shown in Figure 8-10. The software networks for P_1 and P_2 are shown for loci of control through ENDIO and RECEIVE, respectively. The dotted line connects the synchronizing transitions brought about by the kernel. Each place is labeled with pertinent state information as shown: RUNNING, READY, BLOCKED, and the variables of interest COUNT.

P_2 executes the RECEIVE code and finds COUNT equal to zero. Therefore, P_2 is blocked by WAITFOR (NONEMPTY). This causes the kernel to suspend P_2 on the NONEMPTY queue until a GOAHEAD (NONEMPTY) releases P_2. The GOAHEAD operation may not be executed immediately, however.

In the meantime, P_1 executes the ENDIO code and remains in the RUNNING state until it executes the GOAHEAD (NONEMPTY) operation. This causes P_1 to be suspended and P_2 to be unblocked. That is, the kernel *interprets* the GOAHEAD operation for P_1, and P_2 is unblocked by removing it from the NONEMPTY queue and enqueueing it in the READY queue. Then P_1 is put in the READY queue *behind* P_2. Thus, as the kernel dequeues another process from the READY queue, P_2 is eventually allowed to execute before P_1. P_2 continues execution through its RUNNING states until it reaches its GOAHEAD (NONFULL) operation. At this point the cycle starts again.

The example above assumes that P_1 and P_2 both run at maximum speed. This is not the case in general, however, because other processes may intervene and delay either P_1 or P_2. Therefore, we cannot presume an ordering or a priori synchronization of P_1 with respect to P_2. In fact, we must constantly guard against making *any* timing assumptions when analyzing concurrent processes. There is only one assumption that we will need in order to prove concurrent programs correct—that the transitions of a software network are performed atomically; i.e., they are primitive and cannot be divided into operations that could be executed in separate time intervals. This is the fundamental rule underlying the Interleave Principle studied in the final section of this chapter.

DISTRIBUTED KERNELS

The encapsulation of the pseudodata and interrupt structure of a single processor leads to a simplication in the design of concurrent programs. The same encapsulation also leads to a simplification in the design of highly parallel processor systems characterized by distributed processing. Indeed, we can virtualize a network of distributed processors by encapsulation of each processor. This leads to the concept of a system of distributed kernels.

Process Migration

We have discussed how communicating processes are time-multiplexed on a single processor by an encapsulation called the *kernel*. Now, we are faced with a collection of kernels, each executing in parallel on its own separate processor. Figure 8-11 illustrates how a distributed system of kernels might appear logically in a system of N processing sites.

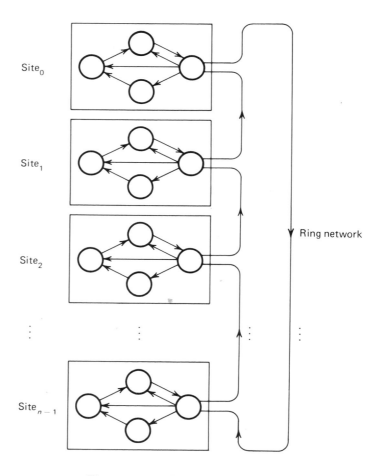

Figure 8-11. Distributed kernels.

In Figure 8-11 we assume identical kernels in each site. The kernels operate just as before, but with three more functions added to their abstract data type operations:

NSEND (message)
NRECEIVE (message)
NCALL (parameters)

The first two of these network operations are "called" by the interrupt structure of each processor. An interrupt from the network interface causes the kernel to perform a NRECEIVE operation, which receives a message from the network and copies it into the "message" argument of NRECEIVE. The NSEND operation is used to send a message from the kernel to another kernel.

The NCALL (parameters) operation is a procedure call mechanism used by an executing program to call a procedure in another processor site. Any process P that executes on kernel K_i is considered a *local process*. Any process Q that executes on another kernel K_j is considered a *remote process*. We designate $P@K_i$ as a local process running under the control of kernel K_i. The NCALL operation provides a way for a local process to call a remote procedure. Let us illustrate this idea by way of an example.

We imagine process $P@K_1$ executing until it calls a remote procedure under the control of kernel K_2 of site 2. Process $P@K_1$ issues

NCALL(K_2, 'card-reader(CARD)') ;

which requests an 80-column card to be read by the "card-reader" procedure on processor two. The NCALL results in a message that must be transmitted to K_2 by K_1. Kernel K_1 does the following on behalf of $P@K_1$:

1. P is suspended by K_1 and put in a blocking queue to await the return message.

2. K_1 sends the request 'card-reader(CARD)' to K_2 using the NSEND operation.

3. K_1 selects another process Q from the READY queue to take the place of P in the RUNNING state.

4. Processor 1 resumes execution of process Q.

At this point in the scenario, P is BLOCKED, Q is RUNNING, and a message has been sent to kernel K_2. After some delay, K_2 is interrupted and is forced to execute its NRECEIVE operation. The kernel at site 2 must process the remote call by activating a substitute process P' on behalf of process P. We say P' is a *clone* of P because it is an exact copy of P, but it runs as if it were a local process under control of K_2. This is what happens at site 2:

5. The currently RUNNING process is interrupted for long enough to execute NRECEIVE. This code causes K_2 to enqueue P' on the READY queue of site 2.

6. The interrupted process resumes execution and eventually either terminates, becomes blocked, or runs out of time.

7. Kernel K_2 repeatedly schedules RUNNING processes until P' is placed in the RUNNING state. P' is time-multiplexed just like any other local process until it finishes executing 'card-reader(CARD).'

8. The value of CARD is computed by the procedure 'card-reader.' Kernel K_2 uses NSEND to return this value back to K_1.

9. Kernel K_2 destroys the clone process P'.

The remote kernel K_2 has done what $P@K_1$ requested. The message containing CARD is returned via the network and kernel K_1 is interrupted:

10. Kernel K_1 is interrupted and processes the return message by executing NRECEIVE.

11. The waiting process P is unblocked, matched with its parameter CARD, and enqueued in the READY list.

12. After working to the head of the READY list, process P is allowed to resume RUNNING. This means P continues execution immediately following the invocation of card-reader:

```
P :(* executable code *)
CARD-READER(CARD);
(* resume after remote call *)
```

This detailed scenario demonstrates the migration of a process from one processor to another. Actually, a clone process was created at K_2 to represent P while the remote call was interpreted by K_2. This method of remote call makes process migration appear to be no different than message-passing. Indeed, we claim that this method is no different from procedure invocation as far as the process is concerned:

Remote Procedure Call: A process P executing on a processor under control of kernel K_1 performs a remote procedure call by message-passing rather than parameter-passing, process cloning rather than procedure activation, and process blocking rather than procedure return mechanisms. However, to the programmer, a remote procedure call is no different than an ordinary (local) procedure call.

This view of distributed kernel encapsulation is a great intellectual aid because it means we can analyze single-processor concurrent programs and multiple-processor parallel programs in like fashion using identical software tools. We need not make exceptions merely because processes are allowed to migrate from one processor to another. In short, we have simplified the study of distributed systems to the study of concurrent processes.

We are now in a position to discuss one of the most useful tools used to analyze concurrent programs, whether they be distributed or centralized. We turn next to the final refinement of the process model.

THE INTERLEAVE PRINCIPLE

A process is modeled by a software network where the transitions in the software network correspond to primitive operations executed by the code segment, and the places correspond to: (1) the state of the process prior to the execution of the next instruction, (2) the values of (shared) data computed by the process up to the point of the place, and (3) the state of the process relative to the kernel, e.g., RUNNING, BLOCKED, READY, or KERNEL.

Suppose we use the following code segments for processes P_A and P_B to illustrate the model. We assume variable B is the name of a shared datum (see Figure 8-12). Thus,

```
process P_A                    process P_B
   var A,B : integer ;            var X,B : integer ;
   begin                          begin
      A:=0 ;                         X:=1 ;
      B:=A ;                         B:=X ;
   end                            end
```

Figure 8-12(b) shows *possible* loci of control through the states of P_A and P_B. The processes begin in the READY state and move asynchronously to the RUNNING state. Since only one process at a time can be in the RUNNING state on a single processor, we must arbitrarily select either P_A or P_B to execute first. That is, P_A and P_B *nondeterministically* transit from the READY state to the RUNNING state and back again. In such cases we say the loci of control are *nondeterministic*.

When either P_A or P_B enters the RUNNING state and executes one or more primitive operations like A:=0 or X:=1, the state of each data segment is changed. The networks of Figure 8-12(b) show the values of A, B, and X after each transition. We have drawn these networks to reflect the *possible timings* between P_A and P_B. Other timings are possible; for example, P_A could run from start to stop without passing through the READY state between execution of A:=0 and B:=A.

The most interesting feature of this example is the effect of timing on the outcome of variable B. The value of B is zero if P_A computes $B:=A$

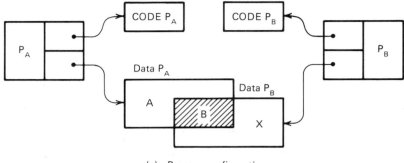

(a) Process configuration

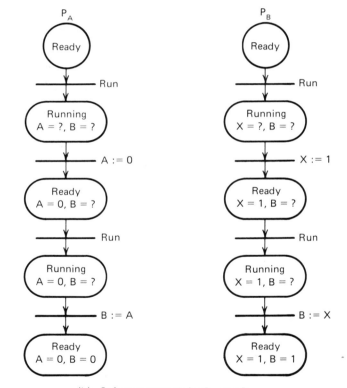

(b) Software network for P_A and P_B

Figure 8-12. Communicating processes P_A and P_B.

after P_B computes $B:=X$. Alternatively, B is one if P_B computes $B:=X$ *after* P_A completes $B:=A$.

If we impose some control on P_A and B_B such that P_A *always* waits for P_B to complete its RUNNING state, then B will always be one. This leads to a deterministic outcome for B. If, as the example shows, we impose only nondeterminism on the loci of control for P_A and P_B, then the outcome of B is sometimes zero and sometimes one. Indeed, we cannot be sure of the outcome for B any time P_A and P_B execute. Thus, we say the value of B is *indeterminate*, and the two processes execute code that leads to indeterminism.

In nearly all applications of concurrent programming, indeterminism is an undesirable side effect of concurrency. In fact, we strive to remove indeterminism from concurrent programs by careful design and implementation of locks. This is the subject of the next chapter.

How do we know that a system of processes like P_A and P_B lead to indeterminate values in shared data? The Interleave Principle is a method of checking concurrent programs for incorrect functioning due to timing problems like the one illustrated above. Before we can apply the Interleave Principle, however, we need to define the process-state matrix.

The Process-State Matrix

Let processes P_A and P_B have code segment software networks represented by Petri networks where the places correspond to states and the transitions correspond to primitive (indivisible in time) operations. Then P_A and P_B are interleaved by merging the two software networks such that a *combined* network results:

$$P_A \text{ interleave } P_B \equiv P_A \times P_B$$
$$\equiv \{(a_i, b_j)\}$$

where a_i, i in $[1 \ . \ . \ n]$ and b_j, j in $[1 \ . \ . \ m]$ are the primitive operations of processes P_A and P_B, respectively.

P_A *interleave* P_B means that all possible timings of P_A and P_B are taken into consideration by interleaving primitive operations from the two processes. That is, we can select a_1 from P_A; then any number of operations from P_B, say b_1; b_2; b_3; and then a_2; a_3; and so on, until P_A and P_B have been completely executed.

As an example, consider the following possibilities for the example in Figure 8-12:

(a) $A:=0$ (This leads to $B=1$.)   (b) $A:=0$ (This leads to $B=0$.)
    $B:=A$ $X:=1$
    $X:=1$ $B:=X$
    $B:=X$ $B:=A$

In this example, only two of six possible patterns are shown, but if we use a *process-state matrix* as shown in Figure 8-13, we can study all six of the interleaved executions of P_A and P_B.

In Figure 8-13 we define a *path* as any combined loci of control through P_A and P_B. A path begins in row 1, column 1 (upper-left hand square), and moves either down or to the right, one transition at a time. Notice the following (exhaustive) paths:

(ROW, COL)

#1: (1 , 1)
     (1 , 2)
     (1 , 3)
     (1 , 3)
     (3 , 3)

#2   (1 , 1)
     (1 , 2)
     (2 , 2)
     (2 , 3)
     (3 , 3)

#3   (1 , 1)
     (1 , 2)
     (2 , 2)
     (3 , 2)
     (3 , 3)

#4   (1 , 1)
     (2 , 1)
     (2 , 2)
     (2 , 3)
     (3 , 3)

#5   (1 , 1)
     (2 , 1)
     (2 , 2)
     (3 , 2)
     (3 , 3)

#6   (1 , 1)
     (2 , 1)
     (3 , 1)
     (3 , 2)
     (3 , 3)

A path is restricted to move either vertically or horizontally. It cannot cross two transitions diagonally because each transition is executed atomically. A diagonal move corresponds to parallel execution of two primi-

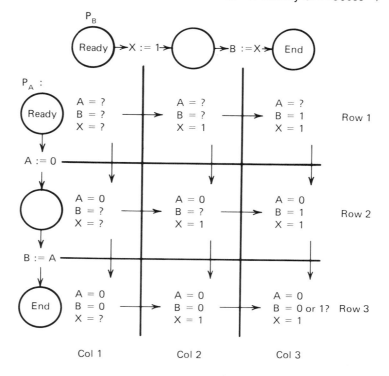

Figure 8-13. Process-state matrix for P_A and P_B.

tive operations. Since only one primitive operation can be executed at a time, diagonal moves are not allowed.

Also notice that the paths are defined by the software network of each process. A path cannot exist unless it corresponds to the locus of control of one of the processes. If we move horizontally, the path must follow the locus of control for the "horizontal" process. If we move vertically, the path corresponds to the locus of control of the "vertical" process.

A path defines a sequence of transitions from one combined state of two processes to another combined state of two processes. Thus, the squares in Figure 8-13 hold all necessary state information for the combined processes P_A and P_B. Indeed, the variables in Figure 8-13 are called the *process-state variables* because their values define the current (combined) state of the system of processes.

A combined state, or simply "state," is *reachable* in the process-state matrix if a path from (1,1) leads to the state. A reachable state is *nondeterministic* if two or more paths lead to it. A state is *indeterministic* if two or more paths lead to it and upon reaching the state, the state variables are indeterminate.

State (2,2) in Figure 8-13 is an example of a nondeterministic state because it can be reached by several paths. State (3,3), however, is indeterminate because its state variable B is indeterminate.

We will strive to remove indeterminate states from the set of reachable states by proper synchronization of concurrent processes. To do so, we must impose synchronization policies on the concurrent processes.

Synchronization Policies

A *synchronization policy* is a set of conditions that must be met by paths defined in a process-state matrix. A *synchronization mechanism* is a program (or hardware device) that enforces a synchronization policy. Examples of synchronization mechanisms discussed in this book are:

Spin locks
Memory interlock
Software encapsulation (monitors)
Message-passing ports
Path expressions
Semaphores (P-V operations)

A synchronization policy restricts the reachability of states in a system of concurrent processes. This is done in a variety of ways, but all methods of synchronization result in constraining the allowable paths through the process-state matrix. Indeed, we can define the main features of synchronization in terms of the allowed paths in *any* process-state matrix (see list below). Let *PS* be a process-state matrix, then a synchronization policy is:

SAFE. Synchronization is said to be *safe* if indeterminism is removed from *PS* by forcing the indeterminate states to be unreachable; i.e., no path leads to an indeterminate state.

FAIR. Synchronization is said to be *fair* if all processes in *PS* are eventually allowed to execute to completion, given that each process is periodically activated. A process *P* is said to be *starved* if there exists a timing pattern that prevents *P* from completing even though it may execute its code segment from time to time.

LIVE. Synchronization is said to be *live* if no reachable state exists such that all paths leaving the state are blocked permanently. Otherwise, synchronization is said to be *deadlock prone*.

The *fair* attribute deserves further explanation. It is very possible that one process might starve another process by executing slightly faster than the other one. If this should occur, it would show up in *PS* as a cyclic path that constantly prevents completion of the starved process, even though the starved process is allowed to execute.

Fairness is a common occurrence in everyday life. For example, suppose customers are waiting to be served at an ice cream store. The second customer might be starved by the first customer if customer #1 was fast enough to:

1. Buy ice cream,
2. Eat the ice cream, and
3. Return to the counter

before customer #2 could approach the counter and ask for service. The first customer might move at high speed while the second customer repeatedly walks to the counter, only to be turned away. Hence, the starved customer spends an eternity trying to get service but always ends up waiting for the faster customer.

Admittedly, starvation may be a rarity in a system of concurrent processes, but we must check for it anyway. The *PS* matrix will reveal starvation as an indefinite postponement of one process by another process that makes repeated passes through the *PS* matrix. Numerous examples of this are shown in the next chapter.

The defnition of *liveness* is also deserving of elaboration. A system of processes can mutually block one another in a manner that causes two or more processes to be "stuck" in a combined state. When this happens, it shows up in the *PS* matrix as a path(s) that cannot leave a state. This typically happens whenever the competing processes are waiting for each other to release control over shared data. Since the competing processes are BLOCKED, they cannot become RUNNING, and so they cannot release their hold on the shared data.

A system of processes is *deadlock prone* if a deadlock state is reachable in the *PS* matrix. Therefore, we will constantly look for deadlock states and paths leading to deadlock states in the *PS* matrix. If no deadlock states exist in the *PS* matrix, then we say the *PS* matrix is *live*.

The examples and counterexamples of Figure 8-14 illustrate possible patterns of *PS* matrix paths. In Figure 8-14(a), indeterminism is avoided by blocking all paths leading to the indeterminate state. In Figure 8-14(b), process P_1 starves P_2 because P_1 quickly reenters the *PS* matrix before P_2 can move horizontally. Such a pattern may be rare, but it cannot be ignored.

In Figure 8-14(e), deadlock can occur if the two processes end up in the deadlock state. Since no path leads out of the deadlock state, both processes are blocked forever. Notice that other paths lead to completion because they do not attempt to pass through the deadlock state. Deadlock may be rare, but it cannot be ignored.

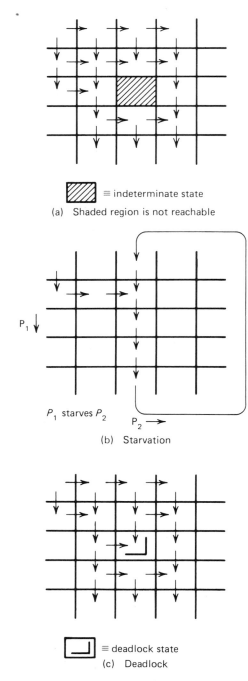

(a) Shaded region is not reachable

(b) Starvation

(c) Deadlock

Figure 8-14. Examples of safe access, starvation, and deadlock.

SUMMARY

We have developed a model and a technique for analyzing concurrent processes. The model is a simple extension of the Petri network model of programs developed earlier. However, the software network of a process contains much more information about the process than does a software network of a program.

A process is a locus of control where the locus is defined by a code segment. A process also has state information. We used the state of a process's data segment and relative timing information to define the state of a process. The idea is simple: the state of a process is the value of is data plus its timing relative to an underlying kernel.

We have also used a form of virtualization to simplify time-multiplexing of processes on a real processor. The kernel of a system of concurrent processes is an encapsulation of pseudodata (virtual machine resources) and operations that only the kernel is allowed to perform. A kernel is an abstract data type with the power to change the state of any other process in the system of processes. For this reason we sometimes consider the kernel a *privileged process* that supervises all other processes.

Virtualization through pseudodata is a method of great intellectual significance. We can ignore all machine level details, e.g., registers, I/O devices, etc., by moving them into the data segment of every process. This means the kernel must map these virtual resources into real resources each time a process enters the RUNNING state. This is done by simply saving registers and other machine resources each time a process leaves the RUNNING state, and then restoring these values each time the process enters the RUNNING state.

The notion of virtualization and encapsulation of the interrupt structure and pseudodata of each processor in a distributed system of processors leads to the concept of distributed kernels. We showed that the problems associated with a collection of distributed kernels can be reduced to the familiar problems of concurrent processes by suitable message-passing and process migration. A local process migrates to a remote processor kernel. The remote kernel "clones" an exact duplicate of the original process for the length of time needed to perform the requested processing. Once the clone has done its job, it is destroyed and its results are sent back to the original process. The original process is then activated and continues as before.

The importance of process migration in a system of distributed kernels is this: We need not invent new language structures to use the distributed system. Existing software can execute on a distributed system by using existing procedure-call and parameter-passing mechanisms as the fundamental message-passing mechanism. The supporting kernel interprets remote calls without notification or bother. This concept is central to distributed processing concepts discussed in later chapters.

Finally, we have developed an Interleave Principle and process-state matrix to be used to test concurrent programs. We can decide if a synchronization mechanism is safe, live, and fair using the Interleave Principle. We need safe access to shared data so that no indeterminism results. We need live access so that no deadlock occurs. We need fair access so that one process cannot indefinitely postpone another process. These three features of a "good" synchronization policy are used to evaluate a number of synchronization mechanisms in subsequent chapters.

PROBLEMS

1. What is a *process? Concurrent process? Parallel process?*

2. Define *SISD, SIMD,* and *MIMD.*

3. Draw a process configuration similar to the configuration in Figure 8-3 for a system of three processes: P_A, P_B, and P_C. Let P_A and P_B share reentrant code, and P_B and P_C share variable X. What do you call this configuration?

4. Give examples of tightly coupled and loosely coupled computer systems.

5. What is an *abstract data type?* How is it used in this chapter?

6. Give an encapsulation wheel like the one in Figure 8-5 for the example in Figure 8-12.

7. Draw a process-state matrix for the two processes shown in Figure 8-10.

8. Draw a system of distributed kernels like the one shown in Figure 8-11 for a network shaped like a star, e.g., one central processing site with spokes radiating out to $(n - 1)$ other processing sites.

9. Draw the state diagrams for two kernels (K_A and K_B) that support the following process activation:

$$P_A : \text{Read-card(CARD)};$$

Here we assume P_A is local to kernel K_A and the code for Read-card is local to kernel K_B. Show all steps in the process migration from K_A to K_B and back.

10. Construct the *PS* matrix for

$$P_A : \textbf{begin} \qquad\qquad P_B : \textbf{begin}$$
$$X := A + B \qquad\qquad\qquad A := 5;$$
$$\textbf{end} \qquad\qquad\qquad\qquad B := 3;$$
$$\textbf{end}$$

where $A = 0$, $B = 0$, $X = 0$, initially, and P_A and P_B share access to A and B. Does this *PS* matrix contain indeterminate states? Which ones?

REFERENCES

Dennis, J. B. and E. C. Van Horn, "Programming Semantics for Multi-programmed Computations," *Communications of the ACM,* vol. 9, no. 9 (March 1966), 143–155.

Tausworthe, R. C., *Standardized Development of Computer Software.* Prentice-Hall, Englewood Cliffs, NJ, 1977 (379pp).

9

Application to Concurrent Programs

INTRODUCTION

In the previous chapter we developed a model of processes that is very useful in analyzing convoluted timing patterns in concurrent programs. In this chapter we apply the model to a variety of concurrent programs. More specifically, we apply the Interleave Principle to the most challenging class of concurrent programs: synchronizing locks.

Concurrent programs are sequential programs containing one or more segments that access shared data. The segments that access shared data are called *critical sections*. Thus, we can simplify the analysis of concurrent programs by focusing attention on the critical sections only.

In order for concurrent programs to function correctly, their critical sections must "cooperate" with one another. The nature and mechanism of cooperation are called the synchronization *policy* and *lock*, respectively. We will be concerned with both policy and lock problems in this chapter.

There are several philosophies for synchronizing access. One method, called the *message-passing dual*, uses duplication of the shared data rather than synchronization of common access for interprocess communication. This will be discussed in greater detail in Chapter 11: The Duality Principle. The philosophy illustrated by the locks discussed in this chapter is called *procedure-oriented dual*. We will adopt the procedure-oriented dual throughout most of this book. However, the reader should be aware of the alternate philosophy.

There are two broad classes of synchronization locks: (1) preemptive and (2) nonpreemptive. Preemptive locks block processes by suspending them (removing them from the RUNNING state), whereas nonpreemptive locks block processes by *spinning*. For this reason, nonpreemptive locks are called *spin locks*.

For example, process *P* executes the spin lock below until condition *C* is satisfied:

while not C **do**

Whereas a preemptive lock might delay process *P* by interrupting it:

if not C **then** WAITFOR (C) ;

The preemptive lock presumes an underlying encapsulation of the interrupt structure, whereas the spin lock presumes nothing more than the ability to evaluate the condition *C*.

Spin locks are the oldest and simplest means of enforcing a *mutual exclusion* policy. The only machine feature needed to implement a spin lock is some form of indivisible operation like memory interlock (one instruction/data access at a time). The preemptive locks, on the other hand, require an interrupt structure, as will be discussed later.

One of the earliest and simplest preemptive locks is the *semaphore* with primitive operations *P* and *V*. The indivisible *P* operation performs a WAITFOR trap to a kernel that places the executing process in a BLOCKED queue, if necessary. The indivisible *V* operation performs a GOAHEAD trap to a kernel that removes the previously blocked process and schedules the current process on the READY list (see previous chapter).

On the surface it would seem that either of the simple locks described above would provide enough control to solve all problems in process synchronization. Unfortunately, these simple locks are woefully inadequate for even the simplest concurrent system. For example, *P* and *V* operations and semaphores fail to provide correct locking when used in multiple-processor systems with a common memory. In such a system, two processes running on separate processors might simultaneously test and set the semaphore without realizing that parallel operations were performed. The only way to prevent parallel *P* operations in this case is to resort to a hardware level primitive-like memory lockout that would permit only one process at a time to access the semaphore.

In the following sections we closely examine a representative collection of spin locks to determine how well they work in terms of safe, fair, and live access. This analysis is then used as a basis for a close study of preemptive locks. Finally, we study how such locks might be used in a network or in concurrent access to a data structure (*B*-tree). Through these examples the reader should gain an appreciation for the strengths and limitations of the Interleave Principle.

SPIN LOCKS

A spin lock delays access of a process to shared data by repeatedly accessing and testing a condition (semaphore) as follows:

```
while C do ;        (* spin *)
C := True ;         (* lock *)
CR ;                (* access *)
C := False ;        (* unlock *)
```

This seemingly straightforward approach is *not valid,* however, for a number of reasons, as shown in Figure 9-1. For example, the lock does not enforce mutual exclusive locking because the test and set operations are separated, as shown below.

```
while C do          (* test *)
```

and

```
C := True ;         (* set *)
```

We might try to improve this lock by separating semaphore variable C into two separate flags as shown in the incorrect lock below:

```
FLAG[me] := True ;       (* set my flag *)
while FLAG[other] do ;   (* test other flag *)
CR ;
FLAG[me] := False ;      (* release lock *)
```

This lock runs with me = 1 and other = 2 corresponding to process one and two, respectively (see Figure 9-2).

The "improved" spin lock is safe because the shaded (CR,CR) squares are not reachable by a path from the beginning square of each process. However, this lock can deadlock P_1 and P_2! Therefore, it is not live.

The correct implementation of a spin lock is more elusive than it appears. In fact, the first published spin lock (Dijkstra) was not altogether successful as we illustrate in the next several sections. (The reader is referred to the list of references at the end of this chapter for further details of these early efforts to implement a correct spin lock.)

Dijkstra's Lock

Dijkstra's lock enforces safe and live access to a mutually exclusive critical section CR but does not guarantee fair access. (See previous chapter for definitions of *live, fair,* and *safe*.) We will examine only the restricted case for $N = 2$ processes. Each process has access to shared variables $b[1] . . b[N]$, $C[1] . . C[N]$, and K. Initially set to True (no request), $b[i]$ is used to signify a request by process i. The value of $C[i]$ is

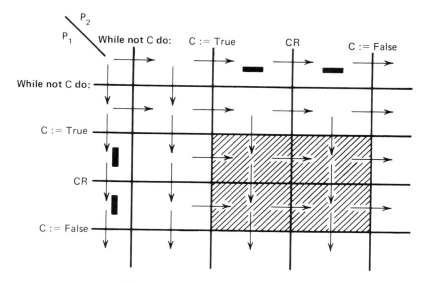

Figure 9-1. A poor spin lock.

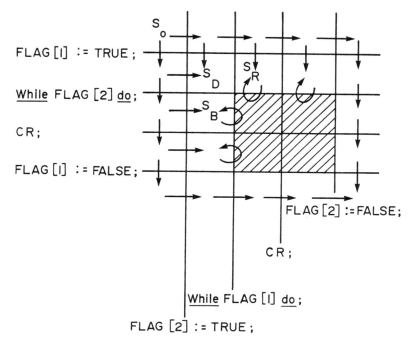

Figure 9-2. The process-state matrix for a simple spin lock.

also False (F) or True (T) and is used to avoid a deadlock configuration like the one shown in Figure 9-2. The value of K designates which process is to be given control next. K is undefined initially.

Dijkstra's program is given below and in software network form in Figure 9-3.

For Process i

```
    b[i] := False;
L1 : if K <> i
        then begin
                C[i] := True ;
                if b[K] then K := i ;
                go to L1
            end (* then clause *)
        else begin
                C[i] := False ;
                for j := 1 to N do
                    if j <> i and not C[j] then go to L1 ;
            end (* else clause *)
    CR ;                (* aha! *)
    C[i] := True ;   (* release *)
    b[i] := True ;
```

The state vector for this lock and $N = 2$ is $\{b[1] := T, b[2] := T, C[1] := T, C[2] := T, K := 1\}$, where we abbreviate True and False with T and F.

Figures 9-4 and 9-5 show that Dijkstra's lock is safe and live for the case where $K = 1$ (process one has first priority), and $K = 2$ (process two has first priority). The value of the state vector $\{b[1], b[2], C[1], C[2], K\}$ is given in each reachable square, and adjacent reachable squares are assumed to be reachable simply because they are adjacent (even though we have not shown an arrow). Therefore, process P_1 is able to move vertically through its CR transition without passing through the mutual exclusion squares (shown as shaded squares).

The "loop-backs" in Figures 9-4 and 9-5 prevent improper access by spin locking. Notice that an unspecified number of loop-backs may occur. Indeed, Dijkstra's algorithm may not be fair to some processes because they may spend all their time spinning rather than entering the critical section.

Figure 9-6 shows why Dijkstra's algorithm is unfair. Suppose process P_1 (vertical) is fast enough to pass through CR and then rapidly request another access. The double-hacked path represents this second pass. If process P_2 cannot break out of its spin lock at the exact place shown in Figure 9-6, then P_2 will continue to wait on P_1. In short, P_1 will starve P_2 if it is fast enough (or lucky enough) to execute the first five rows of the

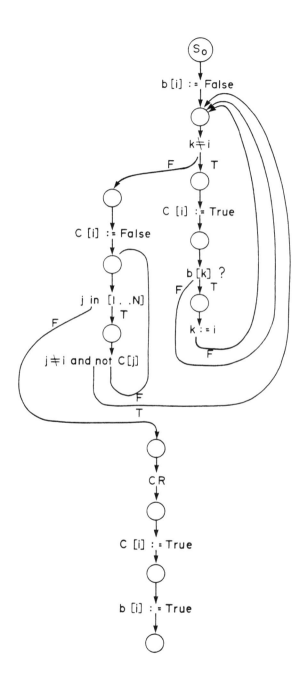

Figure 9-3. Network model of Dijkstra's lock.

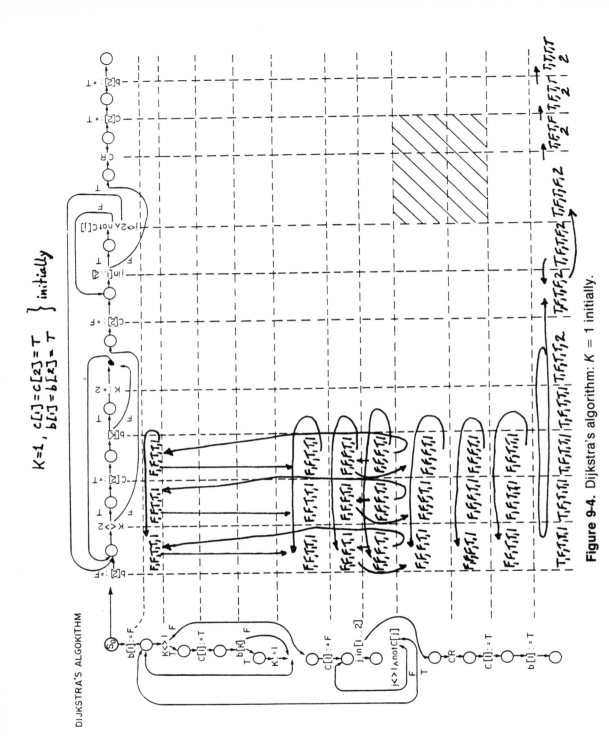

Figure 9-4. Dijkstra's algorithm: $K = 1$ initially.

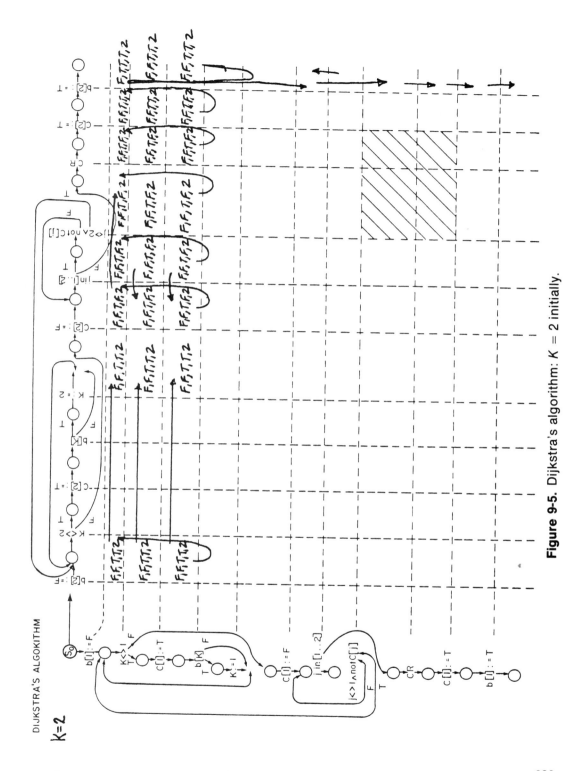

Figure 9-5. Dijkstra's algorithm: $K = 2$ initially.

289

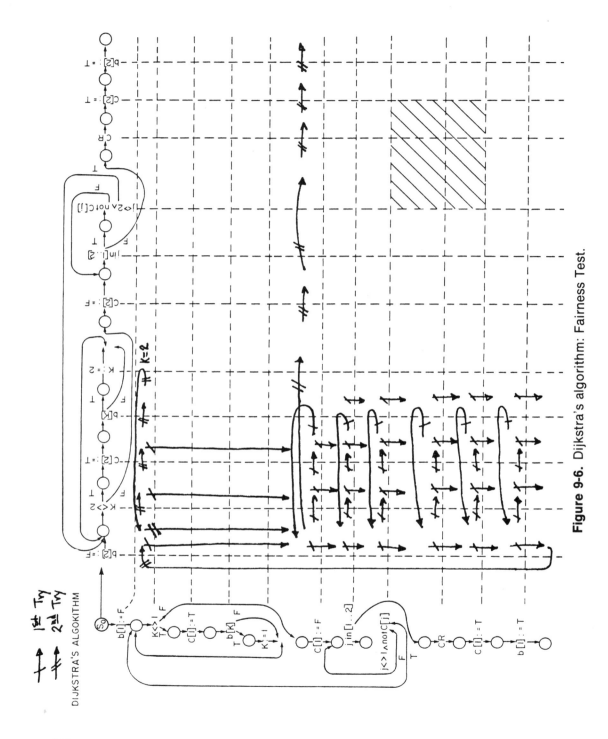

Figure 9-6. Dijkstra's algorithm: Fairness Test.

process-state matrix in the time it takes P_2 to traverse the spin lock loop shown.

A spin lock is unfair if there is at least one path that starves another process. The path may be rare and unlikely to happen; nonetheless, if it is possible, then we say the lock is *unfair*.

It is also possible for one process to starve another process even though they both execute at the same rate. A "harmonic" motion may exist between two processes such that they are out of step with respect to one another. Process P_1 might coincidentally test the lock immediately after P_2 sets it, over and over again.

An improvement to Dijkstra's lock was suggested by Knuth and will be analyzed using the Interleave Principle in the next section.

Performance of Dijkstra's Lock We estimate the performance of a lock by assuming uniform probabilities and unit time delays per operation as shown in the reduction of the network (Figure 9-7). This is a gross approximation, however, because interacting processes may radically alter the probability density functions so that they are not uniform. The results obtained here are merely comparative and cannot be used to estimate the performance of a system of concurrent processes. A more thorough queueing analysis must be done to obtain overall estimates of system performance.

Knuth's Lock

Knuth's modification to Dijkstra's lock overcomes the unfairness defect and simplifies the program. These two improvements are accomplished by using two spin locks, one inside the other, to implement a safe, fair, and live spin lock.

For Process i and $N = 2$

```
L0 : C[i] := 1 ;
L1 : if K = i then goto L2 ;
     if C[other] <> 0 then goto L1 ;      (* spin *)
L2 : C[i] := 2 ;
     if C[other] := 2 then goto L0 ;      (* spin,again *)
L3 : K := i                               (* aha! *)
     CR ;
     K := other ;                         (* avoid starvation *)
L4 : C[i] := 0 ;                          (* release lock *)
```

This is a special version of Knuth's algorithm for two processes (see references at end of chapter). The values ($i = 1$, other $= 2$) and ($i = 2$, other $= 1$) are substituted into the process-state matrix models shown in

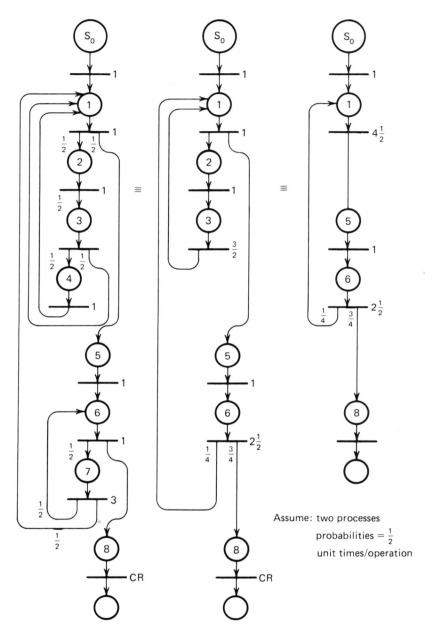

Figure 9-7. Performance analysis of Dijkstra's Lock.

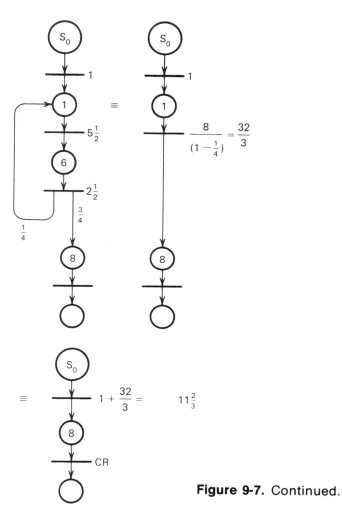

Figure 9-7. Continued.

Figures 9-8, 9-9, and 9-10. The state vector for this lock is $\{C[1], C[2], K\}$, which is initially $\{1,1,1\}$ or $\{1,1,2\}$.

Figures 9-8 and 9-9 show that the lock is safe and live for accesses made by process one or process two. Figure 9-10 shows what happens if we try to starve process P_2 (horizontal) by favoring process P_1. The double-hacked path models what can happen when P_1 rapidly cycles back to make a second request for access. But as we can see, the second pass by P_1 is blocked because $K = 2$. This forces control to be given to P_2 no matter how slow P_2 is relative to P_1.

Subsequently, if P_2 attempts to make a second access at the expense of P_1, the pattern of Figure 9-10 is repeated. Thus, P_2 cannot starve P_1

either. In general, Knuth's algorithm is fair because K takes on subsequent values such that the lock is a round-robin server. Therefore, if $N = 5$ and processes 2, 3, and 5 all make requests while process 1 is in the CR, then the lock enforces the order

1,2,3,5

on the collection of processes. Should process 4 make a belated request, it will be included in the cycle

1,2,3,4,5,1,2 . . .

in round-robin fashion.

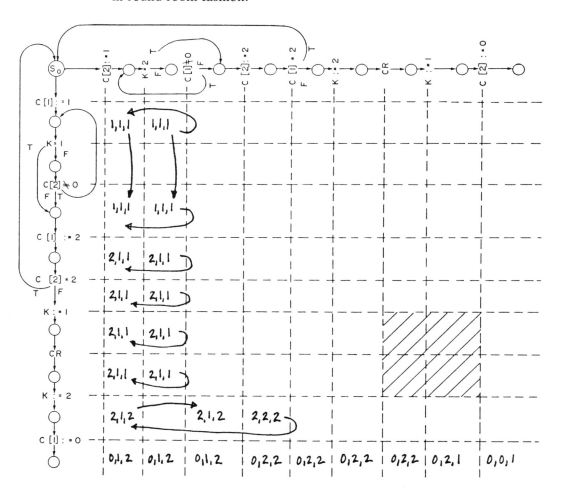

Figure 9-8. Knuth's Modification: $K = 1$ initially.

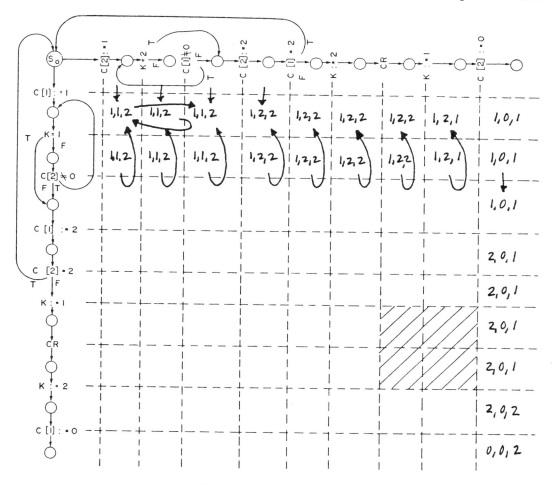

Figure 9-9. Knuth's Modification: $K = 2$ initially.

The "congested square" in Figure 9-10 is very important in determining which process is next in line. If each requesting process is allowed to make a single state transition, then no process will be starved. However, if a single transition is denied a process at this point in its execution, the process may be starved. Therefore, the possibility of starvation is a very subtle feature of locks, based on the assumption that all processes are allowed to execute at least one indivisible transition before being interrupted by the timer (multiplexed in time).

Knuth's algorithm is safe because the shaded squares are not reachable; it is live because there are no deadlock squares; and it is fair because K takes on the values of a round-robin server. In Figure 9-10, K flip-flops between 1 and 2.

Is this the "ultimate" spin lock? Several other proposals have been suggested as improvements over Knuth's lock. In the next two sections we analyze two other proposals: one is "better" in the sense of fault-tolerance, whereas the other is "less desirable" because it is not as fair.

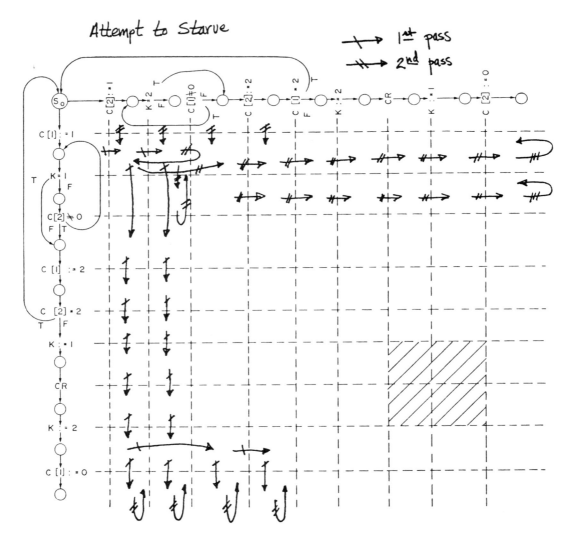

Figure 9-10. Knuth's Modification: Fairness Test.

Dekker's Lock

Knuth's modification to Dijkstra's lock is correct in the sense of safe, live, and fair access, but it is not easily understood or analyzed (even using the Interleave Principle). Is it possible to simplify or structure a spin lock so that it can be easily understood and reliably applied?

Dekker's lock attempts to simplify the implementation of mutual exclusion by using an array of flags, FLAG[1] . . FLAG[N], and a round-robin counter, TURN. The state vector

$$\{FLAG[1], FLAG[2], TURN\}$$

determines the combined state of a pair of processes, P_1 and P_2, each executing the lock as shown below:

Dekker's Algorithm for P_1

```
LOCK    :   FLAG[1] := TRUE
            while FLAG[2] do
                if TURN <> 1 then                    (* my turn? *)
                        begin
                            FLAG[1] := FALSE ;   (* avoid deadlock *)
                            while TURN <> 1 do ; (* spin *)
                            FLAG[1] := TRUE ;    (* make request,again *)
                        end ;
            CR ;
UNLOCK :  FLAG[1] := FALSE ;       (* release *)
          TURN := 2 ;              (*change turns *)
```

The reader can easily show that Dekker's lock is safe and live. The problem with this "simpler" algorithm is revealed in Figure 9-11. The second pass (double-hacked path) through the lock by P_1 may succeed (but only the second pass). P_2 can make two passes through CR before giving P_2 access. Likewise, P_2 can take two turns before giving control to P_1.

This is not exactly starvation because the abused process eventually gets to take a turn. Furthermore, the possibility of this abuse is indeed rare. The reason it occurs (and the cure) is because

```
while TURN <> 1 do ;       (* spin . . . *)
FLAG[1] := True ;          (* and set FLAG *)
```

is a set of divisible "test-and-set" instructions. We can remove the weakness by (somehow) forcing these two instructions to be indivisible. For example, we might implement a primitive test-and-set sequence using a machine instruction that cannot be interrupted by the timer (no time multiplexing allowed during these two operations).

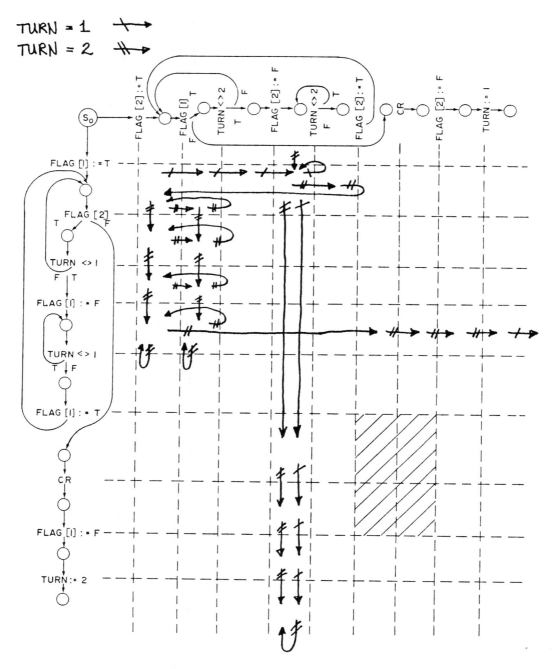

Figure 9-11. Dekker's Algorithm.

Performance of Dekker's Lock   Figure 9-12 shows the steps in reducing the software network for Dekker's algorithm. The expected time delay is considerably lower than the expected delay derived for Dijkstra's algorithm (same assumptions). Thus,

$$\text{Expected delay Dijkstra's lock} = 11\tfrac{2}{3}$$
$$\text{Expected delay Dekker's lock} = 6$$

These estimates do not include the effect of congestion due to competing processes, as we mentioned before. Hence, they cannot be used as throughput estimates.

Lamport's Lock

Lamport's lock is based on the familiar ice cream parlor or bakery algorithm called "Take a number and wait." The analogy is quite exact. An arriving customer in a bakery takes a slip of paper with a number on it. The number is called by the bakery owner when he or she is ready to serve the customer. The bakery algorithm is fair as long as the owner follows the order prescribed by the ticket dispenser and the dispenser avoids handing out indeterminate (duplicate) values to each customer.

Lamport's algorithm also has an added advantage over the spin locks discussed before. That is, if one of the waiting customers decides to leave before being served, then that customer's number is dropped from the sequence. This corresponds to resetting the customer's number to zero.

In the earlier algorithms we could block all processes in the system of processes by allowing a single process to fail while in CR. That is, the process with control of the CR can fail and never notify the other (waiting) processes that it is never going to leave the CR.

In Lamport's algorithm any process may fail while in the CR. If the failure resets the corresponding flags back to zero, the other (waiting) processes are allowed entry into the CR on a first-come-first-served basis. Thus, Lamport's algorithm has the added advantage that it tolerates unreliable processes.

Let the state variables of Lamport's algorithm be ($n = 2$):

$$\{C[1],\ C[2],\ N[1],\ N[2]\}$$

where $C[1]\ .\ .\ C[n]$ are flags for protecting the ticket dispenser, and $N[1]\ .\ .\ N[n]$ are the numbers dispensed by the ticket dispenser. In Lamport's algorithm, the maximum function, MAX, simulates the dispenser.

Note in the algorithm below the order pair comparison:

$$(N[j],j) < (N[i],i)$$

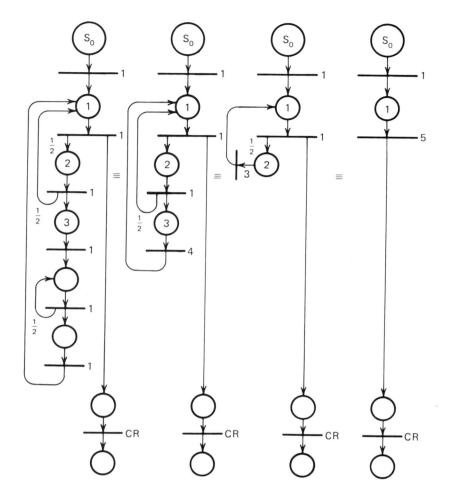

Assume: Each operation takes unit time.
Probabilities all equal $\frac{1}{2}$.
N = 2 processes.

$\tau = 6$ Dekker

Figure 9-12. Performance of Dekker's Algorithm.

which is the same as $N[j] < N[i]$, except when $N[j] = N[i]$, and then it is the same as $(j < i)$.

Lamport's Algorithm

For n processors and common memory containing,

$$C[1 . . n]$$
$$N[1 . . n]$$

where i is the i-th process, and j is a local variable.

```
L1 : C[i] := 1 ;
       N[i] := 1+max (N) ;        (* take a number *)
       C[i] := 0 ;
       for j in [1 . . n] do       (* spin locks *)
         begin
           L2 : if C[j] <> 0 then goto L2 ;      (* spin *)
           L3 : if N[j] <> 0 and (N[j],j)<(N[i],i) then goto L3 ;
         end ;                      (* FOR *)
       CR ;
       N[i] := 0 ;                  (* unlock *)
```

Lamport's algorithm is tested by assuming one of two cases:

$$N[1] >= N[2]$$

and

$$N[1] <= N[2]$$

These two conditions represent all possible cases for a two-process system. Either P_1 is ahead of P_2, or the reverse.

Figures 9-13 and 9-14 show that the lock is safe and live. An attempted starvation of P_1 by P_2 is averted in Figure 9-15 because the "take a number" ordering of processes is correctly implemented by the lock.

In fact, Lamport's algorithm remains fair even if we deny the waiting process a single state transition between successive requests by a single process. A second attempt by P_2, say, is held off by the spin lock because the waiting process P_1 has a lower number than P_2. Lamport's lock appears to be the fairest of them all!

Furthermore, if a process fails, and the corresponding values N[i], C[i] are reset to zero, the lock continues to allow all other processes to execute.

Performance of Lamport's Lock   Figure 9-16 shows the steps in reducing the software network for Lamport's algorithm to an expression for the expected time delay of the lock. This formula leads to an estimate:

$$\text{Estimated delay Lamport's lock} = 8\tfrac{1}{3}$$

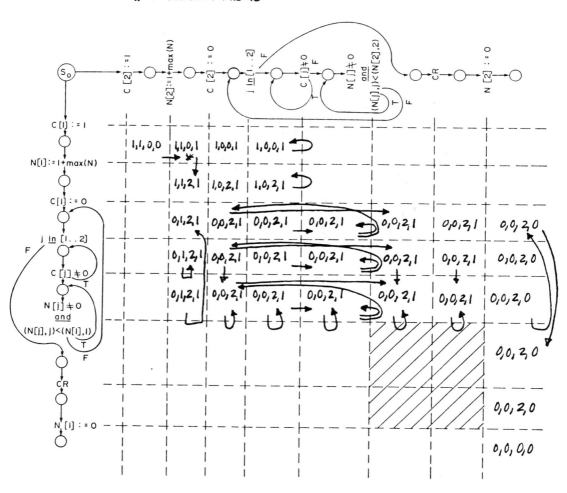

Figure 9-13. Lamport's Algorithm; N[1] < N[2].

$N[2] \geqslant N[1] = 0$
$C[1] = C[2] = 0$ initially

※ ≡ nondeterministic

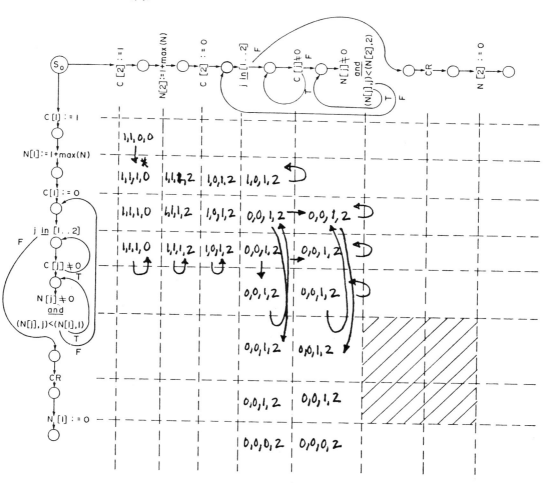

Figure 9-14. Lamport's Algorithm; $N[2] < N[1]$.

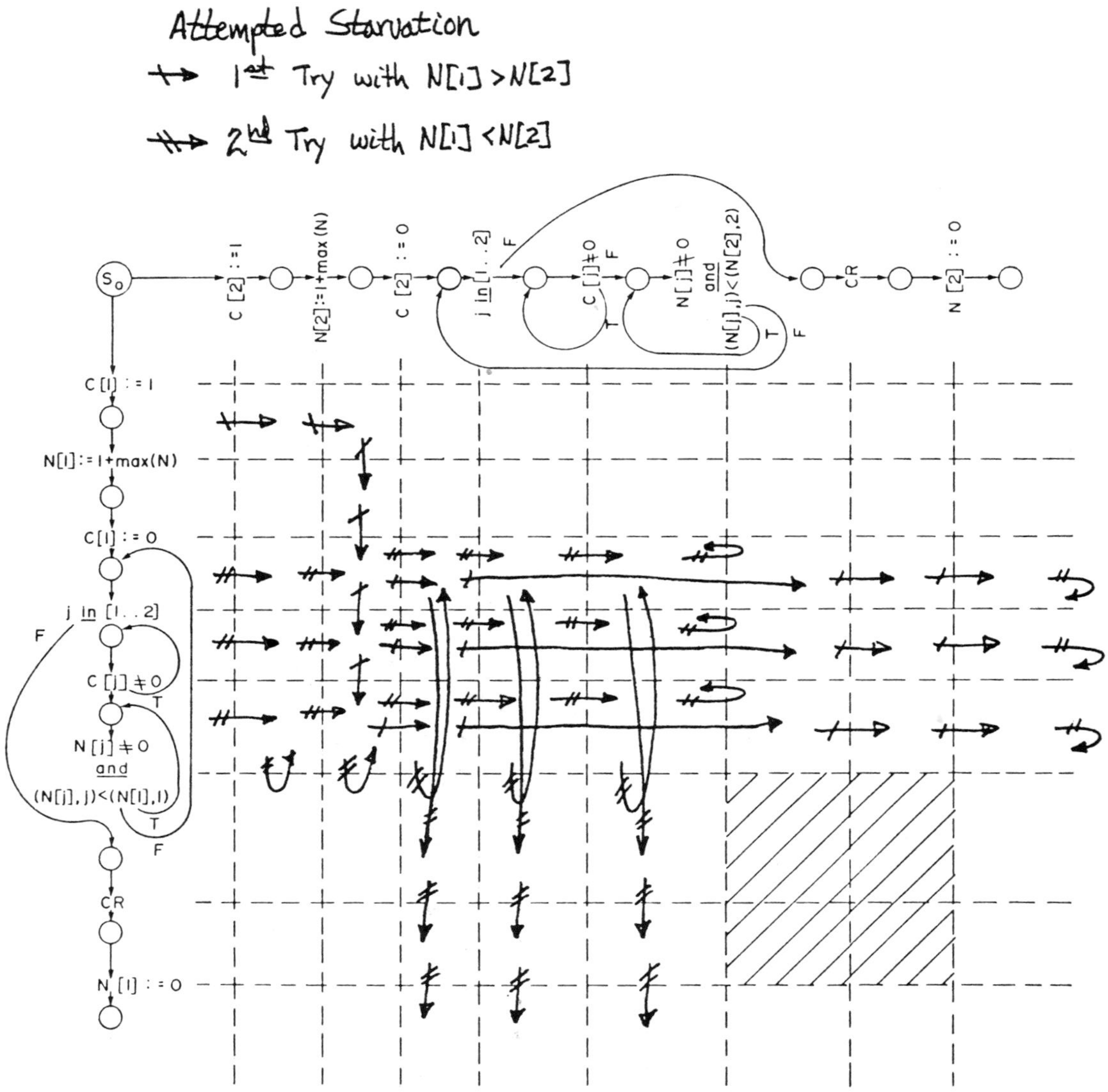

Figure 9-15. Lamport's Algorithm; Fairness Test.

if we assume ($N = n$ = number of processes).
where,

$$p_j = \frac{N}{N + 1}$$ The test is performed $N + 1$ times and succeeds every time except the last time.

$$p_c = \frac{1}{N + 1}$$ We assume a uniform distribution of waiting processes.

$$p_N = \frac{1}{N + 1}$$ Again, assuming a uniform distribution of processes.

Then, $$\text{Estimated delay} = \frac{5N^2 + 2N + 1}{N + 1}$$
$$= 8\tfrac{1}{3} \text{ for } N = 2$$

This estimate also suggests that Lamport's algorithm is $O(N)$ in terms of speed of execution.

Therefore, we have found a spin lock of modest performance, outstanding properties (safe, live, and fair), and tolerant of unreliable processes. Where might such a lock be useful? Since spin locks are best suited to systems where control of an interrupt structure is not required, we can use them to synchronize access to critical regions distributed throughout a network of processors. Although each processor may support an interrupt structure, we cannot assume simultaneous control over *all* processor's interrupt structure. This leads to the distributed lock discussed in the next section.

A Distributed Computer Network Lock

An algorithm for mutual exclusion in a computer network whose nodes (processors) communicate only by messages was first proposed by Ricart and Agrawala (see references at end of chapter). Their algorithm is based on the "bakery algorithm" as explained in the previous section. But since the bakery algorithm is distributed over a network of computers, parts of the Lamport lock are divided into three processing steps as shown below.

First, we assume a shared data segment on each processor as:

me—Unique identifier for the node.

N—The number of nodes in the network.

Our-Sequence-Number—Number in "take a number" (abbreviated OSN).

Highest-Seq-Number—Highest number taken (abbreviated HSN).

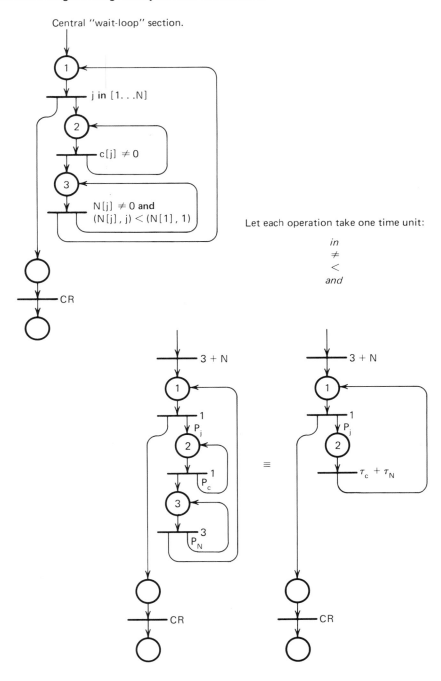

Figure 9-16. Performance of Lamport's Algorithm.

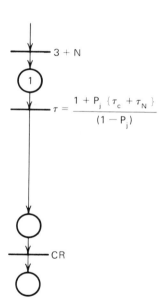

Reduction of Lamport's
Algorithm

Figure 9-16. Continued.

Outstanding-Reply-Count—Number of REPLY messages pending (abbreviated ORC).

Request-Critical-Section—TRUE when a process makes a request (abbreviated RCS).

Reply-Deferred [1 . . N]—TRUE when a reply message is deferred.

Shared-vars—Semaphore to lock access to the other variables in this data segment.

There are three steps to the lock (PWIMEFTN, REQUEST, REPLY). Each processor maintains a separate copy of the shared variables (defined above) and the three processing (code segments) steps:

Step 1 (PWIMEFTN)

PROCEDURE WHICH INVOKES MUTUAL EXCLUSION FOR THIS NODE (abbreviated PWIMEFTN)

```
(* request entry to this node's critical region, CR *)
P(Shared-vars) ;                        (* WAIT semaphore *)
Request-Critical-Section := TRUE ;
Our-Sequence-Number   := Highest-Sequence-Number + 1 ;
V (Shared-vars) ;                       (* SIGNAL semaphore *)
    Outstanding-Reply-Count := N − 1 ;
      for j := 1 to N do
      if j <> me
        then send-message (Request(Our-Sequence-Number,me), j)
Waitfor (Outstanding-Reply-Count = 0) ;
CR ;                                    (* critical section *)
Request-Critical-Section := False ;     (* release lock *)
for j := 1 to N do
  if Reply-Deferred[j]
    then begin
      Reply-Deferred[j] := False ;
      Send-Message (Reply, j)
    end ;
```

The PWIMEFTN process simply takes a number, sends messages to all other nodes in the network telling them it has made a request, and then waits for their approval. Once $(N − 1)$ approvals have returned, the PWIMEFTN process enters the critical section, CR. Then the process releases its exclusive lock by setting RCS := False, and sending REPLY messages to all nodes with waiting processes.

In a sense, the first part of the lock given above as PWIMEFTN does the following:

1. Makes a request and takes a number.

2. Notifies all other nodes that it wants access, and then waits for their approval.

3. Gains exclusive access to CR.

4. Then notifies all waiting processes that they can enter their critical regions in the order provided by the sequence number.

This part of the lock sends messages to other processor nodes to execute either code segment REQUEST or REPLY on its behalf. These messages are accepted by other nodes, and either a REQUEST or REPLY code segment is executed. (Also note that P (Shared-vars) and V (Shared-vars) provide serial access to the shared variables in each node.)

Step 2 (REQUEST)

PROCEDURE WHICH RECEIVES REQUEST (k, j) MESSAGES (abbreviated REQUEST (k, j))
Highest-Seq-Number := Maximum (Highest-Seq-Number, k) ;
P(Shared-vars) ;   (* WAIT semaphore *)
Defer-it := Request-Critical-Section
        and
        ((k > Our-Sequence-Number)
        or
        (k = Our-Sequence-Number **and** j > me))
V(Shared-vars) ;   (* SIGNAL semaphore *)
(* Defer-it = True means we have higher priority over j's request *)
  if Defer-it
      then Reply-Deferred[j] := True
      else Send-Message (REPLY, j) ;

This code tests the request being made by node *j* to see if it should be allowed access or be delayed. If access is allowed a SEND-MESSAGE (REPLY, *j*) is sent to node *j*. Otherwise, the Reply-Deferred flag for node *j* is set to TRUE. This means a message must be sent at some later time; see the "release" section of PWIMEFTN.

Finally, a REPLY message is returned and processed by a procedure for decrementing the Outstanding-Reply-Count.

Step 3 (REPLY)

PROCEDURE WHICH RECEIVES REPLY MESSAGES
(abbreviated REPLY)
Outstanding-Reply-Count := Outstanding-Reply-Count-1 ;

This procedure is executed $(N - 1)$ times in order to let a process go beyond the WAITFOR(Outstanding-Reply-Count = 0) step in PWIMEFTN.

The Ricart-Agrawala lock attempts to synchronize access by N *parallel* processes, using indivisible primitives implemented on each of the N processors. Unfortunately the algorithm fails due to a specific timing pattern that allows a simple network of two processors to deadlock.

Figure 9-17 shows the Interleave Principle applied to an abbreviated Richart-Agrawala algorithm. The process-state matrix shows that the algorithm can deadlock because the REQUEST procedure incorrectly defers message sending. Let us follow the deadlock path in greater detail.

In Figure 9-17 we have used first-letter initials to abbreviate the names of shared variables and procedures. Subscripts refer to the processor node, and T (True) and F (False) represent boolean values. We have also noted process migration from one node to the other as $P_i@N_j$, meaning process i on node j. We need only consider the special case $N = 2$ to show deadlock.

Initially the data base in each node contains $HSN_1 = HSN_2 = 0$; $RCS_1 = RCS_2 = F$; $N = 2$. We begin with $P_1@N_1$, requesting access:

$$P_1@N_1 : \text{PWIMEFTN (me} = 1)$$
$$\text{P(shared-vars)}$$
$$RCS_1 := T$$
$$OSN_1 := 0 + 1 = 1$$
$$\text{V(shared-vars)}$$
$$ORC_1 := 2 - 1 = 1$$
$$\textbf{for } j := 2 \textbf{ do } \text{Send-Message (REQUEST(1,1),2)}$$
$$\text{WAITFOR(}ORC_1 = 0)$$

This segment from $P_1@N_1$ is shown in Figure 9-17 as the path crossing the first line (ME ; Send-Message). At some time later, node two receives the message and begins executing the REQUEST code:

$$P_1'@N_2 : \text{PWRRM} = \text{REQUEST(1,1)}$$
$$HSN_2 = 1$$
$$\text{P(shared-vars)}$$
$$\text{Defer-it}_2 := F$$
$$\text{V(shared-vars)}$$
$$\textbf{if } \text{Defer-it}_2 \textbf{ else } \text{Send Message (Reply,1)}$$

Meanwhile, back at node one, the message is received and REPLY decrements ORC to zero. This unblocks the WAITFOR as shown by the progress of the vertical path in the process-state matrix.

$$P_1@N_1 : \text{``enters critical section, } CR_1\text{''}$$
$$\text{INTERRUPT}$$

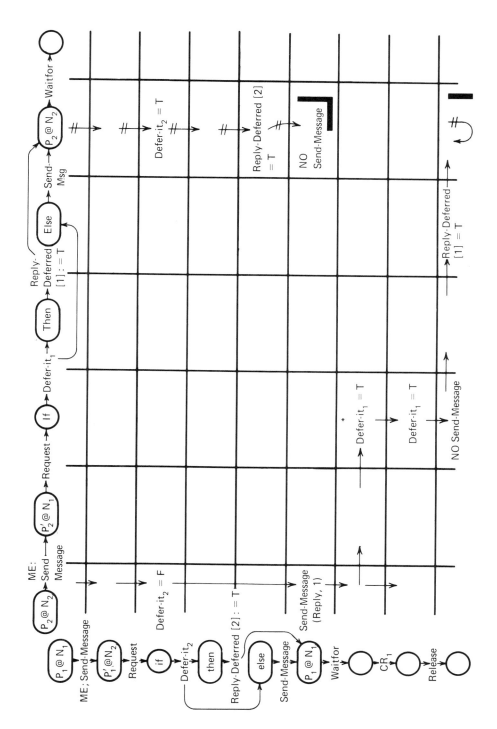

Figure 9-17. Deadlocked Ricart-Agrawala Algorithm.

311

We assume an interrupt occurs anywhere within the CR_1 code because no semaphore is used to guard CR_1.

Meanwhile, process P_2 begins to make a request for CR_2 from node two:

$P_2 @ N_2$: PWIMEFTN (me = 2)
P(shared-vars)
RCS_2 := T
OSN_2 := 1
V(shared-vars)
ORC_2 := 1
for j := 1 **do** Send-Message (REQUEST(1,2),1)
WAITFOR (ORC_2 = 0)

Again, at some time later,

$P_2' @ N_1$: PWRRM = REQUEST(1,2)
HSN_1 := 1
P(shared-vars)
Defer-it$_1$:= T
V(shared-vars)
INTERRUPT

This interrupt corresponds to a context switch that momentarily halts the horizontal path in the square marked "*". Deadlock will occur because of this (unfortunate) interrupt. The reason is simply that Defer-it$_1$ and the value of Reply-Deferred [1] must be exactly the same at every instance in time. However, since Defer-it$_1$ and Reply-Deferred [1] are computed in separate (divisible) operations, no consistency is guaranteed. As we shall see, the result is a failure to Send-Messages, which leads to permanent blocking of both P_1 and P_2.

Meanwhile, $P_1 @ N_1$ resumes execution:

$P_1 @ N_1$: "completes execution of CR_1"
RCS_1 := F
for j := 1 to 2 **do** ;

This corresponds to the RELEASE line in the process-state matrix. Since all Reply-Deferred [j] flags are false, the RELEASE segment does nothing but reset RCS_1 to False. Since no message is sent to the process about to be blocked next, the lock begins to fail. That is,

$P_2' @ N_1$: "continuing in REQUEST(1,2)"
if Defer-it$_1$ **then** Reply-Deferred [2] := T

This step comes too late because Reply-Deferred [2] has already been checked above. Therefore, no message is sent, and the WAITFOR never unblocks. In Figure 9-17 the path is blocked in the lower right-hand square.

The double-hacked path is followed to see what happens after process P_2 is blocked. Meanwhile, back in node one:

$P_1 @ N_1$: PWIMEFTN (second try)
  P(shared-vars)
  RCS_1 := T
  OSN_1 := 2
  V(shared-vars)
  ORC_1 := 1
  for j := 2 **do** Send-Message (REQUEST(2,1),2)
  WAITFOR ($ORC_1 = 0$)

The message now goes to node two and we have

$P_1' @ N_2$: PWRRM = REQUEST(2,1)
  HSN_2 := 2
  P(shared-vars)
  Defer-it$_2$:= T
  V(shared-vars)
  if Defer-it$_2$ **then** Reply-Deferred [1] = T

This last segment corresponds to the vertical double-hacked path in the process-state matrix. Note that no message is sent to remove the WAITFOR block. Therefore, we end up in the deadlock square.

A Correct Bakery Algorithm Figure 9-17 reveals why the Ricart-Agrawala algorithm fails, and thus what can be done to correct it. The problem is the unfortunate context switch that occurred in $P_2' @ N_1$ as indicated by the ``*'' square in the process-state matrix. The solution is to prevent the context switch by enclosing the code for REQUEST in P (shared-vars) and V (shared-vars) semaphores. For example,

PWRequest(k,j) M:
  Highest-Sequence-Number := Maximum (Highest-Sequence-
                Number,k) ;
  P(shared-vars) ;
  if (Requesting-Critical-Section) **and**
  ((k > Our-Sequence-Number) **or**
  (k = Our-Sequence-Number **and** j > me))
  then Reply-Deferred [j] := TRUE
  else Send Message (Reply,j) ;
  V(shared-vars) ;

We should be careful to protect all code, which accesses the shared variables. For example,

314

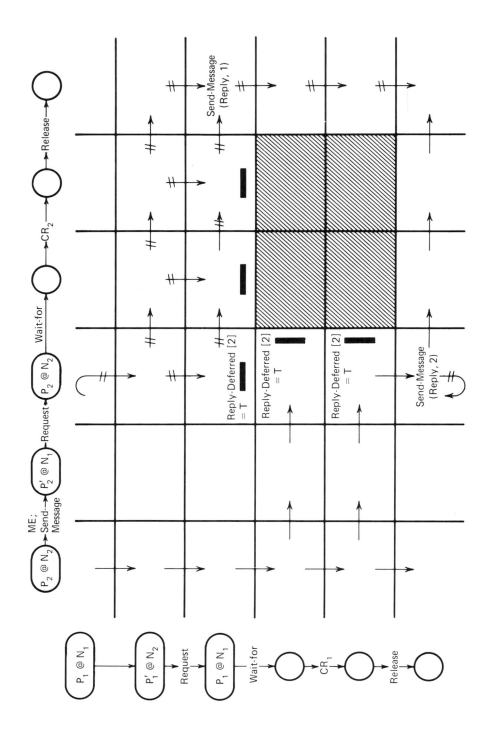

Figure 9-18. Correct Bakery Algorithm is safe, fair, and live.

Process Which Receives REPLY Messages:
    P(shared-vars) ;
    Outstanding-Reply-Count := Outstanding-Reply-Count-1 ;
    V(shared-vars) ;

and we should also enclose the release segment of code in PWIMEFTN with P and V serializers.

Proper grouping of instructions into atomic code segments leads to a process-state matrix as shown in Figure 9-18. The path through CR_1 is similar to the path in Figure 9-17 until we reach the fatal "*" square. In Figure 9-18 this square is removed because the new REQUEST code sets Reply-Deferred [2] to TRUE before any other access to the shared variables is allowed.

In Figure 9-18 we see that the new algorithm is safe because the shaded squares cannot be reached. These squares correspond to the concurrent occupation of CR_1 and CR_2 by both processes. This would violate the mutual exclusion property, but as we see, this cannot occur.

There are no deadlock squares in Figure 9-18; so we say the new algorithm is live.

We attempt to starve process P_2 by allowing P_1 to (rapidly) reenter the lock. This is shown in Figure 9-18 as a double-hacked path. This path is eventually blocked because Reply-Deferred [2] is TRUE, and no message is sent to unblock P_1 at WAITFOR. Thus, P_2 is allowed access to its CR_2 code before P_1 is allowed a second access to CR_1.

The blocking WAITFOR is unblocked by a message sent by P_2 when it executes RELEASE. This occurs because the flag Reply-Deferred has been properly set:

                for j := 1 to 2 do
                    if Reply-Deferred [j]
                    then
                        Reply-Deferred [j] := False ;
                        Send-Message (Reply,j)
                    end ;

So a second access by P_1 is allowed only after P_2 has had access to CR_2. Hence the new algorithm is fair.

PREEMPTIVE LOCKS

A preemptive lock removes a process from the RUNNING state whenever the process must be delayed. Instead of wasting processor cycles performing repeated tests, the preemptive lock blocks the process and passes control to another (waiting) process. This involves putting one process "to sleep" and "awakening" another process.

Semaphore operations WAITFOR and GOAHEAD were used in the previous chapter to synchronize a producer and consumer pair of processes by preemption. These must be performed as indivisible test-and-set operations on the (shared) semaphore variable. Indeed, the ability to perform *atomic* operations (operations that are not preempted) is central to the ability to implement preemptive locks.

Knuth's Atomic Procedures

Knuth proposed a method of mutual exclusion based on a set of atomic procedures. An *atomic procedure* is any code segment that is executed to completion without preemption. An atomic procedure is reusable but not reentrant; i.e., it cannot be shared.

The idea underlying Knuth's proposal is straightforward. A queue for holding process requests is maintained for every critical section protected

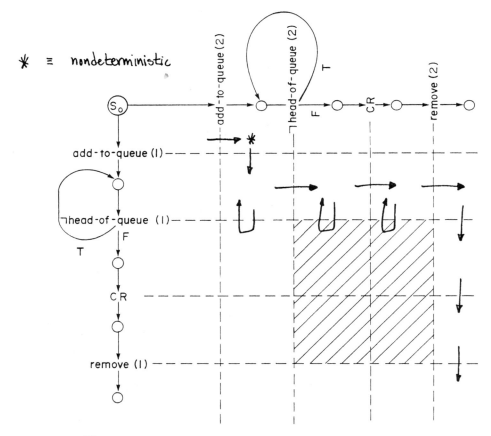

Figure 9-19. Knuth's solution using atomic procedures.

by a lock. The queue has only three allowable atomic operations defined below:

Add-to-Queue (p_i): Add process p_i to the queue.

Head-of-Queue (p_i): True if p_i is at the head of the queue, and false otherwise.

Remove-from-Queue (p_i): Remove process p_i from the head of the queue.

These atomic operations can be used to implement a simple spin lock as shown below.

Spin lock for process p_i

```
L0 : Add-To-Queue (pi) ;
L1 : if not Head-Of-Queue (pi) then goto L1 ;
     CR ;
L4 : Remove-From-Queue (pi)
```

This lock is safe, fair, and live as shown in Figures 9-19 and 9-20, but it is a spin lock and not a preemptive lock. Each process wastes processor cycles while waiting for the timer to preempt it and remove it from the RUNNING state.

An improvement to the spin lock above uses a SUPERVISOR-TRAP to "call" the kernel as soon as a process is blocked. The modification to Knuth's atomic procedure lock continues to use the indivisible operations:

Preemptive lock for process p_i

```
L0 : Add-To-Queue (pi) ;                        (* make request *)
L1 : if not Head-Of-Queue (pi)
        then begin SUPERVISOR-TRAP ;            (* call kernel *)
                   goto L1 ;                    (* check again *)
             end
     CR ;
L4 : Remove-From-Queue (pi) ;                   (* release lock *)
```

This modification is more "efficient" because the waiting process no longer keeps the processor to itself while waiting. As soon as the process discovers that it is not next to enter the critical section, it traps to the kernel. The kernel can reschedule the process on the READY list and select another (waiting) process to run. When the preempted process is once again allowed to run, it executes the **goto** L1 instruction and tries again. This cycle of test, trap, and **goto** is repeated until the test succeeds and the CR is executed.

The queue guarantees fair access to all processes because it establishes a first-come-first-served discipline among the concurrent processes. If N

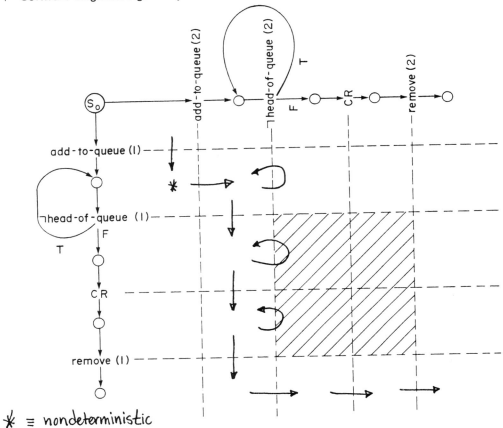

✳ ≡ nondeterministic

Figure 9-20. Knuth's solution using atomic procedures.

processes compete for the same CR, then the queue implements a round-robin scheduling discipline.

There are situations in which unrestricted use of the preemptive lock (or spin lock) can lead to incorrect synchronization, however. Suppose, as a counterexample, we imbed one preemptive lock within another as shown in the example below:

Lock program for process p1

```
LOCK (A-queue,p1) ;
    LOCK (B-queue,p1) ;
    CR ;
    UNLOCK(B-queue,p1) ;
UNLOCK(A-queue,p1) ;
```

The idea here is to access two shared regions of data by first locking one via A-queue, and then locking the other via B-queue. Suppose A-queue holds all processes waiting for or using an input device, and B-queue holds all processes waiting for or using an output device. Then process P1 reads data from the input device and writes it out through the output device. Process P1 has good intentions: it wants to copy values from an input device to an output device. The problem arises when process P2 competes with P1 to do the same thing.

Lock program for process p2

```
LOCK(B-queue,p2) ;
        LOCK(A-queue,p2) ;
        CR ;
        UNLOCK(A-queue,p2) ;
UNLOCK(B-queue,p2) ;
```

Notice the difference between the sequence of nested locks for P_1 and P_2. In P_1 we enter A-queue first, followed by B-queue. In P_2 we do just the opposite: enter B-queue, followed by A-queue. This leads to a potential deadlock state as shown in the process-state matrix of Figure 9-21.

What can be done to avoid improper use of locks? The nesting of one lock inside the critical region of another lock leads to a deadlock situation in the example above. Can structuring rules be used to avoid such abuse? The answer is "yes," and the solution lies in further use of encapsulation.

Monitor Encapsulation

We were able to solve many problems of concurrent processing in the previous chapter by encapsulating the pseudodata of a virtual processor inside a kernel. This idea can be of further use. In fact, a kernel is a special case of a more general encapsulation structure known as a *system monitor*.

A monitor encapsulates shared data by enclosing it within a structure for synchronizing access to the shared data. A monitor defines operations on the data as a collection of atomic procedures that are executed one at a time. That is, only one of the atomic procedures is allowed to execute at any point in time.

If necessary, a process can be preempted while in the act of executing a monitor atomic procedure. This means a queue must be established for holding the preempted processes. In the examples of this book we use kernel calls to:

WAIT (condition): If the condition is true, then do nothing; otherwise preempt the RUNNING process and block it until SIGNAL unblocks it. Select another READY process to run.

SIGNAL (condition): If the queue corresponding to the condition is empty, then do nothing. If not empty, then preempt the RUNNING

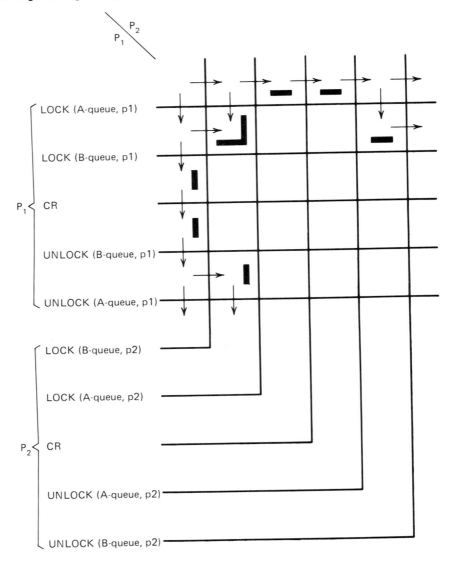

Figure 9-21. Nested locks can deadlock.

process. Remove the waiting process at the head of the condition queue and put it on the READY queue. Select another process from the READY queue and run it.

A monitor encloses all shared data needed to implement a preemptive lock. Furthermore, a system of monitors provides the necessary structure so that improper use cannot occur (a compiler check guarantees this). Hence, a monitor consists of:

Access Queue: A FIFO queue of waiting processes.

Shared Data: Encapsulated data.

Atomic Access Procedures: Allowed operations and synchronized control.

Initialization Routine: A code segment that is executed only once (at the time the system is initialized).

A monitor behaves in an unusual manner. We list some of the properties of a monitor below:

1. Shared (pseudo) data are permanent—they remain in memory before, during, and after the access procedures are executed.

2. Only one access procedure of a monitor is allowed to execute concurrently. All other access procedures must not be allowed to execute while any single procedure is executed by some process.

3. Access procedures are atomic; i.e., they disable all interrupts in the processor. This does not mean a process is not preempted during execution of a monitor procedure. That is, a process can preempt itself but cannot be preempted by any other process.

4. Monitor procedures cannot call other monitor procedures—to do so would risk deadlock. Hence, monitor procedures are not recursive, nor are they reentrant.

5. Monitor procedures cannot be nested inside of other monitor procedures—to do so would risk deadlock.

These rules and restrictions on monitors guarantee safe, fair, and live synchronization. In particular, the SIGNAL primitive assures fair access by enforcing a first-come-first-served discipline on the competing processes. We can see this in the producer-consumer problem discussed next.

A card spooler example We can illustrate the purpose and value of a monitor by example. Suppose a *producer* process reads a deck of cards from an input device and writes them to a buffer BUF of capacity NBUFS = 5 card images. Due to speed differences between the producer process and another process called the *consumer,* access to the buffer must be synchronized so that the consumer does not interfere with the producer.

The consumer process copies card images from the buffer in the same order that they are placed in the buffer by the producer. Both processes, consumer and producer, run asynchronously with respect to one another. It is the job of the buffer monitor to synchronize access by preemption of either process when necessary. Figure 9-22 gives pseudocode for this monitor.

The monitor of Figure 9-22 consists of permanent shared data:

$$BUF, HEAD, TAIL, \#FULL$$

and condition queues:

$$BUFFER\text{-}VACANT, BUFFER\text{-}OCCUPIED$$

These are manipulated by the WAIT and SIGNAL operations enclosed in an underlying kernel.

The access procedures PUTCARD and GETCARD are atomic procedures that define the only allowable operations on the shared variables. The initialization section (**init**) is executed once—when the monitor is initially loaded into the processor's memory.

Suppose we activate producer and consumer processes that call GETCARD and PUTCARD:

```
PRODUCER : begin
             while not EOF(INPUT) do begin
               READLN(CARD) ;
               PUTCARD(CARD) ;
               (* other stuff goes here *)
             end
           end
CONSUMER : begin
             repeat
               GETCARD(CARD) ;
               WRITELN(CARD) ;
               (* other stuff goes here *)
             until DONE ;
           end
```

PRODUCER and CONSUMER are concurrent processes that execute like ordinary sequential processes except when they access the shared data encapsulated inside PROSUMER. When this happens, PUTCARD and GETCARD synchronize access by either process. Figure 9-23 shows that access is safe, live, and fair.

Safe Access: Once GETCARD and PUTCARD get beyond their respective WAIT operations, all interrupts are disabled; thus no interleaving between vertical and horizontal states can occur.

Fair Access: Monitors enforce fairness because SIGNAL is performed before either process exits an access procedure. Hence, one gives the

```
monitor PROSUMER;
  var
    BUF : array[1 . . NBUFS] of CARDS ;
    HEAD, TAIL, #FULL : integer ;
    BUFFER-VACANT, BUFFER-OCCUPIED : CONDITION ;
  access procedure PUTCARD (C : CARDS) ;
    begin
      if #FULL = NBUFS then WAIT (BUFFER-VACANT) ;
      BUF[TAIL] := C ;
      TAIL := TAIL mod #BUFS + 1 ;
      #FULL := #FULL + 1 ;
      SIGNAL (BUFFER-OCCUPIED) ;
    end ;
  access procedure GETCARD (var C : CARDS) ;
    begin
      if #FULL = 0 then WAIT (BUFFER-OCCUPIED) ;
      C := BUF[HEAD] ;
      HEAD := HEAD mod NBUFS + 1 ;
      #FULL := #FULL - 1
      SIGNAL (BUFFER-VACANT) ;
    end
  init
    begin HEAD := 1 ; TAIL:= 1 ; #FULL := 0 end
```

Figure 9-22. A card spooler monitor.

other priority over itself before leaving a procedure. This method of enforcing relative priority among competing processes is effective but expensive. Two context switches are needed to ensure fairness: a context switch occurs when the SIGNAL is executed and then again when the END is executed (return from monitor).

Live Access: Monitors are live because they enforce a first-come-first-served policy without nested critical sections. However, it may be possible to use monitors as locks without enclosing the shared data within the monitor. When this is done, we again must be concerned with deadlock. In this case, the PROSUMER is live because of its proper structure.

Disadvantage of Monitors

The reader must be cautioned about improper use of a monitor to structure access to a critical section. Monitors are best used when the shared data structure is small and simple. In such cases, the encapsulation becomes monolithic (the entire shared data structure is contained within

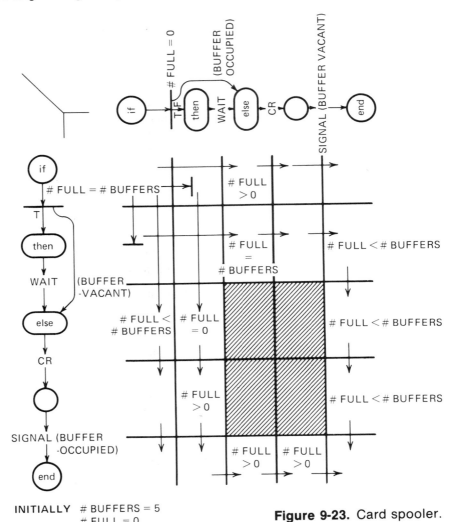

INITIALLY # BUFFERS = 5
FULL = 0

Figure 9-23. Card spooler.

the monitor as permanent data). Monolithic encapsulation means we can use the rules of monitor structuring to guarantee fair, live, and safe access.

There are many cases where monolithic encapsulation cannot be used, however. We first give an example where the critical section cannot be enclosed within a monitor, yet the monitor access procedures succeed in protecting the critical section. Then we will give a counterexample where an improperly designed system results in failure.

The *readers-and-writers problem* is similar to the producer-consumer problem except it allows many readers to simultaneously access CR while only one writer process is allowed access. This problem has important applications in shared data-base design. Suppose we encapsulate a file that is shared by M_R reader processes and M_W writer processes. Only the writers need mutually exclusive access to the file. The readers do not modify the file; hence they can be permitted to access concurrently.

It is not an easy matter to design a fair lock for the readers-and-writers problem. If we allow any number of readers to concurrently acess the file, what is to prevent a collection of readers from starving a waiting writer?

A typical solution to the readers-and-writers problem uses four monitor access procedures:

START-READ: Control access via readers and count the number of active readers in the CR.
STOP-READ: Guarantee fairness to writers and decrement the count of the number of active readers in the CR.
START-WRITE: Control exclusive access via writers.
STOP-WRITE: Guarantee fairness to readers.

The most interesting feature of this application of monitors is that the CR is not encapsulated inside the monitor. The access procedures are used to simply control access to an *external* CR:

```
READER : begin
            repeat
               START-READ ;
               CR ;
               STOP-READ ;
            until FOREVER ;
         (* other stuff *)
         end
WRITER : begin
            repeat
               START-WRITE ;
               CR ;
               STOP-WRITE ;
            until FOREVER ;
         (* other stuff *)
         end
```

The RM monitor shown in Figure 9-24 defines the four atomic procedures used by these competing processes. The EMPTY operation returns true if the condition queue is empty, and false otherwise.

The access procedures START-READ and STOP-READ simply count the number of readers that have entered the CR and exited the CR. The shared variable #READING counts the number of active readers. As soon as a writer requests access through START-WRITE, additional readers are blocked from access. Then, both reader and writer processes wait for the current readers to "clear out" of the CR. When all readers have "cleared out," the waiting writer is given exclusive access to the CR.

Subsequent writers are allowed to enter the CR unless readers are waiting. In this case, one reader is allowed in, and then the waiting writer is allowed in. The pattern of SIGNAL does not guarantee fair access. itor access procedures guarantee safe access, and the monitor (as used) is live.

This example shows how a monitor can be broken up into pieces such that the CR is not encapsulated, yet counters and other variables are protected by atomic access procedures. The only advantage of using a mon-

```
monitor RW ;
  var #READING : integer ;
      ACTIVE-WRITER : boolean ;
      OK-TO-READ, OK-TO WRITE : CONDITION ;
access procedure START-READ ;
  begin
    if (ACTIVE-WRITER or(not EMPTY(OK-TO-WRITE))
    then WAIT(OK-TO-READ)
    #READING := #READING + 1 ;
    SIGNAL (OK-TO-READ) ; (* allow other readers to enter *)
  end ;
access procedure STOP-READ ;
  begin
    #READING := #READING - 1 ;
    if #READING = 0 then SIGNAL (OK-TO-WRITE) ; (* be fair *)
  end ;
access procedure START-WRITE ;
  begin
    if (#READING <> 0 or ACTIVE-WRITER) then WAIT (OK-TO-WRITE) ;
    ACTIVE-WRITER := TRUE ;
  end ;
access procedure STOP-WRITE ;
  begin
    ACTIVE-WRITER := FALSE ;
    if not EMPTY (OK-TO-READ) then SIGNAL (OK-TO-READ)
      else SIGNAL (OK-TO-WRITE) ;
  end ;
init begin #READING := 0 ; ACTIVE-WRITER := FALSE end ;
```

Figure 9-24. Readers-and-writers monitor.

itor in this fashion is the guarantee of an indivisible atomic procedure activation. As the next example shows, this lack of structure can lead to failure.

Suppose we use a monitor to seize a line printer process. A printer process needs to print an entire page of text, one line at a time. If we use the producer-consumer solution, other printer processes might concurrently access the printer device, resulting in interleaved lines of output. Therefore, we need SEIZE and RELEASE procedures for allocating the print buffer to only one process at a time. A monitor containing SEIZE, RELEASE, and PRINT procedures is shown in Figure 9-25.

Now, suppose two processes use this monitor: P_1 is a "good" process, whereas process P_2 is a "bandit."

$$P_1 : \text{SEIZE} ;$$
$$(* \text{ print a page } *)$$
$$\text{RELEASE} ;$$
$$P_2 : \text{RELEASE} ;$$
$$\text{SEIZE} ;$$
$$(* \text{ print a page } *)$$
$$\text{RELEASE} ;$$

The good printer process follows the rule that a SEIZE must be done before a RELEASE. As a result, P_1 is led to believe it has exclusive access to the PRINTBUFFER variables. The bandit printer process P_2 violates the "correct" structure by executing a RELEASE before a

```
monitor PRINTBUFFER ;
  var
    BUF : array[1 . . 132] of char ;
    FREE : boolean ;
    OK-TO-PRINT : CONDITION ;
access procedure SEIZE ;
  begin
    if not FREE then WAIT (OK-TO-PRINT) ;
    FREE := FALSE ;
  end ;
access procedure RELEASE ;
  begin
    FREE := TRUE ;
    SIGNAL (OK-TO-PRINT) ;
  end ;
access procedure PRINT (LINE) ;
  begin (* output LINE to device *) end ;
init begin FREE := TRUE end ;
```

Figure 9-25. A print monitor.

SEIZE. Hence, both P_1 and P_2 are given access to the printer device, and their output lines are interlaced.

What is the cause of the failure in the printer example? The lack of proper structure, i.e., encapsulation of the CR within the monolithic monitor, is what contributed to the failure. Such a possibility always exists whenever the CR is not properly encapsulated within the monitor structure. We could have abused the solution to the readers-and-writers problem in a similar manner by executing the access procedures ''out of order.'' Hence, the disadvantage of monitors is that they either do not provide complete encapsulation or they are too monolithic.

> *MONOLITHIC MONITOR PROBLEM:* A monolithic monitor fully encapsulates data and critical section code. This may make it impossible to synchronize access to shared data without restricted concurrency as shown by the readers-and-writers solution.
>
> Conversely, if we remove the monolithic structure of a monitor, we risk poor structure, and failure may occur as shown in the printer monitor example.

In the next section we study more difficult synchronization problems that aggravate the monolithic monitor problem. Then, in the next chapter we study methods of overcoming the limitations of monitors.

The reader should not be discouraged with the abilities of system monitors. They are extremely elegant structures for implementing simple preemptive locks and should be used in this restrictive case. Furthermore, they provide a basis for study of more powerful methods of structured preemption. A keen understanding of monitors will be necessary to understand the techniques of encapsulation used to implement system *objects* (see Chapter 10, Object-Based Software Design).

CONCURRENCY IN *B*-TREES

Many system resources are described by data with graphlike structure instead of arraylike structure. In such graph-structure applications it may be desirable to access subgraph parts of the structure concurrently. Since monitors prevent multiple access at the same time, they also prevent concurrent access to subgraph parts of more elaborate shared-data structures. In this section we study locking mechanisms that apply to more general situations. In particular, we reexamine the *B*-tree structure that is central to the design and implementation of data-base systems. See Chapter 6, Application to File Structures, for more details concerning *B*-tree operations.

Concurrent Readers-and-Writers Problem

A *B*-tree structure may be shared among a collection of processes that either read or write information to/from the B-tree. Suppose we define a reader process as any process that traverses the B-tree for the purpose of finding a matching key, and when the match occurs, returns a copy of the value of the key and its associated data. Readers do not modify either the structure or the contents of the B-tree.

A writer process, on the other hand, traverses the B-tree for the purpose of inserting a new key (and associated data) into a leaf node. Writers modify the contents of a leaf and, if necessary, the structure too. An insert may result in a node split, followed by ascending inserts and splits on parent nodes. Therefore, writers may have widespread side effects on the B-tree.

We might solve this readers-and-writers problem by encapsulating the entire B-tree structure in a monitor with access procedures called START-BTREE-READ, STOP-BTREE-READ, START-BTREE-WRITE, and STOP-BTREE-WRITE. These procedures could be designed to do exactly what the earlier solution to the readers-and-writers problem did: allow a single writer exclusive access, and multiple readers simultaneous access, to the B-tree.

Unfortunately, the earlier solution is a poor choice for implementation of a "good" B-tree synchronization lock. The trouble with this approach is the monolithic property of the monitor. Only a single writer is allowed access *anywhere within the B-tree,* yet simultaneous access to disjoint subtrees should be allowed.

The scenarios of Figure 9-26 illustrate that a greater degree of parallelism can be achieved in a B-tree than the simple readers-and-writers solution allows. In Figure 9-26(a), a reader and writer can simultaneously access different subtrees without risk of indeterminism. The writer need only gain exclusive access to the subtree that is modified due to an insert operation.

In Figure 9-26(b), we see how three processes can simultaneously access the B-tree without interference. The writer causes a node to be split, but since the side effects of the split are restricted to a subtree, no indeterminism results. Similarly, Figure 9-26(c) shows how two writers can simultaneously insert new keys (and associated data) into *different subtrees* without hazard.

Figure 9-26(d) illustrates what may happen when a writer causes a series of split nodes that propagate to the root node. The writer process in Figure 9-26(d) must be given exclusive access to the *entire B*-tree.

Safe Subtree Locking

In the examples discussed above we noted how writer processes can simultaneously insert new information into the B-tree while other processes access the B-tree. However, we must guarantee noninterference between a writer process and any other process by careful separation of subtree access. We can guarantee noninterference in *safe subtrees*. A safe subtree is a subtree whose root node is safe.

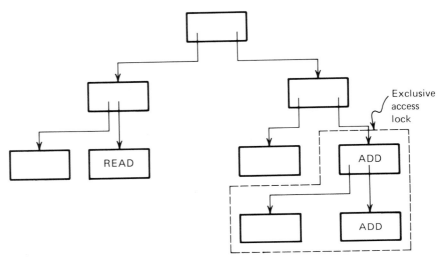

(a) 1 Reader, 1 Writer

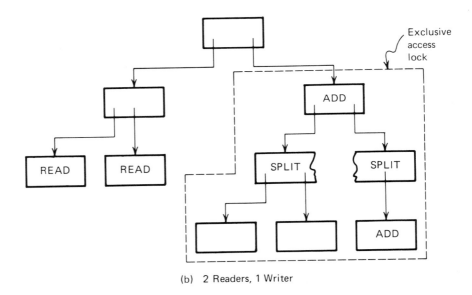

(b) 2 Readers, 1 Writer

Figure 9-26. Concurrent READ/WRITE in a B-tree.

SAFE NODE: A node is safe if it cannot be split due to a writer process that inserts a new key in any node of the subtree defined by the safe node.

A node is safe if it cannot be split, and it cannot be split if it has enough room to accommodate a new key. Hence, we can compute the "safety" of a node by counting the number of writer processes that have scanned the node.

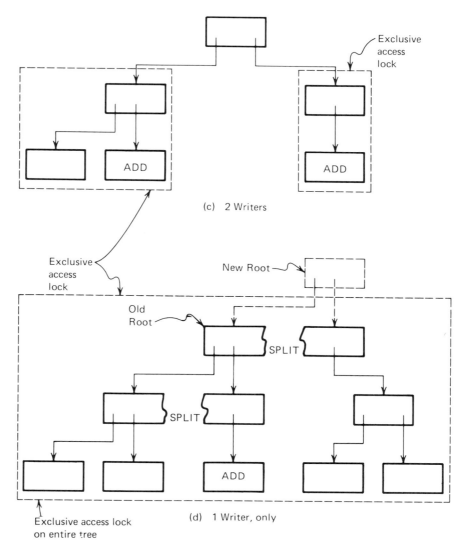

(c)   2 Writers

(d)   1 Writer, only

Figure 9-26. Continued.

WRITER-COUNT: Each node has a writer-count associated with it that counts the number of writer processes that have accessed it.

Let

M = number of occupied items (keys and associated data) in a node.

N = order of the *B*-tree. A node is full when $M = N - 1$ items.

Now, a node is a *safe node* if

$$\text{Writer-count} <= N - M - 1$$

and we say a node is locked if

$$\text{Writer-count} > 0$$

However, it is possible for a node to be full and yet be safe because it cannot be split. How is this possible? A writer process seeks a leaf node in which to insert a new key. Therefore, the writer accesses every node in a path from root to leaf. Every writer-count is incremented along this path, yet the final node may accommodate the new key without splitting. Thus no other (parent) node will be split, and therefore all nodes in the path are safe.

We only need to identify and lock the subtree defined by the lowest safe node. That is, we need only find the *least safe node* that defines the *least safe subtree*. A writer process is given exclusive access to the least safe subtree that is updated by the writer process.

LEAST SAFE NODE: A safe node is least safe if it is the lowest safe node in the *B*-tree (for a given writer process).

Now, as soon as a least safe node is found, all writer-counts above the least safe node are decremented by one. This "clears" the way for other processes to gain access to predecessor nodes.

In order to guarantee safe access to a *B*-tree, we need only lock the least safe subtree that is modified by a writer. Thus, writer processes are given exclusive access to least safe subtrees. Readers are allowed access to any part of a *B*-tree except locked least safe subtrees.

Figure 9-27 illustrates the concept of a least safe node and least safe subtree. In Figure 9-27(a), a writer process searches top–down until the leaf node is reached. At each node in the path from root to leaf, the writer-count is incremented and compared with the inequality

$$\text{Writer-count} <= N - M - 1$$

where $N = 3$. If this inequality holds, the node is marked as SAFE. Otherwise the node is marked as UNSAFE. The third node is UNSAFE in Figure 9-27(a), but since a lower node is SAFE, the lower node becomes the least safe node.

Figure 9-27(b) shows what happens next. The writer-count values in all nodes along the path from least safe node to root node are decremented. The release phase back tracks up to the root node, causing each writer-count to be set to zero. This allows other processes to access those nodes now.

Figure 9-27(c)–(d) illustrates the exclusive lock algorithm for a more interesting case. The top–down phase scans from root to leaf, incrementing writer-count along the way. Finally, when the leaf node is reached, the least safe node is at the second tier of the B-tree; hence only the root node writer-count is decremented in the backtrack phase; see Figure 9-27(d). In this example, the least safe subtree contains four nodes in three levels.

This example shows how complex locking can become when applied to more complex shared-data structures. A monolithic monitor encapsulates the entire data structure that reduces the throughput of readers and writers. Alternatively, an unstructured lock (using atomic procedures) may lead to failure due to starvation or deadlock. The "ultimate" solution to this problem must await advanced techniques; see Chapter 10, Object-Based Software Design.

SUMMARY

This chapter has explored a variety of synchronization locks ranging from the simple spin locks first proposed by Dijkstra and Knuth to the sophisticated locks based on encapsulation. The spin locks require little in the way of hardware support: individual operations and memory interlock. Spin locks, however, waste processor cycles.

A more efficient approach is found in the class of preemptive locks. Preemptive locks assume an underlying interrupt structure and system kernel for maintaining the state of all processes. Structure can be added to preemptive locks so that the system implementer is less likely to construct a "bad" lock.

We defined *safe, live,* and *fair* as properties of "good" locks. Since it is often difficult to analyze the (convoluted) code of locks to determine if they are safe, fair, and live, we resorted to extensive analysis using the Interleave Principle and the process-state matrix. It was possible to distinguish one locking algorithm from another by observing the patterns of control-flow found in the process-state matrix for each lock.

Monitors provide a kind of structure for preemptive locks. This structure was the result of encapsulation of the shared data and critical section code for each lock. Unfortunately, monitors overencapsulate in some applications and lead to the monolithic monitor problem. However, they are excellent programming constructs to use in simple synchronization applications like the producer-consumer problem. Furthermore, their structure guarantees safe, fair, and live access when used properly.

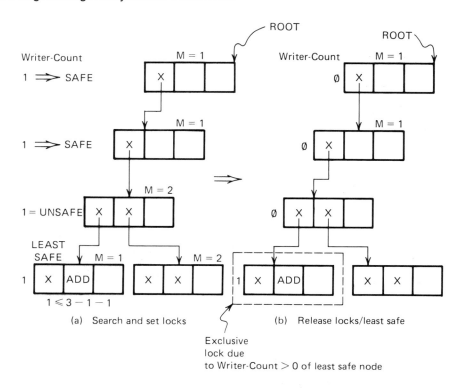

Figure 9-27. Finding the least safe node.

We studied an example of an application of locking to shared *B*-tree synchronization. The *B*-tree readers-and-writers problem illustrated how complex a "real-world" application can become. It also illustrated the inadequacy of the simple locks discussed in this chapter. More powerful synchronization techniques are needed to (elegantly) solve higher-order synchronization problems associated with shared-graph structures.

PROBLEMS

1. Propose a solution to the *B*-tree readers-and-writers problem. Prove your proposal works using the Interleave Principle.

2. Analyze the monitor in Figure 9-24 using the Interleave Principle. Is it safe, fair, and live?

3. Why are pure monitors sure to be fair?

4. What is the largest number N[i] possibly generated in Lamport's lock? What can be done to avoid overflow in this algorithm?

5. Devise a fair lock that solves the readers-and-writers problem using

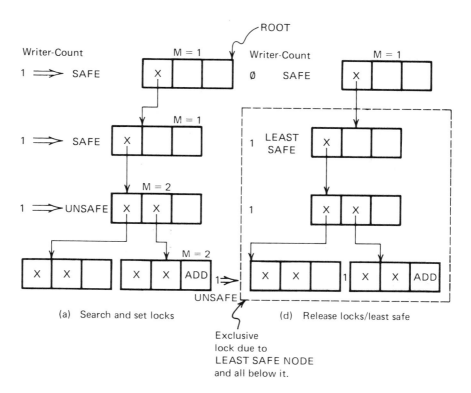

Note: The least safe node is the place where splits stop whenever an inserted item causes splitting.

Figure 9-27. Continued.

Knuth's atomic procedures. Analyze your solution using the Interleave Principle.

6. Analyze the following spin lock using the Interleave Principle (assume $N = 2$ processes only):

For Process i ($i = 1$ or 2)

Flag [i] := True ;
while FLAG [i **mod** 2 + 1] **do** ;   (* spin *)
CR ;
FLAG [i] := False;

Initially, FLAG[1] = FLAG[2] = False, and $N = 2$.

7. Analyze the following spin lock using the Interleave Principle ($N = 2$ and $i = 1$ or 2):

For Process *i*

```
FLAG [i] := True ;
while (TURN <> me) or FLAG [other] do ;
CR ;
FLAG [other] := False ;
TURN := other ;
```

Initially, FLAG[1] = FLAG[2] = False, TURN = 1. In process i = 1; me = 1, other = 2. In process i = 2; me = 2, other = 1.

8. Design and code a monolithic monitor solution for the *B*-tree readers-and-writers problem. Show that your solution is safe, fair, and live. How does your solution differ (or resemble) the proposed solution given in Figure 9-24?

9. Complete access procedure PRINT in Figure 9-25. How might this monitor be modified to handle a two-line buffer?

10. Analyze the following locks using the Interleave Principle to study their properties (Are they live, fair, and safe?).

For Process *i* (*i* = 1 or 2)

(a)
```
if FLAG [i mod 2 + 1] then WAITFOR (OK-TO-ENTER) ;
FLAG [i] := True ;
CR ;
FLAG [i] := False ;
SIGNAL (OK-TO-ENTER) ;
```
FLAG[1] = FLAG[2] = False initially.

(b)
```
FLAG [i mod 2 + 1] := False;
while FLAG [i] do ;
CR ;
FLAG [i mod 2 + 1] := True
```
FLAG[2] = True initially.

REFERENCES

Dijkstra, E. W., "Solution of a Problem in Concurrent Programming Control," *Communications of the ACM,* 8, no. 9 (September 1965), 569–572.

Knuth, D. E., "A Note on 'Solution of a Problem in Concurrent Programming Control,'" *Communications of the ACM,* 9, no. 5 (May 1966), 321–322.

Lamport, L., "Concurrent Reading and Writing," *Communications of the ACM,* vol. 21, no. 11 (November 1977).

Ricart, G., and A. K. Agrawala, "An Optimal Algorithm for Mutual Exclusion in Computer Networks," *Communications of the ACM,* 24, no. 1 (January 1981), 9–17.

10

Object-Based
Software Design

INTRODUCTION

In Chapter 8 we introduced three levels of abstraction:

1. Machine environment to pseudodata
2. Pseudodata to encapsulation
3. Encapsulation to objects

The first two levels have been covered in considerable detail, but only the most rudimentary notions of encapsulation-to-objects have been discussed. In this chapter we clarify and refine the concept of software *object*. A simple object can be thought of as a region in memory that contains a value. The value corresponds to a constant or the value of a variable. A more complex object corresponds to an *instance* of an abstract data type. It is this latter concept that we will emphasize in this chapter.

An abstract data type is an encapsulation of a simple object (region in memory) along with the allowable operations on the simple object. Hence, an abstract data type is an encapsulation of (pseudo) data and the operations allowed to access that (pseudo) data.

An instance of an abstract data type is a complex object. A system monitor (see previous chapters) is an example of a complex object. Since we will be concerned with complex objects in the remainder of this chapter, the term *object* will be used to mean either *simple or complex* object.

An object may encapsulate resources in a distributed or multiprogrammed operating system. In this case it is necessary to synchronize the allowed operations on the object. We call such objects *concurrent objects* because they encapsulate data, operations, and synchronization control mechanisms for guaranteeing safe, fair, and live access.

The major differences between level two virtualization (monitors, locks) and level three virtualization are: (1) the level of abstraction of synchronization mechanisms, and (2) the use of generic types to specify level three objects. We will employ *path expressions* to raise the level of abstraction of the synchronization mechanism of objects, and a data type called *object* to specify a class of objects. Language constructs for expressing these two features are found in an extension to Pascal called *Path Pascal* (Campbell).

A *path expression* is a regular expression containing the names of the operations permitted on an object. Each object has an associated path expression that specifies the order of execution of its operations and the number of processes that may concurrently execute an operation. A path expression is a *separate* specification of synchronization and can be changed without altering the implementation of the operations on the object.

An *object* is an instance of a type; hence the specification of an object is separated from its instance (object), unlike level two encapsulations. For example, in Path Pascal, OBJ1 and OBJ2 are two objects of type SIMPLE, as noted below:

```
type
   SIMPLE = object
               path ADD end ;
               var A,B : integer ;
               entry ADD ;
                  begin . . end ;
            end ;
   var
   OBJ1, OBJ2 : SIMPLE ;
```

Notice in the example above that the type SIMPLE contains data (*A*,*B*), a path (control), and executable code (ADD).

Thus, the instances OBJ1 and OBJ2 also contain data, a path, and executable code. Access to OBJ1 is governed by the allowed operation ADD and the path expression. The executable code segments for OBJ1.ADD and OBJ2.ADD are distinct (duplicate) copies of the code defined in SIMPLE.

The separation of synchronization-from-implementation, and type-from-instance (object) raises several interesting possibilities for improved software engineering using an object-based design methodology. This chapter explores these possibilities by developing a theory of synchronization using path expressions, applying the theory of path expressions to synchronization problems, and then illustrating the theory with an example of a distributed system of objects.

PATH EXPRESSIONS

In Path Pascal a type is defined as a *generic* if it is declared as an object and contains an access path and one or more entry routines for accessing the data encapsulated by the object. Thus, an object contains data, an access path, and operations:

type
　　< type-name > = **object**
　　　　　　　　　　path < path expression > **end** ;
　　　　　　　　　　< data >
　　　　　　　　　　< entry routines >
　　　　　　　　　　< initialization routine >
　　　　　　　　　　end

All access synchronization is done by following the control path defined in the path expression. What is a *control path,* and how is it established in a path expression?

Software Network of a Path Expression

Let *a*, *b*, and *c* be the names of functions and/or procedures declared as *entry routines* in an object. A path expression defines *concurrent* execution of two or more entry routines if ',' separates them, and *serial* execution if ';' separates them. This is illustrated in Figure 10-1. The list below describes the various network paths in Figure 10-1.

1. **path** *a* **end.** Entry routine *a* can be executed concurrently by any number of processes. This corresponds to random, nondeterministic calls to *a*.

2. **path** *a,b,c* **end.** Any number of processes may concurrently execute *a*, or *a* and *b*, or *a* and *b* and *c*. Also, *a* or *b* or *c* may be executed in any order. Altogether there are three ways to follow the control path defined by this path expression.

3. **path** *a;b* **end.** A process cannot execute entry routine *b* until it or some other process has executed *a*. In fact, two or more processes can concurrently execute *a*, but *a* must precede *b* in the flow of control.

4. **path** 1:(*a*) **end.** Only one process can execute entry routine *a* at a time. If two processes attempt to call entry routine *a*, only one is allowed to (nondeterministically) execute *a* and the other must wait.

5. **path** 1:(*a*),*b* **end.** Only one process can execute *a* at a time, but any number can execute *b* concurrently. Execution of *a* and *b* is allowed concurrently.

6. **path** 2:(*a*),*b* **end.** Only one or two processes can execute *a* concurrently. Entry routines *a* and *b* can be active at the same time, but *b* can accommodate any number of processes.

7. **path** 1:(*a*), 1:(*b*) **end.** Only one process is allowed in *a*, and only one process is allowed in *b*. A single process is allowed to execute in *a* at the same time a single process is allowed to execute in *b*.

8. **path** 5:(*a*;*b*) **end.** No more than five processes can execute entry routines *a* and *b*. Entry routine *a* must be executed before *b*. If three processes are active, then two may be in *a* and one in *b*, for example.

9. **path** 6:(5:(*a*), 4:(*b*)) **end.** No more than six processes can be actively accessing the object. A maximum of five can execute *a*, and a maximum of four can execute *b*. Concurrent execution of *a* and *b* is permitted. For example, three processes might be executing *a* while two processes are executing *b*. However, if seven processes attempt to execute *a* or *b*, one must wait.

10. **path** 1:(ToLink; FromLink) **end.** Mutual exclusion between entry routines ToLink and FromLink. ToLink must be executed before From-Link. Typically this path expression is used to serialize access to a shared object (buffer). However, there is nothing to prevent process *X* from executing ToLink, followed by process *Y* executing FromLink.

11. **path** 3:(1:(Bufput); 1:(Bufget)) **end.** Bufput is executed first, followed by Bufget. Only one process is allowed to execute either Bufput or Bufget at a time. No more than three processes are allowed to be (partially) active in the object. Hence, one process may be executing Bufget, one process may be waiting to execute Bufget, and one process may be executing Bufput. If another (fourth) process comes along, it must wait for at least one other process to terminate its access to the object. *Note:* This path expression defines the control paths of producer-consumer processes that compete for and gain access to three buffers concurrently.

An Illustration

The last path expression described above can be used to illustrate an object-oriented design and implementation project. Suppose a three-character buffer is to be used by two processes engaged in producer-consumer interaction. Process Pro supplies characters for the buffer at some undetermined rate, while (concurrently) process Con removes characters from the buffer at some other undetermined rate. The buffer is a simple object as shown in Figure 10-2.

The three-character buffer is an object with associated access routines

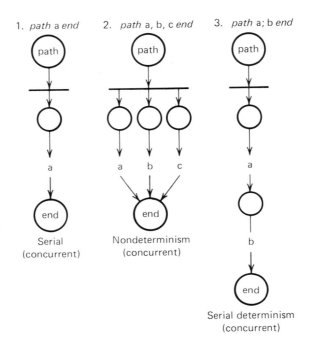

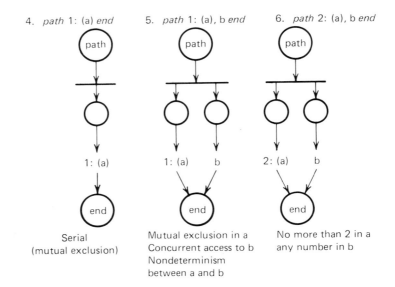

Figure 10-1. Path expressions as networks.

7. *path* 1: (a), 1: (b) *end*   8. *path* 5: (a; b) *end*   9. *path* 6: (5: (a), 4: (b)) *end*

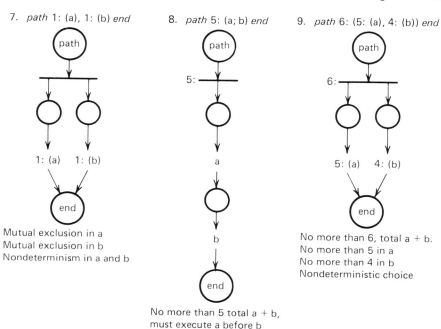

Mutual exclusion in a
Mutual exclusion in b
Nondeterminism in a and b

No more than 5 total a + b,
must execute a before b

No more than 6, total a + b.
No more than 5 in a
No more than 4 in b
Nondeterministic choice

10. *path* 1: (ToLink; FromLink) *end*   11. *path* 3: (1: (Bufput); 1: (Bufget)) *end*

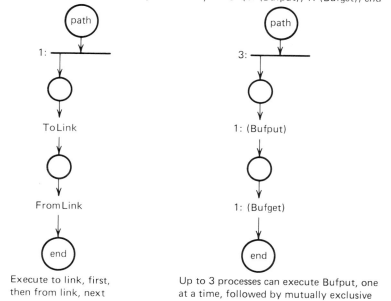

Execute to link, first,
then from link, next

Up to 3 processes can execute Bufput, one
at a time, followed by mutually exclusive
execution of Bufget.

Figure 10-1.   Continued.

Bufput and Bufget. A path expression that synchronizes access to Buf must guarantee mutual exclusion whenever writing to Buf, and yet allow concurrent reads from other parts of Buf whenever a character is available.

path 3:(1:(Bufput); 1:(Bufget)) **end.**

This path expression prevents process Con from executing Bufget more times than Pro executes Bufput. Hence, Con can never read more characters from the buffer than Pro puts into the buffer. Since each routine is limited to one process execution at a time, we never experience a ''race condition'' between accesses (see #11 in Figure 10-1).

A Path Pascal implementaton of this simple producer-consumer problem can be given without additional concern for synchronization. We have separated synchronization from entry routine implementation and thereby used level three abstraction as a software engineering tool.

```
type
  BUFFER = object
            path 3:(1:(Bufput); 1:(Bufget)) end
            var IOBUFFER : array [1 . . 3] of char ;
                In,Outp : integer ;
            entry procedure Bufput (M:char) ;
              begin
                IOBUFFER [In] := M ;
                In := (In mod 3) + 1 ;
              end ;              (* Bufput *)
            entry procedure Bufget (var M:char) ;
              begin
                M := IOBUFFER [Outp] ;
                Outp := (Outp mod 3) + 1
              end ;              (* Bufget *)
            init                 (* initialization routine *)
              begin
                In := 1 ;
                Outp := 1
              end ;
            end ;                (* BUFFER *)
    var
      BUF : BUFFER ;             (* instance = object *)
```

This example hides subtle underlying structure. Therefore, we follow a brief history of the instantiation of Buf along with execution of Pro and Con.

First, the definition of BUFFER includes storage in the form of IO-

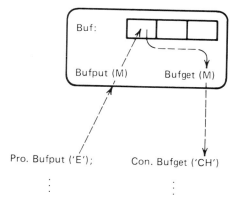

Figure 10-2. Producer-Consumer problem solved using objects.

BUFFER, In, and Outp. This storage is *permanent* once it is instantiated in the **var** statement. The object BUF contains

> BUF.IOBUFFER[1]
> BUF.IOBUFFER[2]
> BUF.IOBUFFER[3]
> BUF.In
> BUF.Outp

In addition, BUFFER defines code in the form of entry procedures Bufput and Bufget. Hence, instantiation of BUF also includes copies of this code:

> BUF.Bufput   (* includes BUF.Bufput.M *)
> BUF.Bufget

If BUFFER were instantiated a second time, say as BUF2 : BUFFER, a duplicate of the data and code would be made for BUF2.

BUFFER also defines a control path by way of the path expression. This expression is implemented (by the compiler) using counting semaphores to guarantee the flow of control stated in the path expression. The counting semaphore for 3:() is incremented each time a process enters the expression (up to 3), and decremented each time a process exits the expression.

Suppose process Con calls Bufget initially:

> Con : **begin**
>
> . . .
>
> Bufget (CH) ;
>
> . . .
>
> **end**

Since the path expression dictates an order (serial) between Bufput and Bufget, execution of Bufget by Con is blocked until Bufput is executed. Therefore, Con is suspended while Pro catches up.

Now suppose Pro quickly executes three Bufput operations:

> Pro : **begin**
>
> . . .
>
> Bufput ('A') ; Bufput ('B') ; Bufput ('C') ;
>
> . . .
>
> **end**

IOBUFFER now contains 'A', 'B', and 'C'.

Since a maximum of three processes are allowed in the path expression, a fourth operation by Pro, Bufput ('D') would be blocked until at least one Bufget is executed by Con. Instead, let Con become active after Pro has completed only two Bufput operations. In this case, IOBUFFER contains 'A' and 'B'. The Bufget routine returns 'A' to Con. Now the path expression will allow either another Bufput, or a Bufget operation. In this case, the buffer would contain 'D', 'B', and 'C'.

If Con is activated a second time, the Bufget ('B') operation is allowed. The buffer would only contain 'C' in this case. (Actually, 'A', 'B', and 'C' are still in IOBUFFER, but In and Outp do not point to them after execution of Bufput and/or Bufget.)

As a final illustration, suppose three Con processes atttempt to issue three concurrent Bufget operations on a single BUF object. All three requests will be blocked in first-come-first-served order. As soon as one or more Bufput operations are performed by Pro, one or more of the waiting Con processes are allowed to execute Bufget.

A comment on path expressions   Path expressions serve to structure the synchronization of access to an object. In this respect they might be viewed as hindrances to the programmer. In reality, a path expression forces the designer and programmer to clearly think through a synchronization problem. Structured programming attempts to minimize the use of **goto** control, and path expressions attempt to minimize the uncontrolled use of semaphores.

Yet, path expressions and objects may prohibit the implementation of needed synchronization mechanisms. Objects may be overly restrictive in much the same way that monolithic monitors are restrictive.

In the next section we show how complete encapsulation via objects can be used to solve the reader-and-writers problem and how the resulting path expressions simplify the problem of showing that the solution is safe, fair, and live. In general, the reader should be warned that objects and path expressions *do not* implicitly guarantee safe, fair, and live solutions. Instead, they only serve to simplify the analysis.

THE READERS-AND-WRITERS PROBLEM REVISITED

In the previous chapter we used a monitor to encapsulate a shared resource. The monitor solution only partially encapsulated the resource in the case of the multiple-readers-single-writer problem (see Chapter 9). For example, to do a read operation, the consumer process had to do two operations as illustrated below:

```
Con : process
        repeat
            START-READ ;      (* first operation *)
            CR ;
            STOP-READ         (* second operation *)
        until FALSE ;
    end
```

Similarly, to do a write operation, the producer process also had to break up access into two phases:

```
Pro : process
         repeat
           START-WRITE ;
           CR ;
           STOP-WRITE ;
         until FALSE ;
     end
```

Failure to execute the proper operations in the prescribed order leads to failure in access synchronization. For example, in the previous chapter we showed how this kind of design leads to failure due to thief processes and/or poor coordination among processes. The question, then, is can object-oriented design improve on this problem?

System of Objects

The following object-oriented design of a solution to multiple-reader–single-writer file access illustrates the utility of level three virtualization using objects. The idea, of course, is to totally encapsulate the file of type T records so that competing processes can access object "myfile" in a safe, fair, and live manner.

For example, shared file

```
var
      myfile : fobj ;
```

is actually an object of type "fobj." The read and write access operations

FREAD and FWRITE are executed from one or more processes as follows:

```
begin
    myfile.FREAD(REC#, REC) ;
    . . .
    myfile.FWRITE(REC#, REC) ;
end
```

where REC# is the record number of file myfile, and REC is the returned record of type *T*.

The access routines must totally control safe, fair, and live access. There are no start and stop operations that are separately executed by the competing process. Instead, competing processes are completely ignorant of the internal structure of object fobj.

The object structure that solves this problem is shown in Figure 10-3. We need the encapsulated file structure of type *T* and three other (internal) nested objects. Objects *R* and *W* are reader and writer semaphores, respectively. They simply serialize access to the file by delaying a process whenever necessary. Two counters, *j* and *i*, are used to keep track of the number of active readers and active writers, respectively.

The following code specifies the entry routines and path expressions corresponding to the objects of Figure 10-3. Notice that *P*, *R*, and *W* are instances of counter and semaphore. Also pay particular attention to the initialization routine and nesting of types.

```
type
  fobj = object path FREAD,1:(FWRITE) end ;
    type
      semaphore = object path SIGNAL ; WAIT end ;
                  entry procedure SIGNAL ; begin end ;
                  entry procedure WAIT ; begin end ;
                  end ;     (* semaphore *)
    type
      counter = object path 1:(INCR,DECR,INCW,DECW) end ;
                var j, i : integer ;
                entry function INCR : boolean ;
                  begin j := j + 1 ; INCR := (i>0) end ;
                entry function DECR : boolean ;
                  begin j := j−1 ; DECR := (i>0) and (j=0) end ;
                entry function INCW : boolean ;
                  begin i := 1+1 ; INCW := (j>0) end ;
                entry function DECW : boolean ;
                  begin i := i+1 ; DECW := (j>0) end ;
                init begin j := 0 ; i := 0 end ;
                end ;     (* counter *)
```

```
var   F  : file of T ;      (* T is some type *)
      P  : counter ;        (* instance of counter *)
      R,W : semaphore ;  (* two instances of semaphore *)
entry procedure FREAD (var REC# : integer ;
                             var REC : T) ;
   begin
     if P.INCR then R.WAIT ;
     SEEK(F,REC#) ;       (* seek record REC# *)
     GET(F) ;
     REC := F↑ ;            (* return the record *)
     if P.DECR then W.SIGNAL;    (* be fair *)
   end ;     (* FREAD *)
entry procedure FWRITE (var REC# : integer ;
                             var REC : T) ;
   begin
     if P.INCW then W.WAIT ;
     SEEK (F,REC#) ;       (* seek record REC# *)
     F↑ := REC ;
     PUT(F) ;               (* store it *)
     if P.DECW then R.SIGNAL ;    (* be fair *)
   end ;       (* FWRITE *)
(* other entry routines like OPEN, CLOSE go here *)
end ;     (* fobj *)
```

Analysis of the System

The solution presented above is claimed to be safe, fair, and live. How can we be sure? First, the top-level path expression guarantees that either zero or one writer is given write access at a time. Thus,

path FREAD,1 : (FWRITE) **end**

Hence only one writer at most can be writing a record into the file.

This top-level path expression does not, however, prevent one or more readers from executing FREAD while a writer is executing FWRITE. We must investigate the inner (nested) structure of fobj before we can show that execution of FWRITE means zero processes can execute FREAD. Suppose process Pro is executing FWRITE when process Con calls FREAD. This leads to the sequence

Pro : **if P.INCW then** . . .   (* i=1,j=0 *)
Con : **if P.INCR then** R.WAIT ;   (* j=1,i=1, so INCR = TRUE *)

Therefore, Con must wait until R.SIGNAL is executed. And R.SIGNAL will not be executed until process Pro completes its access to file F.

myfile: fobj

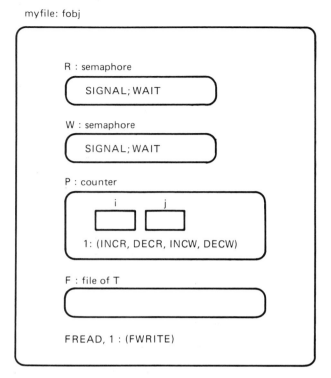

Figure 10-3. Object-oriented design of readers-writers problem.

Pro : **if** P.DECW **then** R.SIGNAL ; (* i=0,DECW = TRUE *)

Hence,

Con : (* enter CR *)

The Interleave Principle process-state matrix shown in Figure 10-4 shows that this solution to the readers-writers problem is safe, live, and fair. The second and third accesses (attempt to starve) are shown as double- and triple-hacked lines in Figure 10-4.

From Figure 10-4 we see that either one writer or one (or more) readers can access CR; at a time. Hence, the solution is safe.

There are no deadlock states; hence the solution is live. Note, the (2,2) square in Figure 10-2 appears to be deadlock prone, but it is not. The second access path is vertically blocked, and the third access path is horizontally blocked. This is what leads to fair access.

An access path that alternately gives control to FWRITE and then FREAD is fair. If several FREADers concurrently execute in the CR; section of the object, then synchronization is still fair if additional

FREADers are held up as soon as a writer makes a request. This is shown by replacing j with n (for n readers) in the process-state matrix. Then as soon as ($i > 0$) becomes true in INCR, the next request for FREAD is blocked. The blocked reader remains blocked until the waiting writer completes FWRITE.

In summary, the object-oriented version of the readers-writers problem totally encapsulates the shared resource object. This is done by completely hiding all underlying structure so that the processes that access the encapsulated object need not be "friendly" toward the object.

Furthermore, path expressions raise the level of abstraction of synchronization. Notice how easy it is to change the synchronization mechanism by simply changing the path expression (almost). Indeed, the explicit nature of path expressions can often be an indispensable aid to formally analyzing an object for correct synchronization. We will show how this is

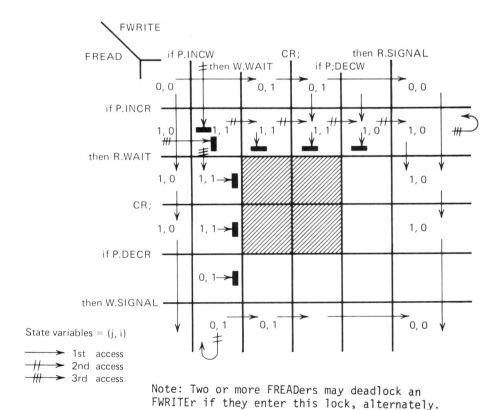

Note: Two or more FREADers may deadlock an FWRITEr if they enter this lock, alternately.

Figure 10-4. Process-state matrix for FREAD versus FWRITE.

done in concert with the Interleave Principle later, but before moving on to another topic, let us see how object-based design is used to guide the design of a distributed system of objects.

A DISTRIBUTED NETWORK OF OBJECTS

A distributed network of computers can be virtualized by encapsulating each machine so that its interrupt structure is hidden within a kernel (see previous chapters). This allows us to view each real machine as a node in a network of kernels. Each kernel handles message-passing throughout the system of kernels in a manner quite analogous to parameter-passing throughout a system of subprocedures. This greatly simplifies both design and analysis of the resulting (distributed) software.

Suppose we use the ideas of distributed kernels, level three abstraction, and object-based design to construct a three-node network. This network will contain objects for network communicating and objects for buffering between communicating process. For example, a process P_A running on node N_A might communicate with process P_B running on node N_B by

1. Producing a message for a local buffer.
2. Calling the local kernel to send the message.
3. Then using an internetwork object to send the message from N_A to N_B.

Figure 10-5 illustrates a ring-structured network containing three processors and a one-way loop that connects the processors together. The three processors are encapsulated as objects of type "machine":

net[1] : machine;
net[2] : machine;
net[3] : machine;

The three network links are encapsulated as objects of type "line":

Lines [1] : line;
Lines [2] : line;
Lines [3] : line;

Of course, we do not know the inner structure of these objects. We can only use machine and line in their most abstract form at this level of the design process. However, we soon discover that each network link must send messages from one buffer object to another. We also suspect that each machine must maintain buffers, nested objects, and so forth, as the suggested design in Figure 10-6 illustrates.

In Figure 10-6 the network consists of an array of three lines of type line and an array of three machines. Each machine (Net) consists of a buffer

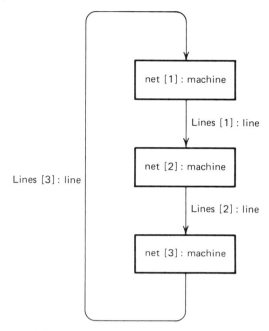

Encapsulations
A. Machine: contains data and functions on data
B. Line: contains messages and functions on messages

Figure 10-5. Example of encapsulation of a network.

object of type buffer, an input object of type inputs, and an output object of type outputs. These are the instantiated objects, however, and do not show all of the operations needed to manipulate the objects.

Figure 10-7 shows both the objects and the operations performed by the entry routines. In addition, each machine contains code for processes and user-called procedures. For example, processes Reader and Writer are used to access (in producer-consumer fashion) the buffer objects. The procedures Send and Receive are user-called procedures that allow a user process to send/receive messages to/from other processing nodes.

The Path Pascal Programs

First we present the code for implementing the objects, and then in the next section we will discuss how the system of objects operates. Also, since the code is lengthy, the objects will be presented in separate pieces, even though they would appear on a progam listing as outlined below:

Outline of Machine Objects

```
type
   Machine = object
                path go end ;
                   type buffer = object path bmax:(1:(bufput);1:(bufget)) end ;
                         ┌─────────┐
                         │ bufput  │
                         │ bufget  │
                         └─────────┘
                   type inputs = object path RespRecd;RespWait and ;
                         ┌──────────┐
                         │ RespRecd │
                         │ RespWait │
                         └──────────┘
                   type outputs = object path RqstRecd;BuildMesg end ;
                         ┌──────────┐
                         │ RqstRecd │
                         │ BuildMsg │
                         └──────────┘
                   var Buf : buffer ; Inp:inputs;Out:outputs ;
                   process Reader (Inline : Line;me:node); begin ☐ end ;
                   process Writer (Outline : Line);begin ☐ end ;
                   entry procedure go (who:node;Inline, Outline:Line) ;
                      begin ☐ end ;
                   procedure Receive (var V : item) ; begin ☐ end ;
                   procedure Send (info : item whoto:node); begin ☐ end;
                   ┌───────────┐
                   │ user code │
                   └───────────┘
   end ;            (* machine *)
```

Each machine object contains duplicate permanent data and duplicate executable code. Notice the path expression **path** go **end** ; which allows each machine to be started by execution of entry procedure "go". In turn, go activates the Reader and Writer processes that constantly look for input and output. If a user process wants to receive a message, it executes Receive. Similarly, a message is sent to another process by executing a Send operation. Synchronization of access to all objects is governed by the path expressions associated with each object.

Outline of Line Objects

```
type
   Line = object
      path 1 : (ToLink ; FromLink) end ;
      var MesgBuf : message ;
      entry procedure ToLink (M : message) ;
         begin MesgBuf := M end ;
      entry procedure FromLink (var M : message) ;
         begin M := MesgBuf end
   end ; (* Line *)
```

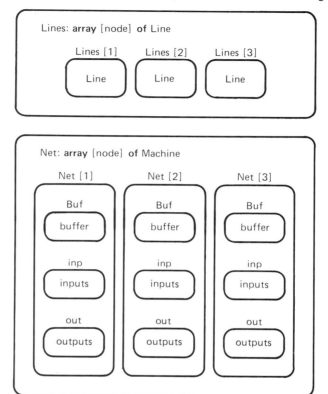

Figure 10-6. Instantiated objects.

Note: **type** message = **record**
                Kind : (Request, Response) ;
                id : node ;
                contents : item ; (* item is a string of char *)
            end ;

The ring network is encapsulated as an array of line objects. The To-Link and FromLink operations simply implement a product-consumer pair with mutually exclusive access. To see how these routines are used, we must look inside the Reader and Writer processes (see below).

Input Process Running on a Machine

process Reader (InLine : Line, Me:node) ;
  var M : message ;
  begin

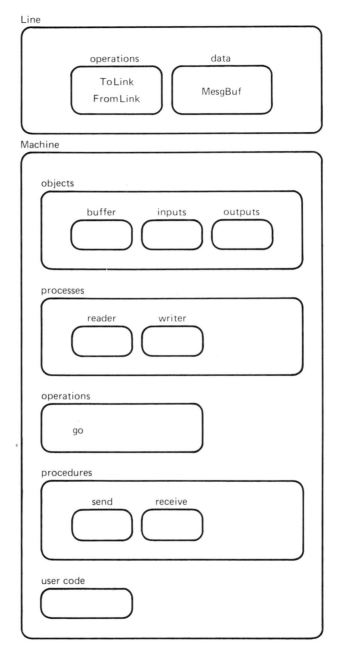

Figure 10-7. Objects and operations.

```
  repeat
    InLine. FromLink (M) ;        (* wait for MesgBuf to fill *)
    if (M.Kind = Response) and (M.id = Me)
      then Inp. RespRecd (M.Contents)      (* wait for and get
                                                 Contents *)
      else
    if  (M.Kind = Request) and (M.id = Me)
      then Out.RqstRecd         (* signal when ready to send *)
      else  Buf. Bufput (M)     (* send message *)
    until FALSE
end ;      (* Reader process *)
```

Note: **type** node = 1 . . 3

Output Process Running on a Machine

```
process Writer (OutLine : Line);
  var M : message ;
  begin
  repeat
    Buf. Bufget (M) ;              (* wait for, then get M *)
    OutLine . ToLink (M)       (* send M out *)
  until FALSE
end :      (* Writer process *)
```

The producer-consumer pair Bufget and Bufput have been discussed in an earlier section. However, we include them again for completeness. Each object of type buffer has its own copy of Bufput and Bufget:

Access to Buf

```
entry procedure Bufput (M:message) ;
  begin
    Iobuffer[In] := M ;
    In := (In mod Bmax) + 1
  end ;
entry procedure Bufget (var M:message) ;
  begin
    M := Iobuffer[outp] ;
    Outp := (Outp mod Bmax) + 1 ;
  end
init ; begin In := 1 ; Outp := 1 end ;
Note: path Bmax:(1:(Bufput);1:(Bufget)) end
     const Bmax = 3
```

Access to Outputs

```
entry procedure BuildMesg(Info:item; var Mesg:message; whoto:node);
  begin
    Mesg.Kind := Response ;       (* response or data? *)
    Mesg.id := whoto ;            (* send to whom? *)
    Mesg.contents := Info ;       (* data *)
  end

entry procedure RqstRecd ;
  begin end ;      (* signal BuildMesg *)

Note: path RqstRecd ; BuildMesg end
```

Access to Inputs

```
entry procedure RespRecd (Info:item) ;
  begin
    MesgContents := Info ;
  end

entry procedure RespWait (var Info : item) ;
  begin
    Info := MesgContents ;
  end ;

Note: path RespRecd ; RespWait end
```

User-Access

```
procedure Receive (var V:item) ;
  var Mesg:message ;
  begin
    Mesg.Kind := Request ;
    Buf.Bufput (Mesg) ;      (* request mesg *)
    RespWait (V) ;           (* grab response *)
  end ;

Procedure Send (Info:item; whoto:node) ;
  var Mesg:message ;
  begin
    BuildMesg (Info, Mesg, whoto) ;      (* format packet *)
    Buf.Bufput (Mesg) ;                  (* send it out *)
  end ;
```

Machine "Start-up"

```
entry procedure go (who:node ; InLine,OutLine:Line) ;
  begin
    Reader(InLine,who) ;      (* start reader process *)
    Writer (OutLine) ;        (* start writer process *)
    Users ;                   (* start user programs *)
  end ;     (* machine activation *)
```

System Activation

```
var
  Net : array [node] of machine ;
  Lines : array [node] of Line ;
begin
  Net[1].go(1, Lines[3], Lines[1]);
  Net[2].go(2, Lines[1], Lines[2]);
  Net[3].go(3, Lines[2], Lines[3]);
end.
```

The system activation step above causes the go procedure of each machine to be executed. When this happens, the ring-structured connections are established, and all processes are activated. Therefore, go activates

```
Reader ( Lines[3], 1 );
Reader ( Lines[1], 2 );
Reader ( Lines[2], 3 );
```

and

```
Writer ( Lines[1] );
Writer ( Lines[2] );
Writer ( Lines[3] );
```

which establishes the topology shown in Figure 10-5. Also, any user processes that execute on the machine are activated by procedure go.

In the next section we will explore the inner structure of this system of objects. Several points should be understood beforehand, however.

1. Access is synchronized by path expressions; therefore process blocking is implied.

2. A user sends and receives messages by executing either the Send or Receive routine in each machine object.

3. Messages are passed from node to node (machine to machine) by the Reader process until the correct destination is reached.

4. Messages can be solicited or unsolicited by processes; this means two kinds of messages are passed around the network: Response and Request.

A Message-Passing Example

A rather detailed example of access control during message-passing is needed to fully appreciate the sophistication of distributed objects. Therefore, the following "blow-by-blow" scenario is offered as an explanation of the example in the previous section. Unfortunately, the details are complex; so we examine only one of several possible actions.

Let a user process on Net[1] request a message from a user process on Net[3]. Then Net [3] must send the message through Net[2] to Net[1]. Initially, the system is in an "idle" state as shown in Figure 10-8. The following list should be used to trace the sequence of actions in Figure 10-8.

Figure Number	Sequence of Actions (Execution Trace)	
10-9	Net[1].Receive (V) ;	(* Request message *)
	Buf.Bufput(Mesg) ;	(* buffer-out Request *)
	RespWait (V) ;	(* block and wait . . . *)
10-10	Net[1].Writer(Lines[1] ;	(* output Request *)
	Buf.Bufget (M) ;	(* copy from buffer *)
	Outline.ToLink (M) ;	(* send it on its way *)
10-11	Net[2].Reader(Lines[1],2) ;	(* pass it on to Net[3] *)
	InLine.FromLink (M);	(* input Request *)
	Buf.Bufput (M) ;	(* **not** for Net[2] *)
10-12	Net[2].Writer(Lines[2]) ;	(* empty Net[2]buffer *)
	Buf.Bufget (M) ;	
	OutLine.ToLink (M) ;	

Comment: At this stage, the "Request" message has traveled from Net[1] to Lines[2]. Next, it is input to its destination Net[3]:

10-13	Net[3].Reader(Lines[2],3) ;	(* is it mine? *)
	InLine.FromLink (M);	(* get it *)
	Out.RqstRecd ;	(* signal so BuildMesg can go *)

The combined actions of Figures 10-9–10-13 are shown in Figure 10-14.

10-15	Net[3].Send(Info,1) ;	(* Respond to Net[1] *)
	BuildMesg(Info,Mesg,1);	(* format Response *)
	Buf.Bufput(Mesg) ;	(* buffer it out *)
10-16	Net[3].Writer(Lines[1]) ;	(* output to Lines[1] *)
	Buf.Bufget(M) ;	(* fetch from Buffer, *)
	OutLink.ToLink (M) ;	(* send it along *)

10-17
Net[1].Reader(Lines[1],1) ;   (* catch Response   *)
InLine.FromLink(M)   ;   (* take from Lines[1]   *)
Inp.RespRecd(M.Contents);(* wait, then get it   *)

Comment: At this stage, the "Response" from Net[3] has been received by Net[1]. This unblocks the user's process that issued a Net[1].Receive(V), and is awaiting RespWait(V). The blocking occurs because of the path expression, below.

path RespRecd ; RespWait **end** ;

10-18
RespWait(V)   ;   (* awakens . . .   *)
User ;   ;   (* return V to user   *)

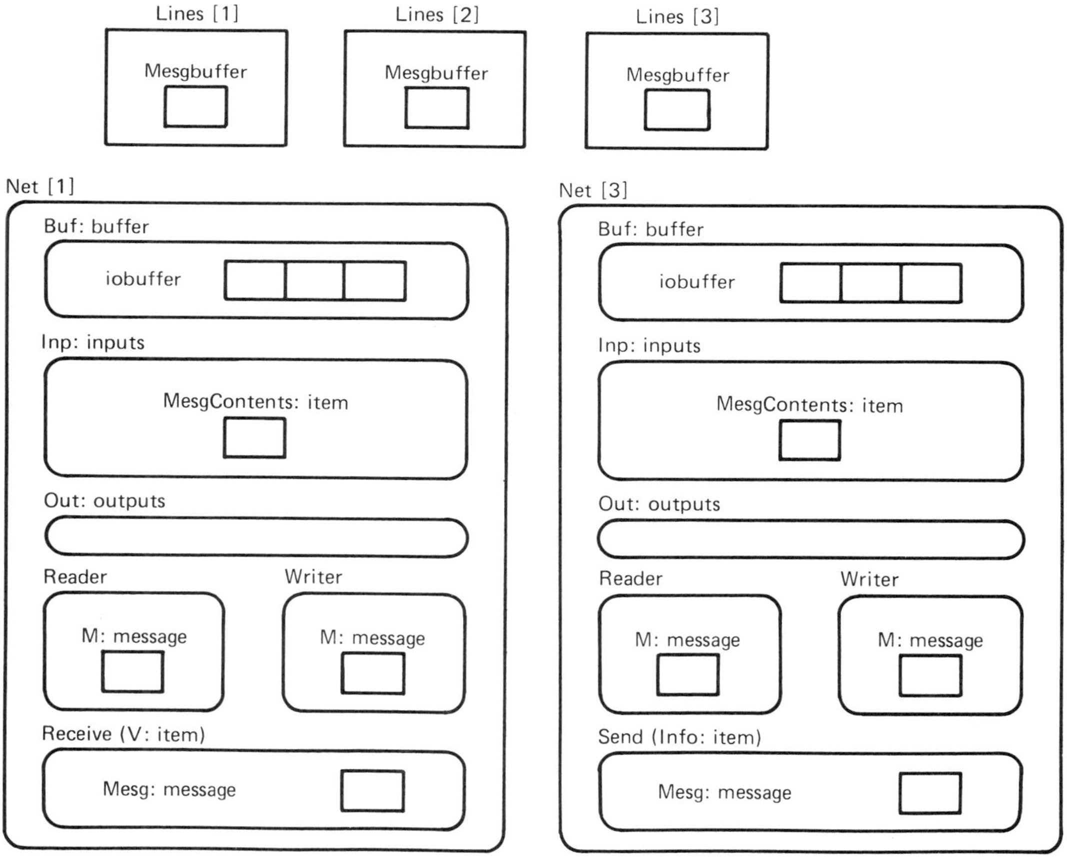

Figure 10-8. Initial state.

The combined actions of Figures 10-15–10-18 are shown in Figure 10-19.

A Path Expression Wheel

The system of distributed objects shown in the previous example can be shown to be safe, fair, and live by careful and detailed analysis of inter-process communication. However, an Interleave Principle analysis is difficult to carry out because the system includes eight system processes, three machines, and possibly many user processes. Instead, a process wheel is used to test the system as shown in Figure 10-20.

Each "pie" in the process wheel supplies control information. At the core, control is provided by Net[2] or Net[3]. Net[1], for example, encompasses the control of a Reader, Receive, and Writer operation for the example. Similarly, a Reader interfaces with operations that are controlled by path expressions as shown in the outer rim of the process wheel. For example, ToLink; FromLink and RespRecd; RespWait and 3:(1:(Bufput); 1:(Bufget)) are used by a Reader to communicate with other processes running on other nodes.

We can investigate safe access of an object by studying the path expression for the object. All path expressions guarantee safe access in Figure 10-20.

Live access is shown in Figure 10-20 because there are no "dead-end" paths through the process wheel. Every "pie" passes control on to another "pie." Of course, this example does not prove liveness for all examples.

Fair access is not shown by the process wheel, but consider this: All path expressions contain ';' serialization. No path expression contains a ',' connector. Therefore, all access is serialized, leading to a fair first-come-first-served discipline. Any process that attempts to starve another process must wait until its turn. Because of this, access is fair.

SUMMARY

An object in Path Pascal is an abstract data type consisting of permanent data, access routines that can be entry procedures or entry functions, concurrently executing routines called *processes,* and a path expression that gives a synchronization rule for ordering the execution of the entry routines.

An object is an instance of a type. Each time an object is created by instantiation of its type, a copy is made of the permanent data and executable code. Thus, an array of objects contains an array of permanent data and an array of (duplicate) executable code.

Objects in Path Pascal are created by the Path Pascal compiler and are activated during execution of the compiled program. This "early binding" of objects during the compilation phase of program development leads to one of the major shortcomings of Path Pascal. All objects must be known and created during program compilation.

Early binding is unacceptable in many applications of real-time control. Instead, the objects of a system (including processes) should be bound during program execution. That is, objects should be allowed to come "on line" and go "off line" dynamically.

A simple operating system should be able to create user processes as dynamic objects whenever a user "logs" onto the system, and then destroy the object whenever the user logs off of the system. In the example of this chapter, user processes were represented as user code segments imbedded inside the machine object. They were assumed to be known before the program was compiled.

A second problem exists for Path Pascal programs. That is, there is no provision for binding objects to real machine resources. For example, pseudodata equivalents of a device register may reside at a fixed memory address (e.g., 177560_8 in the PDP-11). Yet, there is no easy way to encapsulate such pseudodata.

A third problem may be troublesome to real-time application engineers. Path Pascal does not provide a means for scheduling accesses to objects so that deadlines are met. For example, a given device may need to be read once every 100 milliseconds. If access is not completed within 10 milliseconds of multiples of 100 milliseconds, the input data may be lost. This establishes a recurring deadline that cannot be forced on the system of objects. More versatile real-time scheduling is needed before this kind of control can be implemented.

The third level of virtualization using objects gives a structured method of implementing hierarchically organized systems. The use of path expressions simplifies the problem of synchronization, but the designer is still faced with proving that the system of path expressions and objects are safe, live, and fair. Additional research is needed to develop tools for automatically revealing deadlock, for example, in a Path Pascal program.

PROBLEMS

1. Use the process-state matrix of Figure 10-4 to show that the readers and writers problem is solved by fobj; i.e., show that access by three readers and one writer is safe, live, and fair.

2. Explain what the following path expressions mean:
    (a) **path** a,1:(a;b) **end**
    (b) **path** 2:(1:(a),1:(b)) **end**
    (c) **path** 1:(a);1:(b);1:(c) **end**
    (d) **path** 2:(a;a);b **end**

3. Reexamine the example of the distributed network in Figure 10-8. Give a detailed analysis of the case where a user process in Net[3] executes a Send operation *before* a user process in Net[1] executes a Receive operation.

4. Construct a process wheel for the solution to Problem 3.

5. Where (what) is the underlying kernel in the Path Pascal example of a distributed network of three processors?

6. Write a Path Pascal *object* called DISK that allows remote processes (on other processor nodes in a network) to gain multiple-reader-single-writer access to an encapsulated disk file.

7. Is it possible for a system of objects to be unsafe? Deadlock-prone? Unfair?

8. Give an object-based design similar to the design for the following system: one processor with a printer and a user terminal (keyboard and screen). Show the objects, Path Pascal code, and give an example of sending a screen of text to the printer.

REFERENCES

Campbell, R. H., and R. B. Kolstad, *Path Pascal User Manual,* Association for Computing Machinery SIGPLAN Notices, 15, 9 (September 1980), 15–25.

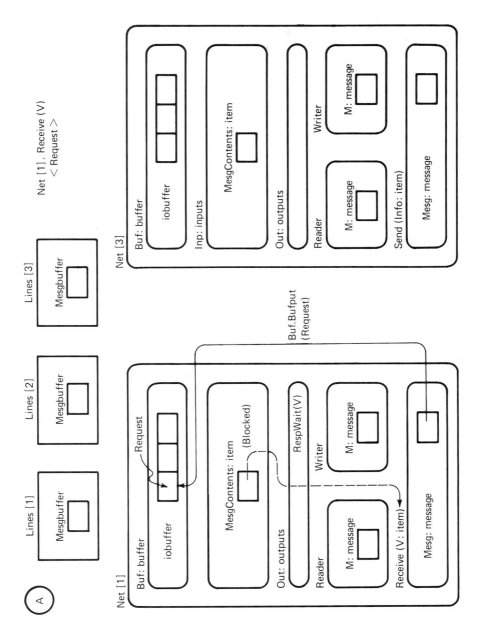

Net [1]. Receive (V)
< Request >

Figure 10-9. Net[1].Receive(V).

365

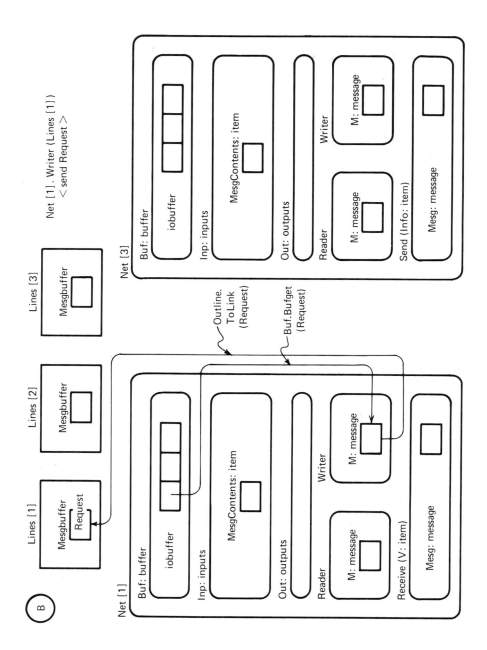

Net [1] . Writer (Lines [1])
< send Request >

Figure 10-10. Net[1].Writer(Lines[1]).

366

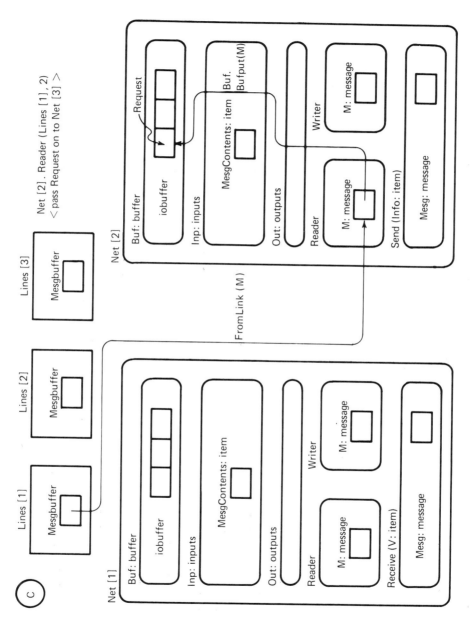

Net [2] . Reader (Lines [1] , 2)
< pass Request on to Net [3] >

Figure 10-11. Net[2].Reader(Lines[1],2).

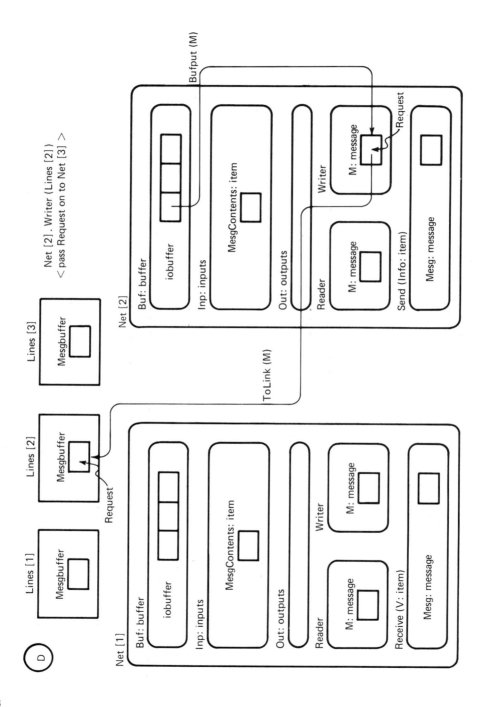

Figure 10-12. Net[2].Writer(Lines[2]).

368

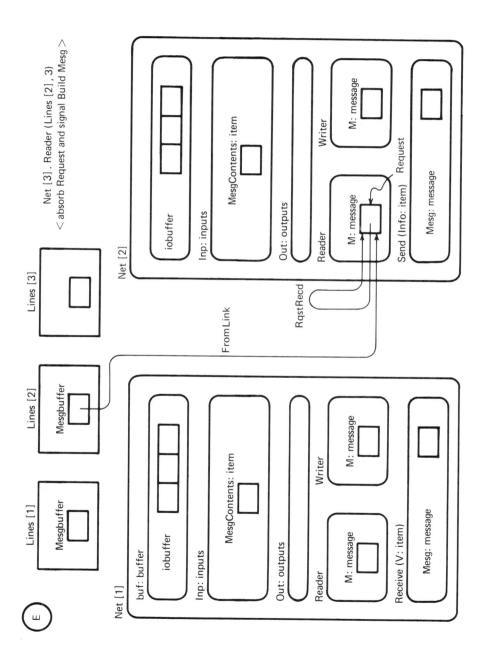

Net [3] . Reader (Lines [2] , 3)
< absorb Request and signal Build Mesg >

Figure 10-13. Net[3].Reader(Lines[2],3).

369

370

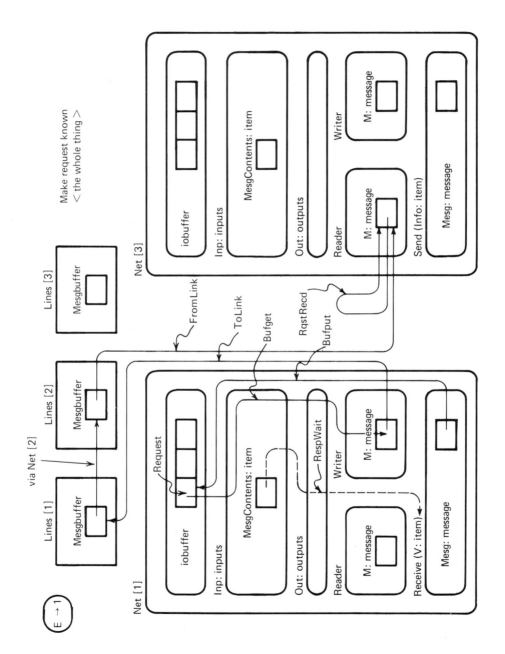

Figure 10-14. Make Request Known.

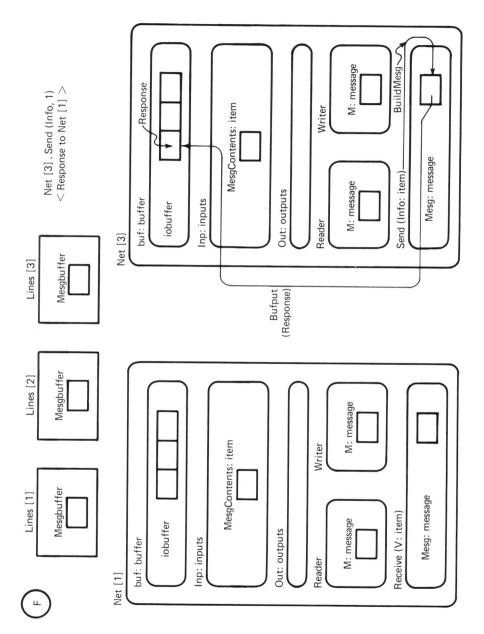

Net [3] . Send (Info, 1)
< Response to Net [1] >

Figure 10-15. Net[3].Send(Info,1).

371

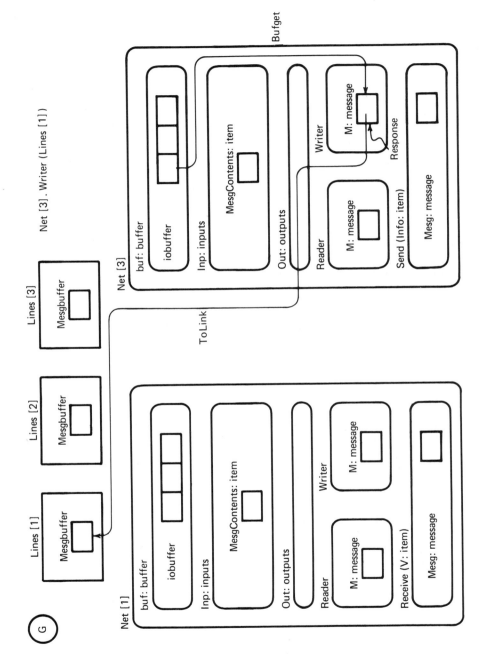

Net [3] . Writer (Lines [1])

Figure 10-16. Net[3].Writer(Lines[1]).

372

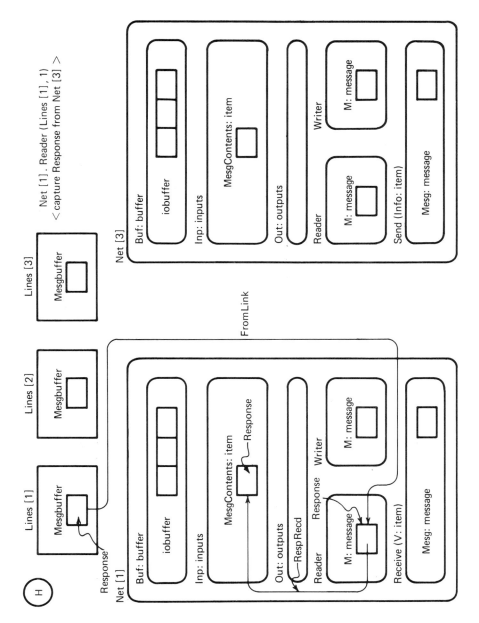

Figure 10-17. Net[1].Reader(Lines[1],1).

373

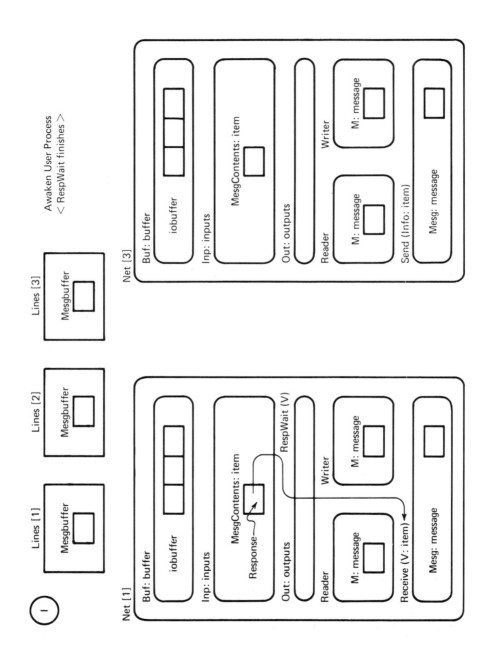

Figure 10-18. Awaken user process after RespWait Finishes.

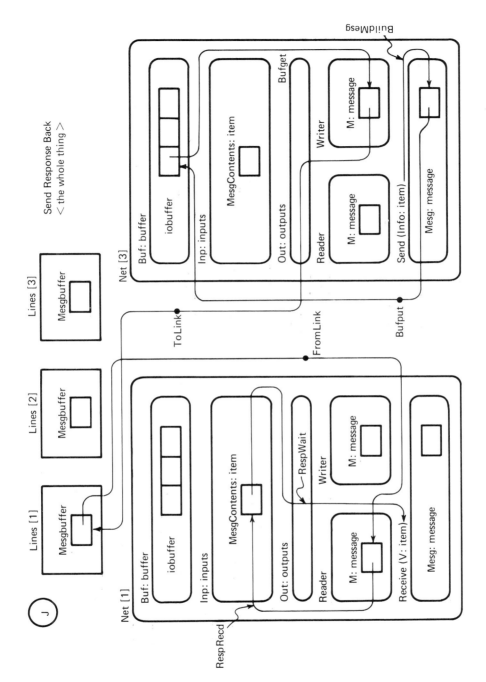

Send Response Back
< the whole thing >

Figure 10-19. Send response back, summary.

375

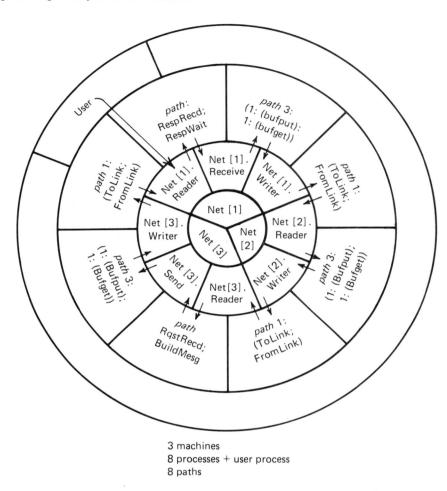

Figure 10-20. Process wheel for distributed objects.

11

The Duality
Principle

INTRODUCTION

The possibility of two distinct design philosophies was first discussed by Lauer and Needham in a fundamental paper on the design of operating systems (see reference list at end of chapter). Lauer and Needham observed that existing operating system software typically followed one of two sets of guidelines. The first set of guidelines adopts a procedure-oriented view, and the second set of guidelines adopts a message-oriented view of software. We will call the first view a *procedure-oriented dual* and the second view a *message-oriented dual* because, as we will show in this chapter, these two views are "opposite sides of the same coin."

In the procedure-oriented dual, a software system is thought of as a collection of many dynamically created (and destroyed) processes that share (common) objects. In a properly virtualized system of objects, process synchronization is needed to correctly access shared data. This is the model used throughout this book.

However, as Lauer and Needham point out, an alternate view of software is possible if we discard the idea of shared data and instead adopt a message-oriented philosophy. In the message-oriented dual, a relatively few statically created processes pass a relatively large number of messages to one another much like a postal service delivers mail to a community of households.

To understand the message-oriented dual, a software engineer must generalize the concept of a message. A message is any information that can be *duplicated, sent* from one process, and eventually *received* by another process. Hence, in the message-oriented dual, an interrupt signal is a message that originates in one process and is received by another process. The receiving process may temporarily halt or resume its execution upon receiving the message (interrupt).

A fundamental difference between procedure-oriented and message-oriented design is the way data are handled. In a procedure-oriented system, permanent data are created and remain in a fixed location of memory throughout the life of the system. In a message-oriented system, data are created and then are duplicated for use by processes. Hence, in a message-oriented system, many copies of the same data are sent to all processes desiring access to the data. In this way the possibility of indeterminism due to incorrect synchronization of access is limited to a small number of message-passing operations.

Figure 11-1 illustrates the two design philosophies. In Figure 11-1(a), two processes concurrently execute separate procedures. Both processes access common (shared) data by executing a critical section in their respective procedures. If the procedures belong to an encapsulated object (see previous chapter), then access synchronization is provided by a lock (semaphore, monitor, object path expression). The important feature of this philosophy is that of *object encapsulation*.

In Figure 11-1(b), two processes communicate through a third agent—one that separates the address space of process P_A from process P_B. A limited "channel" of communication is established between each process pair. This "channel" is used to send a *copy* of the data from one address space to another. Thus, in a message-oriented system, synchronization of access need only be provided at the "ends of the channel."

A common example of a message-oriented system is the U.S. Postal Service. Each house (process) has its own mailbox (port) where envelopes (messages) are placed for delivery. An employee of the Postal Service picks up the letter and delivers it to another mailbox (port). That is, the Postal Service operates like a system kernel for getting and putting messages.

Lauer and Needham have conjectured that the two design philosophies end up with equivalent results. The reason for choosing one philosophy over another may be due to differences in the underlying computer hardware or perhaps in ease of implementation. But the performance and functionality of systems designed in either way will be equivalent.

This book presents a predominantly procedure-oriented view of software systems. However, in this chapter we introduce and give detailed consideration to the message-oriented dual. In this way we present a balanced view of message-oriented versus procedure-oriented software design and implementation. Then the reader can determine which philosophy is best suited to a given situation. But first, let us review what we mean by a procedure-oriented design.

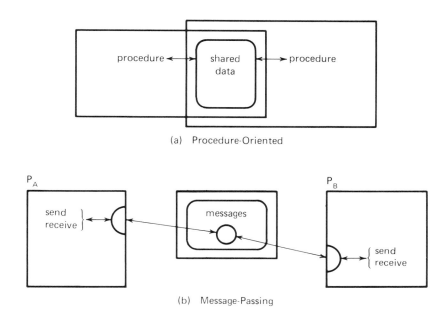

(a) Procedure-Oriented

(b) Message-Passing

Figure 11-1. Process communication in dual systems.

PROCEDURE-ORIENTED DESIGN

The dominant feature of the procedure-oriented dual is that many dynamically created and destroyed processes exist and compete for access to shared data stored in a shared address space. This concept leads to a distinct philosophy of software design.

The Philosophy

In a procedure-oriented system, all peripheral devices, machine resources, and (software) system objects are treated as data with encapsulating structures like monitors, kernels, or managers. These structures are typically composed of pieces of executable code that prevent unauthorized access to the (virtualized) data through locks.

Access to permanent data is a synchronization problem in a procedure-oriented system. *Data* are static, whereas *control* is passed around. Typical access control mechanisms are semaphores, SIGNAL and WAIT primitives inside monitor procedures, or path expressions defined for objects.

Processes inherit priorities dynamically from locks and context switches in a procedure-oriented system because of the way control is passed from process to process. Indeed, due to the sensitivity and importance of managing control (versus data) in a procedure-oriented system, great care must be taken to ensure correct passage of control from one process to another. This is why encapsulating control structures have been devised in the procedure-oriented dual as shown in the outline of a system kernel in Figure 11-2.

The procedure-oriented dual must be able to create and destroy processes because the process is the unit of computation. That is, every time some function needs to be done, a process for doing the function must be "cloned" and placed in the ready state. When the function is accomplished by the "clone" process, the "clone" is no longer needed. In this view, a job is a collection of processes that may be executed in series or concurrently.

The Reality

In reality, a procedure-oriented system is implemented by careful arrangement of code, access control, and scheduling of processes. The following list defines the particular features of the procedure-oriented philosophy.

Procedure: A code structure for transforming information associated with a process.

Synchronous call: Ordinary procedure invocation and its associated parameter-passing.

Asynchronous call: Invocation of concurrently executed procedures, which includes the creation and possible destruction of processes that execute the procedures concurrently.

Encapsulation: Structuring of virtual objects and the code that defines access to the objects in a manner that synchronizes access to the shared objects.

The correct synchronization of access to an encapsulated object has been treated elsewhere in this book. Therefore we will not repeat it here. However, we have not shown how processes are created and destroyed in a procedure-oriented system.

To illustrate creation and destruction of procedure-oriented objects, consider a small system kernel that must create a device-handling process to manage a keyboard and screen (CRT). The CRT device has a keyboard that generates a character each time a key is depressed. This character is placed in a buffer called BUF of length BUFSIZE by a process executing a code segment named CRTIO.

Suppose we instantiate a process called GOCRT to handle the CRT device as follows. Let type DEVICE define the object BUF and all the nec-

```
kernel : Monitor ;
   var
      C : condition;
         .
         .
         .

      begin
              (* initialization *)
      end;
   entry procedure (input : message) ;
      begin
      WAIT (C)
         .
         .
         .

      SIGNAL (C)
      end;
         .
         .
         .
end
```

Figure 11-2. Procedure-oriented encapsulation.

essary code to produce and consume keyboard characters. In type DE-VICE, two low-level device drivers, ECHO and DOIO, are assumed. DOIO returns the character input from the keyboard register, and ECHO causes the keyboard register to be displayed on the screen.

```
type
   DEVICE = object path BUFSIZE:(1:(PUTCHAR);1:(GETCHAR)) end;
            var BUF[1..BUFSIZE] of char;
            entry function GETCHAR : char;
               begin
                  GETCHAR := BUF[Out];
                  Out := Out mod BUFSIZE + 1;
               end;
            entry procedure PUTCHAR;
               begin
                  BUF[In] := DOIO; ECHO; (* display on CRT *)
                  In := In mod BUFSIZE + 1;
               end;
            process CRTIO (* code segment *)
```

```
            begin
               repeat PUTCHAR until FALSE; (* loop forever *)
            end;
        init
            begin
               In := 1; Out := 1
            end;    (* DEVICE *)
```

In a procedure-oriented system, a kernel routine known as NEW is called to create an object containing the buffer and code segments defined by DEVICE. Thus,

NEW(GOCRT,DEVICE);

At this point, GOCRT is an instance of a DEVICE. However, no process has been named to execute the code associated with GOCRT. A FORK routine within the kernel must be executed in order to cause the execution of CRTIO. Hence the FORK causes a process called P1, say, to be created, inserted into the READY list, and eventually executed when moved to the RUNNING state:

P1 := FORK CRTIO ;

In general, the FORK operation can pass parameters back and forth between P1 and the process that executes the FORK operation. In this case, the form of the FORK is as follows:

⟨pid⟩ := FORK ⟨code seq⟩ (⟨parameters⟩);

where

⟨pid⟩ : process identifier
⟨code seq⟩ : code segment to execute
⟨parameters⟩ : input/output parameters to be passed to
⟨code seq⟩.

Notice how P1 does the keyboard and screen operations associated with the CRT. CRTIO is activated as soon as P1 is put into running state and the **init** code is executed. Since CRTIO executes forever (**repeat-until** FALSE) or until destroyed, the PUTCHAR operation is completed each time a character is entered via the keyboard.

The path expression prevents buffer overflow by blocking P1 whenever BUFSIZE characters have been placed in BUF (and none removed). The DOIO routine is executed either as a spin lock that repeatedly tests the status of the keyboard until a character is ready, or else as an interrupt-driven routine.

Other processes execute operation GETCHAR in order to take characters from BUF. That is, interprocess communication betweeen P1 and any other consumer process provides a way to pass a character from the character buffer to the process desiring an input character.

Now suppose the CRT device goes "off line" or for some reason is no longer needed in the system. We could destroy P1 by merging it with another (kernel) process. Thus,

$$[\ ] := JOIN\ P1\ ;$$

This causes P1 to be terminated, and the values in its parameter list are returned to the set on the left-hand side of the assignment statement. In general,

$$[\ \langle results \rangle\ ] := JOIN\ \langle pid \rangle\ ;$$

But since no parameters were involved in this example, no ⟨results⟩ need be returned.

Processes created in a FORK and terminated in a JOIN operation execute asynchronously (concurrently) with the process that "spawned" them. All synchronization is done by passing control from one concurrent process to another.

This example demonstrates how a procedure-oriented philosophy influences the design of a software system.

MESSAGE-ORIENTED DESIGN

The message-oriented dual generalizes the concept of a message so that it encompasses interprocess communication, interrupts, and so on. In a message-oriented system, a relatively small number of statically created processes pass a relatively large number of messages through the system. Since access to shared data is the responsibility of a "delivery service," most message activity is limited to operations that transmit a *copy* of the data. Hence, copies of data are passed around rather than control.

The Philosophy

Figure 11-3 illustrates how process *A* communicates to process *B*. Process *A* is a *sender* process and process *B* is a *receiver* process. Messages are placed in a port to await delivery much like letters are put into a mailbox to await delivery. The kernel is responsible for delivering a message using a channel that connects one port to another. Finally, the receiver process takes its message from its port as shown in Figure 11-3. This leads to the following message-oriented dual terminology.

Message. A data structure for sending information from one process to another. By information, we mean any form of information, including *control* information.

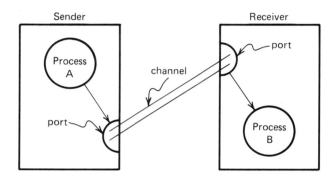

Figure 11-3. Interprocess communication in a message-oriented system.

Channel. An abstract (logical) structure that identifies the source and destination of a message.

Port. A queue capable of holding messages of a certain type while waiting to be received by a receiver process.

A typical system of message-passing processes uses the channel-and-port mechanism to pass information in much the same manner as a system of procedures passes parameters. However, control information may be passed as a message in the message-oriented dual. For example, a kernel designed under this philosophy receives interrupt messages instead of data. The ports of a system kernel are interrupt vectors, and the operations performed by the kernel vaguely correspond to parameter-passing in the procedure-oriented dual.

To clearly see how this model of software design contrasts with the procedure-oriented dual, we need to transform the philosophy into reality. In the next section we define message-passing operations and illustrate by example how they are used to design and implement real-time software.

The Reality

A collection of transmission and receiving operations is used to pass messages between two processes. These operations not only pass messages back and forth between processes, but they block processes when necessary in order to synchronize access to the message. Notice that it is necessary to identify each message so there is no mistake about the message's identity. Thus,

SendMessage (⟨channel⟩,⟨info⟩) returns (⟨mid⟩) ;

A sender process executes this operation when a message ⟨info⟩ is sent to another process connected to the other end of ⟨channel⟩. When Send-Message is executed, the system kernel places ⟨info⟩ at the end of the queue corresponding to the sender's port. The enqueue operation returns a message identifier ⟨mid⟩, which the sender process uses to identify the reply of the receiver process.

An arbitrary length of time may pass before the receiver responds to the sender. Therefore it may be necessary for the sender to wait. The Await-Reply operation causes the sender to block until the ⟨mid⟩ is returned.

$$AwaitReply(⟨mid⟩)returns\ (⟨info⟩)\ ;$$

This operation blocks a process until a message named ⟨mid⟩ is returned along with information stored in ⟨info⟩.

Combining SendMessage and AwaitReply into one construct results in a composite operation similar to the procedure invocation. Suppose we send a message of type **char** to another (receiver) process using the **char** channel. The receiver returns an acknowledgment message as soon as the character is consumed. Thus,

$$Info := AwaitReply(SendMessage(\textbf{char},`A'))\ ;$$

is analogous to

$$PUTCHAR\ (`A')\ ;$$

in the procedure-oriented dual.

A receiver process waits for messages to arrive and then sends an acknowledgment back to the sender. A receiver process can wait for one or more ports to receive a message. Therefore the WaitForMessage operates on a set of ports:

$$WaitForMessage(⟨set\ of\ ports⟩)returns(⟨info⟩,⟨mid⟩,⟨port⟩)$$

The receiver process is blocked until the first message from ⟨set of ports⟩ arrives. When at least one message arrives at a port, ⟨info⟩, ⟨mid⟩, and ⟨port⟩ are returned to the unblocked receiver process.

Typically an unblocked receiver process responds to the sender process by sending a reply along with requested information. For example,

$$SendReply(⟨mid⟩,⟨info⟩)\ ;$$

This operation sends a reply to the channel associated with ⟨mid⟩. For example,

$$[Info,MessId,Port] := WaitForMessage([portA,portB])\ ;$$

and at some later time,

$$SendReply(MessId,NewInfo)\ ;$$

returns NewInfo to the sender.

Figure 11-4 illustrates a small message-passing system similar to the example used to illustrate a procedure-oriented CRT terminal system. In Figure 11-4, two ports, KEYBOARD and SCREEN, are used to interface a CRTIO process to a CRT terminal.

The terminal manager for Figure 11-4 must manage these two ports. When a key is depressed, a character arrives at the KEYBOARD port. The character is copied into variable R and then sent to the process awaiting the input character. Similarly, when a character is sent to the screen, the character is placed in the SCREEN port to wait for output. When the CRT removes the output character and displays it, the sender process is notified that the character is gone. The following is a message-oriented program for managing the terminal shown in Figure 11-4.

TERMINAL MANAGER

```
permanent procedure kernel;
  var
    R,M : messagebody;
      I : messageId;
      P : (Keyboard,Screen);
      S : set of (Keyboard,Screen);
  begin
      S := [Keyboard,Screen] ; (* initialize *)
  repeat
    [M,I,P] := WaitForMessage[S]; (* interrupt? *)
    case P of
    Keyboard : begin
                 S := S-Keyboard ; (* disable *)
                 R := doio (Keyboard,M) ; (* get char *)
                 SendReply(I,R) ; (* send char to USER *)
                 S := S+Keyboard ; (* enable *)
               end;
    Screen :   begin
                 S := S-Screen ; (* disable *)
                 R := doio(Screen,M) ; (* output char *)
                 SendReply(I,R) ; (* status *)
                 S := S+Screen ; (* enable *)
               and
        end ; (* case *)
      until FALSE      (* forever *)
  end.
```

The terminal manager uses a set of ports S to synchronize interprocess communication. Initially, S contains a designator for both ports. However, when an (interrupt) message arrives, M is filled with the value of the

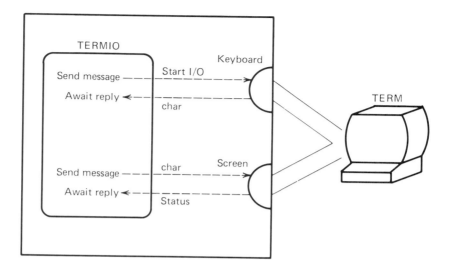

Figure 11-4. Example: Terminal I/O.

character, *I* identifies the message, and *P* designates the first port to get a message. If *P* is KEYBOARD, the KEYBOARD is removed from *S* so that no other input characters are processed until the current character is sent on to the user process. If *P* is SCREEN, the character in *M* is sent out to the screen and the user process is notified.

This example shows how interprocess communication is synchronized by implementing primitive operations that manipulate ports. Since ports are simple first-come-first-served queues, we need not worry about fairness. However, system deadlock and resource allocation problems exist in the message-oriented dual as well as in the procedure-oriented dual.

Furthermore, the number of processes and channels remains static in a message-oriented system. Creating and destroying processes and channels are difficult to do and will not be discussed here.

THE DUALITY MAPPING

Lauer and Needham conjecture that a procedure-oriented system can do anything that a message-oriented system can do and vice versa. Furthermore, the overall performance of a system designed and implemented in either dual is equivalent. In this section we provide a mapping between message-passing and procedure-calling systems.

An approximate correspondence between message-passing and procedure-calling is shown in Table 11-1.

Table 11-1. The Duality Mapping

Message-Oriented	Procedure-Oriented
1. Processes, Create Process	Monitors, NEW
2. Message Channels	External Procedure Names
3. Message Ports	Entry (access) Procedure Names
4. SendMessage; AwaitReply	simple procedure call
5. SendMessage . . . AwaitReply	FORK . . . JOIN
6. SendReply	RETURN from Procedure
7. WaitForMessage . . . *case* . . .	Monitor lock, Entry attribute
8. Case clauses	Entry procedure headings
9. Selective waiting for Messages	Conditions, WAIT/SIGNAL

SUMMARY

We have shown an alternate design philosophy called the *message-oriented dual* to be equivalent to the procedure-oriented dual used throughout this book. The message-oriented dual uses message-passing rather than control-passing to synchronize access to shared objects. Lauer and Needham conjecture that message-oriented systems perform just as well as procedure-oriented systems for the following reasons:

- Sending a message is of the same computational complexity as FORK/JOIN.

A message is sent by invoking a kernel operation on behalf of the sender process, enqueuing the message in a port queue, and then moving the message to another port. This is approximately as time-consuming as creating a process and a copy of its code.

- Leaving an object (monitor) via a SIGNAL and then reentering it to terminate access to the object is of the same complexity as that of waiting for a new message.

If an object is encapsulated in a monitor as illustrated in Figure 11-2, then execution of the SIGNAL operation causes a context switch to the kernel and then back to the process that is executing the monitor procedure. In a message-oriented system, a process must wait for a (control) message instead.

- Process switching, scheduling, and other "overhead" operations are equally fast in either system.

Obviously, if a system implemented in either way runs on a computer with a certain underlying architecture, then context switching and so on will be equally efficient (or inefficient) for both design methods. This applies to memory paging, pipelining of operations, and any architectural feature that is independent of the software methodology used to write programs.

Thus, there are no inherent differences in the two styles of design. However, one style may be conceptually easier to use in designing software for a certain computer system due to compatibility with the design of the computer hardware. For example, a distributed system containing programs resident in physically disjoint memories may be conceptually easier to view as a message-passing system because the message-oriented dual inherently separates the address space of one process from the address space of another process.

PROBLEMS

1. List the characteristics of a message-oriented dual and a procedure-oriented dual.

2. A channel fixes the destination of a message. Design a message-oriented system containing a producer process and a consumer process. Show how the system looks using a diagram like the one shown in Figure 11-3.

3. Consider the system in Figure 11-5. What is wrong with the state defined by processes P_A and P_B, which are blocked by the operations given below:

$$P_A : [MA,IA,PA] := WaitForMessage([A2]) ;$$
$$P_B : [MB,IB,PB] := WaitForMessage([B1]) ;$$

Assume these are the first operations executed by P_A and P_B.

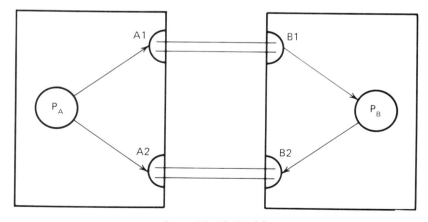

Ports: A1, A2, B1, B2
Processes: P_A, P_B

Figure 11-5. Communicating process in Problem 3.

4. Design a message-oriented system to solve the multiple-readers-single-writer problem. How do you guarantee fair access?

REFERENCES

Lauer, H. C., and R. M. Needham, "On the Duality of Operating Systems Structures," *Proceedings of the Second International Symposium on Operating Systems IRIA*, October 1978. Also reprinted in *Operating Systems Review* (ACM), 13, no. 2 (April 1979), 3–19.

12

Analysis of
System Deadlock

INTRODUCTION

A synchronization lock is *live* if none of the processes that use the lock can become entangled in a deadlock state. This definition of *liveness* was used in the study of locks to investigate the correctness of access to a *single* critical section at a time. However, in a system of multiple resources, there are perhaps many critical sections (and locks), each associated with a resource. In a multiple-resource system, we must be concerned with the interactions among the processes and resources as well as with the interactions of processes in a single lock.

Consider a system of two resources: a printer and a disk device. If only one process at a time is allowed access to the printer and another process allowed access to the disk device, then it is possible for a system deadlock to occur even if the printer lock and disk device lock are live. For example, process P_A may gain exclusive access to the printer while process P_B gains exclusive access to the disk. Suppose both processes request access to the other's device while simultaneously holding on to their own devices. In this case, process P_A requests access to the disk and process P_B requests access to the printer. Process P_A must wait for P_B to give up control to access to the disk since only one process is allowed access at a time. Therefore, P_A is blocked. Similarly, process P_B is blocked because it is waiting for P_A to give up control of access to the printer. Hence, P_B is blocked because of P_A, and P_A is blocked because of P_B. The system of two processes and two resources is deadlocked even though each one has executed a live access lock.

A system of resources can cause a system of processes to deadlock whenever any two or more processes are forced to wait (BLOCKED state). A network of telephones, for example, could become deadlocked if the following rules were used by the telephone company (instead of the busy signal rules actually used). Suppose the telephone being called (callee) is in use when a caller dials its number. Then, suppose the caller is forced to wait indefinitely for the callee to hang up. In this situation, the caller is unable to hang up whenever a busy signal occurs. Instead, the caller must wait for the callee to finish and hang up.

However, under the present rules, a caller hangs up because of a busy signal, thus releasing the line. This is what avoids possible deadlock in the telephone system.

A system of resources can cause processes to deadlock if a pattern of waiting processes is established as follows: a process P_1 is forced to wait for another process P_0. This in turn causes P_2 to wait for P_1, and so on, until a chain of waiting processes is established that leads back to the original process—P_0. That is, a *cycle* is established:

$$P_0 \rightarrow P_1 \rightarrow P_2 \cdots \rightarrow P_0$$

This is a *deadlock configuration* because P_0 ends up waiting for itself. Since P_0 cannot execute (it is BLOCKED), P_0 can never remove itself from waiting.

System deadlock may not be a significant problem in a software system designed to *avoid* deadlock configurations. Avoidance is possible if the resource request pattern for all processes is known in advance, for example. But in most situations, we cannot predict the resource request patterns of a system of processes.

An experiment was conducted to estimate the likelihood of a deadlock in a system of six processes. The frequency of occurrence of deadlock was shown to be as high as 10% in a system of four resources (see Figure 12-1).

In this experiment, one of the six processes was selected at random and made a request for one of the resources at random. If the resource was available (free), the process held exclusive access to it for a period of time sampled from an exponential distribution. If the resource was not available (allocated), the process waited in a first-come-first-served queue, unless this caused deadlock. If waiting would have led to a system deadlock, the process was terminated and restarted after a random time delay.

The loading factor in Figure 12-1 is computed by dividing the average rate of service (from the exponential distribution) into the average rate of requests (set arbitrarily by the experimenter). Thus, a loading factor of 1.0 means that new requests are being made just as fast as old requests are being processed by the processes after they gain access to the randomly selected resources.

We can conclude from the experiment that deadlock configurations can

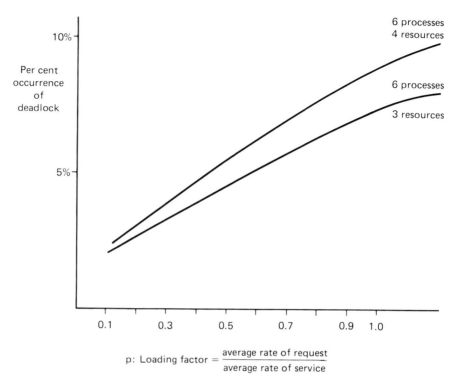

Figure 12-1. Frequency of occurrence of deadlock versus loading factor.

occur with sufficient frequency that software engineers should be concerned with methods of detection. In this chapter we investigate a technique for dynamically detecting deadlock in a system of executing processes. We call this kind of detection *on-line deadlock detection* because it is performed after every request for a resource. Furthermore, since the detection algorithm is performed after each request, it must be very fast. So we will also study the performance of the on-line detection algorithm.

THE CANONICAL DEADLOCK PROBLEM

The process-resource configuration of a system of N processes and M resources can be pictorially represented by a table as shown in Figure 12-2. The processes are listed horizontally as P_1, P_2, . . . , P_N, and the resources are listed vertically as R_1, R_2, . . . , R_M. The entries at location TABLE[I,J] indicate the presence or absence of a request. For example,

Processes

Resources

	P₁	P₂	. . .	Pₙ
R₁	−1	0		1
R₂	1	2		0
. . .				
Rₘ	0	−1		−1

Legend: (−1) empty
         0   allocated
    1 . . . N waiting

Figure 12-2. Process-resource table.

$$\text{TABLE}[1,2] = 1$$

This means process P_1 is waiting for access to resource R_2. Indeed, since the entry is equal to one, process P_1 is first in line (rank is one) while waiting for P_N to release R_2.

$$\text{TABLE}[N,2] = 0$$

This means process P_N is accessing resource R_2. In this case, P_N has exclusive access to R_2 because all other processes in this row are waiting (or have yet to make a request).

$$\text{TABLE}[2,2] = 2$$

This means process P_2 is second in line while waiting for access to resource R_2.

$$\text{TABLE}[2,M] = (-1)$$

This means process P_2 is *not* requesting access to R_M.

A process-resource table is said to be in a *deadlock configuration* if a pattern of values exists such that

1. Starting with a certain process-resource pair, say P_i and R_j,

$$\text{TABLE}[i,j] >= 0$$

2. Moving along row j or column i, we find another process resource pair, say P_{ii} and R_{jj}, such that

$$\text{TABLE}[ii,jj] >= 0$$

3. Continuing in this fashion, we find a chain of entries

$$\text{TABLE}[i',j'] >= 0$$

which leads back to the original process-resource pair, e.g.,

$$\text{TABLE}[i',j'] = \text{TABLE}[i,j]$$

and $i' = i$; $j' = j$.

For example, the table of Figure 12-2 is in a deadlock configuration because

1. Starting with process P_2 and resource R_1,

$$\text{TABLE}[2,1] = 0$$

2. Moving to process P_N and resource R_1,

$$\text{TABLE}[N,1] = 1$$

3. Continuing, we find a chain:

$$\text{TABLE}[N,2] = 0$$
$$\text{TABLE}[2,2] = 2$$
$$\text{TABLE}[2,1] = 0$$

and $i' = 2$; $j' = 1$.

Hence a cycle exists in the table of Figure 12-2 as follows:

$$(P_2,R_1) \rightarrow (P_N,R_1) \rightarrow (P_N,R_2) \rightarrow (P_2,R_2)$$

and back to (P_2,R_1). This is the basis of the horizontal-vertical on-line detection algorithm to be discussed in more detail in a subsequent section of this chapter.

The Dining Philosophers

A classical problem first posed by E. J. Dijkstra has become the canonical form of a deadlock-prone system of processes. In the dining philosophers problem, a system of philosophers (processes) competes for access to forks (resources).

Consider a system of three philosophers as shown in Figure 12-3. Each

Figure 12-3. Three dining philosophers.

philosopher P_i alternately eats and thinks. A thinking philosopher can begin eating by first requesting and getting one fork from his/her immediate left and another fork from his/her immediate right. Philosopher P_1 must get forks F_3 and F_1 before he/she can eat. After eating for an arbitrary period of time, a philosopher releases both forks (one at a time) and resumes thinking. The cycle is repeated indefinitely.

In the dining philosophers problem, N philosophers compete for access to N forks. Since each philosopher must have two forks in order to eat, a shortage of forks leads to waiting. For example, P_1 uses F_3 and F_1 while P_2 and P_3 wait. Then, P_2 uses F_1 and F_2, or else P_3 uses F_2 and F_3 while all other philosophers wait.

The reason this problem has become the canonical deadlock problem is because it is easy to deadlock the philosophers. Suppose each philosopher simultaneously picks up the fork on his/her immediate right-hand side. This results in P_1 holding F_3, P_2 holding F_1, and P_3 holding F_2. Now, all philosophers attempt to pick up their left forks, and become blocked. Since all philosophers are blocked, none of them can put down a fork. Therefore, they all wait for a fork that can never appear. This configuration is shown in the process-resource table of Figure 12-4. The cycle shown as a dotted line is obtained by following a horizontal/vertical search for TABLE[i,j] >= 0 entries as described earlier.

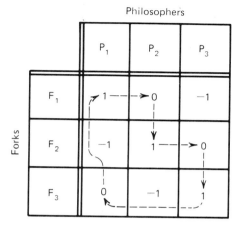

Figure 12-4. Process-resource table for three deadlocked philosophers who pick up their right forks.

Analysis Using the Interleave Principle

Each philosopher in the dining philosophers problem can be thought of as a process that repeatedly accesses a resource. Suppose, for example, we model this activity as follows. Let procedure PICKUP be an access operation that gets a fork and PUTDOWN be an access operation that releases a fork. Thus,

```
Process : repeat
              PICKUP(RIGHT-FORK) ;
              PICKUP(LEFT-FORK) ;
              (* eat *)
              PUTDOWN(RIGHT-FORK) ;
              PUTDOWN(LEFT-FORK) ;
              (* Think *)
         until FALSE ;      (* forever *)
```

Now, suppose we employ the Interleave Principle to study the behavior of a very simple ($N = 2$) dining philosophers problem. Figure 12-5 illustrates how we apply the Interleave Principle to a system of two philosophers. The state variables in Figure 12-5 are the process-resource table entries. The initial values of this process-resource table are shown in the "home" square of the process-state matrix. Initially, TABLE[I,J] = (-1) because no requests have been made.

If we arbitrarily (nondeterministically) permit either philosopher to execute a PICKUP operation, then the next state of the process-state matrix

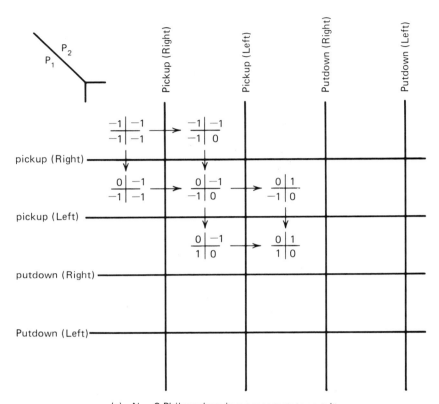

(a) N = 2 Philosophers in a process-state matrix

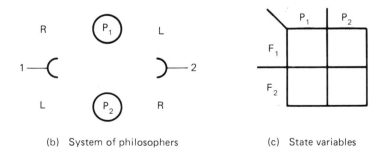

(b) System of philosophers

(c) State variables

Figure 12-5. Analysis of N = 2 philosopher system.

is either in row two or column two. In either case, it is possible to inter-leave the two processes such that the deadlock state at row three, column three is reached. Since a deadlock state is reachable, we say this solution is *deadlock-prone*.

Obviously, what is needed is a solution that *forces* a priority on the phi-losophers so that the deadlock state is not reachable from the initial state. Suppose, for example, we force a philosopher to pick up both left and right forks without intervention of the competing philosopher. Figure 12-6 shows what happens in this case.

In Figure 12-6, either philosopher P_2 gets both forks and blocks P_1 until both forks are released, or philosopher P_1 gets both forks and blocks P_2 until returning both forks. If P_2 executes PICKUP(RIGHT-FORK) ; PICKUP(LEFT-FORK), then P_1 must be blocked when attempting to ex-ecute PICKUP(RIGHT-FORK). This is accomplished with a path expres-sion:

path 1 : (PICKUP ; PUTDOWN) **end**

This expression forces PICKUP to be executed before PUTDOWN *for each fork* (LEFT-FORK and RIGHT-FORK). Furthermore, a fork must be PUTDOWN before it can be PICKUPed again. A program for the solu-tion to the philosophers problem is given in the next section.

Furthermore, the serializing feature of this path expression avoids star-vation of one philosopher by the other as shown in the test of Figure 12-7.

An Object-Based Solution

An object-based design and solution to the dining philosophers problem given by Campbell (see Chapter 10) are analyzed in this section. The ob-jects shown in Figure 12-8 model the solution to $N = 5$ philosophers.

Each philosopher executes routine TABLE.START initially, then eats, and finally executes TABLE.STOP. The path expression for START and STOP forces a serial execution order. This prevents more than five philos-ophers from making requests.

Each fork in the array of objects called FORK contains code for PICKUP and PUTDOWN. The PICKUP and PUTDOWN operations are performed in order, one at a time. Since each fork has its own copy of PICKUP and PUTDOWN, and since mutual exclusion of serial access is guaranteed by the path expression, no race condition, starvation, or dead-lock can occur.

Similarly, a copy of code for each philosopher is executed that simulates request, eating, release, and thinking. Thus, an array of processes called PHILOSOPHER[1..N] is executed concurrently.

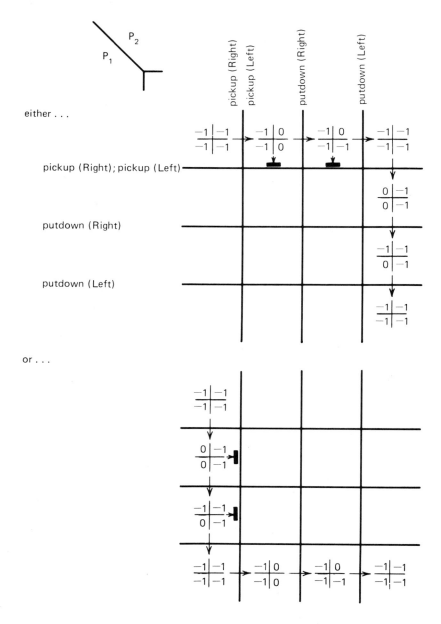

Figure 12-6. A live solution to the dining philosophers problem.

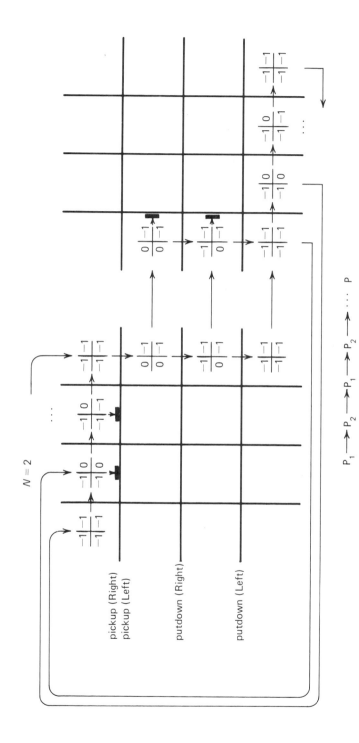

Figure 12-7. Starvation not possible.

401

Objects

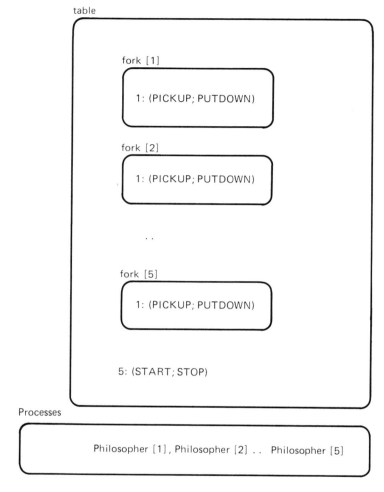

Figure 12-8. Object-based solution to dining philosophers problem.

```
const
   n = 5 ; (* number of diners *)
   max = 4 ; (* maximum active forks *)
type
   diner = 0..max ;
var
   i : integer ;
   table : object path max:(start;stop) end;
           var fork : array[diner] of object
```

```
                    path 1:(pickup;putdown) end ;
                    entry procedure pickup ; begin end ;
                    entry procedure putdown ; begin end ;
              end ; (* fork *)
          entry procedure start(no:diner) ;
              begin fork[no].pickup ; fork[(no + 1)mod n].pickup end;
          entry procedure stop(no:diner) ;
              begin fork[no].putdown;fork[(no + 1)mod n].putdown end;
      end ; (* table *)
process philosophers (who:diner) ;
  begin
    repeat
      table.start(who) ;
      (* eat *) ;
      table.stop(who)
      (* think *)
    until false ;
  end ;
  begin (* activate diners *)
    for i := 0 to max do
      philosophers(i) ;
  end ;
```

Analysis of the Program   A sample software network illustration of the solution above is shown in Figure 12-9. This shows how the path expressions for TABLE and FORK guide each philosopher along an execution path that enforces the needed serialization. In particular, the path expression

$$1 : (PICKUP ; PUTDOWN)$$

prevents two philosophers from simultaneously attempting to pick up the same fork. But of course this path expression is enforced independently for each of the forks so that four philosophers might simultaneously PICKUP the fork on their right, say. Thus, for $N = 5$ philosophers, we have

$$P_0 : FORK[0].PICKUP ;$$
$$P_1 : FORK[1].PICKUP ;$$
$$P_2 : FORK[2].PICKUP ;$$
$$P_3 : FORK[3].PICKUP ;$$
$$P_4 : blocked$$

The last request by P_4 is blocked by the path expression

path 4 : (START ; STOP) **end**

defined for TABLE. Without this expression, P_4 might be allowed to go

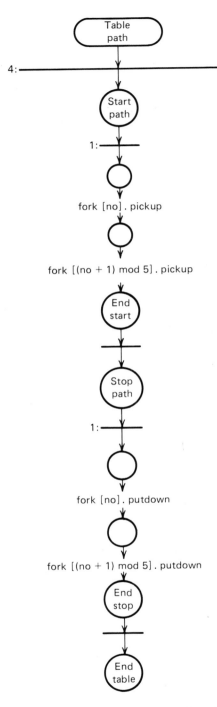

Figure 12-9. Combined path expressions for dining philosophers problem.

ahead and PICKUP fork #4, which would lead to a deadlock configuration as discussed in the previous section. Instead, P_3 is allowed to execute another PICKUP operation:

$$P_3 : \text{FORK[4].PICKUP ;}$$

An analysis of the solution above is given in the form of a sequence of process-resource table configurations; see Figure 12-10. In Figure 12-10(a), philosophers P_0 and P_1 have gained access to both of their forks and are busy eating. Two philosophers are waiting for their first fork, and P_4 is waiting for his/her second fork.

In Figure 12-10(b), we see what happens when P_0 releases both of his/her forks and rapidly requests F_0 again. The path expression for F_0 prevents P_0 from getting F_0 a second time before the waiting philosopher P_4 gets a chance. Thus, P_4 gets F_0, and P_4 can eat. Also, P_1 can now get F_1 and request F_2. Since F_2 is being used by P_2, philosopher P_1 must wait for F_2.

Access to both forks by each of the five philosophers sweeps through the table of Figure 12-10 in a recurring pattern. That is, only two of the five philosophers are able to eat at the same time:

$$\{P_0,P_2\}$$
$$\{P_2,P_4\}$$
$$\{P_4,P_1\}$$
$$\{P_1,P_3\}$$
$$\{P_3,P_0\}$$

This establishes a pattern as follows:

$$P_0, P_2, P_4, P_1, P_3 \cdots$$

First the even-numbered philosophers each take a turn eating, and then the odd-numbered take their turn. This alternating pattern repeats with every other philosopher eating while his/her neighbor is thinking or waiting. If $N = 4$, the pattern would have been

$$P_0, P_2, P_1, P_3 \cdots$$

The object-based solution to the dining philosophers problem is safe, fair, and live. It is possible, however, to arrive at solutions that are not safe, or live, or fair. We illustrated several ways in which a solution will lead to deadlock, but consider the following situations.

Suppose a philosopher feigns eating by PICKUPing a right fork only to PUTDOWN the right fork whenever the left fork is not available. This might occur in a solution that retracts a request instead of waiting (like the telephone system). In this situation it is possible that some philosophers starve while others enjoy eating an unlimited amount.

In another situation we might imagine philosophers falling asleep while

	P_0	P_1	P_2	P_3	P_4
F_0	0				1
F_1	0	1			
F_2			0		
F_3			0	1	
F_4					0

$\{P_0, P_2\}$ busy $\{P_1, P_3, P_4\}$ waiting

(a)

	P_0	P_1	P_2	P_3	P_4
F_0	1				0
F_1		0			
F_2		1	0		
F_3			0	1	
F_4					0

P_0 putdown, then requests pickup, again

$\{P_4, P_2\}$ busy $\{P_0, P_1, P_3\}$ waiting

(b)

	P_0	P_1	P_2	P_3	P_4
F_0	1				0
F_1		0			
F_2		0	1		
F_3				0	
F_4				1	0

P_2 putdown, then requests pickup, again.

$\{P_1, P_4\}$ busy $\{P_0, P_2, P_3\}$ waiting

(c)

Figure 12-10. Analysis using paths.

	P_0	P_1	P_2	P_3	P_4	
F_0	0					
F_1	1	0				
F_2		0	1			
F_3				0		
F_4				0	1	

P_4 putdown, then requests pickup, again

$\{P_3, P_1\}$ busy $\{P_4, P_0, P_2\}$ waiting

(d)

	P_0	P_1	P_2	P_3	P_4	
F_0	0					
F_1	0	1				
F_2			0			
F_3			1	0		
F_4				0	1	

P_1 putdown, then requests pickup, again

$\{P_0, P_3\}$ busy $\{P_1, P_2, P_4\}$ waiting

(e)

	P_0	P_1	P_2	P_3	P_4	
F_0	0				1	
F_1	0	1				
F_2			0			
F_3			0	1		
F_4					0	

P_3 putdown, then requests pickup, again

$\{P_0, P_2\}$ busy $\{P_1, P_3, P_4\}$ waiting

Original State

(f)

Figure 12-10. Continued.

in the middle of eating. Thus, a sleeping philosopher holds two forks, which in turn blocks both right and left neighbors. If the philosopher dies in his/her sleep, the two adjacent neighbors never get to eat. This model simulates unreliable processes that occasionally fail.

A general deadlock detection algorithm is needed just in case a system of processes is implemented without guaranteed live behavior. In the remainder of this chapter we study an on-line detection algorithm called the *horizontal-vertical algorithm*.

ON-LINE DEADLOCK DETECTION

The idea in on-line deadlock detection is to check the process-resource table after every request for a deadlock configuration. If a configuration exists, then one or more requests must be withdrawn in order to remove the deadlock.

One method of on-line detection requires that each process call an avoidance algorithm before attempting access to a resource. For example, each process might execute the following segment of program in order to get access to a resource:

```
begin
    NULL := (−1) ;
    . . .
    repeat
        AVOID(process-id, resource-id, TABLE) ;
    until TABLE[process-id,resource-id] > NULL ;
    if TABLE[process-id,resource-id] > 0
        then SLEEP(process-id,blocking-queue) ;
    . .
end
```

A process continues to try to get access to a resource until the AVOID algorithm returns a TABLE entry value greater than NULL. If NULL is returned, this means the request was refused. If a zero is returned, this means the process has been given access to the resource. If a rank greater than zero is returned, the process must wait for some other process to give up its access. We assume AVOID only returns a rank greater than NULL when *no deadlock* will result from assigning a rank to the requesting process. In other words, AVOID must be able to determine if assignment of a rank greater than NULL would lead to a deadlock configuration. The horizontal-vertical algorithm does this checking.

The Horizontal-Vertical Algorithm

The horizontal-vertical algorithm (HVA) finds a cycle in the process-resource table by scanning for entries greater than NULL using a horizontal-vertical search pattern. The HVA searches a row for an entry equal to zero; then it searches a column for another entry greater than zero, and so on. Eventually the search ends when no entries greater than NULL can be found, or when the starting column is reached.

The HVA is based on the following observations and assumptions:

1. Each time a request by process P_i is made for resource R_j, an HVA scan is done. Therefore, no more than one cycle exists in the process-resource table at any time. This reduces the time it takes to find a deadlock by reducing the process-resource table to a table with zero or one cycle.

2. If process P_i is granted access to R_j, the TABLE[i,j] entry is set to zero. If access is denied, TABLE[i,j] is set to one greater than the row maximum. This is the rank of P_i for resource R_j. Furthermore, process P_i is blocked until its rank is reduced to zero. Thus, every column of the process-resource table contains no more than one entry greater than zero. (However, many zeroes can appear in a column, corresponding to process P_i accessing many resources simultaneously.)

3. We assume each process is given exclusive access to a resource. Therefore, every row of the process-resource table has at most one zero entry. This restriction can be removed to allow multiple-process access to a resource without loss of generality. However, the performance of HVA diminishes when multiple zeroes are allowed in the table.

An illustration of the HVA is given in Figure 12-4. Suppose P_1 requests access to F_1 as shown by an entry TABLE[1,1] = 1. Before HVA allows this configuration in the table, a horizontal scan of row one is performed. The horizontal scan locates a zero at [1,2]. Next, a vertical scan for an entry greater than zero locates a one at [2,2]. Another horizontal scan locates a zero at [3,2]. Another vertical scan locates a one at table location [3,3]. Finally, a horizontal scan finds a zero at [1,3]. Since the HVA has returned to the column that it started in, it has found a cycle in the table. Therefore, allowing P_1 to wait for R_1 leads to a deadlock configuration. Instead, the HVA must mark TABLE[1,1] := NULL and return NULL as a result.

Centralized Solution

One of the pressing problems of deadlock algorithms is protection of the process-resource table itself. The table must be accessed concurrently by "readers and writers" during HVA searching. A reader process, of course, simply reads table entries, whereas a writer process updates table entries each time a request is made. We can synchronize access to the process-resource table by locking it with a multiple-readers-single-writer lock; see Chapter 9.

Furthermore, a simple version of the HVA uses a centralized table even though the HVA may be implemented in a distributed system. This guarantees table *consistency* throughout execution of multiple HVA algorithms.

In the following version of the HVA algorithm, we assume a centralized AVOID program that performs the horizontal and vertical table searching. Version I of the HVA algorithm is shown to be *incorrect* but serves to demonstrate some of the problems inherent in deadlock detection.

Version I In this initial version of the HVA, we use a BACKUP procedure to save the process-resource table before modifying it. The requesting process marks the table and then performs a deadlock configuration search. If the search finds a deadlock cycle in the table, then the saved copy of the table is used to restore the table to its original configuration. The process makes a second, third, etc., attempt to gain access by repeating the steps above.

```
procedure AVOID(I,J : integer ;
                    var TABLE : matrix) ;
    var
        SAVETABLE : matrix ;
        DEAD         : boolean ;
    begin
      repeat
        BACKUP(TABLE,SAVETABLE) ;
        TABLE[I,J] := MAX(TABLE,J) + 1 ;
        DEAD := (HORIZ(VERT(HORIZ(J))) = I) ;
        if DEAD
        then ROLLBACK(TABLE,SAVETABLE) ;
      until not DEAD ;
    end ;     (* Version I. *)
```

This version of the HVA uses BACKUP to make a copy of the TABLE in SAVETABLE, MAX to find the maximum value of row *J*, and ROLLBACK to restore the TABLE with the old copy saved in SAVETABLE. The horizontal and vertical search routines HORIZ and VERT are shown in Figures 12-11 and 12-12.

Notice that Version I of AVOID attempts to find a cycle in the table by finding three corners of a box-shaped path in the table. Since only one zero entry per row is allowed, and only zero or one cycle is assumed each

```
function HORIZ( ROW : integer ) : integer ;
  var
    COL : integer ;
  begin
    if ROW > 0
      then
        begin
        COL := 1 ;
        while ( COL <= N )
                and
              (TABLE[COL,ROW] <> 0)
            do COL := COL+1 ;
        if TABLE[COL,ROW] = 0
          then HORIZ := COL
          else HORIZ := 0 ;
      end     (* then *)
    else HORIZ := 0 ;
  end ;       (* HORIZ *)
```

Figure 12-11. Function HORIZ.

```
function VERT ( COL : integer ) : integer ;
  var
    ROW : integer ;
  begin
    if COL > 0
      then
      begin
        ROW := 1 ;
        while ( ROW <= M )
                and
              ( TABLE[COL,ROW] <= 0 )
            do ROW := ROW+1 ;
        if TABLE[COL,ROW] > 0
          then VERT := ROW
          else VERT := 0 ;
      end     (* then *)
    else VERT := 0 ;
  end ;     (* VERT *)
```

Figure 12-12. Function VERT.

time AVOID is executed, the simple box-shaped path is the only shape expected. This, of course, is not always true; so an improved version that searches for more than a box-shaped cycle is needed. However, this deficiency is not the main problem with Version I.

Figure 12-13 contains a process-state matrix test of Version I. The indeterminism indicated by "?" values reveals that Version I is unsafe. Also, several *livelock paths* exist for the simple two-process test shown in Figure 12-13.

The indeterminism of Version I is due to interleaving of the ROLLBACK/BACKUP operations that may occur due to concurrent execution of AVOID. This can be overcome by locking the table before BACKUP is done, and then UNLOCKing the table after the HVA is successful. This modification appears in Version II.

The second deficiency of Version I reveals a form of starvation called livelock. A livelocked AVOID algorithm repeats its loop forever. Column two of Figure 12-13 can turn into a livelock loop if "?" is set to (-1). What happens is simply this: Each time the HVA is performed, the process is denied access because a deadlock configuration is detected. The ROLLBACK operation resets the table to a nondeadlock configuration, and the HVA is repeated. This happens over and over again without success. In the meantime, process P_2 is waiting for access.

Livelock is a form of deadlock of the deadlock algorithm itself. In an effort to detect a deadlock configuration, AVOID is itself susceptible to deadlock!

Version II   Version II, called LAVOID (L = locked), avoids the indeterminism of Version I by placing locks before and after access to TABLE (see Figure 12-14). However, Version II still contains the livelock flow as shown in Figure 12-15. It is still possible to loop forever while holding onto a resource.

One way out of the ROLLBACK/BACKUP livelock problem is to kill one process involved in deadlock while keeping the other. But which process should we remove, and which one should be kept?

Version III   In Version III we remove a process if it would lead to a deadlock configuration by waiting for a resource. Furthermore, the removed process waits a random length of time before attempting to restart. This is called the *contention resolution* method of deadlock detection and recovery.

The killed process is not so easy to remove from the process-resource table. All resources held by the killed process are released. This leads to updates in the table, which in turn leads to unblocking of some of the waiting processes. This ripple effect is more difficult and time-consuming to implement than the HVA algorithm.

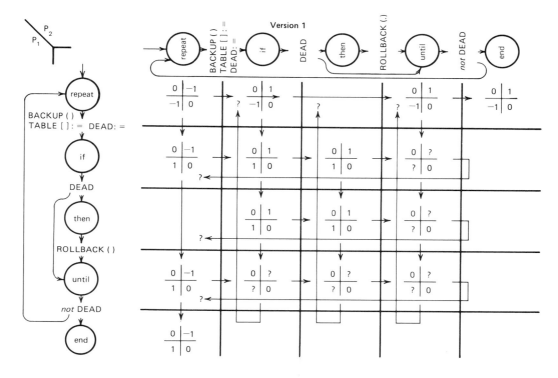

Figure 12-13. Avoid algorithm: Version I.

```
procedure LAVOID (I,J:integer;var TABLE:matrix);
  var
    SAVETABLE : matrix ;
    DEAD        : boolean ;
  begin
      LOCK (TABLE);
      repeat
        BACKUP (TABLE,SAVETABLE);
        TABLE[I,J] := MAX(TABLE,J) + 1 ;
        DEAD := (HORIZ(VERT(HORIZ(J))) = I);
        if DEAD then ROLLBACK(TABLE,SAVETABLE);
      until not DEAD;
      UNLOCK (TABLE);
  end     (* LAVOID *)
```

Figure 12-14. Version II: Locking.

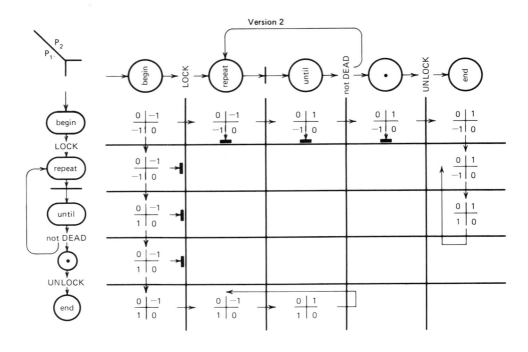

Figure 12-15. LAVOID: Version II.

```
function DAVOID (I,J:integer;var TABLE : matrix):integer;
  const
    TIMEOUT = 10 ;      (* arbitrary delay *)
  begin
    LOCK (TABLE) ; DAVOID := 1 ;      (* assume blocked *)
    TABLE[I,J] := MAX (TABLE,J)+1 ; (* take a number *)
    if TABLE[I,J] = 0 then DAVOID := 2
      else begin if HORIZ(VERT(HORIZ(J))) = I
                then
                begin
                  UNVERT(I,J) ;      (* remove process I *)
                  UNLOCK (TABLE);      (* free TABLE *)
                  WAIT(RANDOM(TIMEOUT));      (* wait a while *)
                  DAVOID := 0 ;      (* signal failure *)
                end ;      (* deadlock avoidance *)
           end;      (* else *)
    UNLOCK(TABLE);      (* no deadlock *)
  end;      (* DAVOID *)
```

Figure 12-16. DAVOID Version III.

414

```
procedure UNVERT (COL,ROW : integer);
  const
    NULL = −1 ;
  var
    I,J : integer;
  begin
    TABLE[COL,ROW] := NULL; (* reset *)
    for J:= 1 to M do
      if TABLE[COL,J] = 0
        then begin
          TABLE[COL,J] := NULL ;
          for I := 1 to N do
            if TABLE[I,J] > NULL
              then begin
                TABLE[I,J] := TABLE[I,J] − 1;
                if TABLE[I,J] = 0 then NOTIFY(I);
              end ;        (* for I *)
end      (* UNVERT *)
```

Figure 12-17. Procedure UNVERT.

Figure 12-16 contains Version III of the deadlock detection and recovery algorithm. The WAIT operation delays the executing process for a random period of time. The UNVERT procedure shown in Figure 12-17 unravels the process from the process-resource table.

In procedure UNVERT we use a NOTIFY operation to awaken blocked processes whenever a killed process releases (or causes release of) a resource. All resources held by the killed process are marked by

$$TABLE[COL,J] = 0$$

These are changed to

$$TABLE[COL,J] := NULL ;$$

and then all other processes in the same row are moved up in rank. If any process is moved up from rank of one to rank of zero, the NOTIFY operation causes it to be notified and put into the READY state.

In summary, Version III uses the following routines to implement a contention resolution HVA:

NOTIFY   Unblock process and place it in the READY state.

WAIT   Block a process for a period of time, and then unblock it when the time has elapsed.

LOCK,UNLOCK   Set mutually exclusive access locks on tables. All other processes must wait for an UNLOCK.

A requesting process executes a CHECKPOINT operation (a recovery point just in case the process is killed) and a CLEAR operation (success) as shown below:

```
CHECKPOINT(process-id) ;          (* recovery point is here *)
case DAVOID(process-id,resource-id,TABLE( of
  0 : ROLLBACK(process-id) ;      (* restart later *)
  1 : SLEEP(process-id) ;         (* block *)
  2 : ;                           (* permission granted *)
end ;
CLEAR(process-id) ;               (* remove restart point *)
```

The CHECKPOINT operation tells the system kernel where to restart the process in the event that it is killed by DAVOID. The CLEAR operation removes the restart information from the kernel since it is no longer needed.

The ROLLBACK routine in this version is a kernel operation that causes the process to restart from the restarting point established by the CHECKPOINT operation. Since DAVOID delays the process by a random length of time, the process restarts after an arbitrary delay.

The SLEEP operation causes the process to remain blocked until its rank is changed to zero. After an arbitrarily long sleep, the process continues execution with access to the resource granted to it.

A brief example of Version III shows how the contention resolution method works. Suppose a two-process and two-resource system is in an initial state defined by the table

$$
\begin{array}{c|c}
0 & 1 \\
\hline
-1 & 0
\end{array}
$$

Let P_1 lock the table and make a request for resource #2. Then,

$$
\begin{array}{c|c}
0 & 1 \\
\hline
1 & 0
\end{array}
$$

a deadlock configuration results; so DAVOID must execute UNVERT. The NOTIFY operation notifies process P_2 that it can go ahead now because P_1 is not blocking it. This is shown below.

$$\begin{array}{c|c} -1 & 0 \\ \hline -1 & 0 \end{array} \text{NOTIFY(2)}$$

Now, P_1 must wait a random length of time before it executes ROLLBACK. When the rollback is executed, suppose P_2 still holds both resources. Then,

$$\begin{array}{c|c} 1 & 0 \\ \hline -1 & 0 \end{array}$$

So P_1 is now waiting for R_1, and P_2 has access to both resources.

Figure 12-18 shows how DAVOID functions in an Interleave Principle test. Every deadlock configuration is removed by UNVERT and ROLLBACK. However, four squares of the Interleave Principle appear to lead to indeterminism.

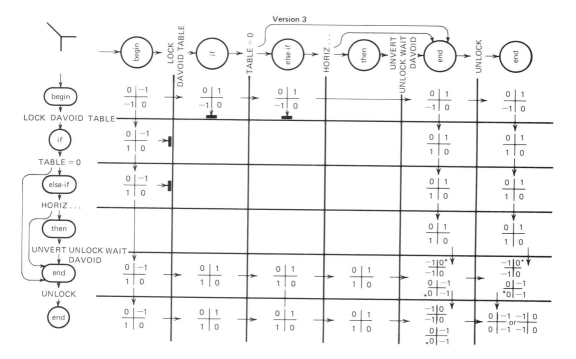

Figure 12-18. DAVOID: Version III. Verification.

If P_1 and P_2 simultaneously reach one of these multivalued states, then the algorithm is unsafe. However, if WAIT delays P_1 and P_2 by differing amounts of time, they reach these states at different times, so that one value only is computed. Therefore, in a special sense, DAVOID is safe.

If P_1 never reaches one of the multivalued states before P_2, then P_1 will always be locked out. This leads to starvation of P_1 by P_2. Conversely, P_2 can be starved by P_1. The probability of this is $(\frac{1}{2})^t$ on the tth request. In the limit,

$$\lim_{t \to \infty} (\tfrac{1}{2})^t = 0$$

But in a practical sense, P_1 and P_2 could be partially starved by being unlucky. Therefore, DAVOID is safe if the random delays are unique for each process that must be restarted, fair in the limit if the number of requests made by a process is unbounded, and live because no deadlock states exist in the algorithm.

Distributed Solution

In the previous section we developed a centralized horizontal-vertical algorithm for detection and rollback of deadlock configurations. One of the limitations of the centralized algorithm is its inability to find cycles other than rectangular or box-shaped cycles. A "stair-step" cycle cannot be detected by Version III, for example.

Another limitation of the centralized algorithm is its inability to distribute parts of the process-resource table to separate processors in a loosely coupled network of parallel processors. In the fourth version of the HVA, we allow the process-resource table to be partitioned into "slices" where each slice of the table is stored in the memory of the local processor responsible for managing the resources attached to the local processor.

Version IV Version IV of the HVA is illustrated in Figure 12-19. Site zero contains resources R_1, R_2, and R_3, and site one contains resources R_4 and R_5. We also assume processes P_1 and P_2 are local to site zero, and processes P_3 and P_4 are local to site one.

Figure 12-19 follows the search path of the HVA during an attempted request for resource $R_1@S_0$ (resource R_1 at site S_0) by process $P_3@S_1$ (process P_3 at site S_1).

According to the HVA, a request is checked by marking the table entry

$$\text{TABLE}[3,1] := 1$$

as shown by a dotted box in Figure 12-19. Then, a horizontal search followed by a vertical search is carried out as follows:

Version 4: Search

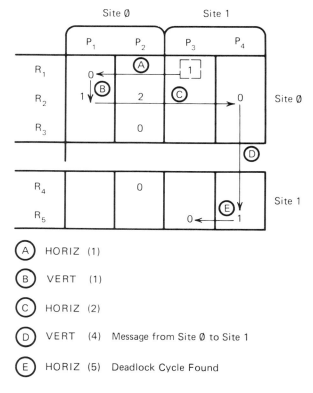

A HORIZ (1)

B VERT (1)

C HORIZ (2)

D VERT (4) Message from Site Ø to Site 1

E HORIZ (5) Deadlock Cycle Found

Figure 12-19. Version IV: Search.

A. Horizontal to entry [1,1]
B. Vertical to entry [1,2]
C. Horizontal to entry [4,2]
D. Vertical to entry [4,5]
E. Horizontal to entry [3,5]

The path established by this search is shown as a chain ending back at column three in Figure 12-19. Since the chain connects process P_3 to process P_3, a deadlock configuration is detected. Therefore, process P_3 must be killed and rolled back for a random period of time.

The partitioned process-resource table for version IV (see Figure 12-19) provides a way to distribute the table to different processor sites. Each processor can then simultaneously perform part of the HVA algorithm in parallel with all other processors in the network. This contributes to an increase in the performance of the HVA, but it also raises an issue.

Since each processor is searching and updating parts of the process-resource table simultaneously, it is also possible that the values stored in a certain part of the table are out of date. We say the data are *stale* when they do not reflect the current state of the table. The possibility of stale data leads to possible inconsistencies in the (overall) process-resource table.

The consistency issue outlined above creates a problem for the HVA. In the following version (IV) of HVA, we adopt a few restrictions and assumptions in order to overcome this problem:

1. Messages from other processors in the network arrive in the order they are sent. No reordering of the messages due to time delays or rerouting is allowed.

2. Sites are ordered and communicate cyclically; e.g., the network forms a logical ring-structured topology.

3. Each resource is managed by a row of the partitioned process-resource table and a resource manager capable of performing the horizontal-vertical search and sending/receiving messages to other processes when necessary.

In the following pseudocode version of the distributed solution, assume n processors arranged in a ring-structured network.

Distributed On-Line Deadlock Detection

Step 1: Process P_i running on site S_j makes a request for resource $R_{k'}$; e.g.,

$$P_i@S_j \rightarrow R_k$$

Step 2: If $R_k@S_j$, then performs local deadlock avoidance algorithm (Version III).

Step 3: If R_k **not** @ S_j, then send a request message to the site containing R_k, say S_t. Meanwhile, block process P_i until an acknowledgment is received.

Step 4: Site S_t receives request from $P_i@S_j$ for R_k:

(a) R_k updates its vector. The horizontal-vertical algorithm is executed on partial information. All partial path information is forwarded to the next site in order, $S_{(t+1) \bmod n}$.

(b) At the next site, $S_{(t+1) \bmod n}$, perform local detection algorithm as before. All path information is forwarded to the next site in order, $S_{(t+2) \bmod n}$.

(c) If the next site, $S_{(t+q) \bmod n} \equiv S_t$, is the site containing R_k, the R_k-request is awakened to compute an acknowledgment message. If *no* cycle has been detected, then $P_i @ S_j \rightarrow R_k$ is accepted. If a cycle is reported, then $P_i @ S_j \rightarrow R_k$ is denied, and P_i is killed (rollback).

(d) If $P_i @ S_j \rightarrow R_k$ is accepted, P_i is blocked until R_k is allocated to P_i. Then P_i is allowed access.

This version (Version IV) of the HVA is as "correct" as Version III because it implements Version III processing at each site, and the ring-structured message system serializes updates. However, Version IV suffers from a subtle flaw called *overavoidance*. Overavoidance is best illustrated by example.

Figure 12-20 shows how Version IV overavoids a deadlock configuration by killing two processes when it is necessary to kill only one process. Suppose two requests for separate resources are made "at the same time":

$$P_4 @ S_1 \text{ requests } R_5 @ S_1$$

and then

$$P_3 @ S_1 \text{ requests } R_1 @ S_0$$

Each request causes a horizontal-vertical search that spans the two-processor network. Since we only require ring-structured message-passing serialization, the two searches proceed at their own rate. Suppose both searches follow the paths shown in Figure 12-20(b) and (c) at about the same rate. We indicate the paths followed by requests for P_3 and P_4 by a "3" or "4" label next to each path.

In Figure 12-20(c), we discover that both searches return to their starting columns; thus both searches claim to have found a deadlock configuration. Actually, only one deadlock configuration exists. The single cycle can be avoided by removing only one process (either P_3 or P_4). However, the rollback step shown in Figure 12-20(d) shows both P_3 and P_4 being removed.

In this example, two processes were killed when only one needed to be removed. Since each HVA search used stale data to make decisions, this overavoidance is not possible to correct in Version IV.

If we modify Version IV so that TABLE[I,J] is *not* updated until the HVA completes its search, then we risk undetected deadlock. For example, both P_3 and P_4 would be kept, thus leading to a deadlocked system.

Performance Analysis

Figure 12-21 shows an HVA search that takes $(M + N - 1)$ probes of the process-resource table to complete. A more detailed performance analysis of the programs used by HVA is covered in this section.

Let

$$P_D = \text{probability of deadlock}$$

$$\text{TIMEOUT} = \text{random time delay in contention resolution algorithm}$$

$$N = \text{number of processes}$$

$$M = \text{number of resources}$$

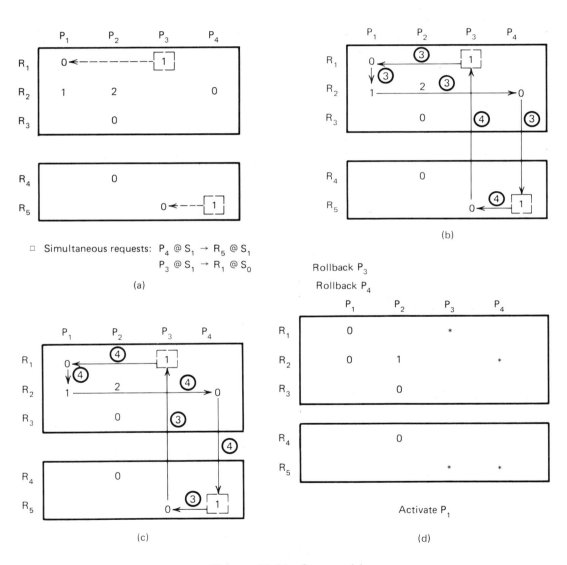

(a)

□ Simultaneous requests: $P_4 @ S_1 \rightarrow R_5 @ S_1$
$P_3 @ S_1 \rightarrow R_1 @ S_0$

(b)

Rollback P_3

Rollback P_4

(c)

(d)

Activate P_1

Figure 12-20. Overavoidance.

Furthermore, we will assume a unit time delay per operation and uniform probabilities unless otherwise indicated.

Figure 12-22 shows a software network model of function HORIZ. The reduction rules for transforming the network yield a performance estimate of

$$\tau_H = 2 + p_I (\tau'_w + \tau'_a) + p_I$$

And if we approximate p_w and p_I,

$$p_w = \frac{N - X}{N}$$

$$p_I = 1$$

where X is a column, e.g.,

$$1 <= X <= N$$

Then,

$$\tau'_w = \frac{4N - X}{X}$$

$$\tau'_a = 2$$

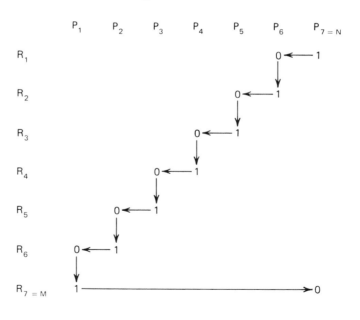

$(M + N - 1) = 13$ comparisons

Figure 12-21. Worst-case analysis.

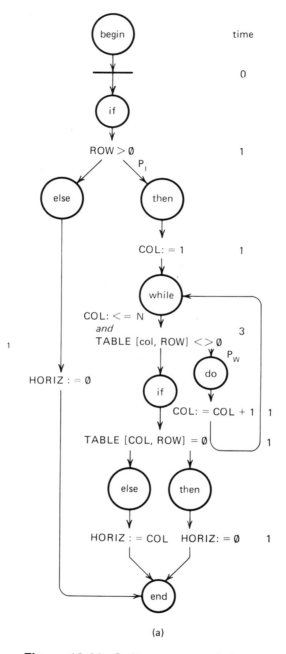

(a)

Figure 12-22. Software network for HORIZ.

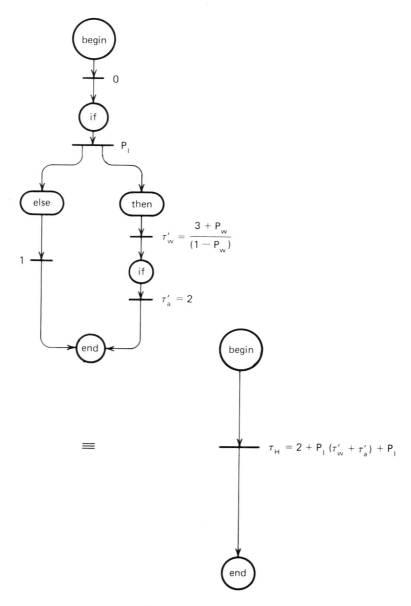

(b) Reductions of HORIZ

Figure 12-22. Continued.

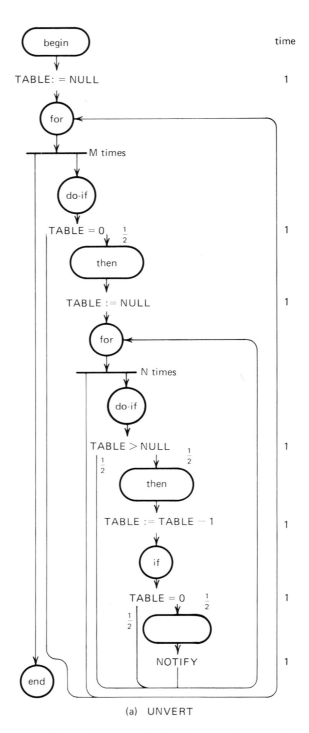

(a) UNVERT

Figure 12-23. UNVERT network.

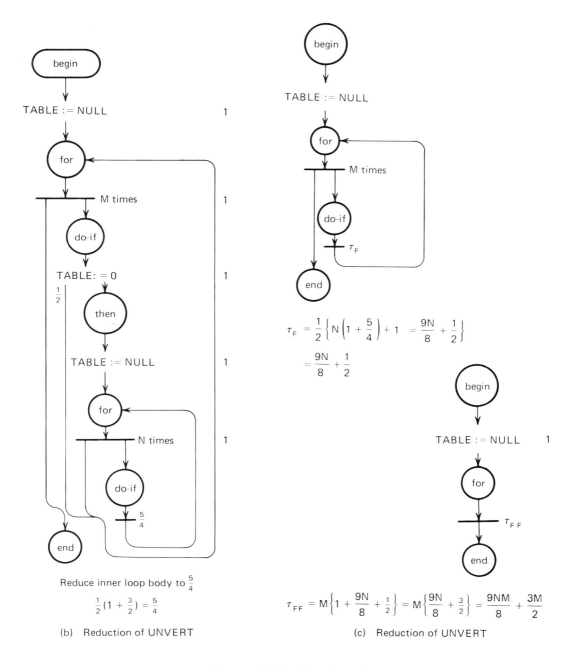

$$\tau_F = \frac{1}{2}\left\{ N\left(1 + \frac{5}{4}\right) + 1 \quad = \frac{9N}{8} + \frac{1}{2}\right\}$$

$$= \frac{9N}{8} + \frac{1}{2}$$

Reduce inner loop body to $\frac{5}{4}$

$$\frac{1}{2}\left(1 + \frac{3}{2}\right) = \frac{5}{4}$$

(b) Reduction of UNVERT

$$\tau_{FF} = M\left\{1 + \frac{9N}{8} + \frac{1}{2}\right\} = M\left\{\frac{9N}{8} + \frac{3}{2}\right\} = \frac{9NM}{8} + \frac{3M}{2}$$

(c) Reduction of UNVERT

Figure 12-23. Continued.

So,

$$\tau_H = 5 + \frac{4N - X}{X} = 4 + \frac{4N}{X}$$

Averaging over $1 <= X <= N$, we have

$$\bar{\tau}_H <= 4(1 + \log_e N)$$

Similarly, the performance of VERT can be derived as

$$\bar{\tau}_v <= 4 (1 + \log_e M)$$

Next, we derive a performance estimate for UNVERT using the software network shown in Figure 12-23. Assuming $\frac{9}{8}$ and $\frac{3}{2}$ are rough approximations to 1, we have

$$\tau_{FF} = NM + M = M(N + 1)$$

Note that UNVERT is more time-consuming than HORIZ or VERT.

Finally, the software network of Figure 12-24 leads to the estimate (using the results for HORIZ, VERT, and UNVERT):

$$\tau_{DA} = \left(\frac{2}{2 - p_D}\right)\left(11 + 2\log_e M + 4\log_e N + p_D\left[\frac{M(N + 1)}{2} + \frac{TIMEOUT}{4} + 1\right]\right)$$

If $p_D = 1$ (worst case estimate), then

$$\tau_{DA} <= 24 + 4\log_e M + 8\log_e N + M(N + 1) + \frac{TIMEOUT}{2}$$

That is,

$$\tau_{DA} = O(MN + \log_e M + \log_e N + TIMEOUT)$$

Therefore, the deadlock detection algorithm executes in time proportional to the product of the number of processes and number of resources. This estimate does not take into consideration the possibility of parallel execution of parts of the HVA on separate processors. For example, if N processors are used to support a system of N processes, then, theoretically,

$$\tau_{DA} = O(M)$$

and the deadlock detection algorithm is quite fast.

SUMMARY

We have used the canonical deadlock problem to study features of a deadlock-prone system of processes. The dining philosophers problem revealed several ways a system might end up in a deadlock configuration.

An object-based solution to the dining philosophers problem illustrated

Reduction of DAVOID

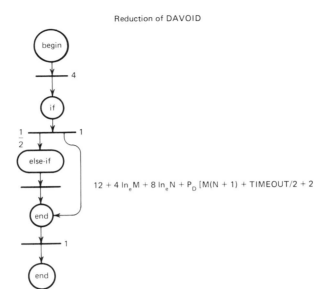

$$12 + 4 \ln_e M + 8 \ln_e N + P_D \ [M(N + 1) + \text{TIMEOUT}/2 + 2$$

$$\tau_{DA} = 5 + \frac{1}{2} \{ 12 + 4 \ln_e M + 8 \ln_e N + P_D \ [M(N + 1) + \text{TIMEOUT}/2 + 2 + \tau] \}$$

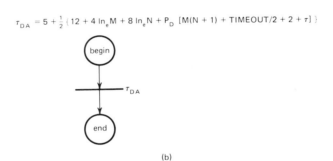

(b)

Figure 12-24. Performance of DAVOID.

how the Interleave Principle is used in combination with the process-resource table to test a solution to deadlock problems. We showed, for example, how careless serialization of access routines can lead to deadlock, livelock, or indeterminism.

The horizontal-vertical algorithm HVA was devised to perform on-line deadlock detection. In on-line detection, each request is checked immediately to see if a deadlock configuration will result if the request is blocked. On-line detection is especially useful for distributed systems where little is known about the request patterns of system processes in advance.

The centralized solution using the HVA leads to a rollback and recovery strategy that removes a process if it contributes to a deadlock configuration. The killed process is allowed to restart at some random delay time later. This is called a *contention resolution method* of restart. Its purpose is to eliminate starvation and livelock.

The distributed solution using the HVA leads to a highly parallel detection algorithm. However, Version IV of the HVA can overavoid a deadlock configuration by removing two blocked processes instead of only one. Overavoidance is tolerated because it is assumed to rarely occur.

Finally, the performance of the centralized solution is $O(MN)$, where M is the number of resources and N is the number of processes. We conjectured that better performance is achieved in the distributed version, but of course it depends on the efficiency of the message-passing network.

On-line detection can be of reasonable time complexity if we make the following assumptions:

1. No more than one nonzero entry appears in each column of the process-resource table.

2. No more than one zero entry appears in each row of the process-resource table.

3. The HVA is implemented with locks and rollback schemes that are safe, fair, and live.

The main achievements of the HVA studied here are

1. Random delays are used to do contention resolution in order to prevent livelock.

2. Interprocessor communication is serialized using network topology control, e.g., a ring-structured network.

PROBLEMS

1. Derive the performance formula for function VERT using a software network similar to the one in Figure 12-22.

2. Repeat the example of the dining philosophers problem shown in Figure 12-10 for $N = 2$ philosophers where P_1 and F_1 are in processor S_1, and P_2 and F_2 are in another processor S_2. Is overavoidance a problem?

3. Suppose the distributed solution uses UNVERT to remove a process whenever a deadlock configuration occurs. Estimate the number of messages sent to remove one process from all partial process-resource tables in a system of N processes with one process per site and N resources, and with one resource per site.

4. In the object-based solution to the dining philosophers problem, suppose we change max to 5. What can happen?

5. Modify the horizontal-vertical algorithm to allow multiple processes

to simultaneously own a resource, i.e., permit more than one "zero" per row of the table.

(a) Show how to check the following configuration of two readers and a single writer (writer must have exclusive access). Reader 2 is allowed access, but writer is *not* allowed to wait. Assume Reader 2 is done first, and the writer attempts to wait.

	Reader 1	Reader 2	Writer
Resource 1	0	0 ①	1 ②
Resource 2	1	-1	0

(b) Give a pseudocode algorithm for your solution.

13

Software
Fault-Tolerance

INTRODUCTION

This book has emphasized the importance of correct software design and implementation, using a variety of software engineering analysis techniques. However, "correct" software may "fail" in spite of all efforts to remove defects. For example, process failure due to a deadlock configuration illustrated in the previous chapter leads to a rollback of the offending process.

Programs may fail to produce desired performance, correct outputs, or correct termination due to

1. Bad inputs, poor network communication, or incorrect interprocess communication.

2. Hardware errors like memory failure or intermittent circuit errors.

3. System recovery procedures like deadlock avoidance or timing limits, etc.

Therefore, fault-tolerance is an important consideration in the design of a system of programs. In particular, we will show in this chapter that software fault-tolerance is a synchronization policy quite similar to the policies discussed in earlier chapters.

Fault-tolerant software is software that continues to give correct outputs despite occasional failures in hardware or in parts of the software. Fault-tolerant software is called *robust* if it is able to continue to execute correctly in an unreliable environment. A *failure* here is any transient or permanent error in calculation due to hardware or software malfunctioning.

A failure is detected in a fault-tolerant software system whenever an *acceptance test* is evaluated and found to be FALSE. In this chapter, any boolean expression employed strictly for the purpose of fault-detection will be considered an acceptance test.

Fault-tolerant software design is based on the concepts of *software redundancy*. A software module (procedure, function) is said to be redundant if it performs a function identical to any other software module. Design of a fault-tolerant system is carried out by carefully placing redundant software modules at critical places in the system so that a failure by a *primary* module can be recovered and corrected by a redundant *standby spare* module.

In the following sections we develop several strategies for fault-tolerant software design and implementation based on the concept of standby spares and synchronization of redundant modules. In each strategy it will be necessary to increase the number of interacting software parts in order to provide robustness. However, the reader is cautioned that increasing the size and complexity of software with additional (redundant) parts is a dangerous solution to any software problem. Therefore, addition of redundant standby spares must be done conservatively and only after careful consideration of system-wide effects.

ROBUST SOFTWARE DESIGN

A software system consists of a collection of routines and sections of code that orchestrates this collection of routines. The original or single implementation of an algorithm that is part of a software system is called a section of *primary code*. Typically, primary code is the programmer's idea of the best way to implement a certain algorithm.

An alternate implementation of a certain algorithm accepts the same inputs and computes the same outputs as the primary code. We call the alternate implementation a redundant *standby spare* when used as part of a robust system of routines. A standby spare may not be as fast as its primary code equivalent, or it may use more memory space, but it returns the same results given the same inputs. This is the idea in fault-tolerance.

Rollback and Restart

Robust software works as follows. Given a primary and one or more standby spares for computing a certain result,

1. The primary code is executed first.
2. An acceptance test is evaluated.

3. If the acceptance test evaluates to TRUE, then the next primary code segment following the current one is executed. Otherwise roll back to a *state* prior to the current state of the program and use a standby spare to perform an equivalent calculation in place of the primary code.

4. Repeat the execution of standby spares until the acceptance test evaluates to TRUE, or else the system fails.

This pattern of executing a primary, testing, and then executing one or more standby spares is shown in Figure 13-1. The primary code is executed, and then an acceptance test is carried out. When the acceptance test evaluates to FALSE, the block of code containing the primary and its standby spares must be *returned to its state before the primary code was executed*. We say the block is *rolled back* to an earlier state if all the variables affected by the primary or its standby spares are returned to their previous values. We say the program is *restarted* at some point in the program if a rollback to the point is followed by execution of the program using the restored values of the program's data.

An *acceptance block* is any segment of program containing a rollback point called a *checkpoint* (place where the variables of a program are saved), a primary code section, an acceptance test, and one or more standby spares. Suppose the following kernel operations are available for backing up to a checkpoint for the purpose of restarting.

BACKUP: Initialize a rollback counter to one, and then copy all variables that may be affected by the recovery block.

CHECK: Perform an acceptance test and if it evaluates to FALSE, increment the rollback counter by one and force the program to roll back to the backup copies and restart the program.

The following is a prototype of a recovery block:

```
begin
    BACKUP (⟨rollback counter⟩, ⟨recovery variables⟩) ;
    repeat
        case ⟨rollback counter⟩ of
        1:  ⟨primary code⟩     ;
        2:  ⟨spare #1⟩         ;
        3:  ⟨spare #2⟩         ;
              . . .
        n:  ⟨spare #(n−1)⟩     ;
    end   ;    (* case *)
    until CHECK (⟨rollback counter⟩, ⟨acceptance test⟩) ;
```

The kernel operations BACKUP and CHECK might consist of the following code:

```
    procedure BACKUP (var rp : integer ;
                          var ⟨list⟩) ;
  begin
    (* ⟨list⟩ is copied into temporary variables *)
    rp := 1 ; (* initially perform primary *)
  end ;      (* BACKUP *)
```

The BACKUP operation creates a new environment for the running program so that recovery is possible using the temporary variables to restart the program at an earlier state. Thus,

```
    function CHECK (var rp : integer ;
                       test : boolean) : boolean ;
  begin
    if test
    then begin (* successful *)
      (* discard copies in temporaries *)
      CHECK := TRUE ;
      rp := 0 ;
    end
    else begin (* failure *)
      (* restore copies from temporaries *)
      CHECK := FALSE ;
      rp := rp + 1 ; (* increment rollback counter *)
    end
  end      (* CHECK *)
```

Suppose we illustrate rollback and recovery using two sorting techniques: QUICKERSORT and BUBBLESORT. Assume the primary sorting routine QUICKERSORT is fast but fails on lists of $N = 2$ elements. The other routine is slower but reliable when $N = 2$. Therefore, QUICKERSORT works correctly "most of the time," and when it fails, BUBBLESORT is called into action.

```
    program ROBUST ;
      var
        DATA : array [1 . . N] of ELEMENTS ;
        RP    : integer;
        . .    (* other data *)
      begin
        (* other instructions *)
        . .
        BACKUP (RP, DATA) ;
        repeat
          case RP of
```

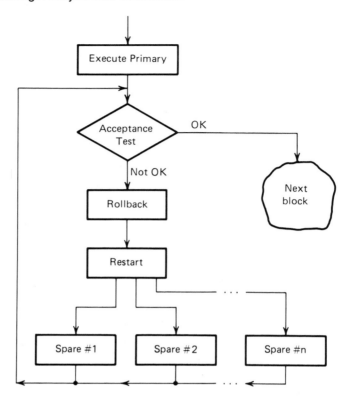

Figure 13-1. Rollback/Restart.

```
            1:  QUICKERSORT (DATA) ;
            2:  BUBBLESORT (DATA) ;
            3:  WRITELN ('ERROR : CRASH !') ;
        end
    until CHECK (RP, SORTED(DATA)) ;
        . .
    end.
```

This program executes BACKUP to make a temporary copy of DATA and then attempts to sort DATA by calling QUICKERSORT. If QUICK-ERSORT succeeds, the temporary copy of DATA is discarded, and execution of ROBUST continues beyond the recovery block. However, if SORTED(DATA) returns FALSE, then CHECK returns FALSE and RP = 2. CHECK also restores the copy of DATA made by BACKUP so that any modifications of DATA made by QUICKERSORT are ignored.

If BUBBLESORT fails, then the program fails also. An error message is returned indicating that primary and standby spare both failed.

A simple algorithm to decide if DATA is sorted or not is provided below. This function returns TRUE if every element of the list is at least as large as the element preceding it. That is, SORTED searches DATA to verify the order property

$$DATA[I-1].KEY <= DATA[I].KEY$$

for $I = 2, 3, \ldots, N$. If this order property holds for every pair of KEYs in the list, then $(I > N)$ is true.

```
function SORTED(X:real):boolean;
  var
    I,N : integer ;
  begin
    N := LENGTH(X) ; I := 2 ;
    while (X[I-1].KEY <= X[I].KEY)
            and
         (I <= N)
      do      I := I+1 ;
    SORTED := I > N ;
  end ;     (* SORTED *)
```

The illustration above shows how software redundancy can be used to insure continued execution of a program despite failures in parts of the program. Recovery blocks can be used everywhere it is essential that correct calculations be completed, *one way or the other.*

However, the simple recovery block model leads to severe problems in real-time concurrent systems of processes where interprocess communication between two processes can have a disastrous effect on recovery. What happens in a system of processes when messages are unreliable?

The Domino Effect

Figure 13-2 shows the familiar multiple-process configuration that uses shared address space to provide interprocess communication. In this configuration, the rollback and recovery variables of two recovery blocks overlap. This coupling of recovery variables leads to a disastrous chain of rollbacks called the *domino effect.*

Randell observed that careless placement of recovery blocks in a system of communicating processes can lead to systemwide failure even though only one process fails (see references at end of chapter). To see why, study the system of three communicating processes in Figure 13-3. The diagrams show the relative progress of three processes through time. The dotted lines indicate interprocess communication between two processes. The square brackets delimit the beginning of a recovery block. A

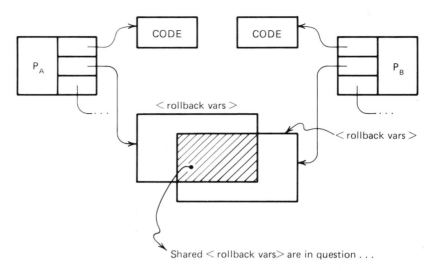

P_A CODE   CODE P_B

< rollback vars >

< rollback vars >

Shared < rollback vars> are in question . . .

Figure 13-2. Recovery of processes.

failure causes a process to roll back to a square bracket and restart (if it can).

Initially the three processes are in a configuration as shown in Figure 13-3(a). We first study the chain of events that occur if process #1 fails as shown. Figure 13-3(b) shows that a failure in process #1 is isolated because it causes process #1 to restart, but all other processes are not perturbed. However, Figure 13-3(c) illustrates what happens when process #2 fails instead.

Rollback of process #2 to its recovery point #4 causes two interprocess communications to become unreliable (perhaps process #2 sent information to process #1). Therefore, process #2 invalidates the communication, and process #1 must restart at the recovery point immediately before the interprocess communication (recovery point #3). The result of a failure in process #2 is a rollback and restart in both processes #1 and #2. This demonstrates how one process can "drag down" another process due to interprocess communication.

Figure 13-3(d) demonstrates a catastrophic chain of restarts called the *domino effect*. A failure in process #3 causes #3 to restart at its recovery point #4. This in turn invalidates the interprocess communication between process #2 and #3. Thus, process #2 must restart at its recovery point #3.

Recovery point #3 of process #2 invalidates the interprocess communication between process #2 and process #1. Therefore, process #1 must roll back to its restart point #3. Now, we have a coupling between process #2 and #3. A sequence of rollbacks follows:

Process #3 to point #3.
Process #2 to point #2.
Process #1 to point #2.

Then,

Process #1 to initial state.
Process #2 to initial state.
Process #3 to initial state.

Hence, the entire system of processes is unable to recover even though the error occurred in process #3 alone.

The domino effect can be overcome by properly structuring recovery blocks of all communicating processes. This can be done using synchronization of recovery and leads to a synchronization theory of fault-tolerance. But first, why did the system of three processes fail in the previous example?

Figure 13-4(a) shows how the system of processes looks in terms of *conversations* between pairs of the processes. A *conversation* is a series of interprocess communications. As the figure shows, the three processes carry on overlapping conversations, and this is what leads to the domino effect.

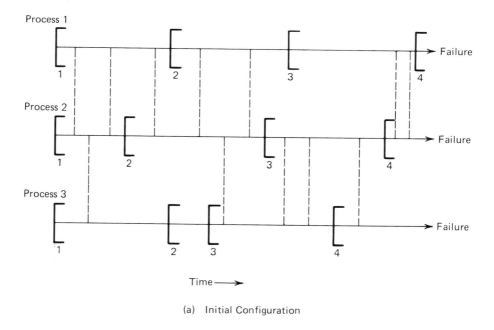

(a)   Initial Configuration

Figure 13-3. Illustration of the domino effect.

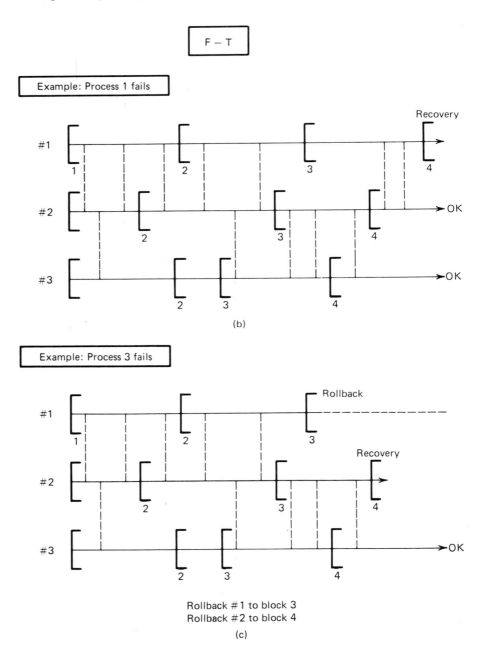

(b)

(c)

Rollback #1 to block 3
Rollback #2 to block 4

Figure 13-3. Continued.

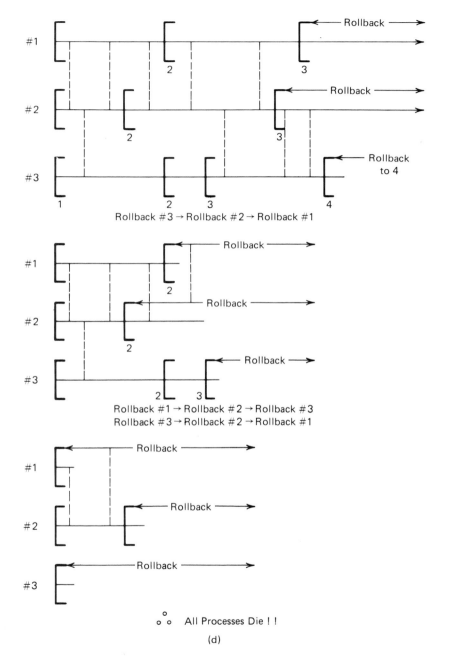

Example: Process 3 fails

Rollback #3 → Rollback #2 → Rollback #1

Rollback #1 → Rollback #2 → Rollback #3
Rollback #3 → Rollback #2 → Rollback #1

All Processes Die ! !

(d)

Figure 13-3. Continued.

Figure 13-4(b) shows the same three processes engaged in *properly structured conversations*. Each conversation is either disjoint from all other conversations, or else completely nested within another conversation.

Properly Structured Fault-Tolerance   A system of processes is properly structured with respect to fault-tolerance if every conversation is either nested or disjoint from all other conversations.

In Figure 13-4(b), a failure in any process affects only the process that is part of the conversation that is going on at the time of a failure. Since nesting and concatenation of conversations isolate one conversation from the other, no chain reaction of rollbacks can occur (outside the conversation).

The rule of properly structured fault-tolerance is easier stated than implemented. In terms of Figure 13-4, the conversations must be timed just

Improper structure — due to intersection of IPC/Rollback regions

(a)

Figure 13-4. Second look at domino effect.

so in order to *force* nesting or concatenation. In the next section we show how to force conversations to conform to this rule.

Synchronized Recovery

Proper rollback and recovery are synchronization problems. Like all other synchronization problems, we can solve the problem of properly structured interprocessor communication by blocking one or more processes while another process is allowed to continue to execute. That is, we can rearrange the processes in time so that their conversations are properly structured.

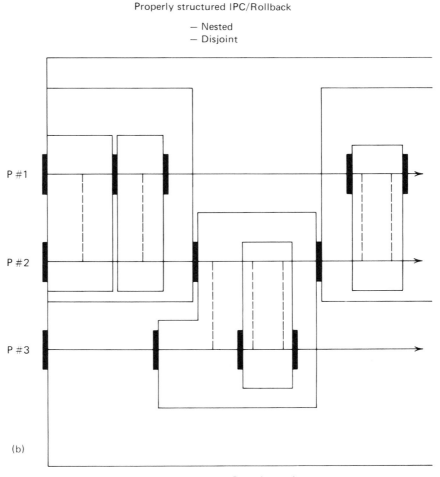

Properly structured IPC/Rollback

— Nested
— Disjoint

Figure 13-4. Continued.

Consider the problem of robust interprocess communication between a producer and consumer pair as shown in Figure 13-5. The producer and consumer processes in Figure 13-5(a) share access to a buffer and its access routines READ and WRITE. Suppose the buffer is an unreliable storage device, however, and so an extra buffer is employed to back up the original. Figure 13-5(b) shows a robust design where BUFFER and COPYBUF are managed by operations called

WRITETWO: Write into both COPYBUF and BUFFER.
COPY: Copy COPYBUF into BUFFER.
CRASH: Notify the user of a system failure.
SIGNAL,WAIT: Synchronization operations.
READ: Retrieve a character from BUFFER.
REREAD: Retrieve a character from COPYBUF.

These operations are used by recovery blocks to put and get characters

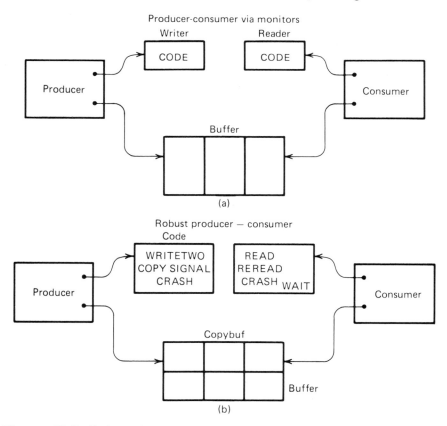

Figure 13-5. Robust interprocess communication between a producer and consumer pair.

from the buffer even though communication might be unreliable. In this illustration we will assume a checksum test of acceptance for detecting failures.

CHECKSUM: TRUE if no errors, FALSE otherwise.

The idea is quite simple: If an attempt to write a character into BUFFER fails, then the producer process writes a second copy of the character into COPYBUF. The consumer process will take one character at a time from the BUFFER, but if the producer detects an error in BUFFER, then the consumer must be told and restarted.

The three conversations shown in Figure 13-6 illustrate how the producer and consumer processes must be synchronized to guarantee proper structure. How is this guaranteed?

A robust producer process executes the following recovery block to send the *j*th character to the shared buffers:

```
PRODUCER:
    r := 1 ;                        (* number tries *)
    repeat
      case r of                     (* restarts *)
      1: WRITETWO (Data) ;          (* double-write to buffers *)
      2: COPY ;                     (* backup copy used *)
      3: CRASH ;                    (* total failure *)
    end ;
    r := r + 1 ;                    (* retry? *)
    until CHECKSUM ;                (* acceptance test *)
    for I := 1 to r-2 do            (* tell CONSUMER its ok? *)
      SIGNAL (J,I,FALSE) ;          (* rollback CONSUMER *)
    SIGNAL (J,r-1,TRUE) ;           (* synchronize CONSUMER *)
```

Similarly, the consumer process takes one character at a time from one buffer or the other and waits for the conversation between it and the producer to be completed. The consumer reads the no-*th* character as follows:

```
CONSUMER
    s := 1 ;                        (* # restarts *)
    repeat
      case s of                     (* restarts *)
      1: READ (Info) ;              (* read BUFFER *)
      2: REREAD (Info) ;            (* read COPYBUFFER *)
      3: CRASH    ;                 (* no way *)
    end ;
    s := s + 1                      (* retry *)
    until WAIT (no,s-1)             (* wait for OK from PRODUCER *)
                                    (* after no-th access *)
```

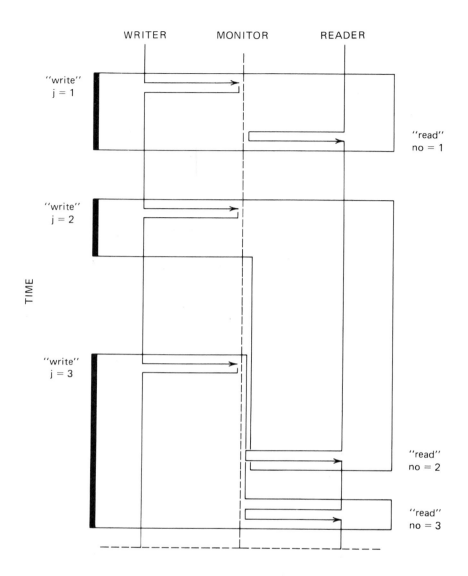

Figure 13-6. Typical conversations in robust producer-consumer pair.

We need two objects to synchronize the accesses defined for producer and consumer. These objects have the following types:

Encapsulations: PROSUMER

type PROSUMER = **object**
    path 3:(1:(WRITETWO);1:(READ)),3:(1:(COPY);1:(REREAD)) **end;**
    const N = 3

```
var   BUFFER,COPYBUF : array[1 . . N] of char ;
   In, Out : 0 . . N ;
entry procedure WRITETWO (Data:char) ;
   begin
      In := (In mod N) + 1 ;
      BUFFER[In] := Data ;
      COPYBUF[In] := Data ;
   end ;     (* WRITETWO *)
entry procedure COPY ;
   begin BUFFER := COPYBUF     end; (* COPY *)
entry procedure READ (var Info : char);
   begin
      Out := (Out mod N) + 1 ;
      Info := BUFFER[Out];
   end ;     (* READ *)
entry procedure REREAD (var Info : char ) ;
   begin Info := COPYBUF[Out] end ; (* REREAD *)
init; begin In := 0; Out := 0 end; (* PROSUMER *)
```

Encapsulations: SYNCHRONIZATION

```
type SYNCH = object
   path 3:(1:(SIGNAL);1:(WAIT)) end ;
   var   OK:array[1 . . 3,1 . . 3] of boolean ;
      I,J : 1 . . 3 ;
   entry procedure SIGNAL(COUNT,TRY:integer;SWITCH:boolean);
      begin OK[COUNT,TRY] := SWITCH end ; (* SIGNAL *)
   entry function WAIT(COUNT,TRY:integer):boolean;
      begin
         WAIT := OK[COUNT,TRY] ;
         if WAIT then OK[COUNT,TRY] := FALSE ;
      end ;     (* WAIT *)
init; begin
   for I := 1 to 3 do
      for J := 1 to 3 do
         OK[I,J] := FALSE ;
   end ;     (* SYNCH*)
```

An example of a conversation involving an error is shown in Figure 13-7. At step #1 the producer has written a correct character into COPYBUF and an incorrect character, A', into BUFFER. The CHECKSUM acceptance test detects the error in BUFFER, but before it can be rewritten, the consumer process READs it.

The consumer must WAIT for approval by the producer before it can go on, however. Therefore, the WAIT(1,1) operation causes the consumer process to block (see step #2 in Figure 13-7).

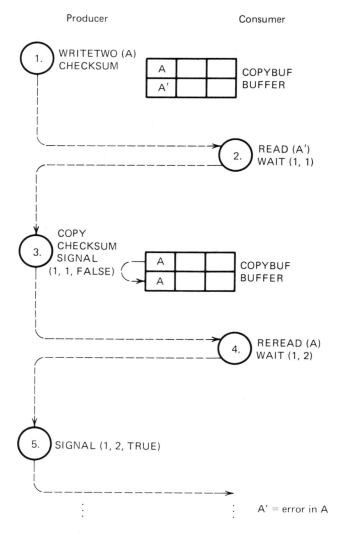

Figure 13-7. Example of producer-consumer conversation.

At step #3 the producer process has executed the COPY operation. This corrects the error and leads to a TRUE CHECKSUM test. The producer can now SIGNAL to the consumer.

At step #4 the WAITing consumer is unblocked by the SIGNAL operation at step #3. The REREAD operation returns the corrected character, and the consumer process is again blocked until the producer signals again.

Figure 13-8 shows the software network equivalent of the test shown in

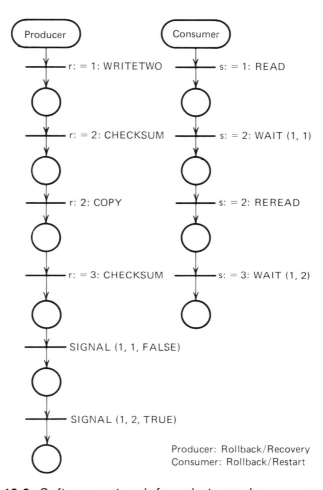

Figure 13-8. Software network for robuts producer-consumer.

Figure 13-7. Figure 13-9 shows the same test in the form of a process-state matrix of the Interleave Principle. The process-state matrix version uses path expressions to demonstrate that producer and consumer processes are properly structured with respect to their conversations.

Finally, a second test of three writes followed by three reads (and no errors) is shown in Figure 13-10. The two processes are allowed to execute concurrently within a conversation, but prevented from executing concurrently if it endangers proper fault-tolerant structuring.

This example demonstrates how redundant storage might be used with recovery blocks and synchronization to increase the robustness of a producer-consumer pair. The weakness of this approach is obviously a di-

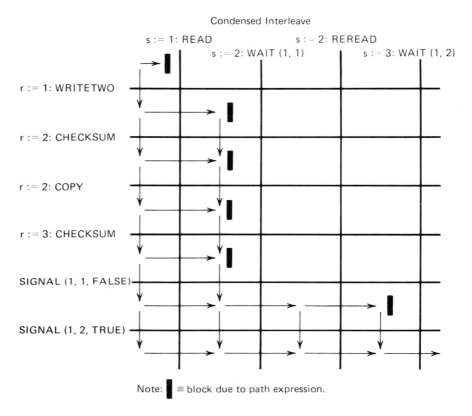

Note: █ ≡ block due to path expression.

Figure 13-9. Verification using a condensed interleave.

minished level of performance (less concurrency). Another approach is to duplicate the processing elements instead of the storage elements and use a technique called *majority voting*.

Majority Voting Systems

Instead of using redundant storage as a hedge against errors, we can use redundant processes (processors) to generate copies of identical inputs. If one or more of the inputs have an error in them, we take the input computed by the majority of the processes and discard the other inputs.

This technique is based on the following:

1. Assume that the majority is always right.

2. Assume identical processes compute identical algorithms.

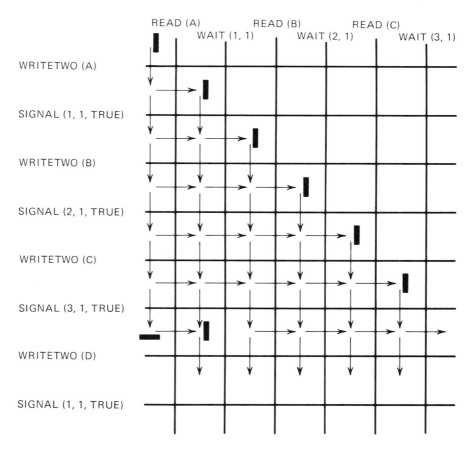

Figure 13-10. Smooth sailing for Three Writes and Three Reads.

Then, the number of faults that can be tolerated without computing incorrect results is a function of the number of redundant processes N:

$$\text{Number of faults tolerated} <= \left\lfloor \frac{N-1}{2} \right\rfloor \qquad (N >= 3)$$

For example, if $N = 5$ processes, each executing identical programs and using exactly identical data, then the correct answer will be obtained even if up to

$$\left\lfloor \frac{5-1}{2} \right\rfloor = 2$$

processes fail.

We can use $N = 3$ processes to compute an algorithm and if one process fails, the result returned by the other two will be correct. Of

Array of producers: Single consumer

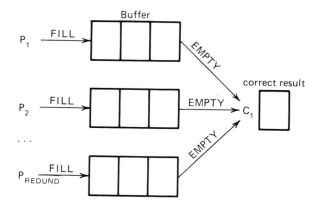

Figure 13-11. Majority voting producer-consumer.

course, if two processes fail, the result will be incorrect, and the majority voting scheme will produce a lie!

Suppose processes A, B, and C compute a single result for a certain algorithm. Let X_A, X_B, and X_C be the value returned by A, B, and C, respectively. Then, if the results are binary numbers, and * means logical **and,** and + means logical **or,** we have

$$\text{Majority result} := X_A * X_B + X_A + X_C + X_B * X_C$$

Thus, majority voting for three processes can be implemented by a simple, fast formula.

This method of redundancy can be applied to the producer-consumer problem too. Suppose three producers write characters into three buffers as shown in Figure 13-11. The consumer process reads from each buffer and then computes the majority result using the formula above. The correct result is obtained if zero or one process fails. Thus,

```
READER:
  begin
    for j := 1 to 3 do
      copy[j].READER(CH[j]) ;
    MAJOR.RESULT := MAJORITY(CH,3) ;
      . .
    end.
  where,
    const
      REFUND = 3 ;
```

```
var
    COPY : array[1 . . REDUND] of buffer ;
    WRITERS : array[1 . . REDUND] of PRODUCERS ;
    READER  : CONSUMER ;
```

and each producer executes the following:

```
PRODUCER:
    begin
        . .
        WRITERS[j].COPY[j].FILL(CH) ;
        . .
    end.
```

This solution uses the following type of objects:

```
type
    buffer = object path 3:(1:(FILL);1:(EMPTY)) end ;
            var
                buf : array[1 . . 3] of char ;
                In,Out : 0 . . 3 ;
            entry procedure FILL(CH:char);
                begin In := (In mod 3) + 1 ;
                    buf[In] := CH ;
                end ; (* FILL *)
            entry procedure EMPTY(var CH:char) ;
                begin Out := (Out mod 3) + 1 ;
                    CH := buf[Out] ;
                end ; (* EMPTY *)
    init; begin
            In  := 0 ;
            Out:= 0 ;
        end ;    (* buffer *)
```

Figure 13-12 illustrates one possible case of concurrent execution of the three producers and the single consumer. Each producer proceeds at its own rate, and the consumer waits until all three characters are available before voting. Notice that the consumer waits for producer #1 before it accepts values from the other two producers. This is a slight inadequacy in the design of the consumer process. How might this be improved?

MESSAGE-PASSING SYSTEMS

According to Russell, reasonable implementation of properly structured fault-tolerance by means of properly structured conversations may be difficult to do. One difficulty mentioned by Russell is the possibility of

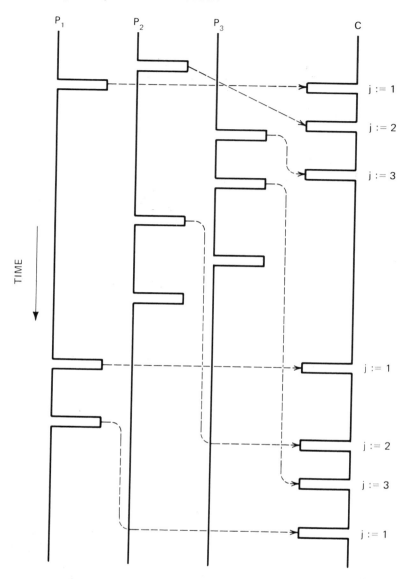

Figure 13-12. Example of **path** 3:(1:(FILL); 1:(EMPTY))**end.**

deadlocked recovery blocks since structuring conversations is a synchronization problem. The main objection to the use of structured conversations, however, is the inefficiency that seems to result from decreased concurrency even when *no* errors are detected. These objections to structured conversations and a complete comparison with other methods of fault-tolerant software design have not been studied extensively at the time this section was written. Therefore it is not clear whether one approach is always superior to another.

In this section we adopt a message-oriented dual philosophy of interprocess communication and investigate how fault-tolerant message-passing might be implemented. As in the previous section, message-passing systems will also be susceptible to the domino effect.

R-Propagation

In the message-oriented philosophy of software design, a distributed system is a finite collection of processes and objects called *messagelists*. All processes interact through messagelist objects with the following operations defined:

MARK(q)   :   Establish a recovery point called q and copy all affected variables for later recovery and restart.

SEND(m,x)   :   This operation puts the value of x into messagelist m.

RECEIVE(m,x): This operation takes a message from messagelist m and puts it into variable x.

In all examples given in this section, the messagelist discipline will be assumed to be first come first served. As long as the system operates without error, the messagelists correctly transfer messages from one process to another. We say the system of messagelists is in a *consistent state* if the sequence of messages received by each messagelist m is a prefix of the sequence of messages sent to m. However, an error in the system of processes leads to an inconsistent state if the prefix property (gap) is lost.

Loss of the prefix property, called a *gap*, is possible in a message-passing system whenever an R-propagation occurs. Figure 13-13 illustrates R-propagation (rollback-propagation) that leads to a gap in the interprocess communication between processes #1 and #3.

In Figure 13-13, the system of three processes and two messagelists communicate as follows:

1. P_1 sends a message x to messagelist M_1:

   $$SEND(M_1,x)$$

2. At some later time, process P_2 takes x from M_1:

   $$RECEIVE(M_1,x)$$

3. Process P_1 continues past its first recovery point and sends another message to process #2 via messagelist M_1:

   $$SEND(M_1,y)$$

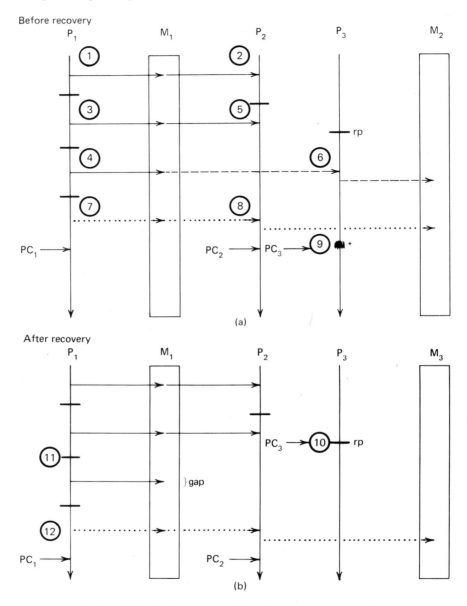

Figure 13-13. R-propagation in message-passing.

4. Process P_1 continues past its second recovery point and sends its first message to process #3:

$$\text{SEND}(M_1, z)$$

5. Meanwhile, process P_2 takes another message from M_1 in the order it was received by M_1:

$$\text{RECEIVE}(M_1,y)$$

6. Process #3 continues past its first recovery point and takes the next available message from messagelist M_1:

$$\text{RECEIVE}(M_1,z)$$

Furthermore, process #3 sends this message on to messagelist M_2;

$$\text{SEND}(M_2,z)$$

7. Process #1 sends a message to process #2 via messagelist M_1;

$$\text{SEND}(M_1,w)$$

8. Process #2 propagates message w to messagelist M_2;

$$\text{RECEIVE}(M_1,w)$$
$$\text{SEND}(M_2,w)$$

9. Meanwhile, process #3 encounters a failure at PC_3. At this point in the computations, the system is in a consistent state because the message received in each messagelist M_1 and M_2 is a prefix of the sequence of messages sent to each messagelist M_1 and M_2.

In Figure 13-13(a), the processes have reached points PC_1, PC_2, and PC_3, respectively. The failure at PC_3 causes process #3 to roll back to recovery point rp. When this is done, the recovery of process #3 is propagated to the messagelist containing invalidated messages. Figure 13-13(b) shows the result of this R-propagation (rollback-propagation).

The "gap" in Figure 13-13(b) may lead to a kind of domino effect. Suppose process #3 requests the "gap" message from process #1 a second time. This forces process #1 to restart from the recovery point designated #11 in Figure 13-13(b). Process #1 will successfully resend the message to process #3 via messagelist M_1. However, it will also send the message at point #12 to process #2, etc. The messagelists no longer retain their prefix property, and so R-propagation may lead to failure of the entire system of processes.

In order to avoid this problem, messages following the "gap" message must also be returned to the messagelist (to maintain the prefix property). The solution to this problem is to avoid R-propagation. Such a system is called *R-normal* because no R-propagation is allowed.

One method of designing R-normal systems of processes and messagelists is to limit the number of processes served by a messagelist to one. Another method of guaranteeing R-normal behavior is to shuffle the messages of a messagelist after every rollback and restart so that the remaining messages are in prefix order.

> *R-Normal Rule (Russell)* If for all messagelists *m* of a system, either (1) the messages in *m* are *received* by at most one process, or (2) *m* is shuffled (reordered) after every recovery involving *m* so that the system of messagelists is returned to a consistent state, then the system is R-normal.

The simplest solution to R-propagation is to reduce to one the number of processes that receive messages from messagelist *m*. Thus each process has its own individual input messagelist as shown in the "before and after" illustration of Figure 13-14. In Figure 13-14(b), each process has its own input messagelist: buffer #1 for process #1 and buffer #2 for process #2. A switcher process is added to handle requests for messages from the processes and to separate incoming messages. Thus, an R-normal system is "simulated" by adding additional processes and buffer objects.

MRS Systems

An R-normal system is designed by limiting the number of consumer processes per messagelist, but the domino effect remains a problem in

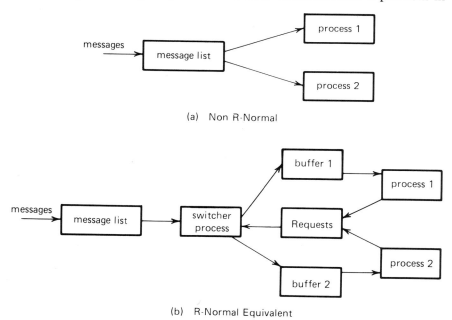

(a)   Non R-Normal

(b)   R-Normal Equivalent

Figure 13-14. Conversion from non R-normal to R-normal.

R-normal systems. To design a domino-free system, we must also restrict the pattern of MARK, SEND, and RECEIVE operations.

A system is said to *domino* if a single rollback by any process leads to an avalanche of rollbacks terminating every process in the system. A system is *domino-free* if the domino effect cannot occur.

We can minimize the domino effect by careful placement of the MARK operation immediately before every sequence of RECEIVE operations in every communicating process. Furthermore, if we assume that every RECEIVE operation accepts *correct* message values from its associated messagelist, then messages need not be sent to a process every time a RECEIVE is executed. The only time a RECEIVE operation needs to be performed a second time is either after a process rollback or after a SEND operation performed by a recovering process. This strategy assumes every message received by a process is correct, unless later proven to be unreliable. If proven to be unreliable after the RECEIVE operation is performed, then the process is forced to roll back over the RECEIVE operation (R-propagation) and execute it a second time.

An MRS process is a process where the MARK, SEND, and RECEIVE operations are performed in an order specified by the following MRS path expression:

path K:(MARK;S:(RECEIVE);[SEND]) **end**

where

K = The maximum number of processes allowed access to the fault-tolerant object.

S = The maximum number of executions of RECEIVE allowed before another MARK is executed.

[SEND] = This means to execute as many SEND operations as needed in order to serve *all waiting* processes (taken as a batch).

Since every path expression is a regular expression, an MRS system is a system of processes where every process obeys the regular expression

MARK ; RECEIVE* ; SEND*

where "*" indicates multiple executions.

For an R-normal system of fault-tolerant processes, local enforcement of the MRS pattern suffices to guarantee the absence of the domino effect.

Figure 13-15 illustrates an MRS system and what happens when process P_1 fails at the point PC_1 (noted by an "*"). Remember the system in Figure 13-15 is R-normal because each process has its own input messagelist (the process and its messagelist have been merged in the figure). The system is MRS because we designed it such that every MARK operation is placed after every sequence of SEND operations and before every sequence of RECEIVE operations. That is, a MARK separates the se-

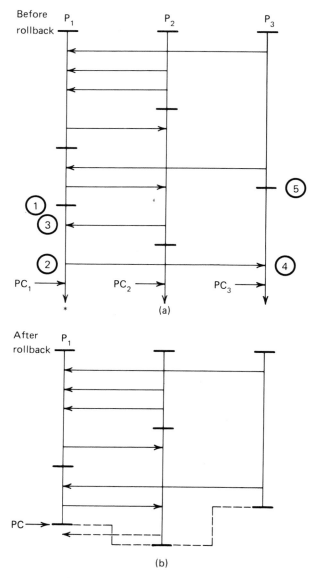

Figure 13-15. An MRS system.

quence of SENDs from the sequence of RECEIVEs in every process.

In Figure 13-15(a), three processes have executed to points PC_1, PC_2, and PC_3, respectively. Suppose process #1 fails an acceptance test at PC_1 and attempts to restart from its MARKed state #1. Rollback to #1 invalidates the SEND operation at point #2, but because we can assume the

Subsequent recovery line for P_1, P_2, and P_3

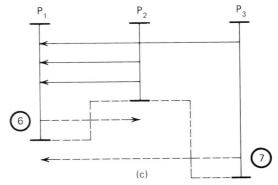

(c)

Last recovery line for P_1, P_2 and P_3

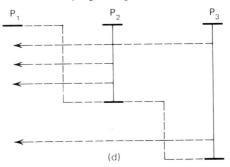

(d)

Figure 13-15. Continued.

RECEIVEd message at point #3 is correct, it need not be recomputed by process #2.

Process #1 restarts at point #1, and process #3 is notified that it received an unreliable message at point #4. Therefore, process #3 must be restarted from its previous recovery point shown in Figure 13-15(a) as point #5.

Process #2 is not affected by the rollback of process P_1 and P_3 since we have assumed it performed correct SEND operations to the other processes. All SENDs from process #2 have placed their values in the input messagelists of their respective consumer processes. However, the "firewall" established by the dotted line connecting the recovery points of the three processes of Figure 13-15(b) represents a *recovery line* for the system of communicating processes. A recovery line marks the earliest points affected by a failure in some process. Hence, the recovery line shown in Figure 13-15(b) limits the R-propagation possible by a failure in process #1 at point PC_1.

The messages represented by dotted lines in Figure 13-15 represent the messages that have already been sent to a consumer and are assumed to be correct. These messages need *not* be sent again because they have been placed in the messagelist of the consumer process independently of the rollback and recovery of the consumer process. Therefore, when the consumer restarts and executes its RECEIVE operation, the messagelist will contain the messages in the order they were sent.

The dotted-line messages are assumed to be correct. However, what happens if they turn out to be invalid? This can happen as shown in Figure 13-15(a) at point #4. The message sent to process #3 by process #1 becomes unreliable when process #1 fails at point PC_1. Hence, process #3 must restart and RECEIVE a new value from the subsequent restarted process #1.

In Figure 13-15(c) and (d), we see how subsequent restarts of process #1 cause a limited amount of R-propagation throughout the system of three processes. At each stage of rollback of process #1, a recovery line is established as a "firewall" against the domino effect.

Figure 13-15(c), for example, invalidates one message sent from process #1 to process #2, but does not invalidate the other message shown at point #6. The message sent by process #3 is also still valid (see point #7). These messages will be waiting for processes #2 and #1 when they restart and execute corresponding RECEIVE operations.

Figure 13-15(d) shows another recovery line established when P_1 restarts at its beginning MARK. Processes P_1 and P_3 need not be restarted because of the MRS pattern of restarting points.

SUMMARY

The theory of fault-tolerant software is in its infancy. We have shown three schemes for designing fault-tolerant software based on redundancy. The redundant software standby spare scheme relies on one or more surrogates to take over the calculations when a primary routine fails. The redundant process model uses majority voting to decide on a correct outcome. Finally, systems of processes can be restarted in a form of *backward recovery* using surrogates or primary routines to attempt a correction.

Systems that employ backward recovery suffer from a propagation trait called the *domino effect*. A system dominos if a failure in a single process propagates rollback to other processes such that no process (subset of processes) can restart. Proper structure of a system can be employed to avoid the domino effect. Such structured systems are called *domino-free*.

One way to design and implement domino-free systems is to structure interprocess communication into conversations. A *conversation* is a collection of interprocess communications that are nested or concatenated such that rollback of one process can only force rollback of other processes that are part of the conversation.

Structured conversation among processes is a synchronization problem, and like other synchronization problems, it must be checked for safe, fair, and live behavior. At the time this section was written, no techniques for analyzing conversations have been developed beyond the Interleave Principle technique. Further research is needed in this area.

Another way to design and implement domino-free systems is to structure the operations MARK, SEND, and RECEIVE defined for objects called *messagelists*. A messagelist contains all input messages for a process. Furthermore, a system of processes are called *R-normal* if each process has its own input messagelist.

An R-normal system is domino-free if every process in the system accesses its messagelist object in MRS order. That is, the accesses are carried out by first MARKing the process (set recovery point), RECEIVEing any number of input messages from other processes, and then SENDing any number of output messages. Each time a sequence of RECEIVEs are executed, they must be preceded by a MARK operation.

An MRS system is designed by placing MARK commands immediately before a sequence of RECEIVE operations. Russell gives guidelines for when and where to remove recovery points using a PURGE operation (p. 194).

PROBLEMS

1. Explain what we mean by the following terms:

   (a) domino effect   (f) majority voting
   (b) recovery line   (g) conversation
   (c) recovery block   (h) messagelist
   (d) MRS   (i) R-normal
   (e) R-propagation   (j) standby spare

2. Design and implement a recovery block for robust searching where the primary code is a binary search routine and the standby spare is a sequential search routine. What is the acceptance test?

3. In Problem #2, suggest a third way to perform the search algorithm and use it to implement a recovery block with one primary and two standby spares.

4. Repeat Figure 13-7 except allow A to be correctly written into BUFFER[1], but B' is an incorrectly written character placed in BUFFER[2].

5. Develop a system similar to Figure 13-5(b) that provides a robust solution to the multiple-readers-single-writer problem. Test your system.

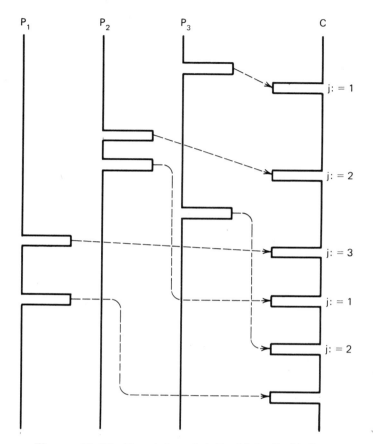

Figure 13-16. Nondeterministic Majority Voting.

6. Introduce nondeterminancy into the majority voting method so that the following may occur (Figure 13-16). That is, allow the reader to read the buffer as soon as at least one writer has provided a value—regardless of the order of writers.

7. Propose a method of testing the solution given to the system in Figure 13-11 and use your method to show that the solution is correct (or incorrect!).

8. Propose a "shuffle" algorithm that would solve the "gap" problem in the example of Figure 13-13.

9. Transform the system in Figure 13-13 into an R-normal system using additional processes and objects as suggested by Figure 13-14.

10. Use the MRS rule to implement a Path Pascal object that solves the producer-consumer problem and is domino-free.

REFERENCES

Kim, K. H., "Programmer Transparent Coordination of Recovering Parallel Processes." Report to HQ Space and Missile Systems Organization, Box 92960, Worldway Postal Center, Los Angeles, CA 90009, August 1978.

Randell, B., "System Structure for Software Fault Tolerance," *Proceedings of the International Conference on Reliable Software,* April 21–23, 1975, Los Angeles, CA, also in ACM SIGPLAN Notices, vol. 10, no. 6 (June 1975).

Russell, D. L., "State Restoration in Systems of Communicating Processes," *IEEE Transaction on Software Engineering,* SE-6, no. 2 (March 1980), 183–194.

Index